Business Cycles since 1820

To Nancy, Dori and Ken

Business Cycles since 1820

New International Perspectives
from Historical Evidence

Edited by
Trevor J.O. Dick

*Professor of Economics, University of Lethbridge,
Alberta, Canada and Visiting Scholar,
University of California at Berkeley, USA*

Edward Elgar
Cheltenham, UK • Northampton, MA, USA

Published by
Edward Elgar Publishing Limited
8 Lansdown Place
Cheltenham
Glos GL50 2HU
UK

Edward Elgar Publishing Company
6 Market Street
Northampton
Massachusetts 01060
USA

A catalogue record for this book is available from the British Library

Library of Congress Cataloguing in Publication Data

Business cycles since 1820: new international perspectives from
    historical evidence/edited by Trevor J.O. Dick.
        Includes bibliographical references.
        1. Business cycles. I. Dick, Trevor J.O.
    HB3711.B9378   1998
    338.5'42—dc21   97–38474
                                                                        CIP

Printed and bound in Great Britain by
Biddles Limited, Guildford and King's Lynn

ISBN 1 85898 350 9

Contents

Figures

Tables

Contributors

Richard C.K. Burdekin, Professor, Department of Economics, Claremont
McKenna College, 850 Columbia Ave., Claremont, CA 91711, USA
email: rburdekin@benson.mckenna.edu

Charles Calomiris, Graduate School of Business, Columbia University, 418A
Uris Hall, 3022 Broadway, New York, NY 10027, USA
Tel: 914-723-6425; *Fax*: 212-316-9180
email: cc374@columbia.edu

Susan B. Carter, Professor, Department of Economics, University of California
at Riverside, Riverside, CA 92521, USA
Tel: 714-787-6352/714-686-8481; *Fax*: 714-787-5685
email: sbcarter@ucracl.ucr.edu

Trevor J.O. Dick, Professor of Economics, University of Lethbridge, Lethbridge,
Alberta, Canada, TIK 3M4
Tel/Fax: 403-381-7829
email: dick@uleth.ca

Christopher Hanes, Mail Stop 59, Federal Reserve Board, 20th and C Streets
NW, Washington, DC 2055, USA
Tel: 202-728-5864/301-564-0119
email:chanes@fed.frb.gov

Toru Iwami, Faculty of Economics, University of Tokyo, 7-3-1 Hongo,
Bunkyo-ku, Tokyo 113, Japan
Tel: 03 3812 2111; *Fax*: 03 3818 7082
email: iwami@e.u-tokyo.ac.jp

John A. James, Professor, Department of Economics, University of Virginia,
Charlottesville, VA 22901, USA
Tel: 804-924-3525; *Fax*: 804-982-2904
email: JAJ8Y@fermi.clas.virginia.edu

Tetsuji Okazaki, Faculty of Economics, University of Tokyo, Hongo, Bunkyo-ku, Tokyo 113, Japan

Jan Tore Klovland, Institute of Economics, Norwegian School of Economics and Business Administration, Helleveien 30, N-5035, Bergen-Sandviken, Norway
Tel: 47 5 95 92 74; *Fax*: 47 5 95 95 43
email: sam_tjk@debet.nhh.no

Albrecht Ritschl, Department of Economics, Universitat Pompeu Fabra, Ramon Trias Fargas, 25-27, 08005 Barcelona, Spain
Tel: 343-542-2509
email: ritschl@upf.es

Pierre L. Siklos, School of Business and Economics, Wilfrid Laurier University, Waterloo, Ontario, Canada N2L 3C5
Tel: 519-884-1970; *Fax*: 519-884-0201
email: psiklos@machl.wlu.ca

Richard Sutch, Professor, Department of Economics, and Director, Institute of Business and Economic Research, University of California at Berkeley, Berkeley, CA 94720, USA
Tel: 510-642-1922; *Fax*: 510-642-5018
email: rsutch@econ.berkeley.edu

Hiroshi Yoshikawa, Faculty of Economics, University of Tokyo, 7-3-1 Hongo, Bunkyo-ku, TOKYO 113, Japan

Preface

Notwithstanding the enormous theoretical and empirical literature produced by past efforts, the explanation, and some would say even the measurement, of business cycles remains elusive. The motivation for this collection of essays lies in the growing recognition that explanation of these phenomena depends partly on our perception of the phenomena themselves. Perhaps in no other area of empirical testing has the advance of economics become more dependent on the collection and interpretation of historical data. It is this recognition that presents economists and economic historians with an unprecedented opportunity to collaborate in their efforts. The purpose of this volume is to underline this opportunity and to stimulate further studies to exploit it.

Earlier versions of these essays were presented in a session at the Eleventh International Economic History Congress held in Milan, Italy, in September 1994, organized to bring together an internationally representative group of scholars working at the intersection of economics and economic history on business cycle topics. We are grateful to the organizers of the Congress for providing the venue at which the ideas for the present volume were firmly planted. For this occasion, we were also fortunate to have the advice and critical remarks of two respected scholars of macroeconomic history, Michael Bordo (Rutgers University) and Tim Hatton (University of Essex). The idea for both the conference session and the volume began to germinate much earlier during the course of a number of seminars at the University of California at Berkeley, where the editor participated as a visiting scholar 1990–91, and again in 1996–7. It became apparent then from the work and presentations of scholars like Christina Romer, Richard Sutch, Susan Carter, Charles Calomiris, Solomos Solomou, and Hugh Rockoff that historical scholarship had a vital role to play in our understanding of business cycle issues.

There are always practical concerns in producing a volume of this kind that sometimes seem insurmountable and often tax the patience of all. First and foremost, I must thank the contributors themselves for their patience and cooperation through the long process of editing and revision which they have endured at my behest. The manuscript now incorporates improvements based an virtually all of the original comments made by the discussants, whose patience and diligence have contributed greatly to the final product. Though much will remain controversial, the authors hope that their investigations are reported with sufficient clarity to offer a basis for ongoing discussion and research.

In addition to those in the front line of this endeavor, there are many others who, by their ideas and encouragement, have in one way or another supported the project. I would like to acknowledge, in particular, the support and encouragement of Barry Eichengreen, Bill Sundstrom, Steve Broadberry, Christina Romer, Anna Schwartz, Marvin McInnis, Michael Edelstein, Joseph Haubrich, and Lars Junung. I also wish to thank the Academic Press for permission to reprint the Calomiris and Hanes article (Chapter 1). Finally, I am grateful to Edward Elgar and his staff for their patient support throughout the project.

Introduction

Trevor J.O. Dick

The study of business cycles has itself been a fluctuating phenomenon and is as old as the collection of data demonstrating the cyclical behavior of business conditions. Indeed the demonstration of cycles depends upon the collection and manipulation of economic data, a principal conclusion of the set of essays contained in this volume. With passing time, new sources of data have been uncovered, old data sets have been revised and reworked, and the techniques available for manipulating data have become more sophisticated. As the potential for generating new data sets has multiplied, it has become increasingly evident that there are important connections between the characteristics of the data implanted by its compilers and the variety of attempts to explain business cycles. It is the purpose of this collection of essays to challenge the reader to assess how well the analysis of business cycles is served by these developments. The essays are organized in two groups: (1) some cross-country examples of business cycles, particularly the Great Depression of the 1930s, and (2) some Phillips curves implied by both macro and micro data.[1]

What are the empirical regularities that need to be explained? In perhaps the most elaborate method for its time, Mitchell and Burns (1935) and Burns and Mitchell (1946) organized the experience of fluctuations around 'reference cycle relatives' basing their measurement on a wide variety of indices or business cycle indicators aggregated into 'diffusion indices' (Zarnowitz, 1992, chs 5–6). Since then, modern time series methods, for example, Hodrick and Prescott (1980), have presented investigators with a new approach using detrending techniques to separate trend from cycle. Such techniques, of course, are more fruitfully employed when the data sets are long. The development of these empirical methods has gone hand in hand with the development of new theories that emphasize not only the role of competitive equilibrium theory but also the integration of the study of business cycles with the study of long-term economic change (Cooley, 1995; Lucas and Stokey, 1989). The premium new techniques place on long data runs has drawn attention to the fact that most long runs of data are not consistently compiled, and their inconsistencies impart bias to the observed patterns to be explained (Romer, 1986a, 1989, 1991; Calomiris and Hanes, 1994 and Chapter 1 in this volume,[2] and Watson, 1994). In addition, new sources of data, both micro and macro, have been uncovered that present some variations in older established patterns (Urquhart, 1986; Carter and Sutch, 1991, 1992; Capie and Webber, 1985, among others). Some of these data extensions include the development of monthly and quarterly, as well as annual, series, raising further issues about new sources and interpolation procedures. The patterns to be explained, therefore, have changed in many details, if not in broader outline.

Calomiris and Hanes illustrate well the dilemma faced by business cycle analysts examining a period as long as the nineteenth century and up to 1914. For the United States over this period, important changes in economic structure occurred, particularly in the relative importance of the agricultural and industrial sectors. Concentration on industry data in the early period when generally acyclic agriculture dominated output leads to an upward bias in volatility. To correct for this, Calomiris and Hanes impose the postbellum relationship they find among series common to the postbellum and antebellum eras to construct an antebellum measure of output consistent with a postbellum measure based on the same series. This results in little or no change in volatility between the antebellum and postbellum eras. Such a procedure, of course, abstracts entirely from the change in economic structure that industrialization represents. The question remains: should one conclude that volatility underwent no change or should one conclude that industrialization made the economy more vulnerable to fluctuation?

One feature of business cycles that has endured successive re-examination of the evidence is their international character demonstrated by similar patterns across many countries (Backus and Kehoe, 1992; Backus *et al.*, 1993; Correia *et al.*, 1992: 459–60). There are, however, some exceptions. Klovland (Chapter 3), using an Hodrick–Prescott filter and a slightly modified Bry–Boschan (1971) procedure (Watson, 1994) finds fewer cycles in Britain than in the United States over the 1850–1914 period, and Chambers (1964) finds greater similarity between Canadian and United States cycles than between Canadian and British cycles. The experience of the Great Depression also was notably milder in Japan than elsewhere (Iwami, Okazaki and Yoshikawa, Chapter 2), while data revision in the German case makes the revival from depression look less dramatic relative to other recoveries than is usually supposed (Ritschl, Chapter 4).

Klovland takes as his point of departure the Friedman and Schwartz (1982) conclusion that it is only a statistical artifact that produces more cycles in the United States than in the United Kingdom between 1867 and 1975. Klovland's main contribution is the construction of monthly series for the United Kingdom that enable a more careful comparison with the United States data. The findings are that these revisions tend to establish a closer correspondence between the United States and United Kingdom chronologies favoring the tentative conclusion that Friedman and Schwartz are warranted in their conjecture about a 'statistical artifact.' Nonetheless, the work of revision to this point leaves substantial departures between the turning points for the two countries in the 1890–1914 period.

Iwami *et al.* use new macroeconomic data constructed by Ohkawi *et al.* (1966–88) to demonstrate that Japan grew slower in the 1920s and faster in the 1930s than many other countries. Rather than attribute this to early Keynesian policies or solely to a military buildup, Iwami *et al.* identify changes in economic structure as the leading cause. Manufacturing, particularly the heavy chemical industries, grew more rapidly than other sectors, such as agriculture. Part of these structural changes, nonetheless, was associated with military spending. In contrast to Hanes and Calomiris, Iwami *et al.* allow this consideration to accentuate the recovery phase of the cycle. Obviously an important next step in business cycle analysis using new data will have to be the emergence of some consensus on how structural and institutional change should be integrated into our view of how volatility may have changed over time.

Finally, Ritschl re-estimates aggregate output for Germany from 1925 to 1938, claiming that Hoffmann (1965), the traditional source of German historical data, gives an upward biased estimate of the volatility of aggregate output and too optimistic a view of interwar German economic performance. Ritschl introduces new data (official output and expenditure data ignored by Hoffmann), particularly for the metal processing industries related to shipbuilding and automobile production, that allow output series to be estimated without using Hoffmann's faulted interpolation procedures involving less satisfactory wage and employment data.

The most challenging observations to explain remain the varied cyclical behavior across countries and time periods of apparently related series used to shed light on cyclical phenomena: prices, wages, consumption, investment, productivity, and the changing volatility of these indicators over time.

One of the oldest themes in the business cycle literature is the tendency for prices to adjust slowly to aggregate shocks, the phenomenon of price inertia. The failure to reach any consensus in theory about this inertia is what has led Keynesian writers to rely on the empirical regularities described by the Phillips curve that makes the rate of inflation depend on current or recent output and inflation in the recent past. It has also motivated New Keynesians to try and develop a more satisfying theory of this inertia. Variability in the nominal rigidities over time has opened the way for economic historians to search for explanations based on long-term changes in technology and institutions, and to explore changes in the characteristics of data that might also account for historical changes in the observation of nominal rigidities.

The earliest attempt to formalize business cycle behavior as a negative relationship between unemployment and wage inflation was, of course, Phillips (1958) who examined British data from 1861. Phillips claimed that a trade-off existed in the United Kingdom between unemployment and wage inflation.

Notwithstanding opposition to this notion in more recent eras, the Phillips curve characterization of business cycles has endured and enjoys some rehabilitation today (King and Watson, 1994). The enormous literature that this idea has generated strangely pays little attention to the empirical foundation on which it was originally built. Phillips relied for wage data on Phelps Brown and Hopkins (1950), Bowley (1900), Bowley and Wood (1906) and Wood (1909), who in turn drew largely on artisan trade union data consisting of 'standard rates' or reservation wages (rather than a measure of actual earnings) for only a fraction of the labor force. The trade union records (containing unemployment benefits paid) were also the source of the unemployment data. The unemployed were conventionally defined as those receiving 'donation benefits' but generally seeking work, much as we define the unemployed today. It remains a question whether more broadly based data can support the standard Phillips curve as originally conceived.[3]

Sachs (1980) was among the first to notice a changing Phillips curve relationship over time in the United States. He found, using macro data, that wage and price rigidity increased over time, diminishing the slope of the short-run Phillips curve, particularly from 1890 to 1930 and again after World War II. Sachs blames long-term contracts and poor aggregate demand policies. James (1989) carries the investigation further back into the nineteenth century where he finds scant evidence of a fall in the Phillips curve coefficients for the United States that would indicate falling rigidity and a steepening of the curve. In fact, Dick (Chapter 6) finds some evidence of increasing price inertia in the United States before World War I that accords with the price inertia results of Gordon (1982a, 1990b), and with the increasing wage rigidity found by Hanes (1993). These somewhat different results obtained with the use of macro data, both old and new, suggest there may be a deeper truth than macro data alone can uncover. They are closely associated with new micro studies of output, wages, and prices described below.

In Dick, the Phillips curves for Canada and the United States are investigated with both old and new annual macro data series for the gold standard era, 1871–1913. Price inertia is examined in a neo-Keynesian framework as an adjustment to excess nominal income growth – the so-called 'triangle model of inflation' (Gordon, 1990a, 1990b, 1982a). The Canadian and American experiences, while offering a contrast, both demonstrate an unstable Phillips curve over the gold standard era. The Phillips curve appears to have steepened for Canada and flattened for the United States. The results for the United States appear to be consistent with other studies (James, 1993; Gordon, 1990b). The contrasting Canadian experience may be related to the relative openness of its economy to trade in both goods and assets that may have accelerated the absorption of nominal shocks into price level changes in the Canadian case as time passed (Hay, 1967; Rich, 1989).

The essays by James (Chapter 8) and by Carter and Sutch (Chapter 5) introduce micro evidence from labor markets that add to similar evidence uncovered by Sundstrom (1990, 1992) for Ohio workers to support the contention that wage rigidity increased in the 1890s. Particular attention has been focussed on the 1893–4 depression. Using monthly New Jersey data, James finds hours reduction by shutdowns rather than short time were important in the 1893–4 depression, similar to the Bernanke and Powell (1986) finding for the Great Depression of the 1930s. Carter and Sutch examine Connecticut labor market data, elaborating further on Carter and Sutch (1990). They find that Connecticut wages were remarkably sticky in the 1890s. Apparently 'short weeks' accounted for a large part of the labor market adjustment (Carter and Sutch, 1991). The possibility for still further work with micro data of other states also exists (Carter *et al.*, 1991).

Another approach to the apparent ambivalence of macro data is to consider how consistently constructed these data are over long periods of time. This enquiry has been undertaken for output, prices, wages, and unemployment starting with the seminal work of Romer (1986a, 1986b, 1988, 1989, 1991). Traditional series tend to be dominated by highly volatile commodity output and prices. Using deviations from trend of GNP and commodity output for the post-1909 period when these data are conceptually consistent, Romer uses an estimated time-varying relationship among these data to backcast GNP before 1908. The result is a discovery of considerably less pre-World War I volatility than found by existing studies using conventional data (DeLong and Summers, 1986b). Further efforts along a similar line tend to confirm these results (Balke and Gordon, 1989). Meanwhile, James (1993), using a VAR approach, has found increasing cyclical severity from the prebellum to the postbellum periods, but this appears to be due to greater sensitivity to monetary shocks rather than to greater volatility of the shocks themselves. While this latter plausibly assumes an explicit IS-LM Phillips curve model, VAR results can sometimes be reconciled with more than one structural interpretation (Keating and Nye, 1994).

More controversial has been the re-examination of the volatility issue with respect to wages, prices and unemployment. A basic paradox noted in the traditional literature appears to have been that over time volatility has declined while prices and wages have become less flexible. It has long been thought that both wages and prices have become less flexible, and therefore less sensitive to the business cycle, over time, particularly in the post-World War II era compared to the interwar period or earlier (Sachs, 1980). This has been attributed to the spread of long-term contracts and the rise of countercyclical policies. More attention to the consistency of times-series construction over long periods of time, however, has revealed that this long-standing view is inaccurate. Gordon (1983, 1988) for the United States, the United Kingdom, and Japan has demonstrated that there was in fact less cyclical responsiveness of nominal wages before 1922.

Using data constructed by Romer (1986b) or Hanes (1992), this type of result is corroborated for the United States by Allen (1992) using average hourly earnings, and by Hanes (1993). Only Schultz (1981), who also claims late nineteenth- and early twentieth-century wage stickiness, finds more stickiness in the post-World War II years. A further anomaly has been the discovery of an apparently smaller increase in wage inertia than in price inertia (Gordon, 1990a, 1990b), a finding that Hanes shows is misleading because it is due solely to non-comparability over time of the price series used. Finally, Dick points out that price flexibility is not necessarily the simple antithesis of volatility of output and employment. Wage and price rigidity may imply unemployment, but they do not alone necessarily imply a more volatile economy.

The issue of changing volatility has been pursued with respect to unemployment data as a corollary to the results for output. Romer (1986a, 1986b) found that the unemployment rate only appeared to stabilize after 1930 because methods of data collection changed. When the postwar data are organized on the same basis as the prewar data, it appears that little change in unemployment volatility occurred between the pre-1930 and post-1948 eras. In essence, Romer transformed postwar employment and labor force data using prewar methods – what has been dubbed as 'turning good data into bad data.' The apparent overturning of conventional views has been controversial since the technique used depends crucially on the assumption that certain relationships among the variables remained relatively unchanged over time (Lebergott, 1992). In an effort to resolve these issues, Weir (1992) dug deeper into the data to confirm Lebergott's unemployment series except for the 1890s when unemployment may have been exaggerated. Carter and Sutch (1992) pay particular attention to the 1890s and find that industrial suspensions and business failures were important causes of unemployment in these years.

In another dimension, related statistical work has explored the co-movements among variables used to characterize business cycles. For example, many older studies appeared to show the movement of prices was procyclical (Burns and Mitchell, 1946; Mills, 1946; Mitchell, 1951), and many business cycle theories have taken this to be a stylized fact (Barro, 1978; Lucas, 1972; Sargent, 1976). More recent studies, including those using VAR techniques, have found no stable pattern in the co-movement of prices and output other than in the interwar period (Cooley and Ohanian, 1991; Kydland, 1987; Backus and Kehoe, 1992; Friedman and Schwartz, 1982). Such new findings cast doubt on any attempt to explain cycles by imposing identifying restrictions that amount to assuming stable aggregate supply schedules while aggregate demand fluctuates (Keating and Nye, 1994). These same findings have also helped to motivate real business cycle theorists and further intensify the search for the data that properly characterizes cycles (Danthine and Donaldson, 1993). There is evidence of positive (negative) association between the trend deviations in output and price levels before (after) 1914 (Cooley and Ohanian, 1991). Backus and Kehoe (1992) obtain similar results before and after World War II. And Siklos and Burdekin (Chapter 9) (find negative correlation for the United Kingdom 1900–1946. Hanes (Chapter 7) and Hanes (1993) show that these anomalies are due to inconsistencies in the construction of wholesale price series over time. By distinguishing between finished and unfinished goods whose relative importance changes over time, Hanes constructs a consistent wholesale price series that rehabilitates the notion of procyclical price behavior, demonstrating price persistence throughout the late nineteenth and early twentieth centuries with somewhat greater persistence after 1914 consistent with a steepening of the Phillips curve. The possibility has also been recognized that different ways of characterizing co-movements in business cycle indicators may reconcile in a robust way differences among some of these findings (Den Haan, 1996; Baxter and King, 1995; Engel, 1993).

In view of these changing covariations of prices and output over time, how should we expect real wages and productivity to move over the cycle? Recognition of variation over time in the absorption of nominal shocks into prices, wages and output leaves room for variation in the behavior of real wages and productivity over the cycle. Much of the past literature is ambivalent about the pattern of real wages over the cycle, although Keynes (1936) took the position that real wages moved countercyclically. More recently, theory and evidence have moved away from this position. A leading explanation of wage stickiness has been the possibility that productivity may depend on wages (Yellen, 1984; Akerlof and Yellen, 1985). Also, the widespread observance of countercyclical markups, taken in combination with sticky wages, tends to generate acyclical or procyclical real wages (Dunlop, 1938; Keynes, 1939). In recent times, wages have been found to be either acyclic or procyclical, and productivity falls during recessions (Geary and Kennan, 1982; Bils, 1985; Bernanke and Powell, 1986; Bernanke and Parkinson, 1991; Allen, 1992; Zarnowitz, 1992: 145–50; Romer, 1986b). Lebergott (1957) implicitly assumes productivity was invariant to the cycle.

In the 1890s, however, Carter and Sutch find that because 'short weeks' and a decline in hours worked per worker accounted for a substantial part of the decline in labor input in Connecticut, real wages and productivity actually rose during the recession. Fatigue reduction, selective retention and extra effort considerations contributed to the productivity result, and countercyclical composition effects account for the wages result. James (Chapter 8) and James (1993) find more evidence of acyclical than countercyclical movement in the productivity of New Jersey workers, and wages were at first more and then less cyclically sensitive in the nineteenth century but experienced no change in cyclical sensitivity in the twentieth century.

These newer results are the direct product of investigating new disaggregated data. Bils (1985) uses a pooled sample of longitudinal surveys of young men over the years 1966–80 to conduct a panel study. Comparing the results obtained by using disaggregated data with the results obtained by using aggregate data reveals importantly that aggregation itself may impart a countercyclical bias. Lower-income persons tend to have procyclical wages and to weigh lightly in aggregates using incomes as weights. The Carter and Sutch results and the James results also depend on new micro data surveys of 500 and 1000 firms in Connecticut in 1894 and 1895 respectively, and several hundred manufacturing establishments in New Jersey in 1892. These labor surveys contain detailed information about wages paid, length of employment, hours worked, productivity, and occupation. The potential for further work along these lines, at least for the United States, is obvious (Carter *et al.*, 1991).

Still another perspective on how nominal shocks get absorbed into prices over time is provided by a literature that identifies the influence of monetary and exchange rate regimes (Alogoskoufis and Smith, 1991). The basic idea is that monetary regimes that are more accommodative of Phillips curve price level change lead to more persistence of inflation or a higher coefficient of lagged inflation (more price stickiness). This implies that regimes like the gold standard with low monetary and exchange rate accommodation experience low inflation persistence, presumably an illustration of the Lucas critique. Alogoskoufis and Smith find this to be true for the United States and the United Kingdom over the 1857–1987 period. This is similar to the findings of Gordon (1990b), except that the emphasis is on the driving significance of the type of monetary regime associated with these results. Siklos and Burdekin find little evidence of this role of monetary regime change in their re-examination of Canada, Sweden, the United Kingdom and the United States, and conclude that inflation persistence has been overestimated in the post-1914 era. Inflation persistence in this study is accounted for mainly by major events like wars, oil shocks, and institutional changes in central banking.

While the essays in this volume are but a small sample of the empirical efforts currently being made to improve our understanding of business cycle phenomena, they give some indication of the variety of empirical efforts being made and how these efforts interact with the attempts to develop better theories of the business cycle. Although the study of cycles is very old, the scope of enquiry that new data and techniques have recently opened up seems to suggest that this enquiry is still only in its early stages.

NOTES

1. At the Milan conference, the papers in group (1) were discussed by Michael Bordo, and the papers in group (2) by Tim Hatton.
2. Reprinting is courtesy of the *Journal of Economic History*.
3. Humphrey Southall (1986, 1989) is developing a database to examine this question more thoroughly (Southall and Gilbert, 1991)

ABSTRACTS

Chapter 1   Consistent Output Series for the Antebellum and Postbellum Periods: Issues and Preliminary Results
Charles W. Calomiris and Christopher Hanes

Existing series for real output that cover both the antebellum and postbellum periods indicate that GNP was more volatile after the War Between the States than before the War. But those series are inconsistent and unsuitable for comparing cyclical patterns across the nineteenth century. More consistent data show that output in cyclically sensitive sectors was no less volatile before the War Between the States than after it, and probably more volatile.

Chapter 2   The Great Depression in Japan: why was it so short?
Toru Iwami, Tetsuji Okazaki, and Hiroshi Yoshikawa

Compared with other major economies, the Great Depression in Japan was shorter and less severe, thanks to the growing export, public deficit-spending and expansionary monetary policy. Most important for these favorable factors was the suspension of the gold standard. Export growth and declining real interest rate stimulated investment, and the robustness of the banking sector contributed to moderate the depression. The expansionary policy in the 1930s facilitated the process of major industrial transformation characterized by the growth of the heavy-chemical industries, which had been hindered under the constraint of the orthodox policy in the 1920s.

Chapter 3   A Reassessment of the United Kingdom Business Cycle Chronology
Jan Tore Klovland

Several new monthly business cycle indicators for the United Kingdom covering the period from 1850 to 1914 are presented. The new monthly indicators comprise indices of real imports of raw materials, real exports, cotton consumption, railway freight receipts, coasting trade and bank clearings. Using the Bry–Boschan algorithm for determining the peaks and troughs of the detrended time series it is found that the new data produce a pattern of turning points that in many cases conforms quite well to the business cycle chronology for Britain derived by the NBER fifty years ago. The new chronology implies a modest increase in the number of cycles in the United Kingdom but there is still evidence of far fewer cycles in Britain than in the United States during the period before World War I.

Chapter 4   Measuring National Product in Germany, 1925–38: the State of the Debate and Some New Results
Albrecht Ritschl

The paper re-examines the widely used industrial and national product data of Hoffmann (1965) for the interwar period. Comparing these to the official industrial production and national income data, there is evidence of systematic upward bias in Hoffmann's estimates. For industrial production the bias is shown to be caused by Hoffmann assuming the wage share in German capital-goods industries to be constant at the level of 1913. Proceeding from sectoral data not used by Hoffmann, the bias between his own and the official industrial production index practically disappears. This implies also that his aggregate output series, which is used by Maddison (1995), must be adjusted downwards. Similar corrections apply to Hoffmann's expenditure series. Re-examining the components of national expenditure and completing the time series with archival data from Nazi Germany suggests a downward revision which puts Hoffmann's expenditure estimate even slightly below the official figures. It is argued that for the time being, the latter are the most reliable existing estimate, and a complete expenditure account is provided.

Chapter 5   The Labor Market a Hundred Years Ago: New, Micro-level Evidence on Long-term Change from the Depression of 1893–4

Susan B. Carter and Richard Sutch

Recent revisions to long-run annual series on unemployment and average hourly earnings seem to suggest that macroeconomic labor market outcomes have been remarkably uniform over the past 100 years. Our analysis of new, firm-level survey data from the severe depression of 1893–4 reveals significant differences. We find that in the 1890s downturn about half the reduction in labor inputs was achieved by short weeks; labor productivity rose; and average hourly wages rose despite the fact that no firm that cut employment increased wage rates. These empirical results point to important changes in labor market outcomes over time and suggest flaws in the estimation procedures used to construct the standard series on unemployment and average hourly earnings for the pre-World War I period.

Chapter 6   Phillips Curves under the Gold Standard Regime: Canada and the United States Compared

Trevor J.O. Dick

The short-run interaction between changes in prices and output in the United States and Canada is investigated using a modern approach to the Phillips curve that permits inertia in the adjustment to excess nominal income growth to be observed. Price stickiness is observed using annual data for the 1871–1913 period in both countries. A trend break in the Canadian data around 1895 marks a parameter change lessening the impact of excess nominal income growth on output (steepening the Phillips curve). In the United States, by contrast, there is less evidence of a trend break and output appears to have become more sensitive to nominal income change over time (flattening the Phillips curve).

Chapter 7 Consistent Wholesale Price Series for the United States 1860–1990

Christopher Hanes

Existing wholesale price indices and GNP deflator series for prewar decades put much more weight on prices of raw materials and intermediate goods than do postwar series. That affects their behavior over business cycles, and comparisons to behavior of postwar series, because prices of less-finished goods are more flexible than prices of more-finished goods. I present a consistent wholesale price index based on the same set of goods from 1860 through 1990, and compare the cyclical behavior of this series to that of the standard wholesale price index.

Chapter 8 The Cyclical Adjustment of Hours and Employment in the Prewar United States: Evidence from the Depression of 1893–4

John A. James

This paper examines the relative importance of hours reductions and employment cuts in the cyclical adjustment of labor input in the United States before World War I, using monthly firm-level data reported by the New Jersey Bureau Labor Statistics for the Depression of 1893–4. The data indicate that, as in the postwar period, layoffs and dismissals were the principal means by which firms reduced labor inputs. Although to be sure hours reductions were larger then than now, there seems to have been little fundamental change over the last century.

Chapter 9 Central Bank Behaviour, the Exchange Rate Regime, and the Persistence of Inflation in Historical Perspective

Pierre L. Siklos and Richard C.K. Burdekin

The present study considers how inflation has evolved since the late 1800s in the mirror of commonly used specifications of the Phillips Curve. We also aim to quantify the impact of various important economic and institutional events on inflation developments. Novel features of our analysis include the following: estimation of a pooled data set from four industrialized countries; examination of the sensitivity of our results to how the data are filtered; and exploration of how inferences about the slope of the Phillips curve are affected by the source of the relevant time series. We find that inflation persistence is considerably reduced if allowance is made for large unusual events in economic history as well as changes in government–central bank relations.

PART I

Recasting Business Cycles with New Data:
a Cross-country Sampling

1. Consistent output series for the antebellum and postbellum periods: issues and preliminary results

Charles Calomiris and Christopher Hanes*

INTRODUCTION

Time-series data on aggregate output can reveal historical changes in the characteristics of business cycles: patterns in output movements and relations between output and financial events or other macroeconomic variables like price levels. Associating changes in cyclical patterns with developments in economic structure and institutions is an important job for economic historians and may bear on issues in macroeconomic theory. Comparisons across historical periods require series that are consistent across those periods, constructed in the same way from the same kinds of information. Otherwise, incomparabilities in the data may be mistaken for changes over time in economic behavior. Christina Romer and others have constructed output series for postbellum decades – the years between the War between the States and World War I – designed to be consistent with postwar twentieth-century series and allow comparison between late nineteenth-century and postwar cycles (Romer, 1986a, 1989; Balke and Gordon, 1989; Miron and Romer, 1990).

But some of the most important changes in economic structure took place *before* or shortly into the postbellum period. By the 1880s the more developed regions of the United States had already undergone their industrial revolution. Firms supplied concentrated markets through reliable distribution networks (Chandler, 1977). Establishments (plants) were already large; Anthony O'Brien (1988: 645) shows that 'almost two-thirds of the increase in factory size [employment] that was to take place between 1869 and 1929 had occurred by 1889.' Thus, the effects on business cycles of the rise of large-scale industry may show up most clearly in series that span the nineteenth century, covering both antebellum and postbellum periods.

* Thanks to Thomas Senior Berry, John James, and especially Robert Gallman for advice and data.

Rare attempts to push back the frontier of macroeconomic history, like those of John James (1989, 1993) have been hampered by a lack of consistent antebellum–postbellum data. The standard National Bureau of Economic Research (NBER) chronology of peaks and troughs is based on different information and criteria before and after 1854 (Moore and Zarnowitz, 1986: 755). Robert Gallman's unpublished annual series on real GNP begins in 1834 and has been used to compare antebellum with postbellum and even twentieth-century cycles. But the briefest glance at Gallman's notes reveals that the information behind his annual 'interpolations' between census-year benchmarks varies enormously from decade to decade. The antebellum data are much scantier than those for the 1870s and 1880s, which are in turn less reliable than those for the 1890s.[1] Indeed, Gallman has refrained from publishing the series precisely because he does not trust its year-to-year movements. Thomas Berry's annual real GNP series is derived from a nominal GNP series using deflators that were 'smoothed slightly so as to yield GNP series over 1789–1889 … with comparable volatility before and after 1889' (Berry, 1988: 6). The nominal GNP series is in turn based on a mix of nominal and real series, with many components absent before the 1860s (Berry, 1968: Table 3).

We have begun a project to create a peak–trough chronology and an output series covering both antebellum and postbellum years through 1914, consistent and comparable throughout. This chapter discusses some issues associated with the construction of the output series and presents some preliminary answers to one of the questions the series will be designed to answer: did the amplitude of business cycles change from the antebellum to the postbellum period?

As John James (1993: 710) found, the Gallman series suggests that 'There was a substantial increase in the degree of business cycle severity of economic fluctuations in the United States over the nineteenth century.' This can be seen in Table 1.1, which shows statistics on the Gallman series' deviations from two different trends: simple quadratic time trends (time and time squared), separate for each period, and the Hodrick–Prescott trend.[2] The antebellum period is restricted to its last two decades because the data relied on below will not allow us to say much about years before 1840. Consistent with James's observation, the Gallman series appears more volatile over 1870–1914 than over 1840–59. Dividing the postbellum period at 1890, the period from 1891 to 1914 appears more volatile than from 1870 to 1890 but both appear more volatile than from 1840 to 1860. Table 1.1 also shows statistics for the Berry real GNP series. The Berry series is only slightly more volatile over 1870–1914 than over 1840–59, and is less volatile over 1870–90 than over 1840–59.

What answer do we get from more consistent output series? That depends on one's definition of 'output,' in a way that has been largely ignored by the literature following Romer.

Table 1.1   Volatility of existing series

Trend: Period	Standard deviation of deviation from trend in log of			
	Gallman real GNP		Berry real GNP	
	Quadratic time	Hodrick–Prescott	Quadratic time	Hodrick–Prescott
1840–1859	0.0365	0.0361	0.0344	0.0354
1870–1914	0.0553	0.0461	0.0396	0.0383
1870–1890	0.0519	0.0442	0.0276	0.0276
1891–1914	0.0572	0.0469	0.0483	0.0464

Sources: Gallman series provided by Robert Gallman; Berry series from Berry (1988).

WHAT DO WE MEAN BY 'OUTPUT'? GNP VERSUS INDUSTRIAL PRODUCTION

In 1950 Simon Kuznets observed that sectors vary in their sensitivity to business cycles. Hence the cyclical behavior of aggregate output and employment might change over time as a result of shifts in the relative importance of different sectors, even if 'there are no marked secular shifts within each sector in responsiveness to business cycles. … For example, a decline in the weight of agriculture, combined with a lack of responsiveness of agricultural output to business cycles, would mean, other conditions being equal, a widening of business cycle amplitudes' (Kuznets, 1951: 159). Wesley Mitchell, George Burns, and other National Bureau researchers had shown agriculture to be *uniquely* acyclical:

> the basic industry of growing crops does not expand and contract in unison with mining, manufacturing, trading, transportation, and finance. … In no other great industry for which we have records are the cyclical fluctuations so irregularly related to business cycles as in crop husbandry. (Mitchell, 1951: 56, 58)

Farm output and employment 'undergo cyclical movements, but they have little or no relation to business cycles' (Burns, 1951: 7).

This had been especially obvious during the Great Depression: from 1930 to 1932 employment fell in every major non-agricultural sector, including trade and services; aggregate employment fell by 14 per cent. Meanwhile farm employment *increased* by 3 per cent.[3] But it had also been true in earlier decades. In his study of the period between the War between the States and World War I, Edwin Frickey (1942: 229) found:

> agricultural production patterns traced out short-term fluctuations bearing little resemblance to those for other major production groups. The causal relationships

between the agricultural and non-agricultural groups certainly did not express themselves in the form of any simple correlation.

That is not to say that agricultural *incomes* are acyclical. There may be cyclical patterns in the relative price of farm output.

Table 1.2 demonstrates these points for the postbellum and twentieth-century postwar periods, with regressions of deviation from trend in real GNP on deviation from trend in sectoral employment and output indices (all in logs). For the postbellum period we use both the Romer and the Balke and Gordon series on real GNP and Frickey's indices of output in manufacturing and transportation. The Frickey manufacturing index runs from 1861 through 1914 but is not consistent until the 1870s (several of its component series are missing before that decade) (Frickey, 1947). There are no reliable annual data on employment for most of the postbellum period. For the postwar period, manufacturing is represented by the Federal Reserve Board Index of Materials Production, which is comparable to the Frickey manufacturing index (Romer, 1986a). For employment the sample ends with 1980 because the farm data were not collected from 1981 through 1984.

The first part of the table shows postwar patterns. Regressing real GNP on manufacturing production gives a significantly positive coefficient. For agricultural output the coefficient is zero and insignificant. Employment levels in all non-agricultural sectors are strongly procyclical, but agricultural employment is countercyclical. The second part of the table shows results for the postbellum period. Regressing either real GNP series on either the manufacturing or transportation indices gives a significantly positive coefficient. Regressing output on the crop index gives a much smaller and insignificant coefficient. The Frickey manufacturing index is closely correlated with the transportation index but not with the crop index.

The fact that agricultural fluctuations are independent of business cycles has not received enough attention in the literature on macroeconomic history. DeLong and Summers (1986b: 685) argue that cyclical volatility might have fallen over time because 'agriculture, which is notoriously unstable, has shrunk rapidly as a share of GNP'. Romer treats volatility of industrial production and real GNP including agriculture as more-or-less equivalent indicators of business cycle severity. Whether or not this is justifiable for comparisons between periods since the 1870s, it is probably not for antebellum and postbellum periods. The shift out of agriculture was especially rapid across the nineteenth century. From 1840 to 1900 farm gross product (output value minus value of inputs excluding capital depreciation) fell from about one-half of GNP to about one-fifth. Agricultural employment fell from 63 per cent of total employment to 40 per cent. Meanwhile the share of manufacturing in GNP or employment doubled.[4]

Table 1.2   Agriculture and business cycles[1]

Post-1947

Output 1947–90. Real GNP regressed on output indices

Manufactures	Agriculture	
Materials, production	Crops and livestock	Crops only
0.4312	–0.0291	–0.0363
(12.831)	(–0.275)	(–0.493)

Employment 1947–80. Real GNP regressed on employment

	Non-farm			Farm	
All non-farm	Services	Other, incl. manuf.	Manuf. only	All	Hired only
1.0091	1.2440	0.6741	0.6407	–0.3896	–0.2522
(8.159)	(4.552)	(10.147)	(10.262)	(–3.046)	(–3.823)

Pre-1914

Output 1869–1914. Real GNP regressed on output indices

Romer GNP			Balke & Gordon GNP		
Manuf. Frickey	Transp. Frickey	Agric. Crops only	Manuf. Frickey	Transp. Frickey	Agric. Crops only
0.2311	0.2203	0.0076	0.4136	0.4918	0.0562
(4.847)	(3.147)	(0.111)	(7.397)	(6.053)	(0.582)

Frickey manufacturing index regressed on output indices

Transport Frickey	Agriculture Crops only
1.0651	0.0357
(9.157)	(0.204)

Note:
1.   Variables are deviations of logs from Hodrick–Prescott trend *t*-statistics in parentheses.

Sources: Postwar real GNP, 1982 dollars, from US Council of Economic Advisors. Postbellum GNP from Romer (1989) and Balke and Gordon (1989). Postwar manufacturing and output indices from US Council of Economic Advisors. Employment from US Bureau of Labor Statistics. Postbellum farm output index from United States Department of Agriculture (1935). Frickey indices from Frickey (1947).

We intend to construct a consistent antebellum–postbellum *index of industrial production* along the lines of the postbellum Frickey manufacturing index and twentieth-century Federal Reserve Board production indices. We believe it is impossible to construct an adequately consistent series for real GNP, if only because antebellum data on many important components of farm production are fragmentary or missing altogether.

DATA FOR A CONSISTENT OUTPUT SERIES

Our first job was to collect all data that began by 1840, ran through the postbellum period, were consistent throughout, and indicated the movements of variables that might be correlated with industrial production. That includes quantities of just about any industrial output or input, including transportation services and imports.[5] We excluded data on prices, financial and monetary series, and *nominal* output values in the absence of reliable and consistent deflators. Many such series show relations to real output, but we wanted to use the output index to examine those relations and look for changes over time. To indicate cyclical movements the data must be observed at least annually.

We found seven annual series on outputs and inputs that met the requirements; none on a shorter frequency. Most are products of considerable research by others. We are fairly certain that no more can be constructed from primary sources. The series are listed and briefly described in the appendix. Two – pig iron production and cotton consumption – are components of the postbellum Frickey manufacturing index and may be fairly direct indicators of output in two important industries: cotton textiles and iron and steel products, which by themselves made up more than 10 per cent of manufacturing employment in the 1840s and 1850s, and slightly less than 10 per cent after the war (Lebergott, 1966: Table 1). There is no series on the real value of total imports, but we found consistent import volume data for 25 individual goods.[6] Some are consumption goods, hence a function of aggregate income; others are inputs, more directly linked to industrial production. The import series is interrupted in 1843, when the fiscal year shifted from ending September to ending June.

It is useful to think of each series as made up of three components: a cyclical component, correlated with economy-wide output movements; an idiosyncratic component reflecting sector- or product-specific shocks to demand or supply; and errors in measurement, presumably independent across the series. For many of the domestic series there is reason to believe that antebellum observations contain larger errors. Import series appear about as reliable in antebellum as in postbellum years, but may be subject to relatively large idiosyncratic shocks associated with changes in tariffs. It is hard to account for the effect of these on import levels. There is no index of general tariff rates. The usual proxy, aggregate tariff revenue relative to aggregate import value, varies with the composition of imports as well as changes in protection. Nineteenth-century tariffs were a bizarre mix of nominal per-unit duties and *ad valorem* rates, often applied to the same good at the same time. Reclassification of a good from one schedule to another could change effective protection without any change in official rates. Legislative changes in rates or classifications were often peculiar to certain goods; sometimes rates were dropped on some goods and raised on others. Taussig (1931a) gives many examples. Imports could be affected by *expectations* of rate changes that had not yet taken place. Consider wool in the 1890s, described by Taussig (1931b: 299):

> The [duty-]free admission of wool in 1894 and the re-imposition of duties three years later necessarily caused great shifts. In the year just before the act of 1894, when it was almost certain that wool would become [duty-]free, imports naturally shrank to almost nothing. They then rose abruptly as soon as the abolition of the duty went into effect. Again, after the election of McKinley in the autumn of 1896 it became in turn almost certain that the duty would be restored. Consequently during the fiscal year 1896–1897, imports were rushed in from every possible quarter while wool was still free. They then fell abruptly after the passage of the tariff act of 1897 … Not until 1900 were the effects of this abnormal situation out of the way.

A wool import series would probably give a fairly inaccurate indication of woolen production, much less aggregate production, over the 1890s.

In this chapter we restrict our focus to a couple of imports for which changes in tariffs and substitution between domestic and foreign supplies are not a problem: coffee and tea. Both were free of duty from 1830 through the War between the States and again after 1872 (Taussig, 1931a: 184, 188). These series are described in the appendix. In future work we will examine the other import series.

CHANGES IN VOLATILITY IN THE SET OF CONSISTENT SERIES

An increase in the volatility of industrial production from the antebellum to the postbellum period should show up as an increase in the volatility of each series, unless it is swamped by reductions in the volatility of idiosyncratic shocks and measurement errors. The first part of Table 1.3 shows volatility measures for the series over 1840–59 and 1870–1914. The break in import data at 1843 prevents us from calculating Hodrick–Prescott trends for those series. (Quadratic trends were estimated with that year excluded from the sample.)

With the exception of anthracite coal production, each of the series, including cotton and pig iron, appears *less* volatile in the postbellum period. The result for lead depends on the definition of trend. Coffee and tea imports, gross or net of re-export, appear less volatile in the postbellum period than over 1840–59 or a longer antebellum period, 1821–59. Thus, the behavior of the series taken one at a time suggests that output volatility *decreased* from the antebellum to the postbellum period.

Table 1.3   Volatility in consistent antebellum–postbellum series

Individual series

Standard deviation of deviation from trend

		Quadratic		Hodrick–Prescott	
	1821–59	1840–59	1870–1914	1840–59	1870–1914
Anthracite coal		0.0609	0.1059	0.0925	0.0981
Bituminous coal		0.0810	0.0797	0.0831	0.0763
New York Canal traffic		0.1720	0.0985	0.1699	0.0924
Erie Canal traffic		0.1571	0.1499	0.1679	0.1380
Cotton consumption		0.1374	0.0858	0.1378	0.0779
Lead production		0.1401	0.1601	0.1413	0.1105
Pig iron production		0.2246	0.1686	0.2214	0.1637
Imports (excludes 1843)					
Coffee, gross	0.1526	0.1209	0.1199		
Coffee, net	0.1807	0.1340	0.1138		
Tea, gross	0.2422	0.1892	0.1059		
Tea, net	0.2451	0.2033	0.1153		

Output deviation indices

	1840–59	1870–1913	1870–90	1891–1913
Quadratic				
Standard deviation	0.1073	0.0826	0.0875	0.0784
R^2 (Frickey on proxy)		0.913	0.917	0.907
Hodrick–Prescott				
Standard deviation	0.1072	0.0780	0.0821	0.0757
R^2 (Frickey on proxy)		0.920	0.913	0.930

Unfortunately, as mentioned above, the antebellum observations of some of the series may be more affected by measurement errors, though the fact that nearly all, including the import series, show greater antebellum volatility suggests that alone cannot account for the difference between periods. To deal with the problem directly, we can construct an index of movements in the individual series. An index might have different volatility properties from any or all of the component series, since they are not independent. There are several ways to construct an index. Here we will construct a couple suitable for the question at hand.

Romer and others have used deviations from trend in the Frickey manufacturing index to indicate postbellum business cycles. Taking that as our standard, we can choose weights for deviations in the individual series so as to best reproduce deviations in the Frickey index. The weights can be taken from a regression of deviations in the Frickey index on deviations in the set of antebellum–postbellum series. Applying the estimated coefficients to the series over both the antebellum and postbellum periods gives the regression's predicted value of deviations from trend in the Frickey series for both periods – a consistent, comparable index of deviations from trend in output. This procedure is reasonable if we can believe that the relation between the set of series and manufacturing production as measured by the Frickey index was stable across the nineteenth century. We do not have enough data to check that, but we can at least make sure that the relation between the antebellum–postbellum series and the Frickey index is stable within the postbellum period. Applying the procedure to deviations from both quadratic and Hodrick–Prescott trends gives two consistent indices.

There are a couple of complications. First, we cannot use the import series in this exercise since they break at 1843. Second, the Frickey index is on a calendar-year basis, but some of the input and output series are not. The observations of a given series may be most closely correlated with the Frickey index at the leading or lagging year. We regressed the Frickey series on each series individually to see which timing was best (again, all expressed as deviation from trend). All gave the closest correlation relative to the same year except anthracite coal production, which was best at the leading year, and lead production and cotton consumption, which were best at the lagged year.

Then we regressed the Frickey index on *all* the series (current-year, lead or lag as appropriate) and applied the estimated coefficients to construct the two antebellum–postbellum indices. Figure 1.1 shows the values for these indices over postbellum years, along with the corresponding deviations from trend in the Frickey index. The two sets of series show similar peaks and troughs. The second part of Table 1.3 shows R^2s from the regressions. In either case the set of consistent series can predict more than 91 per cent of the variation in deviation from trend in the Frickey index. To check that the relation is stable within the postbellum period, we regressed the Frickey index on the antebellum–postbellum indices in two subsamples from the postbellum period

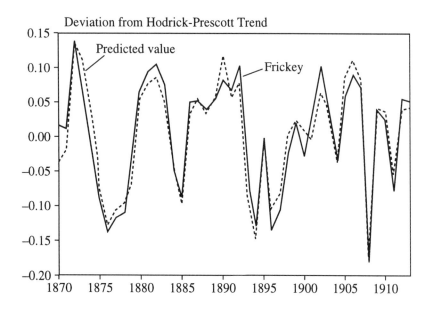

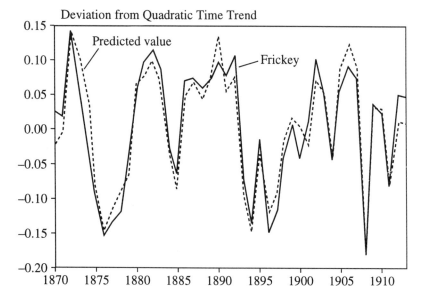

Figure 1.1   Antebellum–postbellum indices and Frickey index, 1870–1913

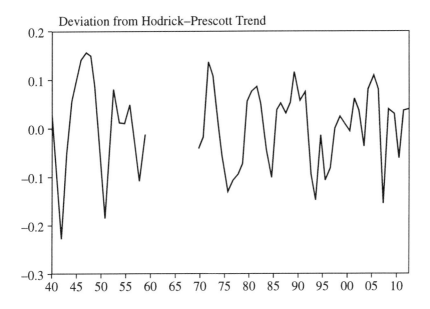

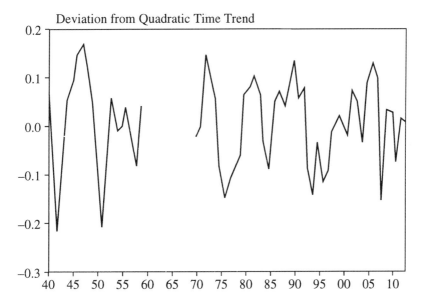

Figure 1.2   Antebellum–postbellum indices, 1840–59 and 1870–1913

and observed the R^2s shown in Table 1.3. The relation appears quite stable from 1870–90 to 1891–1914, so it *may* have been stable into the antebellum period as well.

What about the change from the antebellum to the postbellum period in the overall volatility of output? (Note that the antebellum index must be compared to the postbellum index constructed in the same way, rather than to the Frickey index.) Figure 1.2 shows the series over both periods. Neither appears more volatile in the postbellum period. The second part of Table 1.3 confirms this judgement: the standard deviation of either series is smaller in the postbellum period.

CONCLUSION

The set of consistent antebellum–postbellum series clearly indicates that cyclical movements in industrial production were no larger, and were probably smaller, in the postbellum period than in the last two decades of the antebellum period. The cyclical volatility of GNP could nonetheless have been greater in the postbellum period, only because the share of cyclical sectors in aggregate output had grown relative to the share of acyclical agriculture. Would that constitute an increase in the severity of business cycles?

APPENDIX: ANTEBELLUM–POSTBELLUM SERIES

This appendix gives the series in italics, the source in brackets, and the starting year of the series.

Bituminous coal production, 1000 tons (Eavenson, 1942: 426–34) 1800.

These and the anthracite data are from many sources of different kinds. The numbers seem to be much better in the later antebellum decades (1840s and 1850s).

Pennsylvania anthracite coal production, 1000 short tons (Eavenson, 1942: 426–34) 1808.

Lead production from domestic and foreign ores, short tons (US Bureau of Mines, 1929: 12–14) 1821.

New York State canal tonnage, All and *Erie* only (*Historical Statistics* Q556, Q557) 1837.

Cotton consumption (US Department of Commerce, 1929: 57) 1826.

Pig iron production, thousand gross tons (1840–53: Fogel, 1964: 166; 1854–1914: American Iron and Steel Institute 1917) 1840.

Coffee and tea imports (US Treasury Department, Bureau of Statistics, 1896; US Bureau of the Census 1907, 1917) 1821.

NOTES

1. The series is described in Gallman (1966). Examples of its use include James (1989, 1993) and Temin (1969).
2. This is described in Kydland and Prescott (1990). If x is the time-series variable, the trend $\hat{x}$ is defined as the solution to

$$\min_{\hat{x}_t} \sum_{t_0}^{t_1} (x_t - \hat{x}_t)^2 + \lambda \sum_{t_0+1}^{t_1-1} [(\hat{x}_{t+1} - \hat{x}_t) - (\hat{x}_t - \hat{x}_{t-1})]^2$$

   with λ set at 400 for annual data.
3. See United States Bureau of the Census (1975): non-agricultural sectoral employment series D127-141, total employment series D5, farm employment series K174.
4. Farm gross product from Towne and Rasmussen (1960). Manufacturing value-added from Gallman (1960: 43). GNP from Gallman (1966: 26) and Balke and Gordon (1989: Table 10). Employment from Lebergott (1966: Table 1).
5. Mitchell found that 'imports conform closely to business cycles while exports do not' (Burns, 1951: 7). See Mitchell (1951) for discussions and examples of other variables.
6. Total nominal value deflated by a price index would be suitable only if we had a consistently constructed import price index *and* the composition of imports were acyclical or held a consistent cyclical pattern between the antebellum and postbellum periods.

2. The Great Depression in Japan: why was it so short?

Toru Iwami, Tetsuji Okazaki, and Hiroshi Yoshikawa[*]

INTRODUCTION

The Great Depression in the 1930s was a global phenomenon, but individual countries experienced differences in the depth and width of the slump. Compared internationally, the depression in Japan was undoubtedly short and 'mild' in terms of the decline in GNP. The present study attempts to identify those factors which made the depression less severe than elsewhere, and enquires how economic policies contributed to recovery from the depression in Japan.

The Japanese literature on the economic situation in the 1930s has traditionally tended to emphasize difficulties in Japan compared with those in other countries. This tradition is still alive in the more frequent use of the term *Kyokoh* (economic crisis) than *Fukyoh* (depression), which partly reflects the strong influence of Marxist economics on economic historians. Economic historians in Japan prefer a term such as *Showa Kyokoh*, with an implication that the economic downturn was so severe that the resulting political instability constituted the background to the military elites' takeover of power, leading to the war with China and subsequently to World War II.

The *Estimates of Long-term Economic Statistics of Japan since 1868* (hereafter abbreviated to *LTES*), edited by K. Ohkawa *et al.* and published from 1966 to 1988 now provides the basis for more objective macroeconomic analysis of the Japanese economy than was previously possible. The present study depends largely on this series. However, some of its limitations are discussed in the Appendix.

In the next section we review whether or not this traditional assessment of the depression in Japan is actually supported by statistical data. Next we consider the causes of the economic recovery, examining each demand factor. The role of economic policy in the recovery is discussed before our concluding remarks.

[*] This is a revised version of the paper presented at the 11th International Economic History Congress in Milan, September 1994. We appreciate comments and suggestions by Takafusa Nakamura, Dieter Lindenlaub, Gerold Ambrosius, Michael Bordo, and Trevor Dick.

STYLIZED FACTS AND QUESTIONS ARISING

International Comparison of Growth Performance

Table 2.1 presents an international comparison of growth performance among major countries. The growth rate in Japan belongs to the lower group, in fact the third lowest in the 1920s after Britain and Italy. In the 1930s, however, it was by far the highest. Germany recorded the second highest growth in the 1930s, but her economic situation was not as good as the average growth rate might imply; as Figure 2.1 illustrates, Germany experienced sharp decline from 1930 to 1932, while Japan showed only a slight fall in GDP (with no decline in terms of GNP).

Table 2.1   Average GDP growth rate of the major countries (%)

Period	Britain	Germany	France	Italy	US	Japan	Japan (GNP)
1919–29	1.03	5.16	5.79	1.66	3.42	2.39	1.80
1929–39	1.79	4.11	0.34	2.10	0.12	4.64	4.69

Note: Average growth rate is calculated as $(\ln Y_t - \ln Y_0)/10 \times 100$; data from Maddison (1991).

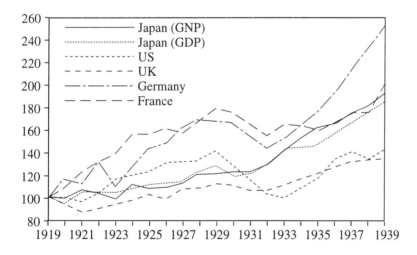

Source: As Table 2.1.

Figure 2.1   GDP (GNP) movements of the major countries (1919 = 100)

Prices in Japan, on the other hand, fell remarkably within a short period. But here we simply note that prices declined to a lesser extent in the heavy and chemical industries than in the textile and food industries and in agriculture (Table 2.2). This contrast is related to the emerging 'dual structure of the economy' which we will discuss below.

Table 2.2   Growth performance in each industrial sector

Year	Heavy and chemical				Textile and food				Agriculture			
	O	E	P	RW	O	E	P	RW	O	E	P	RW
1929	100	100	100	100	100	100	100	100	100	100	100	100
1931	102.6	92.8	77.7	111.7	100.0	91.7	63.9	114.3	94.9	99.7	60.6	82.6
1936	236.5	213.2	151.3	99.3	135.2	91.7	86.4	92.8	108.8	98.3	93.5	76.0
Annual rate of change (%)												
1929–31	1.3	–3.7	–12.6	5.5	0.0	–4.3	–22.4	6.7	–2.6	–0.1	–25.0	–9.6
1931–36	16.7	16.6	4.7	–2.4	6.0	0.0	3.9	–4.2	2.7	–0.3	8.7	–1.7

Notes:
O = real output; E = employment; P = price; RW = real wage rate, deflated by CPI.
Heavy and chemical is an arithmetic mean of metal, machine and chemical.

Source: LTES, 2, 8, 9, 10.

A popular explanation for Japan's good performance in the 1930s is the 'Keynesian policies as early as 1932 without a Keynes' (Kindleberger, 1973: 17).[1] These 'Keynesian policies' were, however, not unique to Japan, but shared by other developed countries where the depression was more severe. As is well known, the New Deal government adopted public-deficit spending through a series of public works and relief expenditure. Currency depreciation and easy monetary policy were pursued in Britain.[2] Therefore, it is a question why the seemingly similar policies brought about different outcomes in the United States, Britain, and Japan.

On the other hand, Japan and Britain illustrate a similar contrast between the two decades: the growth rate was low in the 1920s and high in the 1930s. It suggests the importance of the foreign exchange and monetary policies; the currency overvaluation in the 1920s might have depressed the economy, whereas the suspension of the gold standard relieved it of deflationary pressures. Similarly, the reason given for the German slump being so severe and the depression in the United States and France lasting so long is often related to the traditional policy stance under the gold standard.[3]

Although we discuss below the ways in which economic policy contributed to recovery in Japan, the growth performance seems to depend more on other factors, such as the economic structure, than on economic policy.

Industrial Structure

There was a widening gap between the 'modern' sector, represented by large firms, and the traditional sector as well as agriculture. Nakamura (1971) and others stressed the emergence of the 'dual structure of the economy.' Within the modern sector, the industrial structure changed drastically away from the textile industry toward the heavy and chemical industries.

Particularly noteworthy is the contrast between stagnating agriculture and growing manufacturing, on the one hand, and between light (textile and food) industry and heavy and chemical industries, on the other (see Table 2.2). While employment in every sector showed a decline from the peak of 1929 to the trough of 1931, the heavy and chemical industries alone recorded a slight *increase* in real output during the slump and a rapid increase in both output and employment thereafter. A significant contrast is observed for price as well as for output. In the heavy and chemical industries, the price fell only slightly between 1929 and 1931 and its level actually stood 50 per cent higher in 1936 than in 1929. In both light industry and agriculture, on the other hand, prices had not recovered to the 1929 level by 1936. How is this difference among sectors to be explained? How did it affect the growth performance of the Japanese economy during the 1930s?[4]

Second, why did the growth potentials of the heavy and chemical industries not materialize in the 1920s, but had to wait until the 1930s?[5] Japan seems to have had technological potential even in the 1920s, and yet the development of heavy and chemical industries did not take place until the 1930s, when importing the necessary technology was more difficult than in the 1920s; the realization of this potential must have been some what hindered in the 1920s. We will take up this issue, discussing the relationship between investment and economic policy.

Third, why did the textile and other traditional sectors stagnate? As we discuss below, the textile industry had been suffering from a fall in exports prior to the general downturn that began in 1929. But it still continued to be the most important export item through the late 1930s. It remains, therefore, an issue why the textile industry declined despite the growth in total exports and the rising real income in the modern sectors.

Finally, Japan maintained the share of agriculture in GDP and in total employment at a higher level than did most of the major countries. Did this large share of agriculture help economic recovery or worsen the depression? Although agriculture was hit most severely in the depression, the roundabout effect is not self-evident.

More specifically, there was a substantial transfer of income from the depressed agricultural sector to the urban modern sector in the interwar years. The relative productivity (and income) of agriculture decreased substantially throughout the 1920s and 1930s, after long-run stability from the 1880s onwards.[6] The terms of trade between agriculture and other industrial sectors turned in favor of the latter. As Table 2.2 demonstrates, agricultural prices declined substantially, due to various reasons such as a good harvest in 1930, increasing imports of rice at a time of poor crops, and a sudden fall in the export of silk products to the United States. The agricultural area, heavily dependent on rice and silk, suffered seriously from the decreasing income; there are a number of gloomy images of the depression, such as the tenant farmers' riot, and their daughters being sold to brothels.[7]

Did the income transfer from agriculture to other sectors of the economy affect the recovery positively or negatively? How did private consumption actually behave during the 1930s?

Given stylized facts and the questions arising, the following analysis focuses on the period from the beginning of the slump in 1929 to the outbreak of the Chino-Japanese War in 1937; thereafter, the government took over general control of the economy, and the market mechanism was fundamentally impeded.

EXPLANATIONS

Growth Accounting Using Demand Factors

Tables 2.3 and 2.4 show the relative contribution of each demand component to the growth in real GNP for the United States and Japan, respectively. In the United States, both private consumption and investment declined substantially from 1930 to 1933. In Japan, on the other hand, both declined only slightly and recovered as early as 1933. In addition, Japan recorded large increases in both exports and government expenditure.

Focusing on the critical years 1931–2 (Table 2.4), we find a remarkable contribution by increased public expenditure (fixed capital formation and consumption, including military) in 1931 and by exports in 1932. The share of public expenditure, however, declined after 1932. Private consumption and exports, on the other hand, continued to grow in the following years. Although the contribution of private fixed investment was smaller than that of export, it stayed at a high level in 1934 and 1935, which was naturally reflected in the early recovery of the capital goods (heavy and chemical) industries.

In sum, the pump-priming effect of public expenditure worked well in the initial stage of recovery; this was followed by exports, which had a much longer effect, and then by fixed capital formation. Private consumption seems to have been sustained by the higher incomes enjoyed in the more stable modern sector (in particular, heavy and chemical industries), and not by the depressed traditional sector. But why did such large fluctuations in private consumption occur, in particular the remarkable growth in 1933 and 1934? We will discuss below the behavior of private consumption. As for the question of what determines output, standard neoclassical theory tells us that, under perfect competition and given capital stock, the level of output is determined by the real prices of labor and other production factors such as raw materials and energy. Higher real wages, for example, would lower output. The assumption that goods market are imperfectly competitive, however, leads us to the conclusion that the firm's output simultaneously responds to changes in *both* real input prices *and* demand constraints. It justifies a regression of output on real input prices and demand variables.

Table 2.3   Growth accounting by demand factors: the United States (%)

Year	Y	C_p	G	I_p	CA	X	M
1930	−9.9	−4.5	1.1	−4.4	−0.0	−0.7	−0.6
1931	−7.7	−2.3	0.6	−4.8	−0.3	−0.8	−0.6
1932	−14.8	−6.7	−0.7	−4.9	−0.2	−1.1	−0.8
1933	−1.9	−1.4	−0.6	−0.8	−0.4	0.0	0.3
1934	9.0	3.7	2.3	1.7	0.2	0.1	0.0
1935	9.9	4.8	0.3	2.3	−0.8	0.3	1.0
1936	13.9	7.6	2.8	3.1	−0.1	0.3	0.4
1937	5.3	2.4	−0.5	1.9	0.3	0.8	0.6
1938	−5.1	−1.4	1.5	−2.5	1.3	0.0	−1.2

Note: Y = gross national expenditure; C_p = private consumption; G = public expenditure, sum of C_g and I_g; C_g = government consumption; I_g = government fixed capital formation; I_p = private fixed capital formation; I = fixed investment = $I_g + I_p$; X = export; M = import; CA = current account of the balance of payments.

Source: US Department of Commerce (1975).

Table 2.5 presents simple regressions of output by industry on the unit labor cost (real wages deflated by average product of labor) of each industry, and *macroeconomic* demand variables such as exports, government expenditures, and investment:

$$\log Q_{it} = C_i + \alpha \log Q_{it-1} + \beta \log UL_{it} + \gamma \log X_t + \delta \log G_t + \zeta \log I_t + \varepsilon$$

Table 2.4 Growth accounting by demand factors: Japan (%)

Year	Y	C_p	G	C_g	I_g	Military	Non-military	I_p	I	CA	X	M
1920	-0.46	-1.14	1.71	0.28	1.43	0.63	0.80	0.21	1.64		-1.61	-0.37
1921	6.40	4.96	5.00	0.11	4.89	4.03	0.86	-3.33	1.56	-0.23	-0.82	-0.60
1922	-2.65	4.66	-0.25	0.61	-0.86	-1.33	0.47	-1.34	-2.21	-5.71	0.55	6.26
1923	-4.56	1.43	-1.67	-0.14	-1.53	-1.83	0.30	-2.68	-4.21	-1.64	-1.26	0.38
1924	3.23	1.82	-0.64	0.14	-0.78	-0.89	0.11	2.28	1.50	9.04	2.44	2.67
1925	5.79	1.70	0.18	-0.97	1.15	0.68	0.47	0.33	1.48	-4.96	2.02	-1.55
1926	0.75	1.18	1.02	0.64	0.38	-0.49	0.88	0.54	0.92	-1.99	0.88	2.87
1927	3.37	2.42	2.03	1.80	0.23	-0.01	0.24	0.23	0.46	-1.31	1.59	2.91
1928	6.46	2.43	2.59	2.27	0.32	0.12	0.19	-0.53	-0.21	1.98	0.96	-1.02
1929	0.45	-0.54	-0.44	-0.45	0.01	-0.12	0.14	0.98	0.99	0.45	1.41	0.96
1930	1.07	0.36	-0.82	-0.41	-0.41	-0.09	-0.32	-0.13	-0.54	1.66	0.19	-1.47
1931	0.43	1.74	2.82	2.64	0.18	0.20	-0.02	-1.86	-1.68	-2.28	0.82	3.10
1932	4.42	-1.16	2.77	1.00	1.77	1.26	0.51	-1.02	0.75	3.83	3.12	-0.71
1933	10.08	5.20	1.47	1.33	0.14	0.11	0.03	1.66	1.81	1.75	1.07	-0.68
1934	8.72	4.66	-0.93	-0.71	-0.22	0.07	-0.30	2.66	2.43	2.33	5.06	2.73
1935	5.42	-0.05	0.75	0.26	0.49	0.01	0.48	1.81	2.30	2.91	3.62	0.70
1936	2.16	1.80	0.39	0.15	0.24	0.14	0.10	0.87	1.11	-0.89	0.62	1.52
1937	6.32	3.50	4.13	1.64	2.49	3.35	-0.85	1.60	4.09	-2.91	0.53	3.44
1938	3.83	-2.56	7.02	2.94	4.08	4.52	-0.45	1.23	5.31	-1.86	-0.99	0.87
1939	5.99	1.82	-1.26	-2.41	1.15	1.24	-0.08	6.19	7.34	-0.76	-2.18	-1.42
1940	4.07	0.20	5.28	3.86	1.42	1.13	0.29	-0.68	0.74	-0.33	0.62	0.96

Note: Y = gross national expenditure; C_p = private consumption; G = public expenditure, sum of C_g and I_g; C_g = government consumption; I_g = government fixed capital formation; I_p = private fixed capital formation; I = fixed investment = $I_g + I_p$; X = export; M = import; CA = current account of the balance of payments.

Source: LTES, 1, 3.

We assume that each industry is small enough relative to the whole economy so that *macro* demand variables on the right-hand side do not cause a simultaneity problem. The sample period is 1901–36; in order to keep the degrees of freedom large enough, we take a sample period longer than the depression period we are actually investigating. We also experimented on regressions using real wages rather than unit labor cost. The results are broadly similar to those shown in Table 2.5, but in some cases, the coefficients for real wages exhibit the wrong positive sign. This wrong sign may be due to a positive correlation between output and real wages which might be generated by productivity shocks. For this reason, we use unit labor cost rather than real wages. We could not include raw material cost because the price index separating raw material from finished goods is not available.

Table 2.5   An analysis of factors determining output (annual data, 1901–36)

Q_{it}	Constant	Q_{it-1}	UL_{it}	X_t	G_t	I_t	Adj.R^2 DW SER
Total manufacturing	0.88	0.66	0.04	0.26	0.04	–0.00	1.00
	(2.77)	(8.86)	(0.88)	(5.74)	(1.14)	(–0.25)	1.88
							0.04
Food	–0.41	0.94	–0.08	0.03	0.06	0.04	0.98
	(–0.46)	(9.67)	(–1.20)	(0.89)	(0.94)	(1.82)	2.31
							0.06
Textiles	0.10	0.55	0.14	0.35	0.09	–0.01	0.99
	(0.45)	(4.74)	(2.10)	(3.91)	(1.67)	(–0.38)	2.49
							0.07
Wood	–0.88	0.30	–0.12	0.43	0.31	–0.10	0.97
	(–2.71)	(1.94)	(–2.26)	(4.58)	(3.55)	(–2.32)	2.71
							0.09
Chemicals	–0.73	0.77	–0.04	0.26	0.11	–0.06	0.99
	(–1.99)	(7.52)	(–0.98)	(3.13)	(1.68)	(–2.15)	2.34
							0.06
Ceramics	–0.86	0.78	–0.07	0.18	0.11	0.00	0.98
	(–1.77)	(7.19)	(–0.49)	(2.01)	(1.36)	(0.11)	2.11
							0.11

Table 2.5   continued

Iron and steel	−2.27	0.79	−0.16	0.24	0.29	−0.01	0.99
	(−1.77)	(8.91)	(−2.03)	(1.54)	(2.40)	(−0.21)	2.35
							0.14
Non-ferrous	−1.49	0.78	−0.24	0.38	0.11	−0.05	0.97
metal	(−1.57)	(9.53)	(−2.55)	(3.44)	(0.63)	(−0.61)	2.20
							0.17
Machinery	−2.50	0.34	0.03	0.59	0.06	0.33	0.99
	(−5.32)	(3.34)	(0.29)	(7.32)	(0.72)	(4.00)	1.69
							0.09
Printing	0.09	0.94	−0.10	0.05	0.05	−0.04	0.98
	(0.19)	(8.96)	(−1.04)	(0.45)	(0.58)	(−0.78)	2.03
							0.11

Note: Ordinary least-squares estimates; *t*-statistics in parentheses. Q = output; UL = unit labor cost; X = exports; G = government expenditure; I = investment. All in real terms and expressed in natural logarithms.

Source: Yoshikawa and Shioji (1990: Table 3), original data are from *LTES*, 2, 8, 10.

Table 2.5 demonstrates that exports are a much more important factor than real labor costs. It also suggests that the Japanese economy was demand constrained and its macroeconomic growth and fluctuations were basically determined by aggregate real demand. Given this finding, we next enquire more closely how each demand component was determined.

Fixed Investment

To examine factors which affect investment, we begin with the interest rates. Figure 2.2 illustrates loan rates in both nominal and real terms. The real rate is calculated from the inflation rate (GNP deflator) of the same year. Although nominal rate declined only gradually throughout the 1920s and 1930s, the real rate shows large fluctuations due to changing inflation rates. In the 1920s, the real rate stood between 10 per cent and 20 per cent on average, while it showed a downward trend in the 1930s, reaching negative levels at the end of the decade. The declining real rate from the peak in 1930 probably promoted investment.

Figure 2.3 shows an investment cycle with a peak in 1920, followed by stagnation until 1932, and accelerated growth subsequently. The contrast in the average growth rate between the stagnant 1920s and the booming 1930s corresponds well to the level of real interest rates in Figure 2.2.

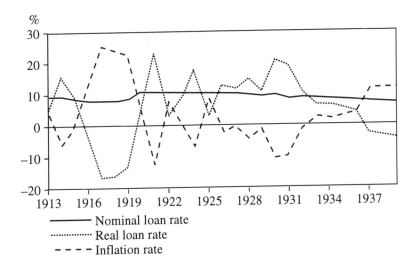

Sources: Toyo Keizai Shimpo, *Keizai Nenkan*; *LTES*, 1.

Figure 2.2 Movements of loan rates, 1913–39 (%)

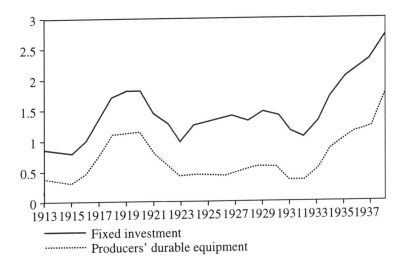

Source: *LTES*, 1, Table 21.

Figure 2.3 Private fixed capital formation, 1934–6 prices (million yen)

We estimated a private investment function with lagged private fixed capital formation, government expenditure, export and loan rates, all in real terms, as independent variables. The estimation procedures, such as the sample period and taking the logarithm of real variables (except interest rates) are the same as in Table 2.5:

$$\log I_{pt} = C + \alpha \log I_{pt-1} + \beta \log G_t + \gamma \log X_t + \delta r_t + \varepsilon$$

Table 2.6 shows that export was the most important demand component that determined private investment, as Table 2.5 shows for manufacturing production. Surprisingly small *t*-statistics (and minus signs) for public expenditure as a whole and military fixed investment in particular imply that these factors had very limited impact on private investment. Another finding to note is that the coefficients for real interest rates reveal minus signs as expected, with enough statistical significance.

Table 2.6   *An analysis of factors determining private fixed investment (annual data, 1901–36)*

Dependent variable I_p, sample 36

Constant	$I_{p(-1)}$	G	X	r	Adj.R^2	DW	SER
0.82	0.71	−0.00	0.18	−0.01	0.94	2.17	0.12
(1.65)	(8.87)	(−0.03)	(2.84)	(−2.96)			

Constant	$I_{p(-1)}$	Mi	X	r	Adj.R^2	DW	SER
0.79	0.72	−0.01	0.18	−0.01	0.94	2.17	0.12
(2.26)	(7.68)	(−0.09)	(3.52)	(−3.00)			

Note: Ordinary least-squares estimates, *t*-statistics in parentheses. I_p = private fixed investment; G = public expenditure (sum of consumption and fixed investment); Mi = military fixed investment; X = export; all in real terms and expressed in natural logarithms; r = real loan rate; deflated by GNP deflator.

Sources: LTES, 1, 3, 8. The loan rate is from Toyo Keizai, *Keizai Nenkan*, various issues.

Private Consumption

While private consumption grew, on average, slower than GNP in the interwar years, it fluctuated to a greater extent than GNP. This surprising fact appears, however, due mainly to the estimation procedures.

The major items of private consumption are food (50 per cent), clothing (13 per cent), and housing (12 per cent) for the period 1931–40: the Engel coefficient (the share of food in private consumption) was quite high. Moreover, rice and other cereals occupied about a third of the food consumption.[8] The estimated consumption of rice is basically equal to domestic supply (mainly domestic production supplemented by net imports and changes in stock). The supply of agricultural products naturally fluctuates with the state of crops, leading to volatility in consumption. The decreased consumption in 1932 and 1935, for example, corresponds to bad crops; by contrast, the large increase in consumption in 1933 and 1934 corresponds to good crops in the previous years.[9] Thus, estimated private consumption is almost an exogenous variable, dependent on natural conditions.

Private consumption is likely to reflect the emergence of the 'dual structure of the economy.' Farmers were not better off even with good crops when price movements accelerated downward, partly reflecting world prices. The rice market encountered oversupply from the mid-1920s, due to increased imports from the colonies. The government introduced protective measures such as restrictions on cultivation and price controls.[10] The large share of agriculture in the national economy did not contribute to the economic recovery, but rather hindered it.

Most of the discussions on the 'dual structure' focus on the gap in wages and income. Despite increasing employment during the recovery, money wages declined as a whole, because the new employment consisted largely of younger workers and part-timers.[11] Real wages in manufacturing, on the other hand, rose during the economic downturn, due to declining consumer prices. Whereas the real wage rate subsequently declined in every sector as the economy recovered, those in the heavy and chemical industries remained at almost the same level in 1936 as in 1929 (Table 2.2).

The negative effect of unemployment on consumption was not so large, because the number of unemployed was actually lower than contemporary impressions might suggest. The unemployed workers were absorbed in traditional urban sectors (retail trade and service).[12] Moreover, employed workers could increase their consumption, because real incomes did not decrease substantially, particularly in the manufacturing sector. According to the composition of private consumption, however, the increase in real incomes would not have brought about so much increase in the demand for superior goods other than food. Assuming a reverse correlation between the propensity to consume and income levels, income transfer from the depressed agricultural sector might have hindered rather than helped recovery.

Exchange Rates and Export

As the regressions for both output and private investment demonstrate, growth and fluctuations of the prewar Japanese economy were basically export-led. The analysis of exports is, therefore, very important. We begin by considering the relationship between the exchange rate and exports. Since product differentiation was not so important for prewar export goods, such as textiles, the exchange rate seems to have had a larger impact on exports than it does today.

Figure 2.4 shows nominal and real effective exchange rates, and real export growth not only for the rest of the world, but also for those minus colonies. ('Colonies' in this case include Taiwan, Korea, Manchuria and Rhea Province.)

The nominal effective exchange rate changed remarkably within a short period: an appreciation from 1929 to 1931, followed by a sharp depreciation until 1933. It thereafter stabilized with the exception of a slight appreciation in 1934. The real exchange rate in Figure 2.4 shows a downward trend until around 1934, longer than the nominal effective exchange rate. Corresponding to this decline,

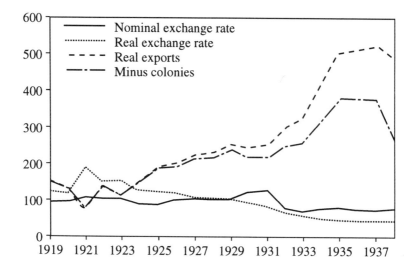

Notes:
1. The nominal effective exchange rate is defined as the weighted average of sterling, the US dollar, the rupee, and the tael per yen. The weight is the export share to Britain, the United States, British India and China of each year.
2. The real effective exchange rate is defined as Japanese export price divided by import price of Japan's major trading partners. The latter is calculated as $P = (P_\$/E) \times (\$_{35}/\$_t)$
3. P = import price in yen; $P_\$$ = import price in US dollars as of 1935 (taken from *LTES*, 14, Table 24); E = exchange rate expressed as US dollars per yen; $\$_{35}$ = US dollars in terms of gold in 1935; $\$_t$ = US dollars (in terms of gold) of the year concerned.

Sources: Bank of Japan, *Hompo Keizai Tokei*; *LTES*, 14.

Figure 2.4   Effective exchange rates and real exports (1913 = 100)

export growth accelerated from 1933 to 1935. These facts suggest that price competitiveness explains the remarkable growth in real exports.[13]

The effects of depreciation, however, were not uniform, but depended on trading partners. The yen depreciated from its peak of 1931 when sterling began floating in September. The fact that the yen depreciated to a larger extent than sterling generated complaints on the part of the British and Indian cotton industry and intensified pressure for protective measures in British Empire countries. After April 1933, when the United States allowed the dollar to depreciate, Japanese export goods slightly lost their price competitiveness, not only against British but also against American products.

The relation of the yen with silver standard currencies is more complicated. India stabilized the rupee in 1926, and returned to the gold exchange standard in April 1927. Silver sales from India as well as Thailand (1928) and Indochina (1929) depressed the silver price, and accordingly the yen appreciated against the silver standard currencies, most importantly against the Chinese tael. However, from April 1934, when the United States enacted the Silver Purchase Bill, the silver price rose again, thereby depreciating the yen against silver standard currencies. This tendency continued until the Chinese government introduced currency reform in November 1935.[14]

The effects of depreciation varied, depending on the export goods. Raw silk yarn and products, Japan's main export goods to the United States, had large income-elasticity. The depression (accompanied by the shift in consumption towards synthetic fibers) in the US market reduced silk exports, deepening the agricultural depression in Japan. The depreciation of the yen did not help silk exports to recover, because of its low price elasticity.[15] Cotton exports to East Asian countries, on the other hand, had a larger price elasticity than silk, and yen exchange rates naturally had a larger impact. The sharp appreciation of the yen against the tael from 1929 to 1931 reduced cotton exports to China, while the yen depreciation from 1931 to 1933 stimulated export growth.

Breaking down Japan's real exports by area, we find that the growth of total exports is more remarkable than that of exports minus those to the colonies (in other words, exports to foreign countries). In this sense, trade with the colonies played an important role in economic recovery. Japanese direct investment promoted the import of heavy and chemical products from the home country. Since trade with the colonies was transacted in yen, its remarkable growth after 1933 is not inconsistent with the stability in the effective exchange rate.

But it is also worth stressing that real exports to foreign countries showed substantial growth from 1933 to 1935, the highest growth rate during the interwar years. From 1934 to 1937, exports to the foreign market shifted gradually from the East Asian countries to developed countries, such as North America and Britain.[16] Economic recovery in the developed countries, however weak it may have been, increased imports from Japan.

The growing export market was sustained by textile products: by cotton goods from 1931 to 1934, and subsequently by silk and synthetic fiber products. These textile products were exported mainly to the Asian market, except silk which was dependent on the US market. Japanese cotton exports stagnated from the mid-1930s, because it encountered strict protective measures in the British Empire countries and at the same time competition from the Chinese firms including *Zaikabo*, Japanese subsidiaries operating in China.[17]

The composition of exports gradually shifted from textiles towards heavy and chemical products during the 1930s, due to increased exports of the latter products to the colonial market. Textiles, however, still remained the main export industry, accounting for nearly a half of total exports in the mid-1930s. The export share of metal and products, machinery and chemicals increased from 13.0 per cent in 1929 to 24.1 per cent in 1935 while those of textiles decreased from 61.2 per cent to 48.7 per cent.[18] As Tables 2.5 and 2.6 suggest, the transformation of the industrial structure was brought about not only directly by export growth itself, but also indirectly in the sense that the growing exports promoted fixed capital formation, which in turn increased demand for capital goods manufactured in the heavy industries.

THE ROLE OF ECONOMIC POLICY

Government Expenditure and Monetary Policy

With the aim of re-establishing the gold standard at prewar parity, the government in the 1920s pursued, generally speaking, tight macroeconomic policy (see, for example, Patrick, 1971). Although the Bank of Japan provided special credit to financial institutions in difficulties after the earthquake in 1923, and in particular during the financial crisis in 1927, and as Itoh (1989: 205–7) added, the specie reserves held abroad (*Zaigai Seika*)[19] worked as a cushion to counteract deflationary pressures caused by current account deficits, the relatively high level of real interest rates (Figure 2.2) suggests a tendency towards tight monetary policy.

In particular at the end of the 1920s, the government held to its deflationary stance in order to prepare for the liberalization of gold exports (the gold bullion standard), which finally came into force in January 1930. In short, the macroeconomic situation of the 1920s failed to facilitate the promotion of the new industrial structure. The suspension of the gold standard, on the other hand, constituted the basis for expansionary public expenditure and for the depreciation of the yen which accelerated exports in the earlier stage of the recovery.

The expansionary fiscal policy undertaken by Korekiyo Takahashi, *Takahashi Zaisei*, commenced in December 1931, when Takeshi Inukai formed a Seiyukai cabinet and gold exports were prohibited again (31 December). Indeed, in 1933 and 1934, fiscal policy shifted to tighter controls on military expenditure, but economic growth did not show a downward trend, possibly because the pump priming had already taken effect.

The Keynesian character of the *Takahashi Zaisei* is relatively well known.[20] The political circumstances of the warfare in Manchuria promoted military expenditure. The finance minister, Takahashi, was assassinated in the attempted military *coup d'état* of February 1936, because he tried to restrain the ever-increasing requirement for military expenditure. His death finally broke the moral support for the government to restrain continued military expansion, which stimulated continuous fixed capital formation and the growth of heavy and chemical industries. In this sense, the economic recovery in Japan had common features with Nazi Germany.

Government deficits were monetized by the Bank of Japan. Most of the literature on Japanese macroeconomic policy in the 1930s, Nakamura among others, stresses the role of the central bank in financing the government deficits.[21] The gradual decline of the nominal loan rate in Figure 2.2 implies that the Bank of Japan was successful in avoiding the crowding out which otherwise would have been brought about by large issues of deficit bonds. But more interesting to note is the movement of *M2* and behavior of the money multiplier.

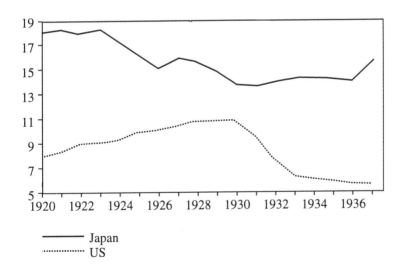

Japan
US

Source: Gordon (1986: app. B); Asakura and Nishiyama (1974).

Figure 2.5   The money multiplier (M2/base money): the United States and Japan

The contraction of *M2* in Japan was substantially shorter and smaller than in the United States. The decrease in Japan was 8.2 per cent from 1929 to 1931, while it amounted to 33.5 per cent from 1929 to 1933 in the United States.[22] As Friedman and Schwartz (1963: 332ff) discuss, monetary contraction (*M2*) in the United States was caused by changes in the money multiplier, which in turn resulted from the decrease in the ratios of commercial bank deposit both to bank reserves and to the currency held by the public. In contrast, the money multiplier was quite stable during the depression in Japan (Figure 2.5), because the public did not change their portfolios away from deposits and towards currency as in the United States. This public behavior probably reflected the stable state of the banking system.

Before World War I, most of the depression in Japan was accompanied by financial panics, in which the ratio of bank deposits to currency held by the public fell sharply. After the war, however, this ratio became stable. The primary reason for this stability was the concentration in the banking sector; a number of small banks had either gone bankrupt or been acquired by a few big banks. As a result, the Big Five banks came to enjoy the great confidence of the public. In case of bank runs, deposits merely shifted from smaller banks to the Big Five. The second reason was banking regulation introduced by the Banking Act of 1927. Prior to this law, the Japanese financial system had been close to a state of free banking. The Banking Act facilitated concentration by imposing a minimum level of paid-in capital. It also legalized banking inspection by the Ministry of Finance.[23]

The Effects of Devaluation

The depreciation of the yen strengthened the price competitiveness of Japanese exports, on the one hand, and enabled the government to pursue expansionary macroeconomic policy, on the other. It is a controversial issue which of the two was the more important in alleviating the depression in Japan.[24]

Sato (1981: 25–6) claims that the depreciation of the yen did not necessarily contribute to recovery in the trade balance, and that expansionary public expenditure was more important.[25] Indeed, depreciation led to higher import prices of raw materials, such as raw cotton, thereby canceling out the favorable effects on exports. But this disadvantage turned out to be not so serious in fact, because the price of raw materials declined considerably, reflecting the world depression.[26] Contrary to Sato's assertion, Table 2.4 shows that the contribution of net exports to the growth of real GNP was substantial for the 1932–5 period.

As discussed above (pp. 39–42), the devaluation undoubtedly contributed to increasing real exports in the initial phase of the recovery, and at the same time it set a basis for the government to introduce an expansionary fiscal policy. In this sense, the devaluation was certainly a major factor for economic recovery in Japan.

However, the continued growth of exports was also promoted by the demand in the colonial market, on the one hand, and in foreign countries, for example the United States and Britain, on the other. In the later phase of the recovery, rising demand itself was important for Japanese exports.

As for the second effect of devaluation, Table 2.4 shows that the effect of increased public expenditure did not last longer than a few years. Military expenditure stayed at a lower level after the initial rise in 1932, until the outbreak of the Chino-Japanese war in 1937. But we would like to stress that the military elites influenced increasingly on the government after the warfare in Manchuria and that this regime would have raised expectations of a continued growth in military expenditure, thereby promoting investment in the heavy and chemical industries. In addition, the declining real interest rate which stimulated private investment was sustained by the easy monetary policy. In this sense, the suspension of the gold standard contributed to economic recovery through monetary channels as well.

CONCLUDING REMARKS

Compared with other major economies, the depression in Japan was shorter and less severe. Real GDP hardly declined and recorded the highest growth rate in the 1930s. This chapter has attempted to explain these characteristics of the Great Depression in Japan from various angles.

With a bit of exaggeration, we can summarize our findings by saying that growth and fluctuations of the prewar Japanese economy were dominated by exports. A sudden decline in silk exports to the United States directly hit the agricultural area, generating gloomy episodes in the depression. The most important factor for economic recovery was exports which substantially affected both the manufacturing output and fixed investment. The depreciation of the yen stimulated Japanese exports, but the growing demand for Japanese goods in the colonies and the developed countries also sustained its growth.

Most fundamental for the 'Keynesian policy without a Keynes' in Japan was the suspension of the gold standard at the end of 1931. Japanese policy-makers had attempted to stabilize the yen exchange rate at pre-World War I parity. As soon as this policy goal was given up, the yen began to depreciate considerably, and at the same time it allowed the government to pursue expansionary fiscal and monetary policies. As already explained, export growth led the economic recovery and the significant decline in real interest rates stimulated fixed investment. Needless to say, the active fiscal policy of the finance minister

Takahashi would not have been possible under the constraint of the gold standard.

In addition to the vigorous demand, both private and public, we can cite the robustness of the banking sector as a factor mitigating the depression in Japan. In contrast to the United States, Japan did not suffer from bank runs and financial panics in the 1930s, thereby stabilizing the money supply through banks.

Finally, the Japanese economy in the 1930s was in the process of major structural transformation characterized by the growth of the heavy and chemical industries. The impact of the Great Depression was hardly seen in these sectors. Japanese agriculture, on the other hand, experienced long-run stagnation from the mid-1920s through the 1930s, compared with the recovery in manufacturing sectors. The expansionary policy of the 1930s finally realized the potential of new industrial development which had been hindered under the constraint of orthodox policy. It is worth recalling that this policy stance was associated with the 'new regime.' It raised expectations on the part of business leaders for increased military expenditure and the subsequent demand for heavy industries, similar to Temin (1989: 102–3), who argued for the German recovery under Hitler's government.[27]

APPENDIX

We have relied on the following volumes of the *Estimates of Long-Term Economic Statistics of Japan since 1868* (*LTES*):

1. *National Income*, ed. K. Ohkawa *et al.*
2. *Manpower*, ed. M. Umemura *et al.*
3. *Capital Stock*, ed. K. Emi
6. *Personal Consumption Expenditures*, ed. M. Shinohara
8. *Prices*, ed. K. Ohkawa *et al.*
9. *Agriculture and Forestry*, ed. M. Umemura *et al.*
10. *Mining and Manufacturing*, ed. M. Shinohara
14. *Foreign Trade and Balance of Payments*, ed. I. Yamazawa and Y. Yamamoto.

Note that important variables in macroeconomic movements, such as private consumption and investment, have limitations due to estimating methods.

Private consumption is estimated from commodity-flow analysis (in this case production minus export plus import, thereby including inventory stocks). Except for rice from 1914 to 1940, which is adjusted with changes in stocks, these data tend to overestimate fluctuations in private consumption.

Investment data exclude changes in inventory stocks of consumption goods, which are included in the estimation of private consumption. Fixed investment is estimated from both commodity-flow analysis and public statistics. Commodity-flow analysis is applied to private equipment and partly to public equipment; the latter is supplemented by the government's statements of accounts. Private construction is calculated from the stock data reported in the municipal annual statistics, while public construction is estimated from the government's statements of accounts. To the extent that estimated fixed investment is not adjusted for inventory stocks, the data have similar shortcomings to those for private consumption.

NOTES

1. Nakamura (1971: ch. 8) stressed the recovery effect of deficit spending, before the *LTES* was fully available, while Yamamura (1972: 202–3), also argued the 'Keynesian' character of the military expenditures without the data of this series. Nanto and Takagi (1985) is another study which discusses the macroeconomic impact of Japanese policy in the 1930s.
2. For the economic policies in the 1930s, see Arndt (1944) and Temin (1989), among others.
3. Orthodox macroeconomic policy in Germany was mainly pursued by the governments of the Weimar Republic, notably Brüning's cabinet. Hitler left this tendency as soon as he took power and made a success of economic recovery through 'a new policy regime', as Temin (1989: 103) named it.
4. Sato (1976) stressed that large-scale firms in the modern sector showed a decline not only in prices, but also in output and employment, whereas the traditional sector exhibited the typical phenomena implied by classical economics; the decline was mainly in prices and not so much in output and employment. But his argument is not supported by specific data, in particular the changes in output are not reported.
5. The share of the heavy and chemical industries in overall manufacturing production expanded during World War I, but stagnated in the 1920s. It increased again in the 1930s, from a third to nearly 60 per cent (Nakamura, 1978: Table 12).
6. Nakamura (1978: 118).
7. Since the problems of the agricultural area have been widely researched by Japanese economic historians, there is a large literature, including Shimizu and Nishida (1987).
8. *LTES*, 6, Tables 1–2, 5, 9, and 10.
9. In Japan, the harvest of rice is usually in autumn.
10. Shimizu and Nishida (1987).
11. Hashimoto (1984: 245ff) gives a detailed discussion of (nominal) wage movements.
12. Sato (1976) and Hashimoto (1984: 246ff).
13. Shinohara (1961: ch. 10) stressed that declining terms of trade (in other words, the relative prices) promoted export, which worked as an engine for economic growth in prewar Japan.
14. Hashimoto (1984: 169–70).
15. Sato (1981: 24).
16. Itoh (1989: 286–9).
17. Hashimoto (1984: 214–25); Itoh (1989: 283–94).
18. Calculated from the trade statistics in *LTES*, 14.
19. This reserve was initially built up with the Chino-Japanese War Indemnity and later accumulated by the large current account surplus during World War I. Despite its name, it included foreign exchange reserves.
20. See the literature in note 1.

21. The experience of the subsequent inflation, in particular during the war, constituted the basis of public opinion against the deficit bond issues, which were excluded by Article 4 of the Public Finance Act of 1947.
22. Calculated from the data in Gordon (1986: App. B) Asakura and Nishiyama (1974).
23. For more details, see Okazaki (1993).
24. For a more general discussion and an international comparison of the devaluation effect, see Eichengreen and Sachs (1985).
25. Takagi (1989) similarly does not fully assess the contribution of the depreciation.
26. The price of raw cotton, for example, declined sharply until the autumn of 1931 (see Takamura, 1987: 179).
27. Arndt (1944: 175) also emphasized the psychological effect of the political change, stating that 'one of the main reasons for the revival of business confidence in 1933 was that German business men had no doubt whatever that, as soon as internal and international conditions permitted, the Nazis would embark on a vast rearmament programme. In the eyes of the German capitalists who helped Hitler to power, his rearmament programme, together with his anti-socialist policy, provided the *raison d'être* of his regime.'

3. A reassessment of the United Kingdom business cycle chronology

Jan Tore Klovland

INTRODUCTION

More than a century ago W. Stanley Jevons claimed to have 'found the missing link required to complete the first outline of the evidence' on the relationship between sunspots and commercial crises in Britain.[1] This relationship formed the core of his famous theory of economic fluctuations, which Jevons built around the proposition that 'the secret of good trade in Lancashire is the low price of rice and other grain in India.'[2] Yet today many aspects of business cycles in Victorian Britain are controversial and some important issues are still relatively unexplored despite a vast accumulation of theoretical and empirical knowledge since Jevons' pioneering *Investigations* into the subject.

Measuring business cycles, particularly with a higher frequency than annual national income data permit, is an important but somewhat neglected empirical issue with respect to the pre-1914 economy in the United Kingdom. The need for a monthly or quarterly indicator of economic activity often arises in empirical studies of financial markets and macroeconomic fluctuations, but such data barely exist for the Victorian economy. Better data on the short-term fluctuations in economic activity may be particularly important in cases where modern time series techniques are applied in testing hypotheses from business cycle theory.

This chapter presents several new monthly business cycle indicators covering the whole period from 1850 to 1914. The new monthly indicators comprise indices of real imports of raw materials, real exports, cotton consumption, railway freight receipts, coasting trade and bank clearings. As a test of the properties of the new data a composite index derived from these indicators will be used in the reassessment of business cycle turning points in this period.

The most important reference guide to the cyclical behavior of the pre-World War I economies is undoubtedly the business cycle chronologies constructed by Burns and Mitchell (1946) at the National Bureau of Economic Research (NBER). These chronologies provide monthly dates of peaks and troughs for the United States, United Kingdom, Germany and France since 1854.

Friedman and Schwartz (1982) brought attention to a particular feature of the NBER chronologies: between 1867 and 1975 there are 53 turning points for the United States and only 39 for the United Kingdom. Most of the extra cycles in the United States are located before World War I. Starting with the common trough in December 1854 there are 30 turning points before August 1914 in the United States compared to only 20 in the United Kingdom. The explanation suggested by Friedman and Schwartz (1982: 308) is:

> The extra United States turning points have generally been regarded as evidence of more marked cyclical movements in the United States than in the United Kingdom, leading to both briefer and larger cycles in the United States than in the United Kingdom. Our examination of the data leads us to enter a caveat. The extra United States turning points may simply reflect a greater plenitude of statistics for the United States than for the United Kingdom and a more searching examination of the United States ... The concentration of extra turning points in the pre-1914 period strengthens the suspicion that we may be dealing with a statistical artifact ... There is a far greater difference between the statistical data available for the United States and the United Kingdom, and also between the effort that has been devoted to their analysis, for the pre-1914 than for the post-1914 period.

The reassessment of the UK business cycle pattern between 1850 and 1914 undertaken here may shed some light on Friedman and Schwartz's suggested interpretation of the NBER chronology. By comparing the cyclical features of the new data with the established chronology and qualitative historical evidence on economic fluctuations a more solid basis for the determination of turning points in the UK should be obtained. In this process important information on the reliability of the new indicators may also emerge.

EXISTING BUSINESS CYCLE INDICATORS 1850–1914

This section presents a brief review of monthly indicators that have been available to researchers trying to identify the cyclical movements in pre-World War I Britain. Then some features of the annual gross domestic product series and production indices that have been used in historical analyses of the business cycles in this period are discussed.

Monthly Business Cycle Indicators

The lack of high-frequency data on real economic activity in Victorian (and Edwardian) Britain has often led analysts to work with financial market data and nominal series in this period. The famous article by Kitchin (1923) employed nominal indicators only: bank clearings, commodity prices and interest rates.

Of the 15 series used by Persons *et al.* (1922) in their study of business cycles in the years 1903–14 there were only four real series (unemployment, export quantity of iron and steel, number of blast furnaces in blast, pig iron stocks); the rest were nominal (railway freight traffic receipts, foreign trade, commodity prices, clearings and financial market variables). This presents a problem because ideally the procyclicality of, say, commodity prices and interest rates is a hypothesis to be tested; it is not obvious that it is an intrinsic property of business cycles.

In general, few quantitatively oriented studies deal in any detail with *intrayear* fluctuations in business activity, particularly before the 1890s. A major exception is the painstaking work by Hughes (1956, 1960) on the 1850s, which is an invaluable source of information on economic fluctuations in this decade. There are many studies which contribute greatly to our understanding of various aspects of the business cycles between 1860 and 1890,[3] but apparently none that is wholly devoted to analyzing the fluctuations in economic activity on a finer grid than annual data can provide. The short article by Thomas (1926) presented several business cycle indicators on a quarterly basis from 1855 to 1914, but without discussing the data from an economic or historical perspective.

The only *real* series that figures in Thomas's (1926) tables before 1887 is the percentage of unemployment among 'The Friendly Society of Ironfounders' originally published by Dessauer-Meinhardt (1940). This is apparently the only *monthly real* series that was used by Burns and Mitchell (1946) in setting turning points for this period.[4] These data represent only one small sector of the economy, however.[5] Two other real indicators became available towards the end of the century: unemployment for 'all trades' in 1887 and the number of blast furnaces in blast in the 1890s. Reference must also be made to the data on railway freight traffic receipts, which is formally a nominal series, but which will be shown below to give valuable information on real economic activity.[6]

There is thus a gap between studies which did not go beyond 1850 (Silberling, 1923; Gayer *et al.*, 1975) or 1860 (Hughes, 1960), on one side, and the study of the Edwardian economy by Persons *et al.* (1922) on the other side. For the intermediate period our knowledge of business cycle fluctuations is largely based on annual national accounts data, indices of industrial production and unemployment.

Information Based on Annual Data

For modern time periods national accounts data and production indices have largely replaced the use of traditional business cycle indicators in econometric modelling, to some extent also in descriptive business cycle analysis. This fact is obviously related to the broad coverage and the extensive efforts made in measuring variables such as gross domestic product.

With respect to the period considered here the choice of data is less obvious. There are two main problems with using national income data, for both modelling and descriptive purposes. In contrast to more recent time periods no GDP or production index exists on a quarterly or monthly basis for the United Kingdom. In dating business cycle turning points, in particular, this fact is of course a serious drawback. Second, it is an unquestionable fact that the quality of the national accounts data is poorer for the more distant time periods, a fact that has been duly stressed in the sources of the original data.

Feinstein (1972) presented a thorough discussion of the reliability of his three alternative estimates of gross domestic product. This analysis clearly shows how fragile inferences on *short-term* movements in economic activity are to the choice between GDP estimated from the income, expenditure, or output side. While improvements subsequently have been made to the income estimate of GDP,[7] which is judged to be the best guide to cyclical movements,[8] Solomou (1994: 249) notes that national income data 'contain pitfalls for the study of cycles.'

Because data on annual variations in output are lacking for many sectors, aggregate industrial production indices may also face problems in tracking the cyclical movements in the economy. The output estimates of some sectors have been derived from raw materials consumption data without correction for changes in stocks. In revising the production index made by Hoffmann (1955), Lewis (1978) had to resort to various *ad hoc* assumptions regarding the interpolation of annual production figures between Census of Production benchmarks: constant growth rates, moving averages, and even imposing 'the same cyclical fluctuation as marriages' for some sectors (commercial property building, printing and chemicals). Using these data in assessing turning points may be hazardous; on the other hand, it should be pointed out that this feature should not materially affect the estimation of long-run growth rates.[9]

In order to illustrate the degree of comovement of various indicators in the short run, Table 3.1 presents simple correlation coefficients between annual growth rates of various GDP measures over the 1856–85 and 1886–1913 periods.

The correlation coefficients serve to highlight the relatively low degree of correlation between the various measures of gross domestic product. The expenditure estimate, in particular, deviates from the other versions, which is consistent with the discussion in Feinstein (1972). Table 3.1 also includes two indicators based on railway freight receipts (RAILFR) and ton-miles (RAILTM). These are further discussed below, but it may be noted here that there is a relatively high degree of correlation between RAILFR and the industrial production index. It may also be noted that in the period 1856–85 the correlation coefficient between this variable and the income version of GDP is higher than between the output or expenditure estimates of GDP and the income data.

Table 3.1   Correlation coefficients between annual growth rates: 1856–85 in lower triangle, 1886–1913 in upper triangle

	GDPI	GDPO	GDPE	INDPRO	RAILFR	RAILTM
GDPI	1	0.794	0.488	0.630	0.549	NA
GDPO	0.251	1	0.577	0.841	0.627	NA
GDPE	0.030	0.716	1	0.519	0.116	NA
INDPRO	0.415	0.909	0.517	1	0.525	NA
RAILFR	0.395	0.565	0.255	0.650	1	NA
RAILTM	0.284	0.504	0.253	0.606	0.810	1

Notes and sources: GDPI = real gross domestic product, income based (Feinstein, (1972: T18–19); GDPO = real gross domestic product, output based (ibid.); GDPE = real gross domestic product, expenditure based (ibid.: T14–15, as revised and extended in Mitchell, 1988: ch. 16, Table 6); INDPRO = industrial production (Crafts *et al.*, 1989); RAILFR = railway freight traffic receipts (this chapter); RAILTM = railway freight output (Hawke, 1970: Table III.03).

Implications for Data Construction Strategy

What kind of data would be most fruitful with a view to increasing our knowledge of the course of business cycles in Victorian Britain? The discussion above has highlighted the fact that national income data do not play on home ground in retracing the very short-run fluctuations of economic activity. In this regard they are severely handicapped by their broad coverage (including sectors for which data are poor) and low frequency (annual figures only). The fast play on the narrow pitches in the business cycle matches often favours the more specialized local teams, the old-fashioned business cycle indicators that were never promoted to the national accounts league.

The brief review of the existing indicators has revealed that there are very few high-frequency indicators of real economic activity spanning the whole period from 1850 to 1914. Hence the efforts made here have been directed towards constructing such series.

THE NEW MONTHLY INDICATORS

The Business Cycle Indicators Used by Contemporary Analysts

It may be useful first to turn to the pages of one of the best-informed contemporary sources, *The Economist*; in order to get a view of the business cycle indicators that were considered to be the most important ones at the time. *The Economist* regularly reviewed the state of trade throughout the period considered here, skillfully presenting and analyzing a variety of economic statistics. From the early 1880s a distinct pattern of analysis emerged, which was retained until World War I; there was a set of three main economic indicators that were nearly always considered: UK railway traffic receipts, bank clearings, and foreign trade. In addition, other indicators relating to particular trades, commodity prices, and financial markets were sometimes discussed,[10] but the three main indicators were the ones that were consistently used as a barometer of the overall activity of home and foreign trade.

The use of cyclical indicators in contemporary sources will now be reviewed together with a discussion of some of the more important features of the new indicators presented here. Further details on the definition and sources can be found in the Appendix.

The Individual Indicators

Foreign trade
The use of monthly exports and import values as indicators of fluctuations in real economic activity has previously presented two major problems: the lack of monthly import values before 1870 and the non-existence of appropriate monthly price deflators before 1880. The first problem arises from the fact that the Board of Trade's monthly returns provided import *values* of only some of the main commodities in the period from 1856 to 1870; with respect to import *quantities* there was a far more detailed enumeration throughout the period.[11]

A new monthly index of raw materials import based on import quantities of 35 commodities is presented in this chapter, covering nearly all enumerated raw materials as well as some goods referred to as 'mainly unmanufactured.' This index excludes cotton, which is dealt with separately. The index may then be linked with the deflated values computed for the subsequent periods.

The Economist's discussions of foreign trade data as an indicator of trade activity were often accompanied by an elaborate analysis of the price and quantity components of the changes in import and export values. However, no appropriate monthly price deflators were generally available until Silverman (1930) presented fixed-weight index numbers of British export and import prices for the period 1880–1913. The usefulness of these data is somewhat limited by the fact that monthly values are only available on an aggregate level.

Extending the data base used in Klovland (1993), monthly price indices have been constructed for the present purpose, with a view to computing continuous monthly series of real exports and imported raw materials for the entire period 1850–1914. These price indices are fixed-weight geometric indices, with separate weights for the period before and after 1880. The number of commodity descriptions (excluding cotton) included before 1880 is 171 for imports and 82 for exports; after 1880 the figures are 129 and 62, respectively.[12]

Data on merchandise imports and exports have been widely used as indicators of economic activity – perhaps more because of their availability than because of their representativeness. Even in the relatively open nineteenth-century British economy the share of domestic merchandise exports only ranged between 15 per cent and 23 per cent of national income. Crouzet (1982: 119) estimates the share of industrial output which was exported to 'about 40 per cent around 1870, and somewhat more at the beginning of the twentieth century.' Imports were in the order of 30 per cent of GDP, of which the share of raw materials and semi-manufactured goods fell from roughly one-half to one-third over the years to 1914.[13]

These considerations regarding the relative size of the foreign trade sector imply that, although of great importance, the role assigned to such indicators should not be exaggerated. Even if information on the state of home trade may be harder to obtain, real exports should not be assigned additional weight on the assumption that export quantities and domestic business cycles exhibit parallel movements.[14]

As to empirical evidence from the United Kingdom, Ford (1983: 35) has noted that the turning points of total exports and income from abroad 'accorded more closely with fluctuations in output and employment than did those of investment.' This observation is consistent with a view which focuses on the causal role of exports in generating cycles in a domestic economy that is generally characterized by underemployment of resources. On the other hand, to the extent that the Victorian economy was fully employed, the argument put forth by Harley and McCloskey (1983: 62) is a plausible hypothesis: 'An increase in demand for exports can cause little increase in total output, merely a reallocation of resources and a restructuring of output.' Only further empirical analysis can decide which of these views is the more fruitful one in the case of Victorian Britain.

In addition to theoretical caveats there are several measurement problems that should be borne in mind when the indicators based on foreign trade data are being used. Deflating nominal values by fixed-weight deflators is one source of uncertainty.[15] The most serious problems, however, arise from the lack of data on stocks, both with respect to raw materials and manufactured goods. On the export side, sales are less than perfectly synchronized with output. Inputs of raw materials have been extensively used as indicators of domestic output, but their usefulness may be severely limited by changes in stocks, particularly regarding short-run movements.[16]

The use of raw materials input is otherwise attractive for such British industries as textiles (except wool), building, rubber, seed oil and non-ferrous metals (but less so early in the period) where a substantial proportion of the basic raw materials was imported. For the most important of these industries, cotton manufactures, weekly data on imports and stocks held in ports as well as end-of-year data on mill stocks have been combined to form a monthly series of raw cotton consumption. Along with a series of deflated exports of cotton manufactures, this provides a firmer basis for studying short-run movements in the activity of the cotton industry than is the case for other industries.

Home trade

On many occasions *The Economist* complained that 'in dealing with our home trade, there are no such complete statistics available as those relating to our oversea commerce.'[17] The statistics that were considered as useful were primarily bank clearings, being largely superseded by railway freight traffic as from the 1880s; occasionally, coastal shipping returns were also considered. Consistent monthly data series have now been derived for these indicators for the whole period.

Railway freight receipts   Despite all its apparent weaknesses this indicator was considered as the major barometer of short-run fluctuations in home trade in contemporary sources. *The Economist* (September 2, 1899) put it thus: 'In regard to the home trade, the railway returns constitute almost the only guide to the general position of affairs, as there are no statistics embracing the whole industrial area.' Subsequent analyses by economists have confirmed its usefulness. Hultgren (1948, 1953) examined the relationship between various measures of railway output and NBER's reference dates, both for the United States and the United Kingdom (only on an annual basis before World War I). His general conclusion for the UK confirmed the findings from US data as to the parallel movements of these output measures and the general state of trade:

> From 1857 to 1913, the railways carried more tonnage in each year of every business expansion than they did in the preceding year ... Indeed in every general business contraction the annual average change was either a fall or a smaller rise than in the preceding or following phase.[18]

The monthly data series on railway freight traffic used here are based on receipts (the only information available before 1920) rather than ton-miles, which is the output measure usually preferred. It is thus a nominal series. Compared with a physical output measure, such as ton-miles, it has one major disadvantage as an indicator of business cycles: it is affected by changes in railway rates; but it has also one advantage: it is less dominated by coal transport. The rates charged for freight traffic were set by individual companies or by agreements between several companies, being far less variable than the general price level. It should nevertheless be pointed out that it did occasionally happen that the freight receipts presented a distorted picture of the volume of physical transport activity because of a significant general increase in rates charged by the companies.[19] But apart from a few exceptional episodes, railway freight rates seem in general to have followed a relatively smooth downward trend from 1850 and well into the 1880s, possibly beyond this as well.[20]

For the purpose for which the data series are used here, a relatively smooth trend in the level of railway rates is not a major problem, because only deviations from trend, that is, growth cycles, are studied. By using a flexible method for trend estimation (see p. 60 below), any long-run drift in railway rates charged will be reflected in the estimated trend. This method seems to work reasonably well for the indicator used here, which is computed as railway freight receipts per workday divided by miles of line open for traffic. There are significant variations in the estimated trend, most of which are presumably due to long swings in traffic expansion, particularly in the early years of the railway era. Between the mid-1870s and mid-1890s the trend rate of growth is low, reflecting the falling general price level of the period; when the long-run price level started to rise again in the second half of the 1890s the trend of nominal railway freight receipts rises as well.[21]

The enormous rate of expansion of freight traffic in the 1850s does present some difficulties with respect to extracting the cyclical component of the time series. This was indeed a period of strong growth in the economy; according to Hughes (1960: 4): 'aggregate economic activity showed a recurring tendency to rise steeply.' Following the huge investments in the 1840s, a nationwide system of railways was already in place, and nearly all of the major trunk lines were established by the early 1850s.[22] Hawke (1970: 169) maintains that the inland trade in coal was captured by the railways at least by the 1850s, but sea-borne coal still had a hold on the London market in this period; only in 1867 was more than 50 per cent of London's supply brought by rail. There is no doubt, however, that the rapid expansion of the early 1850s does make the railway freight indicator a more uncertain guide to business cycle movements than in later periods when the railway system became more mature. An argument can be made for analyzing movements in this indicator in conjunction with the volume of the coastal shipping trade in this period.

Around 1870 mineral freight accounted for more than 60 per cent of tonnage carried by rail, but only 39 per cent of total freight receipts. In the 1860s receipts per ton on mineral traffic was only about one-fourth of the receipts on general merchandise. About 75 per cent of the mineral carried by railways consisted of coal and coke.[23] The predominance of coal increased steadily towards the end of the prewar period. In this respect the freight receipts data provide a more balanced indicator of the flow of goods conveyed by the railways than does a series based on ton-miles.[24]

Referring back to Table 3.1, some indirect evidence may be obtained on the reliability of the railway freight series, RAILFR, as an indicator of *real* economic activity. Compared with the annual estimates of real railway freight output derived by Hawke (1970), who used information on freight receipts, tonnage carried, as well as ton-miles in constructing this series, RAILFR performs rather well, exhibiting a higher degree of correlation with all GDP variables and industrial production than the physical output measure RAILTM. As noted above, it is also well correlated with GDP and industrial production throughout the period. This lends some support to the central role assigned to this variable as an indicator of fluctuations in home trade.

Bank clearings   When Sir John Lubbock, the Secretary of London Bankers, announced in a letter to *The Economist* in 1867 (May 11) that the daily totals of cheques and bills passing through the Clearing House henceforth would be published, *The Economist* enthusiastically remarked that this information would be invaluable in identifying 'the ebbs and flows of the internal trade.' In a similar vein, W. Stanley Jevons, in a letter to the same journal the following week, expressed the opinion that 'these accounts will throw light upon much that is now dark.'[25]

After some years, however, it became clear that this statistic was so much affected by financial market transactions that its value as an indicator of home trade was not as great as first believed. More emphasis was initially placed upon the clearings recorded on the 'fourths' of the months, on which date domestic bills matured, but the importance attached to these figures diminished as the volume of inland bills declined.[26] Towards the end of the century increased attention was paid to provincial clearing returns;[27] later also to metropolitan and country clearings in London, for which separate figures only became available after the turn of the century.

The clearings indicator derived here is based on the only series for which continuous data exist since 1867, total London clearing figures minus amounts cleared on the half-monthly Stock Exchange settling days.[28] These figures were divided by the number of business days per month and deflated by the monthly wholesale price index derived by Sauerbeck (1886), extended back to 1850 by Klovland (1993). Ideally, a cost-of-living index and a security price index would also be appropriate for this purpose.[29] Because of the uncertainty implied by the deflation procedure the cyclical clearings series will be presented on an undeflated (nominal) basis as well. Compared with the index of clearings outside New York city derived by Snyder (1927), which is known to be a useful business cycle indicator, relatively less confidence should probably be attached to the London Clearing House series than the US series in this respect.

Coasting trade   The shipping returns published monthly by the Board of Trade provided data on the volume of shipping engaged in the foreign trade as well as in the coastal trade (including traffic between Great Britain and Ireland). The latter series, deflated by the number of workdays per month, is the one used here. The volume measure does not reflect the tonnage of goods carried but rather the tonnage of ships entered and cleared at United Kingdom ports with cargo. This may imply that it is not a particularly reliable indicator of long-run growth in the coastal shipping trade, but the short-run deviations from trend of this variable may be assumed to have some bearing on fluctuations in the activity of coastal transport. As such it is of some importance, particularly in the early years when the railway system was not yet fully developed.

Blast furnaces in blast Monthly data covering more than 90 per cent of the total furnaces in blast were published in the *Labour Gazette* beginning December 1893. For previous periods data available from other sources are far less complete. It is difficult to construct a reliable series for the whole of the period covered here; hence it will not be considered in this connection.

A Composite Cyclical Indicator (CCI)

In the subsequent determination of turning points use will be made of a composite cyclical indicator, referred to as CCI. This indicator is intended to give a summary measure of the fluctuations in the economy. The weights assigned to the individual indicators reflect *a priori* beliefs about the relative importance, reliability, and coverage of these indicators as outlined above; hence the CCI indicator is a rather crude index of economic activity.[30]

In general, indicators of home trade were assigned a weight of 60 per cent, and foreign trade series (including imports of raw materials) the remainder. The first three variables represent home trade (railway freight receipts, coasting trade, and deflated clearings), the other foreign trade (raw materials import volume, real non-cotton exports, raw cotton consumption, and real cotton exports). The following definition was employed:

$$CCI = 0.50 \times RAILFR + 0.05 \times COASTR + 0.05 \times CLEARR +$$
$$0.15 \times IMPRMR + 0.15 \times EXPNCR + 0.05 \times COTRAR + 0.05 \times COTEXR$$

These weights apply to the 1868–1910 period. Slightly modified weights were used in other subperiods as follows: RAILFR 0.45 before 1860, 0.55 beginning 1911; COASTR 0.15 before 1860, 0.10 between 1860 and 1867, zero after 1910; EXPNCR 0.20 before 1868; COTRAR and COTEXR 0.025 before 1868; CLEARR was not available before 1868. The main considerations underlying this pattern were the diminishing role of coastal shipping relative to railway transport and the increasing share of cotton exports after the late 1860s. The indicator was constructed from the cyclical components (actual minus trend) with all variables having a standardized variance of unity.

STATISTICAL METHODOLOGY

Trend Estimation

The starting point of the empirical analysis is the assumption that the actual time series can be divided into a trend and a cycle component. It is the latter that is of interest here, but following established procedures the cycle component is derived as the residual after estimating the trend.

A number of methods are available for the estimation of the trend of a time series, ranging from simple log-linear regressions on a time trend variable to more sophisticated structural time series methods.[31] For the purpose of the exploratory data analysis performed here the trend component was estimated using the Hodrick–Prescott filter,[32] which has been extensively used in recent analyses of 'the stylized facts' of business cycles. The trend component, τ_t, of a time series y_t is estimated by minimizing:

$$\sum_{t=1}^{T}\left(y_t - \tau_t\right)^2 + \lambda \sum_{t=2}^{T-1}\left[\left(\tau_{t+1} - \tau_t\right) - \left(\tau_t - \tau_{t-1}\right)\right]^2$$

for a chosen value of λ. This parameter determines the degree of smoothness in the trend component, with higher values of λ giving a smoother trend for a given data frequency. Conventionally, the value of this parameter has been set at 1600 on quarterly data, but in order to produce a relatively smooth time trend for monthly data it must be much higher. This follows automatically from the higher frequency of the data, that is, monthly instead of quarterly. If the monthly data contain a relatively large irregular component, which is typically the case for such business cycle indicators, a reasonably smooth trend requires a further increase in the value of λ. This parameter can be given an interpretation as the ratio of the variance of $(y_t - \tau_t)$ to the variance of the change in the growth rate of τ_t per period. The conventional value of λ was initially chosen by Hodrick and Prescott (1980) on the assumption that a 5 per cent deviation from trend was comparable to a one-eighth percentage change in the trend growth rate in a quarter.[33]

After some experimentation it was decided to use a value of 57 600 for λ, which is consistent with a 10 per cent deviation and 1/24 percentage change in trend per month. However, too much significance should not be attached to this particular value; the main point is that a value of λ of, say, 20 000 and upward is required to produce a relatively smooth trend. The results do not appear to be sensitive to the choice of λ within a wide range around the chosen parameter value.[34]

The trend component was estimated by this method for all business cycle indicators except the unemployment rate, which is a stationary variable. Although the procedure seems to give sensible results, at least corresponding to our *a priori* notion of the trend and cycle components, it should be borne in mind that other decomposition methods may result in somewhat different estimates.

Growth Cycles

With the exception of the unemployment rate, the empirical measure of cycles used here is the growth cycle, that is, the deviation from trend. Given the estimate of the trend component, $\hat{\tau}_t$, the growth cycle is then computed as $y_t - \hat{\tau}_t$.

The use of detrended data in dating the turning points, rather than looking for turning points in data with the trend included (classical cycles), is consistent with the established tradition for Britain. If there is a significant upward trend in the series the peak in the detrended data will tend to be located before the peak in the classical cycle. Conversely, the trough in the growth cycle will come after the corresponding trough in the non-adjusted data. On average, with a positive rate of growth, the recession periods of such cycles thus tend to be somewhat longer than classical cycles.

The turning points identified for Britain by Burns and Mitchell (1946) were derived within a framework that focused on classical cycles only. However, regarding the reference dates set by the NBER for the United States, Romer (1994) has drawn attention to the fact that the main series were analyzed in detrended form before 1927. Consequently, the cycles identified in this period may conform to the growth cycle concept. A somewhat similar effect could apply to the case of Britain, particularly before the 1890s, when the unemployment rate and financial variables, in which the trend component is absent or very weak, constituted the basis for the dating procedure done by the NBER.

The Identification of Turning Points

The monthly turning points were identified by the NBER through a complicated procedure, subjecting a large number of business cycle indicators to statistical analysis. The drawback of this procedure is that it is not replicable by other researchers. However, the computerized method for finding turning points developed by Bry and Boschan (1971) has been shown to produce estimates of peaks and troughs that are broadly consistent with the NBER chronology when applied to comprehensive indicators, for example industrial production indices.[35]

A slightly modified version of the Bry–Boschan procedure is applied to the data series studied here. The basic modification consists of rules intended to weed out minor cycles, which may be a problem in identifying the turning points in the detrended data. Otherwise the procedure retains the duration requirements of cycles attributable to Burns and Mitchell (1946) as well as the filters applied to the data by Bry and Boschan (1971).[36] The steps involved are:

1. *Replacement of extreme values*: this was only done for two series, railway freight traffic and the unemployment rate during some months in 1893 and 1912 were severely affected by strike (see Appendix for further details);
2. *locating turning points in 12-month moving average of the series*, eliminating double peaks and troughs by choosing the highest peak and lowest trough;
3. *determination of corresponding turns in the Spencer curve*:[37] the selected turns are to be within ±5 months of those determined in the previous step. Cycles whose duration (from peak to peak or trough to trough) is less than 15 months are eliminated;
4. *determination of corresponding turns in 5-month moving average*, using the same procedure as in the previous step. Minor cycles are eliminated according to the following criteria:
   (a) duration is less than 15 months;
   (b) the absolute value of the difference between alternating turning points is less than 2 standard deviations of the 5-month averages of the series;
5. *determination of final turning points in weakly smoothed data* (3-month average with weight 0.5 for actual value and weights 0.25 for lag 1 and lead 1). As before, no cycle is accepted if the duration of the whole cycle is less than 15 months; in addition, each cycle phase has to be no less than 5 months in this final step.

Application of this procedure was guided by inspection of the graphs of the cycle indicators described below.

A REASSESSMENT OF THE BUSINESS CYCLE CHRONOLOGY IN THE UNITED KINGDOM

The Plan of the Data Analysis

This section presents an overview of the results obtained from applying the methods outlined above to the set of business cycle indicators derived here. The discussion will focus on the identified turning points in Table 3.2 and the accompanying graphs of the unemployment rate (representing the NBER chronology) and the CCI indicator (summarizing the new chronology), which are shown for three subperiods: (A) 1850–70, (B) 1870–90 and (C) 1890–1914.

Table 3.2   Turning points in UK business cycle indicators, 1850–1914

	NBER	UNEMP	CCI	RAILFR	COASTR	CLEARR	IMPRMR	EXPNCR	COTRAR	COTEXR
Trough					1851:10		1851:10		1851:5	
Peak			1851:12		1853:4		1851:11		1851:12	
Trough			1852:7	1852:7	1853:12		1852:7		1852:12	
Peak			1854:2	1854:3	1854:7		1854:2	1853:10	1853:5	
Trough	1854:12	1855:2	1855:2	1855:3	1855:2		1855:10	1855:2	1854:4	1854:1
Peak	1857:9	1857:2	1856:11	1857:1	1857:4		1857:11	1856:11	1857:6	1855:12
Trough	1858:3	1858:5	1858:3	1857:12	1858:2		1858:3	1858:1	1857:11	1857:12
Peak	1860:9	1860:5	1860:8	1860:5	1860:3		1860:3	1859:3	1861:7	1860:12
Trough	1862:12	1862:7	1862:10	1862:2	1864:9		1861:6	1861:7	1862:9	1862:11
Peak	1866:3	1865:11	1866:2	1866:3	1867:8		1865:12	1865:12	1868:2	1867:11
Trough	1868:3	1868:6	1869:9	1868:6	1868:3	1870:9	1869:11	1867:12	1869:9	1869:9
Peak	1872:9	1872:2	1871:12	1873:7	1871:10	1872:3	1871:10	1871:9	1871:12	1871:4
Trough					1872:11	1873:4	1873:1	1873:6	1872:7	
Peak					1876:10	1875:2	1874:5	1875:2	1876:12	
Trough							1875:12	1876:4		
Peak							1876:11			
Trough	1879:6	1879:5	1878:12	1879:9	1879:5	1877:1	1878:12		1878:11	
Peak	1882:12	1882:8	1883:8	1883:8	1883:7	1881:6	1884:12	1882:1	1882:6	
Trough	1886:6	1886:4	1886:3	1886:4	1887:9	1885:9	1887:2		1885:4	
Peak	1890:9	1890:1	1890:6	1889:12	1888:9	1890:8	1889:10		1888:6	
Trough		1893:1	1893:2	1893:2	1892:5	1891:8	1893:1	1892:5	1893:2	1893:3
Peak		1897:4	1896:1	1894:2	1893:11	1895:9	1897:2	1895:9		1894:11
Trough	1895:2	1897:11	1898:6	1895:2	1895:2	1897:5		1898:5		1895:12
Peak	1900:6	1899:1	1899:5	1900:6	1897:10	1899:3		1899:5	1899:6	1897:11
Trough	1901:9		1900:10	1901:1	1901:4	1900:5	1899:6	1900:10	1900:9	1900:10
Peak	1903:6		1902:11	1902:11		1902:2	1902:3	1902:9	1901:8	1902:11
Trough	1904:11	1904:5	1903:10	1904:12		1904:3	1905:7	1904:1	1903:9	1903:10
Peak	1907:6	1907:4	1907:3	1907:7	1906:4	1905:11	1907:11	1910:8	1905:6	1908:1
Trough	1908:11	1908:10	1908:11	1908:12	1907:12	1907:12	1912:5	1912:4	1908:10	1910:4
Peak	1912:12	1913:3	1912:9	1912:6	1912:9	1910:5	1913:2		1912:7	1911:11

Notes:

NBER = reference dates determined by Burns and Mitchell (1946); UNEMP = unemployment rate (ironfounders July 1854–December 1886, all trades thereafter); CCI = composite cyclical indicator; RAILFR = railway freight receipts; COASTR = tonnage of ships engaged in coasting trade; CLEARR = deflated bank clearings; IMPRMR = quantity index of raw materials import, beginning 1871 value index in constant (1880) prices; EXPNCR = value of non-cotton exports in constant (1880) prices; COTRAR = raw cotton consumption; COTEXR = exports of cotton goods in constant (1880) prices.

In order to get some notion of the performance of the new indicators reference can be made to Table 3.3, which shows the correlation coefficients between the cyclical components of annual gross domestic product and industrial production, on the one hand, and annual average values of the monthly business cycle indicators, on the other. The cyclical components upon which the correlations are based were derived by estimating the trend by the Hodrick–Prescott filter, using the conventional value of λ equal to 400.

Table 3.3   Correlation coefficients between annual cyclical components of gross domestic product, industrial production, and the new indicators

	CCI	RAILFR	COASTR	CLEARR	CLEARN	IMPRMR	EXPNCR	COTRAR	COTEXR
1850–69									
GDPI	0.544	0.565	–0.232	NA	NA	0.333	0.226	0.168	0.114
INDPRO	0.613	0.601	0.249	NA	NA	0.624	0.065	0.158	–0.019
1870–89									
GDPI	0.696	0.513	–0.131	0.697	0.705	0.489	0.150	0.606	0.431
INDPRO	0.897	0.668	–0.175	0.544	0.717	0.685	0.332	0.714	0.441
1890–1914									
GDPI	0.762	0.588	0.327	0.377	0.463	0.322	–0.028	0.590	0.583
INDPRO	0.684	0.672	0.306	0.372	0.548	0.228	–0.141	0.447	0.414

Note: See note to Table 3.2 for explanation of variables.

In general, these correlation coefficients show a high degree of comovement between industrial production or GDP and CCI, the Composite Cyclical Indicator. Among the individual indicators the railway freight series is performing well in all three subperiods. The raw materials index also exhibits relatively high correlation coefficients with the industrial production index in the first two subperiods. A somewhat surprising feature is the very low degree of correlation between real non-cotton exports and industrial production or GDP. It thus seems to perform poorly as a coincident indicator; its role as a leading indicator is yet to be explored.

New Evidence on the Business Cycle Chronology

(A) The 1850s and the 1860s

An important result evident from Figure 3.1 and Table 3.2 is that the turning points of the NBER chronology are close to the peaks and troughs in the unemployment rate of ironfounders as identified by the computer program described above. This method picks exactly the same number of turning points in this series as the NBER chronology. At the business cycle peaks in 1857, 1860, and 1866 (troughs in the unemployment data) the new method shows a lead relative to the NBER dates of four to seven months; at business cycle troughs

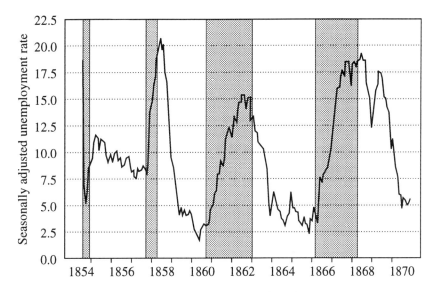

Figure 3.1   Unemployment rate: ironfounders, July 1854–December 1870

in 1854, 1858, and 1868 there is a lag of two or three months, 1862 forming an exception with a lead of five months. It is likely that the NBER modified the turning points of the unemployment series slightly in the light of information from Thorp's *Business Annals* (1926) and other information, presumably mostly financial series.[38]

Figure 3.2 graphs the movements of the Composite Cyclical Indicator (CCI) along with turning points of this series determined by the procedures outlined above. Inspection of Table 3.2 at once reveals that the turning points of the CCI indicator are remarkably close to the NBER dates. In fact, the new reference dates suggested here are closer to the NBER dates than the ones implied by the unemployment rate of ironfounders in four out of seven turning points in the 1850s and 1860s; in one case (the trough in 1854–5) the two indicators give the same date. In the peak of 1857 the turning point of the CCI indicator precedes the NBER peak by ten months. In the trough of 1868–9 the components of CCI diverge markedly with respect to the location of the turning point. Referring to Figure 3.2 it will be noted that there is a another marked local trough in the CCI indicator early in 1868, corresponding to the NBER trough in March 1868.

This finding is noteworthy because the two chronologies have been derived using quite different methods and basically different sets of business cycle indicators. The data series differ because there is no evidence that the NBER

Recasting business cycles with new data

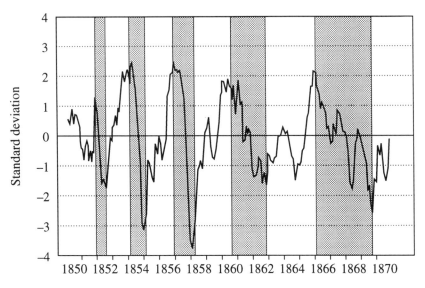

Note: Shaded areas designate contraction periods (CCI chronology).

Figure 3.2   Five-month moving average of composite cyclical indicator (CCI), March 1850–December 1870

collected monthly railway freight data or quantities of raw materials import for this period; monthly nominal export series might have been consulted, but real exports were definitely not computed.[39] The striking similarity of these two monthly sets of reference dates points to the conclusion that the pattern of business cycles in this period is fairly well established. This result also conforms to the lists of peak and trough years that were derived by Beveridge (1944), Rostow (1948) and Aldcroft and Fearon (1972) working with annual data, although there are minor differences as noted below.

Our data begin with 1850 but the cycles identified for the first two or three years must be regarded as decidedly more uncertain than the subsequent ones. The first clearly identifiable turning point in CCI is the trough in July 1852. Two of the most important indicators, railway freight receipts and raw material imports, both have an unambiguous trough in this month, while other indicators show a less distinct pattern. However, both non-cotton exports and the cotton industry were rather buoyant at this time, although the latter sector seemed to experience a slacker demand towards the end of 1852. In the early summer of 1852 commodity prices ended a period of weakness, starting to rise steeply in the strong expansion period which then followed.

The new data analyzed here do point to a likely cyclical trough in the middle of 1852, but this must only have been a weak and short-lived retardation of growth. Hughes (1960: 28) considers the years 1849–53 as 'one continued expansion, although it is possible that it might properly be divided into three shorter periods – a strong recovery in 1849–50, a moderate downswing in prices and trading activity in 1851, with the boom beginning in the summer of 1852 and reaching its peak in the third quarter of 1853.' From Figure 3.2 it may seem that a peak around the final months of 1850 would be consistent with our data, but it should be emphasized that this date is really too close to the beginning of the data series for the trend and cycle components to be determined with much precision.

The spectacular boom that started in the summer of 1852 continued unabated through 1853, ending in February 1854 according to the CCI indicator. A more disaggregated analysis would show, however, that some sectors, particularly textiles, experienced difficulties as from the second part of 1853.[40] From Table 3.2 it will be seen that cotton consumption peaked already in May 1853. According to the circular of Wm. Peel and Co.[41] the first symptoms of change in the worsted trade appeared around July 1853: 'and Bradford, in all interests, has during 1854 passed through an ordeal of great severity.' The aggregate picture, as represented here, fairly unambiguously locates the peak in early 1854, although it seems clear that the export trade peaked somewhat earlier.

The decline during 1854 is visible in all the major indicators. So is the subsequent trough in the early months of 1855. The contraction was apparently more severe in the foreign trade than in the home trade, as represented by the railway freight indicator and the ironfounders' unemployment rate. This is consistent with the fact that the iron industry was still prosperous in 1855, although 1854 was the peak year of the Scottish iron industry.[42]

Many aspects of the great commercial crisis occurring in the final months of 1857 are well known;[43] only two features implied by the new data will be noted here. First, the cyclical movements of the monthly indicators around the peak late in 1856 or early in 1857 and the trough about a year later are very evident in all the series. Although these fluctuations are quite well synchronized, there is some displacement of foreign trade relative to the aggregate series: raw materials import lagging and exports leading the development. The second important conclusion regards the exact dating of the 1857 peak. According to the CCI indicator the turning point was in November 1856, eleven months earlier than the NBER reference date and well ahead of the commercial crisis in October 1857.[44] The underlying monthly data give an impression of a less distinct difference in timing; economic activity held up quite well through July of 1857, but fell off significantly thereafter.

The first three turning points of the 1860s seem to be well determined by our main indicators. Peaks in August 1860 and February 1866 are clearly identifiable in the aggregate CCI indicator, being fairly well synchronized with railway freight and raw materials import. The trough in October 1862 is close to the NBER date, but the underlying indicators exhibit less-similar movements. The tendency is for a somewhat earlier dating of the trough, but the extreme movements in cotton pull the trough toward the autumn of 1862. With the exception of the 1865 peak, non-cotton exports conform to the evidence from the 1850s, often being a leading indicator at turning points.

It is of some interest to note the cyclical movements in 1864, which are common to several indicators but not sufficiently persistent to be classified as a separate cycle. It appears that the economy was rather buoyant at the beginning of the year but that a setback occurred later. This was most marked in raw materials import and exports, also being evident from the CCI indicator and from commodity prices. 1864 was a year of recurrent monetary stringency; three periods of monetary pressure with bank rate at 8 per cent or more were recorded (January–February, April–May, September–October). According to contemporary trade reports many industries were initially rather busy but the monetary squeeze did not fail to leave its depressive marks on economic activity.[45]

The years from 1867 to 1869 constituted a period of slack trade in many industries, one notable exception being the revival of the cotton industry following the return to more normal supply conditions after the American Civil War. It is difficult to determine a unique trough: both the early months of 1868 and the autumn of 1869 are candidates. Here, the latter date was identified as the trough in the CCI indicator, most heavily influenced by the strong decline in raw materials import and cotton consumption. Further research may be able to move the date of the trough back to the first months of 1868, perhaps also finding an additional minor cycle within this period.

(B) The 1870s and 1880s

According to the CCI indicator there are only two clearly defined turning points in the 1870s: the peak in December 1871 and the trough in December 1878 (Figure 3.3). The existence of a long period between a monumental peak early in the decade and a deep trough in 1879 is consistent with the NBER reference dates, the unemployment series and nearly all attempts at inferring business cycle chronologies on the basis of national income data. Technically, a large proportion of the 1870s is therefore characterized as a recession period, but this may be rather misleading. In most of this period aggregate economic activity held up quite well; the economy did not deviate much from a reasonably high growth path.[46] Several turning points are determined for the individual indicators in Table 3.2, particularly in the foreign trade series, but in the aggregate these are too unsynchronized and too weak to generate movements in the CCI indicator. Hence these may not be classified as genuine cycles according to the criteria outlined above.

A somewhat surprising feature is the dating of the peak as early as December 1871 (Figure 3.4). Traditionally, it has been later, in 1872 (Burns and Mitchell,

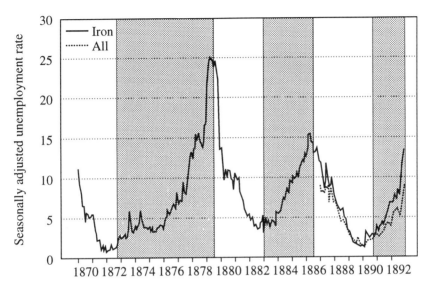

Note: Shaded areas designate contraction periods (NBER chronology).

Figure 3.3   Unemployment rate: ironfounders and all trades, January 1870–December 1892

1946), 1873 (Rostow, 1948), or even 1874 (Beveridge, 1944; Aldcroft and Fearon, 1972). It is evident from annual real GDP figures, though, that there was little or no growth in 1872 and 1873.[47] It should therefore be no real surprise that Capie and Mills (1991), using modern time series techniques in the estimation of the trend, found that the growth cycle peak of annual real GDP was in 1871. In this perspective the location of this peak in December 1871 on a completely independent data set is of some interest.

The problem with this result relates primarily to a reconciliation with the great inflationary boom of the iron and coal industries in 1872 and 1873, which lasted until the winter months of 1873.[48] Evidently there were supply bottlenecks in these industries, which fuelled the enormous inflation of iron and coal prices. Real output in these sectors appears to have peaked in 1872. It should be noted that the ironfounders' unemployment series was at its lowest level already in February 1872.[49] Much of the further rise in nominal values after this may thus have been due to price increases only. As noted above, the railway freight data are susceptible of being distorted by the increase in freight rates in October 1872, which may explain the late peak recorded in the RAILFR series.

The trough early in 1879 (or perhaps in December 1878) is a major one. The unemployment among ironfounders reached 25 per cent (seasonally adjusted)

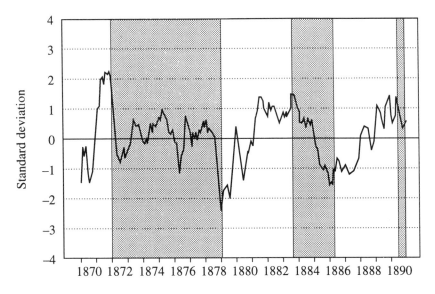

Note: Shaded areas designate contraction periods (CCI chronology).

Figure 3.4   Five-month moving average of composite cyclical indicator (CCI), January 1870–December 1890

in May 1879, the highest figure recorded for the whole period. The severe downturn is reflected in all indicators of home and foreign trade, the latter ones once again leading the development.

The recovery from the deep trough early in 1879 was exceptionally strong in the second half of 1879. The source of this is clearly identified in *The Economist's Commercial History and Review of 1880*: 'It is now clear that, stimulated by the sudden and large American demand, first for iron and steel, and then for other commodities, which appeared after Sept. 1879, there arose, in nearly all the considerable markets in this country a violent speculative fever.' Nearly all trade reports reproduced in this source, however, point out that the year 1880 proved disappointing in the end, after opening with 'considerable hopes.'[50] In the majority of industries the course of events was the same: 'The very considerable improvement and general rise of prices which marked the close of 1879 and the first three months of 1880 was not maintained during the summer of the year.'[51] This summary applied to such industries as iron and steel, woollen and worsted, silk, linen and leather; only cotton seemed not to experience any marked setback.[52]

The observations made here are duly reflected in most of the new monthly indicators; in fact, the fluctuations are so distinct that a separate cycle is close to being identified in the CCI indicator. There is a local peak around February 1880 and a subsequent local trough in the second half of 1880. Although there is not yet firm evidence to classify this episode as a separate cycle, the widespread surge of activity in a variety of trades and the sudden reversal of expansive forces in these months may nevertheless warrant some attention. It should be noted that because the period of extraordinarily high economic activity was so short, being divided between two years, 1879 and 1880, the cyclical fluctuations in this period are hardly discernible in annual data.

The CCI indicator identifies a peak in August 1883, somewhat later than the NBER date. The first half of 1882 and summer and early autumn of 1883 are also periods of buoyancy in many indicators, the latter period especially in the railway freight series. The dating of the peak of the corresponding classical cycle would presumably have fallen in 1884, as the CCI indicator seemed to exhibit growth rates above trend well into 1884.[53]

There are few problems with the next trough. Here it is determined to have taken place in March 1886, three months earlier than the NBER reference date. A short period of renewed slackness early in 1887 is also a common feature of nearly all indicators, in particular the foreign trade series.

(C) The period 1890–1914

The deviations between the NBER turning points and the chronology implied by the new monthly indicators are not extensive from 1854 and until the end of the 1880s (Figure 3.5). The peak occurring in 1890 is also confirmed by the new data. On the other hand, the evidence from the rest of the 1890s and the first half decade of the twentieth century presents another picture. Comparing the first three columns of Table 3.2 it will be seen that there is an extra cycle in the 1890s in both the ironfounders' unemployment series and the CCI indicator. Otherwise the NBER dating does not correspond well to the course of the CCI indicator or the unemployment data between the peaks of 1890 and 1907.

The evidence in Figure 3.5 explains why a trough was determined by the NBER in February 1895, but the new data show that February 1893 represents a lower point.[54] The economy apparently recovered somewhat during 1893, but suffered a setback in the second half of 1894, reaching a new low in the winter of 1895. In some indicators (RAILFR, COASTR, COTEXR) this bulge is identified as a separate cycle, but not in the aggregate CCI indicator (Figure 3.6).[55]

The various indicators do not portray a unified picture as to cyclical movements in the remainder of the 1890s. Cycles in aggregate economic activity were short but not particularly severe. Peaks are identified in the CCI indicator in January 1896 and May 1899, the latter year corresponding to the results in Capie and Mills (1991). Trough dates are June 1896 and October 1900. These dates seem to be heavily influenced by fluctuations in exports; note that turning points of

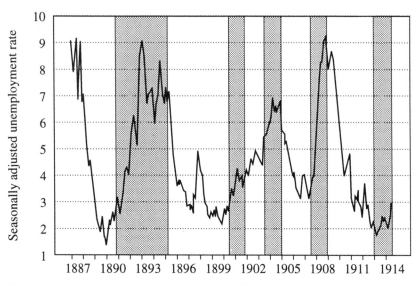

Note: Shaded areas designate contraction periods (NBER chronology).

Figure 3.5   Unemployment rate: all trades, January 1887–July 1914

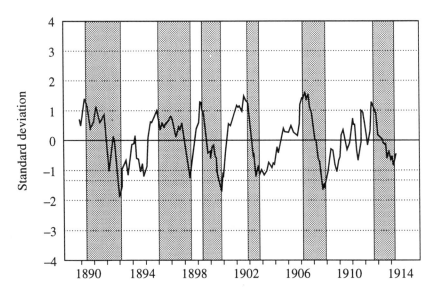

Note: Shaded areas designate contraction periods (CCI chronology).

*Figure 3.6   Five-month moving average of composite cyclical indicator (CCI),
January 1890–May 1914*

RAILFR, the main indicator of home trade, are identical to the NBER reference dates in the period 1895–1900.

Capie and Mills (1991) argued that the choice of 1903 as a peak year, as implied by the NBER chronology, was quite unfortunate because this year was known as one of widespread complaints about the slump in economic activity. The course of the CCI indicator gives support to this view, signalling a peak in November 1902 and then falling rapidly to a trough in October 1903. The cotton industry was particularly badly hit at this time, experiencing sagging demand for cotton goods and sharply increasing raw material prices. The home trade was just as sluggish in the greater part of 1904; hence the turning point might very well have been located in this year.

The three remaining turning points of this period are well determined, corresponding closely to the NBER reference dates. The 1907–8 turning points are among the least doubtful ones, being on the short list of every business cycle chronology in Britain. March 1907 was the peak and November 1908 marks the trough. A feature of these years is the relatively stability of non-cotton exports, which is somewhat puzzling in view of the international character of this cycle.

The movements toward the final peak in September 1912 were quite irregular, possibly due in part to several episodes of labour disputes.[56] The final years before World War I were a recession period, but as the monthly data series end in July 1914, it is not possible to tell when the trough of this cycle phase occurred. When September 1914 came, the month of the NBER reference trough, railway companies had already been taken over by the government, the publication of traffic returns had been discontinued in August and foreign trade was severely disrupted by the actions of war.

CONCLUDING REMARKS

The new monthly business cycle indicators were derived with a view to providing a consistent quantitative basis for analyses of short-run economic fluctuations in Victorian Britain. When evaluating the results based on these data the various defects of the individual indicators should be duly taken into account, however. Some indicators are based on sales or inputs to the production process, and the main series are inferred from transport activity, which is truly an indirect way of measuring commodity production. It turns out, however, that the new indicators are generally consistent with the cyclical pattern that has been established in the previous literature; in some cases where deviations occur contemporary sources give some support to the revised views presented here.

Although most reference dates determined by Burns and Mitchell (1946) have been modified slightly by using new data and new statistical methods, the general impression is that the NBER chronology emerges largely unscathed during substantial periods. There is, however, a tendency for the new turning points to be located a few months earlier than the monthly NBER dates, a feature which is more consistently present at peaks of the cycle than at troughs.

Only between the peaks of 1890 and 1907 are there any major discrepancies between the turning points determined by the new data and the established chronology. There is evidence of several additional cycles in this period, most notably at the beginning of the 1880s and one in the 1890s, but only the latter is formally confirmed as a cycle by the procedures adopted here. This makes a slight increase in the total number of pre-World War I turning points in Britain, from 20 to 22, which is in the direction anticipated by Friedman and Schwartz (1982). However, the number of business cycles in Britain is still well below the number recorded for the United States during the period studied here.

Whether the key to understanding the causes of bad or good trade can be found in the shadow of sunspots is perhaps less obvious now than Jevons once imagined. But the search for a full explanation of business cycles in Victorian Britain still goes on in the light of new theories and, equally important, new data.

APPENDIX

The Rate of Unemployment

Data series
Unemployment data relating to the 'Friendly Society of Ironfounders' are available on a monthly basis, beginning July 1854. A monthly data series on the unemployment rate for 'all trades' has been published back to January 1887. It should be noted that the industries covered in this series do not remain the same throughout the period (see Persons *et al.* 1922).

Transformations
The published ironfounders' data consist of a monthly series of the number of members reported to be unemployed at the end of the month and figures giving total membership number at the end of each year. The unemployment rate was computed as the number of unemployed relative to the number of union members, the latter series being linearly interpolated between December figures.

The unemployment rate for 'all trades' was taken directly from the sources, except the March 1912 observation, which was severely affected by a labour dispute. A linearly interpolated figure of 3.2 per cent was substituted for the actual figure, which is 11.3 per cent.

Sources
The ironfounders' data used here are from Dessauer-Meinhardt (1940). The other unemployment series were taken from the following sources: *1887 and*

1893–1904: *Labour Gazette* (1887 figures were read off the chart on page 161 of the November 1893 issue); *1888–1892* were found in *British Parliamentary Papers* 1895 (365: Appendix 28, p. 547); *1905–14* are from *The Economist's Commercial History and Review* of 1909–14.

Volume of Imported Raw Materials

Data series
This series consists of two main parts: (a) an index based on physical import quantities for the years 1850–70, (b) import values deflated by an import price index for the period 1871–1914. The two series were linked together in 1871. This index covers seven main groups of imported raw materials and partly manufactured goods: metals, chemicals and dyestuffs, oil seeds and oils, wool, other textiles except cotton, wood and timber and sundry raw materials. Note that imports of raw cotton are not included here – they are covered by the separate time series of raw cotton consumption described below. A description of the volume index covering the period 1850–70 and the nominal import values beginning 1871 is included in this section. The import price index is explained separately below.

Index of import quantities, 1850–70   Monthly returns of import quantities exist for the whole period, but information on the computed real (that is, market) value of imports first appeared in 1856. In the beginning the returns covered only a few main commodities, but the range of items included increased gradually towards 1871. In order to construct a reasonably complete index of the volume of raw materials imported for this period it is hence necessary to work directly with physical import quantities. An index was constructed from 35 monthly time series of imported raw materials and semi-manufactured goods, using the average of value shares in 1855, 1860, 1865, and 1870 as weights:

1. *Metals*: copper ore, copper regulus, copper unwrought, iron bars, lead, spelter, tin;
2. *Chemicals* and *dyestuffs*: brimstone (sulphur), saltpetre, nitrate of soda, cochineal, indigo, madder (including madder root and garancine), gambier, valonia;
3. *Oil seeds* and *oils*: linseed, rapeseed, fish oils, palm oil, olive oil, linseed oil, tallow;
4. *Wool*: gross imports of sheep wool minus re-exports;
5. *Other textiles*: flax, hemp, jute, raw silk;
6. *Wood* and *timber*: hewn timber, sawn wood;
7. *Sundry raw materials*: caoutchouc, dry hides, wet hides, tanned hides (leather), mahogany, staves.

Nominal import values 1871–1882 Beginning January 1871, the monthly trade returns were significantly expanded. The new returns contained *declared* values of all main import items, whereas previously only estimated values of selected commodities were published. The commodities were entered alphabetically, however, not grouped according to main classes of commodities. In constructing a nominal series consistent with the volume index for the previous period the import values of the following 63 commodities were extracted and grouped together:

1. *Metals*: copper ore, copper regulus, copper unwrought, iron ore (included in the monthly returns only from June 1876; prior to this annual values were distributed evenly over the year), iron bars, steel unwrought, lead, pyrites, quicksilver, tin, zinc;
2. *Chemicals* and *dyestuffs*: alkali, bark for tanners' use, brimstone, chemicals unenumerated, cochineal, gambier, indigo, madder (including madder root and garancine), nitrate of soda, saltpetre, valonia;
3. *Oil seeds* and *oils*: cotton seed, linseed, rapeseed, fish oils, palm oil, coconut oil, olive oil, seed oils, turpentine, petroleum, rosin;
4. *Wool*: sheep wool, alpaca and similar wools, goat's wool (mohair), woollen rags minus re-exports of sheep wool;
5. *Other textiles*: flax, hemp, jute, raw silk, thrown silk, waste silk;
6. *Wood* and *timber*: hewn wood, sawn wood;
7. *Sundry raw materials*: bark Peruvian, bristles, caoutchouc, gum arabic, gum lac etc., gutta percha, dry hides, wet hides, tanned hides, rags of linen and cotton for paper making, esparto and other vegetable fibres, tar, elephant's teeth, staves, mahogany.

Nominal import values, 1883–1914 For the years 1883–1902 the returns contained total values of commodity groups corresponding closely to the classification used above. In addition to the commodities listed above, these group totals also included the value of unenumerated articles, which implies a broader coverage of goods than in the previous periods. A reclassification of a few items was undertaken in order to obtain consistency with the commodity group definition used for the previous period.

In 1903 the commodity groups in the monthly returns were altered. After some manipulation it is possible to link these data to the previous groups. The main difference is that some commodity groups now contain more semi-manufactures than previously. The metals group, for example, now comprises other manufactures (that is, plates and angles for shipbuilding as well as iron and steel rails, girders, beams, and so on.) in addition to iron bars and unwrought steel already included in the previous periods. On the other hand, more highly manufactured goods, such as cutlery and hardware, machinery and telegraphic cables, were not included.

Transformations

The data were adjusted for the number of workdays in each month. Until March 1855 the Board of Trade returns were not made up to the end of the calendar month, but rather to the 5th of the next month (October 10 in the case of 'September'). The number of workdays per month equals the number of days minus the number of Sundays and holidays falling within the month covered by the returns. In conformance with contemporary practice, only Good Friday and Christmas Day were counted as holidays before 1871; thereafter Easter Monday, Whitsun Monday and additional holidays during Christmas were included. Special bank holidays, such as the Queen's Jubilee in June 1887, were also taken into account, using *The Economist*'s weekly reviews of the money market as a guide.

Before 1871 an adjustment was made to the December figures, of which 25 per cent was transferred to the following January. The rationale for this is that the December figures were unduly inflated, and January figures were very small. This is explained by *The Economist* (February 11, 1871) thus: 'By one of the anomalies of the old system, January only included from fourteen to twenty-one days, and in consequence there was always a great diminution in the month of January as compared with the month of December.' As a consequence of the transition to the new system in 1871 the effective month of January 1871 included in the returns was 'some days shorter than that of January 1870' (ibid.). Here, it has been reduced by four days, corresponding to the 'no extravagant estimate' of one-seventh employed by *The Economist*.

Because the various parts of the series overlap at each break point, splicing could be done by the simple ratio method. After deflating nominal import values for each commodity group in the 1871–1914 period and removing the breaks in each of the series, the next step was seasonal adjustment of the seven commodity group series. This was done separately for the 1850–70 and 1871–1914 periods because of the various differences in the construction of the data for the two periods, as explained above. Finally the data were aggregated to form a series of total raw materials imported, excluding cotton.

Source

The primary data were found in *UK Trade and Navigation Accounts*, published monthly by the Board of Trade.

Price Index of Imported Raw Materials

Data series

Separate price indices were computed for the 1850–80 and the 1880–1914 periods. The weights applied to the first period reflect average import shares within each commodity group in the years 1856–8 and 1876–8; for the second period weights were calculated from average import shares in 1886–8 and 1906–8. Both indices are computed as geometric averages of price relatives with 1880 as base year. The two indices were spliced in 1880 by gradually increasing the weight of the second index each month by steps of one-twelfth beginning January 1880, and reducing the weight of the first index correspondingly, thus phasing out this index by December 1880.

The following list contains the imported commodities included, giving in parentheses the *number* of descriptions within each subgroup of main commodities.

1850–80

1. *Metals*: copper (2), tin (2), lead (1), spelter (1), quicksilver (1), antimony (1), Swedish iron bars and steel (2);
2. *Chemicals and dyestuffs*:
   (a) *Chemicals* (52.2 per cent): brimstone (2), pearl and pot ashes (2), alkalis (6), ammonia salts (4), metallic salts (including bichromate of potash, prussiate of potash, borax) (10), organic chemicals (including acids, cream of tartar and quinine) (6), saltpetre (1), nitrate of soda (1), guano (1);
   (b) *Dyestuffs* and *tanning materials* (47.8 per cent): indigo (4), cochineal (3), dyewoods (5), madder root (1), other dyestuffs (3), tanning materials (including gambier and valonia) (3);
3. *Oil seeds* and *oils*: linseed (2), rapeseed (2), cottonseed (1), linseed oil (1), rapeseed oil (1), cottonseed oil (1), palm oil (1), olive oil (1), coconut oil (1), fish oils (4), lard oil (1), turpentine (2), rosin (1), tar (1), petroleum (1), tallow (2);
4. *Wool*: Australian merino wools (10), Cape wools (3), low wools (including East India wools and Russian Donskoi) (3), alpaca (1), mohair (1);
5. *Other raw textile materials*: flax (2), jute (1), hemp (2), silk (5);
6. *Wood* and *timber*: fir timber (6), oak (3), teak (1), sawn wood (8);
7. *Sundry raw materials*:
   (a) *Hides* (60 per cent): raw hides (9), butts, kips and prepared hides (5);
   (b) *Drugs* and *drysalteries* (40 per cent): shellac (2), gums (3), essential oils (3), drugs (13), plumbago (1), India rubber (1), gutta percha (1), elephants' teeth (1), mother-of-pearl shells (1).

1880–1914

1. *Metals*: copper (1), tin (1), lead (1), spelter (1), quicksilver (1), antimony (1), iron and steel manufactures (approximated by British prices) (7), iron ore (3);
2. *Chemicals* and *dyestuffs:*
   (a) *Chemicals* (50 per cent): brimstone (2), pearl and pot ashes (2), metallic salts (including bichromate of potash, prussiate of potash, borax) (10),

organic chemicals (including acids, cream of tartar and quinine) (6), saltpetre (1), nitrate of soda (1);

(b) *Dyestuffs, tanning materials, drugs and drysalteries* (50 per cent): indigo (2), cochineal (1), dyewoods (5), other dyestuffs (2), tanning materials (2), shellac (2), gums (3), essential oils (3), drugs (13), gutta percha (1), elephants' teeth (1);

3. *Oil seeds and oils*: linseed (1), rapeseed (1), cottonseed (1), linseed oil (1), rapeseed oil (1), cottonseed oil (1), palm oil (1), olive oil (1), coconut oil (1), fish oils (4), lard oil (1), turpentine (2), rosin (1), tar (1), petroleum (2), tallow (1);

4. *Wool*: colonial merino wools (5), Cape wools (2), colonial crossbred wools (2);

5. *Other raw textile materials*: flax (2), jute (1), hemp (2), silk (5);

6. *Wood and timber*: fir timber (3), oak (2), teak (1), sawn wood (6), staves (2);

7. *Sundry raw materials*:
    (a) *Hides* (40 per cent): raw hides (7), butts, kips and prepared hides (3);
    (b) *Rubber* (40 per cent): India rubber, para (1);
    (c) *Drugs and drysalteries* (10 per cent): see under item 2 above;
    (d) *Chemicals* (10 per cent): see under item 2 above.

Sources

Price quotations were found in a number of sources, including *The Economist, London Mercantile Prices Current, Princes' Prices Current, London New Prices Current, Iron and Coal Trades Review, Colliery Guardian*, the *Grocer, Mark Lane Express*, the *Chemist and Druggist*, the *Statist*, and *The Times*.

Exports of Non-cotton Goods

Data series

Monthly nominal values of non-cotton exports were calculated as total nominal value of exports of British and Irish goods minus exports of cotton goods (see below, p. 81). This series was then deflated by a price index of non-cotton exports, which is explained below.

Transformations

Before January 1854 the monthly returns did not contain an estimate of the value of unenumerated exports. In this period the monthly totals were inflated by the ratio of total export value from the annual returns to the sum of the export figures from the monthly returns. Beginning 1854 the accumulated annual figures from the monthly returns correspond to the complete annual export values.

The real export series were adjusted for the number of workdays per month (taking into account the alterations in the Board of Trade reporting procedures, see pp. 77 above) and then seasonally adjusted.

Source
UK Trade and Navigation Accounts, published monthly by the Board of Trade.

Price Index of Non-cotton Exports

Data series
Separate price indices were computed for the 1850–80 and the 1880–1914 periods. The weights used for the first period reflect average shares of each commodity group of non-cotton exports in the years 1856–8 and 1876–8; for the second period weights were calculated from average export shares in 1886–8 and 1906–8. Both indices are computed as geometric averages of price relatives with 1880 as base year. The two indices were spliced in 1880 by gradually increasing the weight of the second index each month by steps of one-twelfth beginning January 1880, and reducing the weight of the first index correspondingly, thus phasing out this index by December 1880.

The following list contains the *weight* of each commodity group and the *number* of commodity descriptions within each subgroup of main commodities. Monthly prices of most descriptions are available for the whole period. In some cases where quotations could not be found for part of the period (for example, steel rails before 1870) the price series was linked to a near substitute series (for example, iron rails). With the exception of woollen and worsted manufactures and other textile manufactures, where unit prices of exports were used, individual price quotations refer to market prices.

1850–80
1. *Coal* (6.2 per cent): steam coal (2), manufacturing coal (2), house coal (1);
2. *Iron and steel* (32.9 per cent): pig iron (3), iron bars (4), iron and steel rails (2), other iron manufactures (iron hoops, rods, sheets, ship angles, ship plates) (5), tinplates (1);
3. *Non-ferrous metals* (7.7 per cent): copper (3), tin (1), lead (1), zinc sheet (1);
4. *Woollen and worsted manufactures* (24.7 per cent): woollen and worsted yarn (1), woollen cloths (1), worsted stuffs (1);
5. *Other textile manufactures* (16.2 per cent): linen yarn (1), linen manufactures (1), jute yarn (1), jute manufactures (1), silk manufactures (broad stuffs) (1), silk yarn (1), thrown silk (1);
6. *Chemicals* (6.6 per cent): heavy alkalis (6), metallic salts (including copper sulphate, refined borax, arsenic powder, sugar of lead and bichromate of

potash) (10), wood ashes (2), ammonia salts (4), organic chemicals (including acids) (6);
7. *Oils, tallow and naval stores* (2.2 per cent): linseed oil (1), rapeseed oil (2), cottonseed oil (2), turpentine (1), rosin (1), pitch (1), tallow (1);
8. *Leather* (3.5 per cent): hides (4), leather butts (3), calf skin (2).

1880–1914
1. *Coal* (14.3 per cent): steam coal (5), house coal (4), gas coal (1);
2. *Iron and steel* (37.3 per cent): pig iron (4), iron bars (1), iron ship plates and angles (2), steel ship plates and angles (2), steel rails (1), tinplates (1);
3. *Non-ferrous metals* (5.8 per cent): copper (2), tin (1), lead (1), zinc sheet (1);
4. *Woollen and worsted manufactures* (20.7 per cent): woollen and worsted yarn (1), woollen cloths (1), worsted stuffs (1);
5. *Other textile manufactures* (9.6 per cent): linen yarn (1), linen manufactures (1), jute yarn (1), jute manufactures (1), silk manufactures (broad stuffs) (1), silk yarn (1);
6. Chemicals (7.3 per cent): heavy alkalis (5), metallic salts (including copper sulphate, refined borax, arsenic powder, sugar of lead and bichromate of potash) (10), wood ashes (2), ammonia salts (3), organic chemicals (including acids) (6);
7. *Oils, tallow and naval stores* (1.7 per cent): linseed oil (1), rapeseed oil (1), cottonseed oil (1), linseed cakes (1), tallow (1);
8. *Leather* (3.5 per cent): hides (3), leather butts (1), calf skin (1).

Sources
See notes to the import price indices (p. 79).

Exports of Cotton Manufactures

Data series
Cotton exports include cotton yarn and twist, thread for sewing and all manufactures (piece goods, lace and patent net, hosiery and other goods).

Transformations
Nominal export values were deflated by the price index of cotton exports (see below) and adjusted for the number of workdays (see notes to the import series) and then seasonally adjusted.

Sources
The primary data were found in *UK Trade and Navigation Accounts*, published monthly by the Board of Trade.

Price Index of Cotton Manufactures

Data series
This index is constructed in the same way as the other price indices described above, comprising price quotations of yarn and twist (two series in the first period and three in the second) and grey cotton cloth (six and four series, respectively). The basic data series are the same as those used by Sandberg (1968), who provides an extensive discussion of these data.

Sources
Price quotations were taken from *The Economist*'s 'Comparative Statement of the Cotton Trade'. Supplementary data on cotton yarn in the 1880s and 1890s were found in *The Economist*'s *Commercial and History Review* and in the *Commercial and Financial Chronicle* (New York).

Cotton Consumption

Data series
Weekly data on the number of cotton bales imported, re-exported, held as stocks in ports and delivered to home consumption are available throughout the period. These figures are largely dominated by transactions in the Liverpool cotton market, but the London market was also of some importance regarding trade in East Indian cotton during the 1860s and 1870s. In 1864 the London market accounted for 14.1 per cent of the number of bales delivered to home consumption, but this percentage fell to 8.8 in 1874 and further to 4.5 in 1880. London market transactions are explicitly included prior to 1881; thereafter, the monthly data are taken from Liverpool market reports only. It appears that the Liverpool based data included imports and stock holdings in some other ports (such as Hull) as well.

Transformations
The original weekly data are given as accumulated totals from January 1 each year (September 1 beginning 1908). The data used here were computed as *average* cotton consumption *per week*. The monthly averages include data for all full weeks falling within the month plus any week falling partly within the previous month.

To arrive at an estimate of the volume of cotton consumed – and thus of yarn produced – it is desirable to make adjustments for two factors that are not reflected in the weekly data: (a) changes in stocks held by spinners at the mills, and (b) changes in the weight of cotton bales:

(a) The published estimates of stocks held at the mills indicate that these were about one-third of the size of the stocks held in ports towards the end of the nineteenth century, but rather smaller – about 20 per cent – in the late 1860s. End-of-year estimates of mill stocks are available through 1908.

(b) The weight of cotton bales differed significantly across the country of origin. In 1870 it ranged from 164lb for Brazilian to 434lb for American and 517lb for Egyptian cotton. The average weight also tended to drift upwards; in 1900 the corresponding weights were 283lb, 484lb and 743lb, respectively.

An adjustment for these two factors was made using a series of annual estimates of average cotton consumption per week that was adjusted for changes in mill stocks and expressed in standardized bales of 400lb. There is thus an implicit assumption that any changes in mill stocks were evenly distributed throughout the year and that the pattern with respect to the country of origin of the cotton consumed (but not imported) remained constant through the year. The necessary data for making this adjustment was not available after 1908. It was then assumed that the average weight of bales was the same as in 1908.

Sources
The weekly consumption data were published in *The Economist*. Annual estimates of the corrected average consumption of cotton per week were published in *The Economist's Commercial and History Review*, the original sources of which were the circulars of Messrs Ellison and Co., Liverpool. Before 1855 estimates (not adjusted for the weight of bales) can be found in *A Handbook of the Cotton Trade* by Ellison, reproduced in *The Economist*, January 15, 1859. These data were converted to bales of 400lb each by interpolating between an estimated weight of 388lb of cotton consumed in 1850 (from McCulloch, 1882) and 399.4lb in 1855.

Railway Freight Traffic Receipts

Data series
The data are derived from the weekly returns on railway freight receipts from general merchandise, mineral and livestock traffic. No *aggregate* figures of *freight* traffic receipts were published until 1884. Consequently, monthly figures had to be constructed from weekly figures relating to individual railway companies in this period.

January 1850–February 1884   In January 1856 there were 74 weekly reporting railway companies in the most comprehensive returns published by the *Railway Times*. Many companies published separate figures for passenger and goods receipts, but this did not apply to all companies. This was particularly the case for the small companies, and during some intervals even the more important ones, as only total receipts were given. Further complications were due to the fact that the number and the composition of the group of non-reporting companies were changing all the time. Because of this it was decided to estimate total freight receipts from (1) total receipts (passenger and goods) from *all companies*, multiplied by (2) an estimate of the average ratio of goods traffic receipts to total receipts from a *sample of companies*. A further adjustment was made for (3) the length of miles open.

1. *Total weekly receipts for all weekly reporting companies* were given in contemporary sources. Because missing reports, provisional estimates and 'sweepings' (periodical receipts from jointly run lines, and so on) distorted the current figures, the revised data published the subsequent year were always used (cf. Goodhart, 1972: 76–7). It should be noted that regarding the two sources of total receipts used here, the *Railway Times* and *The Economist*, these presented quite similar figures around 1860 but discrepancies grew larger later in the 1860s.

2. *The sample of railways used to estimate the average weekly freight receipts share* consists of 16 of the largest companies which separated goods receipts from passenger receipts in their weekly returns These were:

    1. Bristol and Exeter (ending December 1870; this company was taken over by the London and North Western in January 1876);
    2. Caledonian;
    3. Great Eastern (Eastern Counties & Norfolk and Eastern Union until August 1862);
    4. Great Northern (estimated January–September 1850 and August–December 1853);
    5 Great Southern and Western (Irish);
    6. Great Western (estimated January 1850–May 1854);
    7. Lancashire and Yorkshire (data relating to East Lancashire were used in some periods in the 1850s);
    8. London, Brighton and South Coast;
    9. London, Chatham and Dover (beginning January 1871);
    10. London and North Western;
    11. London and South Western (beginning January 1871);
    12. Manchester, Sheffield and Lincolnshire;
    13. Midland (estimated January 1850–June 1855 and July 1858–December 1860);
    14. North British (reporting jointly with Caledonian February 1868–May 1869);

15. North Eastern (before August 1854 consisting of (a) York, Newcastle & Berwick, (b) York & North Midland and (c) Leeds Northern (Leeds and Thirsk until August 1851);
16. South Eastern.

All the great trunk lines and the largest passenger lines are represented in this sample; in addition, some regional lines are represented, including two Scottish and one Irish. These railways accounted for about 73 per cent of the total receipts of weekly reporting companies in January 1856 and 79 per cent in September 1870. No single company of any importance is excluded from the sample. The three largest companies not included in the above sample before 1871 were London and South Western, Glasgow and South Western, and London, Chatham and Dover. Neither of these companies accounted for more than 2 per cent of total receipts. After 1871 similar positions were held by Glasgow and South Western, Great Northern of Ireland and Taff Vale or Furness, of which the Glasgow line was by far the largest, representing between 1 and 2 per cent of total receipts. Average freight shares were computed using weights derived from the relative size (percentage of total receipts) of the companies in every fifth year, beginning with 1853. As indicated above, three railways did not present separate figures for freight receipts during part of the 1850s (Great Northern, Great Western, Midland). In these cases their freight shares were estimated from regression equations run on nearby sample periods. The weekly freight shares of lines within similar categories were used as explanatory variables. The freight shares exhibited a quite regular and very marked seasonal pattern, with strong comovements between the freight receipts of individual lines, which facilitated the interpolation.

3. Data on the length of lines open for traffic were taken from the weekly returns.

March 1884–July 1914   For this period weekly aggregate freight receipts were published in the *Railway News*. The data covered nearly all UK railway companies, but there were still some companies that did not divide their passenger and goods receipts. In 1893 these amounted to about 3 per cent of the total of the weekly reporting lines. The data were used with no further adjustment, except for two periods during which the figures were severely affected by labour disputes: 1893, August to October; 1912, March and April. For these months data were estimated by the exponential smoothing procedure contained in RATS.

The length of lines open was linearly interpolated between end-of-year data.

Transformations
The weekly data on freight receipts were aggregated to monthly totals; weeks extending into the subsequent month were split in proportion to the number of workdays falling within each month.

Total monthly freight receipts were then divided by miles of lines open and the number of workdays. Adjustment for the number of workdays follows the principles outlined above (p. 77), using calendar months throughout.

The data from the two sample periods were spliced together using the ratio between the two series in March 1884.

Sources

Data on individual railway companies, from which freight receipt shares were computed, were taken from the weekly returns in *The Economist* and the *Railway Times*, supplemented by *Herapath's Railway Journal*. The *Railway Times* also provided the data for total aggregate passenger and freight receipts before 1860; in the 1860s *The Economist* was the preferred source; between August 1870 and March 1884 a continuation of this series was found in *Herapath's Railway Journal*. Weekly data on total aggregate freight receipts beginning January 1884 were taken from the *Railway News*.

Coasting Trade

Data series

This series represents the tonnage of vessels employed in the coasting trade of Great Britain and between Great Britain and Ireland. The figures are the sum of the tonnage of vessels entered inwards and cleared outwards with cargoes at UK ports each month.

Transformations

The tonnage measure reported in these returns were altered several times. The most significant ones were as follows:

1. Beginning in 1856 the returns contained an expanded registration of the trade between Great Britain and Ireland. The ratios between the new and old series in the overlapping year 1856 (1.2040 for entries and 1.1317 for clearances) were used to adjust the tonnage entered and cleared before 1856.
2. Beginning in 1873 a number of commodities previously exempted from Coast Regulations (thus being omitted from the returns) were included. Among those were bricks, chalk, clays, manures (ashes, bones, coprolites), gravel, sand, slates, British quarried stones and tiles, British timber and wood intended for pit props and railway sleepers, iron ore, fresh meat, live fish, hay and straw. There is no exact information upon which splicing of the old and new series can be made. As a rough approximation the old series was adjusted in accordance with the growth rate of tonnage entered and cleared in the foreign trade between 1872 and 1873.

3. Beginning in April 1898 trade between places in the estuary of the Thames 'situated westward of an imaginary line drawn from Revulver Towers to Colne Point' was no longer included in the returns. It was stated in the notes to the returns that this entailed an estimated decrease of 1 200 000 tons in the tonnage of vessels entered and 600 000 tons for vessels cleared. The data were adjusted accordingly.

Source
UK Trade and Navigation Accounts, published by the Board of Trade.

Bank Clearings

Data series
The returns of the amount of cheques and bills cleared daily at the London Bankers' Clearing House begin with May 2, 1867. The data used here are total clearings minus the amount cleared on the two monthly Stock Exchange settling days. Separate figures for 'town clearing' and 'country clearing' were published on a weekly basis beginning in July 1905. In order to retain comparability with previous periods no use was made of this information.

Transformations
The monthly series is calculated on the basis of average clearings per business day.

Sources
The Economist published the weekly returns throughout the period. Because these returns no longer specified the total clearings on a daily basis after February 1885, the monthly totals were taken from the *Bankers' Magazine*.

NOTES

1. Letter to the editor of *The Times*, April 19, 1879. The missing link which Jevons referred to was a series of prices of wheat in Bengal.
2. Ibid. These studies are collected in Jevons ([1884] 1964).
3. See, *inter alia*, Clapham (1932, 1938, 1944), Rostow (1948), Ford (1963), Hawtrey (1965), Aldcroft and Fearon (1972), Church (1975), Lewis (1978), Collins (1988) and Cottrell (1988).
4. This is stated explicitly in Burns and Mitchell (1946: 74). The qualitative information contained in the *Business Annals* collected by Thorp (1926) and financial variables were used as additional input to the analysis.
5. Hughes (1960: 27) is sceptical of relying too much on these data in marking off the reference cycle turning points. Work by Southall (1991) has shown that it is possible to extract monthly unemployment series for some trade unions other than ironfounders back to the 1850s (engineers) and 1860s (carpenter and joiners).

6. The quarterly railway data in Thomas (1926) go back to 1881. Goodhart (1972) constructed a monthly series of railway freight receipts starting in 1893 that was used by him, and later by Pippenger (1986), as an indicator of economic activity in their econometric analysis of bank behaviour. The recalculated series contained in the present paper has been used for similar purposes in Klovland (1994).

7. Greasley (1986) and Feinstein (1989, 1990).

8. Feinstein (1972: 16–17) compared the turning points of the income and expenditure side estimate of GDP with the NBER reference dates, finding that the income estimate conformed best to the NBER dates.

9. It may affect the time series properties of the data, however, and thus the way in which decomposition into trend and cycle is made. Crafts *et al.* (1989) used the Lewis index with some revisions in the early years to investigate the long-standing issue of variations in long-term growth rates of the British economy. As a byproduct of their trend estimation the cycle component could be extracted, suggesting a cycle period of about seven years for the period after 1815. This result must be viewed on the background of the fact that Lewis *imposed* a cycle of nine years in some industries. See Solomou (1994) for a further discussion of this issue.

10. From a modern perspective it is somewhat surprising that unemployment data were so infrequently considered, even after becoming publicly available on a monthly basis in the late 1880s. Along with data on pauperism it was more often regarded as an indicator of social conditions.

11. No monthly import values were published before 1856. Publication of the *annual* value of imports, based on actual market prices, only began with the year 1854. Imlah (1958) provides a full discussion of issues relating to annual trade statistics.

12. The import price index for 1880–1914 is more comprehensive than Silverman's (1930) index; the export price index has about the same number of commodity descriptions. On the other hand, it is doubtful whether the present version of the export price index for the post-1880 period yet presents any improvement upon Silverman's index. The indices used here are preliminary estimates, reflecting work in progress on wholesale prices in Britain in the period 1845 to 1914.

13. See Deane and Cole (1969: 29 and 310) and Crouzet (1982: 112–21) for a further discussion.

14. Such considerations led Goodhart (1972) to reject indicators based on foreign trade in favour of the railway freight receipts as the single best indicator of economic activity.

15. This does not imply that deflators based on unit prices would be an improvement in all respects; the uncertainty regarding declared values, inhomogenous commodity items and quality changes over time may create grave measurement problems. Sandberg (1968) presents an example of such problems with regard to UK export of cotton goods.

16. The new monthly industrial production index for the United States constructed by Miron and Romer (1990) relies on input data for many of the industries covered. This index seems to exhibit somewhat more irregular short-run movements than the previous indexes derived by Babson and Persons.

17. *The Economist, Commercial History and Review of 1906*: 2.

18. Hultgren (1953: 4).

19. One such episode occurred in October 1872 (see *The Economist*, November 30, 1872: 1460), when goods rates were increased following the general rise of prices, which was particularly marked with respect to coal and metals.

20. Hawke (1970: 69). *The Economist* reported on several occasions in the late 1880s (July 2, 1887; February 18 and March 31, 1888; September 14, 1889) that railway rates were still falling. There was a major restructuring of railway charges in 1888 and in 1893 following new legislation, bringing much complaint from traders of increases in rates, which was refuted by the railway companies. *The Economist*'s (January 14, 1893) verdict was: 'The balance, on the whole is not likely to be unfavourable to traders.' The railway freight indicator derived here moved in line with annual GDP and industrial production even in these years: rising in 1888 and falling in 1893.

21. Since annual data on freight receipts per ton loaded exist from 1856 (except 1868–70, see Mitchell, 1988: 545–7), it might be suggested that some crude deflation procedures involving this variable as a proxy for freight rates could be performed. However, freight receipts per ton

are affected by three main factors: the rates charged by railway companies, the length of the 'lead' (that is, average distance for which freight was carried), and the composition of traffic. As documented in detail by Hawke (1970: 55–92), there are distinct cyclical movements in all these factors, which makes this variable a poor indicator of the general level of railway freight rates.

22. Sherrington (1934).

23. Hawke (1970: 73–4 and 174).

24. Goodhart (1972: 79–82) provides a discussion of the possible distortions to the railway freight indicator caused by the heavy influence of coal and pig iron after the turn of the century.

25. *The Economist*, May 18, 1867.

26. This is discussed by King (1936: 274). See also Nishimura (1971) for a further analysis of the decline of the importance of internal bills. It should also be noted that it happened that Consol pay days fell on the fourth of the month (which might be the third or fifth), which tended to inflate the figures significantly, cf. *The Economist*, October 1, 1887: 1241.

27. Publication of weekly clearing returns from provincial centres did not seem to attain a reasonably broad coverage until 1894; by then returns from Manchester, Birmingham, Newcastle, Leicester, Leeds, and Liverpool were available.

28. The only other correction for the influence of purely financial transactions that can be made is the deduction of clearings on the monthly Consols pay days, but this would not have affected the figures to any significant extent.

29. Keynes (1930: 76) suggested to deflate clearings figures by 'wholesale prices for a period three months earlier and of wages for the current period.' In the present case it turned out that an average of wholesale prices lagged one and two months produced a slightly lower variance of 12-monthly growth rates than other alternatives and was therefore chosen.

30. An alternative, which may be exploited in further research, is to apply modern time series techniques to determine the composition of the indicator. This was done on US data by Stock and Watson (1991). In the present case, working with a set of indicators that vary substantially with respect to data quality, reliability, and coverage, it is not obvious that such an estimation technique would have produced a satisfactory indicator. Note also that Watson (1994) rejected using a dynamic factor model in order to extract a single factor from his set of US business cycle indicators because of the lack of robustness of this method.

31. See, for example, Mills (1992) and Crafts and Mills (1994) for an introduction to these methods.

32. This procedure is explained in, for example, Kydland and Prescott (1990), which is a more accessible source than Hodrick and Prescott (1980). Some aspects of business cycles in the United Kingdom in the period 1956–90 using this method are presented in Blackburn and Ravn (1992).

33. The value of λ can then be computed as $5^2/(1/8)^2 = 1600$.

34. The Hodrick–Prescott filter has been found to produce estimates of trend that are quite close to those that can be derived by fitting structural time series methods. However, it is known that mechanically detrended series may give rise to spurious cyclical behaviour in some cases. See Harvey and Jaeger (1993) and Crafts and Mills (1994).

35. Recent studies using this method include Wynne and Balke (1993) and Watson (1994).

36. As a rough check of the new procedure it was applied to the Miron–Romer (1990) production index for the United States over the period 1884–1914. The number of (growth cycle) turning points identified was 19, which is exactly the number of reference dates set by the NBER for this period. Although the implications of this particular result should not be stretched too far it does give some indication that the new method identifies about the same number of cycles as the NBER procedures.

37. The Spencer curve is calculated by applying a symmetric filter to seven lags and leads. The weights from lag 0 to 7 are 0.2313, 0.2094, 0.1438, 0.0656, 0.0094, −0.0156, −0.0188, −0.0094.

38. Differences in seasonal adjustment procedures may of course also account for some of the discrepancies in reference dates. The unemployment series used here is expressed as a percentage of union members rather than the actual number of unemployed workers as in the original data.

39. The railway freight traffic series in Thomas (1926) are quarterly, beginning in 1881. Note also that the monthly trade returns did not contain estimates of aggregate import values before 1870.

40. This fact has been emphasized by Hughes (1960: 27): 'Since Burns and Mitchell date the first stage of their monthly reference cycle in November 1854 they must have considered the 1854 peak as occurring earlier in the year. This may have been true for iron but for cotton and other textiles, in addition to other sectors of home trade, the first months of 1854 were months of depression and slack production.'

41. Published in *The Economist*, January 6, 1855.

42. Campbell (1957).

43. See King (1936) and Hughes (1956). An extensive collection of material relating to the crisis was published by Evans ([1859] 1969).

44. Hughes (1960: 27) was puzzled by the fact that the NBER reference trough was determined to be as late as September, surmising that 'If this is based upon the iron founders' data it represents a seasonal phenomenon peculiar to the iron trade which is in no way representative of their industries.' This is not really the case, however. As will be seen from Table 3.2 the trough of this indicator occurs as early as February 1857.

45. See *The Economist's Commercial History and Review of 1864*.

46. Lewis (1978: 21) characterizes the recession of the 1870s in Britain as 'shallow but long,' while that which succeeded 1883 was 'deep but short.'

47. The stagnation of the growth of gross domestic product after the great leap in 1870 and 1871 is evident in the new expenditure estimates derived by Feinstein (Mitchell, 1988: National Accounts, Table 6) as well as the income based version presented by Greasley (1989).

48. Prices of British pig iron peaked in February and iron manufactures in April 1873 according to the data underlying the export price index described in the Appendix.

49. The annual industrial production series covering iron and steel constructed by Lewis (1978) show a fall in output in 1873 compared with 1872 for pig iron and steel ingots and a significant reduction of the growth rate of iron and steel manufactures.

50   Such was the characterization of the woollen trade of 1880 in the *Leeds Mercury*, reproduced in *The Economist*'s *Commercial History and Review of 1880*. The same source noted further that 'Many mills in this neighbourhood worked overtime, the cost of materials rose, and in anticipation of a further advance in prices, numerous large orders were given out in the early spring for the home as well as the foreign trade. This expected advance only partially took place, being checked by a considerable falling off in the American demand.'

51. This was *The Economist*'s own evaluation of the year 1880 in *Commercial History and Review of 1880*.

52. The strong revival is also clearly reflected in the monthly price index shown in Klovland (1993).

53. This observation is only partially corroborated by estimates of real gross domestic product. Feinstein's compromise estimate (in Mitchell, 1988: table 5A of ch. XVI) grows 1.1 per cent in 1883 and 0.5 per cent in 1884.

54. Capie and Mills (1991) also found that the trough in the gross domestic product data was in 1893.

55. 1893 was a year of many unfavourable exogenous events impinging on trade in a negative way: strikes in cotton and coal industries, banking crisis in Australia and currency crisis as well as protective tariff legislation in the United States. *The Economist* (*Commercial History and Review of 1893*) summed it up thus 'The condition of trade throughout 1893 was … one of suppressed energy. There was a continued tendency to expansion, which asserted itself whenever anything like an opportunity was afforded, but which was ever being repressed by some new and grave misfortune.'

56. Only RAILFR and the unemployment series have been adjusted for the distortions caused by these events.

4. Measuring national product in Germany, 1925–38: the state of the debate and some new results

Albrecht Ritschl*

INTRODUCTION

Traditional business cycle measurement with historical data has been rooted in the national accounts produced by an international community of scholars in the 1960s under the coordination and guidance of Simon Kuznets. The German group associated with this project produced an impressive wealth of national product data (Hoffmann, 1965) that soon became the universally accepted database for research on German macroeconomic history.[1] For the interwar period, these data suggest a rather favorable perspective on the dynamics of the German economy. According to these data, the Great Depression of the 1930s hit an economy that was basically sound, having experienced its own Weimar Germany version of the Golden Twenties in the second half of the decade. This impression of a basic soundness of the German economy reappears in the data during the Nazi recovery from 1933 onward, when a sustained upswing set in that by the year of 1938 had carried Germany to levels of output far higher than the 1928 peak of the pre-depression boom. In this perspective, the severity of the depression appears as more or less exogenous to the fundamentals of the German interwar cycle, suggesting that its causes lay in things like international spillovers and the deflationary policies adopted by the pre-Hitler administrations in Germany during the slump (Haberler, 1937; Kroll, 1958; Kindleberger, 1973). Indeed, the depression of the early 1930s is known to the Germans under the label of '*Weltwirtschaftskrise*', or world economic crisis.

Revision of this standard interpretation has gone hand in hand with a critical reappraisal of Hoffmann's national account data. Temin (1971) concluded from the official investment figures that recession was well under way in 1927–8,

* I am grateful to Steve Broadberry, Albert Carreras, Herman de Jong, Angus Maddison, and Mark Spoerer for helpful comments. Financial support from Deutsche Forschungsgemeinschaft, from Dirección general de investigación científica y técnica (DGICYT), project PB94–1001, and the Posthumus Institute is gratefully acknowledged.

triggering a debate about the reliability of German investment data.[2] Borchardt (1979) employed time-series evidence on unit labor cost based on official national income data to argue that between 1925 and 1929 wage pressure attained a historical high that was never reached again in the postwar period. He concluded that in Weimar Germany the reconstruction of a bourgeois society after World War I[3] had rested on a precarious compromise between organized labor and capital, which set in motion a vicious circle between high wages, low productivity and profitability, and low investment. Consequently, the Great Depression would to a far lesser extent be the result of exogenous shocks and misguided macroeconomic policies. Rather, fundamental weaknesses already existed in the German economy before the depression, and the intensity of the depression itself might well be related to the rather precarious performance in previous years.

This view soon gained recognition and is now almost standard internationally (see James, 1985, 1986; Eichengreen, 1992). Within Germany, however, this shift in perspective, with its apparent implications for the economic causes of the rise to power of German fascism, provoked intense scholarly controversy in Germany, a debate which has struck recent observers as an academic *stellungskrieg*, or war in the trenches (Riemer, 1995). Holtfrerich (1984) questioned Borchardt's evidence on supernormal unit wage cost, invoking Hoffmann's series again. Kruedener (1985) used industry-specific data from Hoffmann (1965) to defend the case for increasing wage pressure at least within the late 1920s, as did Corbett (1991). In Ritschl (1990), I compared the available national product estimates to argue that Hoffmann's (1965) data might overstate output and productivity. Indeed, the results for unit labor cost I obtained varied considerably with the respective product series. Balderston (1993) again employed the Hoffmann data to argue for high-productivity, export-led growth during the late Weimar years, a result echoed in Voth (1994).[4] Broadberry and Ritschl (1994, 1995) argued from alternative data sources that during the second half of the 1920s, prices, wages, and unit labor cost in Germany evolved almost identically to their British counterparts when put on a 1913 basis. They conclude that the difference in aggregate performance between Germany and England must be sought in international capital movements and other demand-side factors influencing aggregate activity. Holtfrerich (1996) doubts the evidence presented by Broadberry and Ritschl and suggests that their productivity estimates might be downward biased.

The present chapter, which has grown out of a larger project on a recuperation of national account data from official sources and archival data,[5] aims to separate the issue of business cycle measurement for interwar Germany from the context indicated above and to focus on the technical aspects. I will evaluate the estimates of national output and expenditure of Hoffmann (1965) in the light of the official figures produced by the German statistical office, *Statistisches*

Reichsamt, at the time, and with results from later research. Examining the methods which underlie Hoffmann's estimates I argue that for the interwar period his two most commonly employed national product and expenditure estimates exhibit marked upward bias. I present revisions of Hoffmann's estimates which partly correct these defects. For the expenditure account, the difference from the official figures disappears almost entirely, while for the output series we attain a partial correction. These results imply a marked downward revision of GNP levels and provide further evidence of the view that Germany's interwar business cycle was much less a dynamic growth cycle than is suggested by conventional wisdom.

The rest of this chapter is organized as follows. The next section provides a brief survey of the different existing estimates. This is followed by an evaluation of the expenditure series of Hoffmann against the official data from which it is constructed, and an examination of Hoffmann's national output series. The final section presents conclusions and implications.

EXISTING ESTIMATES OF GERMAN NATIONAL PRODUCT, 1925–38: A QUICK REVIEW

Viewed in international comparison, Germany is well endowed with estimates of national income and product for the inter-war years. There exist national income statistics calculated by the statistical office, which employ an output approach for agriculture and a personal income approach for the non-farm economy.[6] This series, which the *Reichsamt* calculated backward to the year of 1890, has been revised by West Germany's Statistical Office in 1954 (Statistisches Bundesamt, 1954) and further refined in an earlier contribution by Hoffmann (see Hoffmann and Müller, 1959, which includes a survey of earlier research).

Independently, Hoffmann (1965) produced three more estimates. These cover aggregate expenditure, national output, and the distribution of national income. The expenditure series, expressed as net national expenditure at market prices, is widely accepted as the standard estimate of historical national product in Germany. As such, it is reproduced in international comparisons as Mitchell (1975) but also in a historical database released by the Bundesbank (Deutsche Bundesbank, 1976).[7]

Hoffmann's output-based series (expressed as net domestic output at factor cost) enters into the data of Maddison (1991, 1995) as the national product estimate for the nineteenth century. In Maddison (1991) it is spliced into the official national income series mentioned above in the year of 1925, while Maddison (1995) gives up the official data entirely and works with Hoffmann's output data to the year of 1938. Moreover, because of its detailed sectoral breakdown, this time series is well accepted for studies of sectoral growth of

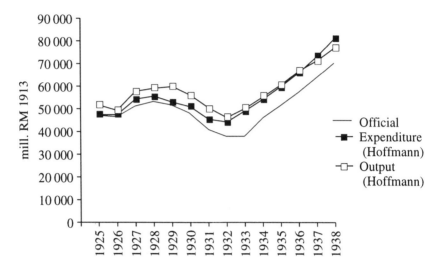

Figure 4.1   Three estimates of national income

the German economy (see, for example, Kruedener, 1985; Corbett, 1991; and Balderston, 1993, for interwar Germany). The series is also employed by Holtfrerich (1984) in his refutation of Borchardt's wage pressure hypothesis and has thus taken center stage in recent debates about the German interwar cycle.

In contrast, Hoffmann's income distribution series has found only limited acceptance, which may be due to its extreme results: for example, a wage share in national income that exceeds unity during the depression years of 1931–2. Hoffmann himself (1965: 170) expresses skepticism regarding the validity of that series. As it has played no role in subsequent debates, it is omitted from the discussions that follow. Figure 4.1 presents the personal income series ('official') along with Hoffmann's estimates of net aggregate expenditure and output.

Two major effects stand out from Figure 4.1. First, throughout the interwar period the aggregate output series is systematically higher than the other two. Second, while there appears to be a satisfactory fit between Hoffmann's expenditure series and the official personal income based data for the Weimar years, a systematic gap opens during the slump and remains throughout the Nazi years. These deviations are dismissed by Hoffmann (1965: 170) as the inevitable result of observation errors and the underestimation problem inherent in personal income data. In the following it will be shown that this intuition is probably misleading[8] and that systematic defects in his calculations exist. In the next section I discuss methods of reconciling the expenditure and the official series with one another. Examination of Hoffmann's output approach is left for the penultimate section.

RECONCILING THE EXPENDITURE ESTIMATE WITH THE OFFICIAL DATA

Consider again Figure 4.1. While for the Weimar years there is no systematic deviation between the expenditure series and the official data, a widening gap opens during the depression. Searching for the possible causes, this effect could not be ascribed easily to a deteriorating quality of the national income series during the Nazi years, as the coverage of the tax system even increased and as tax fraud may, if anything, have decreased (see Spoerer, 1996, with micro evidence on corporate profits). However, there is good reason to assume that it was the quality of the expenditure series which declined instead.

Hoffmann (1965) calculates national expenditure from estimates of private consumption plus data on investment, the balance of payments, and public consumption. Publication of official figures on the three latter items was restricted or even completely suspended during the Nazi years, to the effect that Hoffmann relied on indirect estimates. However, as the Nazi administration did continue to produce such data, albeit in classified form, postwar research has been able to close some of the gaps in official publications. Much of this work had already been published in the late 1950s but it is almost ignored by Hoffmann (1965).[9] Thus, an obvious correction is to replace Hoffmann's estimates for the 1930s with the available data that Hoffmann missed. A second correction suggests itself from methodological weaknesses in Hoffmann's work which again induce upward bias. I consider the main entries of national expenditure in turn.

Aggregate investment data in interwar Germany were compiled by the Reichsamt, which employed a somewhat discretionary approach that blended examination of corporate balance sheets with commodity-flow estimations and, at times, direct surveys of investment (procedures and results from 1924 on are documented in Keiser and Benning, 1931; a reappraisal is Balderston, 1974). Publication of these data was partly suspended by the *Reichsamt* in 1935.

For the years to 1934, Hoffmann (1965) employs the same database but ends up with different results. Partly this is due to the way Hoffmann estimates public investment, which he calculates from public budgets item by item rather than employing the official data on public investment and on public construction activity. Hoffmann's intentions behind this are not made explicit. One motivation may lie in his attempt to separate structural and civil engineering from one another, a distinction which was not made consistently in German official statistics at the time. However, this does not explain why Hoffmann does not use the official data on public investment but accepts the same data source for other sectors. Nor is it clear why Hoffmann does not control his estimates by the figures on construction activity, which fit the official investment data very well (Gehrig, 1961; Ritschl, 1992).

For the period of war preparation during 1935–8, official publications included only manufacturing investment along with data on investment in transportation. However, aggregate data on fixed investment exist in the business cycle reviews of the Reichskreditgesellschaft (Erka), a public bank in the hands of the economics ministry; these are identical with the official data for previous years (see Figure 4.2) and have been used in the work of Ehrlicher (1956), Erbe (1958), Klein (1959) and, above all, by Gehrig (1961), to reconstruct sectoral and aggregate investment data. Gehrig (1961) constructs a commodity-flow estimate of investment from output and construction data for the whole period from 1924 to 1938 to show that these data are indeed consistent with one another. Using archival evidence from the economics ministry, which are again consistent with this evidence, Ritschl (1992) revises and completes the sectoral estimates of Ehrlicher (1956). These data also help improve Gehrig's (1961) estimate of public investment, thus arriving at a full data set which is consistent with the official data for previous years.

Hoffmann's (1965) own approach for the late 1930s is to close the gaps by extrapolating investment in the missing sectors with investment in manufacturing while continuing to show a series of public investment that he claims is derived from public budgets. Again it is not obvious what motivates Hoffmann's choice, as no reference to either the Erka data or the aforementioned postwar research is made.

As Figure 4.2 shows, the official series as continued in the Erka reports suggest a more modest increase in investment for the later 1930s than the data of

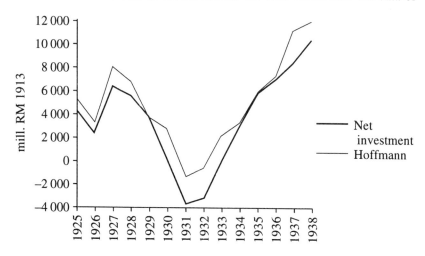

Figure 4.2   Net aggregate investment

Hoffmann, which in turn implies that investment in industry from which Hoffmann extrapolates the missing parts of the series was more dynamic than the aggregate economy. This is precisely what research on Nazi industrial policy (Petzina, 1968; Mollin, 1988; Plumpe, 1990; Erker, 1994) and capital market regulation (Stucken, 1964; Barkai, 1990; Spoerer, 1996) suggests. As Hoffmann's estimations are basically taken from a subset of the available information, there seems to be no clear justification for preferring them to the data elaborated earlier.

A second correction comes through the balance of payments. For the years after 1935, published data on the balance of payments were lacking. Hoffmann (1965) employed estimates based on capital flows instead. Comparing this estimate with his own current account estimate for the period 1925–35, major discrepancies arise, as the current account estimate is far lower than the capital account. To overcome this problem, Hoffmann (1965: 827–8) actually provides two estimates of national expenditure at constant prices, one employing his capital account series, the other the current account which is only available to him up to 1935. As the resulting national product series exhibits a gap for 1936–8 it enjoys less popularity; compilations like Mitchell (1975) and Maddison (1982, 1991, 1995) include only the more complete series in spite of its inferior quality.

As the Reichsamt did continue to produce balance of payments data after 1935, albeit in classified form, the gap can be bridged using archival information. Ritschl (1991) reports balance of trade data compiled by the Reichsamt for 1936–41 which survived in the files of the German commerce ministry. Converting the now completed current account balance to constant prices, additional deviations arise through the fact that Hoffmann (1965) deflates the balance of payments items employing Laspeyres indices of export and import prices. Using implicit (Paasche) deflators from Germany's foreign trade statistics instead, I arrive at a current account balance at constant prices for 1924–38 which in most years to 1935 is below Hoffmann's own series (Figure 4.3).

As Figure 4.3 shows, the deflating procedure indeed makes a difference: Hoffmann's price series seem to fail to account for the changing composition of Germany's foreign trade. Moreover, it becomes apparent that Hoffmann's attempt to construct a deflated capital account series produces grossly misleading results, particularly in the 1930s. This implies major corrections to both of Hoffmann's estimates of national expenditure. With respect to his more complete series starting from the capital account, a marked downward adjustment results for the whole period in question. For his 1925–35 series of national expenditure based on his current account estimate, corrections only matter from 1929 onward.

Bias is also introduced through Hoffmann's (1965) series of public consumption, although the source of the difficulty is apparently not a data problem. For the years from 1934, Hoffmann takes his data on central government

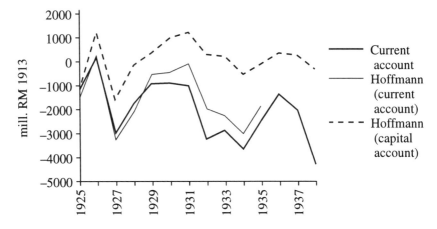

Figure 4.3   Estimates of the current account

budgets from Stuebel (1951), who had access to the – then still classified – public budget balance sheets of the Nazi administration. The problem arises when converting the original data which conform to Germany's rather complex budgetary rules to more meaningful concepts of public spending. One aspect of this is adjusting for fiscal transfers between the several levels of government and filtering out transfer items. A second and equally difficult problem is introduced by the failure of most contemporary German budgetary statistics properly to separate interest payments on public debt from repayment of the principal. Last, numerous shadow budgets and other budgetary manipulations have to be accounted for.

Some such budget manipulations had already been discovered by contemporaries, notably by the allied reparations agent in Berlin who carefully traced the attempts of the Germans to hide away their public budget deficits from reparation creditors (Gilbert, 1930).[10] Employing the now fully available set of central government balance sheets and recalculating public sector budgets for the total period 1925–38, in Ritschl (1996) I obtain results for the German budget concept which are basically identical to Gilbert (1930). Information on the shadow budgets of the Nazis, that is, extra-budget expenditure on work creation and clandestine rearmament, became available in the war crime trials held after the war; it is reproduced in Stuebel (1951).[11] Less easy to overcome are the aforementioned difficulties in converting data from German budgetary definitions to a spending concept in the national accounting sense. Again, Hoffmann (1965) is not very explicit about the way in which he arrives at public expenditure.

In order to calculate public consumption from the public expenditure data, investment must yet be subtracted. Hoffmann (1965) solves this problem by checking public budgets for investment expenditures item by item and then assuming that all such expenditure is net investment. Despite its obvious weaknesses, this procedure may work satisfactorily for state and municipal governments for which contemporary summary statistics of investment expenditure exist. It works less well for the central government, and invariably fails during the Nazi years when Hoffmann did not have access to the detailed budgets. Figure 4.4 compares the data on public consumption from Hoffmann (1965) with my own recalculations using the full information set. As can be seen, both series are reasonably close to one another for the Weimar period up to 1933 but display major divergencies later. It is particularly noteworthy how different the profile looks for 1935 and 1936, where my revision indicates that Hoffmann's data grossly exaggerate the increase in public spending.

To some extent these results carry over to private consumption. No reliable, independent estimate of private consumption exists for the period; Hoffmann (1965) works from his own estimate of consumer goods production. For the 1930s, lack of data induces him to assume that the total commodity flow of consumer goods is divided between private and public consumption according to the proportions prevalent in the late 1920s. If this was right, National Socialism would have been the first golden age of consumerism in Germany, a result which hardly fits the evidence apportioned by historians, which characterizes the mid-1930s as a period of low wages, increased rationing, and stagnant living standards (see, for example, James, 1986; Hachtmann, 1989).

A first check consists in comparing Hoffmann's time series on private consumption with companion data from the official national account data. For this, I calculate a series of private consumption as the residual from subtracting all previous items from the official national income series shown in Figure 4.1. If the official accounts are not too wrong and the problems in Hoffmann's consumer series for the 1930s matter, large discrepancies should arise in the 1930s

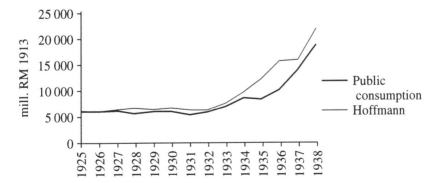

Figure 4.4   Public consumption

but not before. Data on private consumption are shown in Figure 4.5, and indeed show a gap between both estimates of private consumption during the 1930s; during the 1920s Hoffmann's data are in fact slightly lower than the residual series from the official statistics. Both series intersect around 1929, which is the year in which Hoffmann splices his data into public consumption. Thus, evidence indeed indicates a weighting problem for the 1930s. However, more research is needed in order to spot more precisely the sources of the deviation.

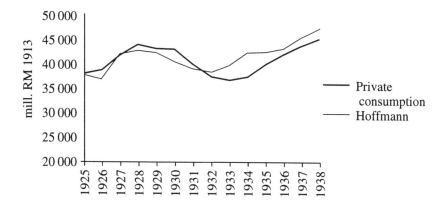

Figure 4.5   Private consumption

To conclude this section, in Figure 4.6 all previous revisions except for private consumption are combined to provide a revised series of national expenditure. This includes Hoffmann's data on private consumer expenditure as the only remaining item of his original estimate, as this is the only series to which no easy improvement could be made just by using the full amount of data available also to Hoffmann. As all other discrepancies have been explained by the weaknesses in Hoffmann's way of dealing with the official data, the resulting revised national income series is much closer to the official national income data than to its own two originals. Like the official national income data, the revision of Hoffmann's expenditure series suggests that after 1929, the performance of the German economy was much less favorable than Hoffmann's original estimates would suggest. Although the timing of the business cycle peaks and the trough of the depression do not change, the amplitude of the cycle does. Whereas Hoffmann's capital account based series says that the peak of the previous cycle was reached again by 1934, our revision indicates that it took the Nazi economy two years longer to recover to the 1928 level. This timing is also what would be indicated by the employment data; indeed all existing research agrees that full recovery was reached in 1936 but not before.[12]

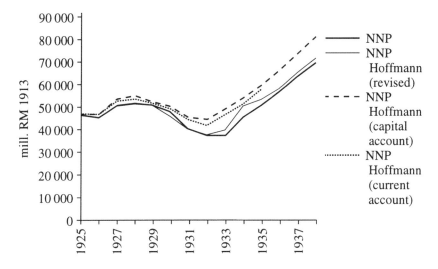

Figure 4.6   A revision of Hoffmann's aggregate expenditure series

HOFFMANN'S OUTPUT SERIES: A FIRST REVISION

Hoffmann's (1965) main effort was directed toward recalculating a detailed estimate of output, prices, and value added by sectors, subsectors, and even by hundreds of individual products like honey, haircuts, and bank transfers. Contemporary and later work exists for manufacturing (Wagenführ, 1933; Gehrig, 1961) and agriculture (Decker and Wagenführ, 1936–7; Grupe, 1957). While Hoffmann follows the latter, he dismisses the former, but without stating his motivation very clearly. With respect to value added in the non-farm, non-manufacturing sectors of the economy, to this day no estimates other than his exist. Therefore, the following section is restricted to a very limited purpose: I will reassess the production of capital equipment, which in his index accounts for some 17 per cent of manufacturing and construction.

The dynamics of manufacturing output have played a pivotal role in controversies about the performance of the Weimar Republic (see Balderston, 1993), as there exists the same discrepancy between Hoffmann's index of industrial production and the official data that is now familiar from Figure 4.1 (see Figure 4.7a).

Looking at industry groups, striking differences exist for metal processing (Figure 4.7b). If Hoffmann's estimates were correct, the output of this industry – which is largely machinery, shipbuilding, automobiles, and electrical

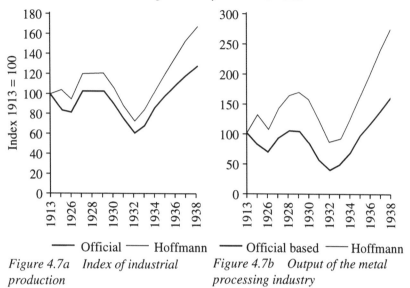

Figure 4.7a   Index of industrial production

Figure 4.7b   Output of the metal processing industry

products – would almost have tripled between 1913 and 1938. Such an enormous boom, in turn, would have left its traces in investment or in consumption of durables, which is at odds with the evidence on aggregate expenditure examined above.

In spite of an abundance of data on the sectors in question, Hoffmann (1965) employs a rather indirect method of estimating output. Starting out from census data on employment in metal making and metal processing, he nets out the iron and steel industry, using the census employment shares of 1907, and then extrapolates output of the metal-processing industry by means of the employment series and a wage rate he calculates from his distribution account. Balderston (1993) provides an attempt to reconstruct this calculation method. This approach is justified if (a) the structure of employment between metal making and metal manufacturing was constant over time; and (b) the wage share in net value added, or real unit labor cost, remained unchanged as well. It is precisely this second point which was controversial in the aforementioned debates about unit labor cost in the late 1920s. It is apparent that any cost estimate based on Hoffmann's data on manufacturing output data is biased toward the hypothesis of no change, as one of its major entries is calculated under just this assumption.

Ritschl (1995) combines the series of shipbuilding and automobile production provided (but not used) by Hoffmann with the official data on machinery output (which again is not employed by Hoffmann) and a series of output in the electrical industry derived from official data by Gehrig (1961) to construct a more reliable series of output of the metal-processing industry (termed 'official based' in Figure 4.7b). The result turns out to be consistent with all other available data: the figures on investment in machinery, commodity flow estimates on domestic absorption of machinery, foreign trade in machines, and the consumption of iron and steel all are consistent with one another but do not support the results obtained by Hoffmann. Inserting the revised index of metal industry output into Hoffmann's index of industrial production, Ritschl (1995) obtains a revision of Hoffmann's index of industrial production (Figure 4.8).

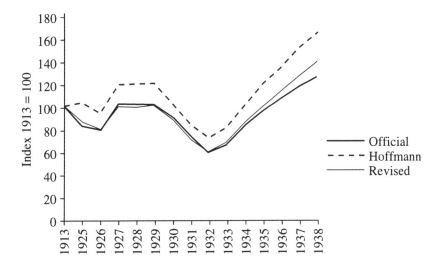

Figure 4.8   A revised index of industrial production

The result of this exercise is striking: up to the year 1934, the revised Hoffmann index mimics the behavior of the official one almost exactly, which implies that the Weimar productivity puzzle that has plagued research so much is just a data artifact. Once the capital goods series are corrected, the controversial discrepancy between the Hoffmann series and the official data disappears entirely, which in turn supports the more pessimistic perspective on industrial productivity in the Weimar Republic set out in Borchardt (1979, 1990). What introduces the deviation for the 1930s is still an open question. Two obvious candidates are textiles and chemical products, where Hoffmann's index is based strongly on the more dynamic subsectors of synthetic textiles and organic chemistry, while the official index might seems to be more conservative. This issue must be left for future research.

As a last step, I insert the result from Figure 4.8 into Hoffmann's output-based net national product (NNP) series and compare results with the original and the official series from Figure 4.1 above (Figure 4.9). As Figure 4.9 shows, the resulting series of NNP lies between the official data and the Hoffmann output series. Its striking feature is that, except for the 1926 slump, the amplitude of the interwar cycle is dampened when compared to Hoffmann's original data. This result is still provisional, and more research needs to be directed towards evaluating Hoffmann's sectoral output data against other evidence. However, it shows that even with the single revision at hand, the business cycle peaks indicated by Hoffmann's original output series become markedly flatter and there is a tendency to reconfirm the results from the official income-based aggregate expenditure accounts.

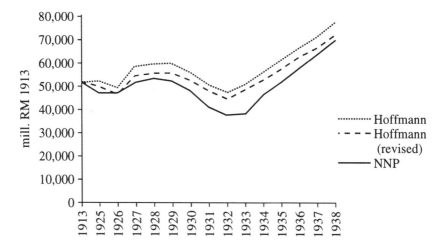

Figure 4.9   A revised aggregate output series

CONCLUSIONS AND IMPLICATIONS

Measurement of Germany's aggregate performance in the interwar years has been the subject of intense, at times emotionally loaded, debates. In this chapter we have attempted to isolate the quantitative issue of national product measurement from the context of these discussions and to establish a number of revisions to previously well-accepted stylized facts. I have argued from an evaluation of rival data series that Germany's interwar cycle exhibited less growth dynamics than was hitherto accepted.

The evidence presented in this chapter supports a more pessimistic perspective on Germany's interwar performance than the one which has been traditional. Employing the official data on national income and industrial production,

Broadberry and Ritschl (1994, 1995) had argued that, looking at the supply side of the economy, interwar Germany followed the British slow-growth pattern of poor productivity performance, combined with high wage increases and, consequently, supernormal unit wage cost. The results I obtain here reinforce this result by showing that for the interwar period, the rival GDP data from the national accounts of Hoffmann (1965) are upward biased, and along with them, the data appearing in Maddison (1991) are upward biased. Making adjustments for these biases and correcting sometimes major methodological flaws in his calculations, I obtain revisions of his estimates of national income and product which are far closer to the official data than to Hoffmann's own original estimates.

The question might arise to what extent the results presented here carry over to Hoffmann's estimates of national product in the nineteenth century, and a word of caution is in place. Hoffmann's series start in 1850, and some have been calculated backwards into the 1830s (Spree, 1977). Indeed, criticism of Hoffmann's methods for the nineteenth century data also exist (see Fremdling, 1988, 1995; Holtfrerich, 1983). However, the impact of the methodological defects discussed in the above sections on the nineteenth century is not likely to be equally high. As to Hoffmann's expenditure series, the problem for public investment can hardly be major, given the small overall size of the public sector before World War I. With regard to the output estimates, no easy answer can be given because of the immense complexity of Hoffmann's work. However, it should be stated that neither of the revisions discussed above is automatically applicable to the nineteenth century. As far as manufacturing is concerned, Hoffmann's method is largely that of a chain index, and most of the calculation methods for the pre-1913 period differ from those for the interwar years. Even where this is not true, as in machine building, the discrepancy between Hoffmann's data and the results from other sources do not seem to be as manifest as in the interwar period. Hence, for the time being and for the lack of better estimates, Hoffmann's data may continue to be a valid source for German macroeconomic data of the nineteenth century, although its use for the interwar period seems very limited and may in fact be misleading.

The results presented above open a new avenue for future research. Given that the official accounts are more reliable than previously thought, it seems straightforward to extend the time series backward and forward, using information of the same or similar varieties. In this way, an internally self-consistent series of output and its components might be arrived at which hitherto has been missing and which might allow for a full assessment of German economic growth in the early twentieth century.

APPENDIX: DATA FOR FIGURES 4.1–4.9

All figures are in millions of Reichsmarks (1913 value), unless otherwise indicated.

Table A4.1   National product

| Year | Official | | Hoffmann | | | |
| | | | Expenditure | | Output | |
	Gross	Net	Cap. acc.	Curr. acc.	Original	Revised
1913		51,493	52,440	52,440	51,550	51,550
1925	50 305	46 532	47 426	46 897	51 515	48 216
1926	50 797	46 790	47 491	46 587	49 115	46 130
1927	55 579	51 208	54 670	53 108	58 040	54 250
1928	57 478	53 142	55 936	53 950	59 124	55 325
1929	56 353	51 948	52 563	51 694	59 523	55 650
1930	52 499	48 032	50 708	49 289	55 894	52 509
1931	45 196	40 707	45 232	43 913	50 180	47 465
1932	41 835	37 083	44 082	41 760	46 269	43 946
1933	45 575	40 619	49 829	47 375	50 436	47 785
1934	50 446	45 569	54 581	52 102	55 512	52 223
1935	56 603	51 262	60 352	58 658	60 564	56 698
1936	63 107	57 287	66 226		66 814	62 440
1937	70 069	63 978	73 167		71 377	66 500
1938	76 676	70 350	81 335		77 391	72 029

Sources: Official: Ritschl (1996); expenditure and output: Hoffmann (1965).

Table A4.2   Investment

Year	Gross	Net	Net (Hoffmann)
1925	8 035	4 262	5 380
1926	6 258	2 251	3 300
1927	10 733	6 362	8 070
1928	9 873	5 537	6 880
1929	8 225	3 820	3 550
1930	4 642	175	2 790
1931	766	−3 723	−1 360
1932	1 549	−3 203	−680
1933	4 807	−149	2 310
1934	7 919	3 042	3 250
1935	10 789	5 448	5 790
1936	12 659	6 839	7 260
1937	14 419	8 328	11 200
1938	16 743	10 417	11 950

Table A4.3   Current account

Year	Official	Hoffmann	
		Current account	Capital account
1925	−1337	−1758	−1229
1926	117	238	1142
1927	−2958	−3262	−1700
1928	−1756	−2143	−157
1929	−902	−575	294
1930	−854	−397	1022
1931	−997	−78	1241
1932	−3234	−1997	325
1933	−2883	−2255	199
1934	−3583	−2994	−515
1935	−2443	−1788	−94
1936	−1390		380
1937	−2008		280
1938	−4211		−320

Table A4.4   Industrial production

Year	Official	Hoffmann	Hoffmann (revised)
1913	100	100	100.0
1925	84	103	86.8
1926	81	94	78.7
1927	103	119	99.8
1928	102	119	100.0
1929	103	121	101.9
1930	91	106	89.1
1931	74	85	71.5
1932	60	73	61.1
1933	67	83	69.8
1934	85	103	86.6
1935	98	121	101.8
1936	109	137	115.1
1937	119	153	128.4
1938	127	168	141.2

Table A4.5   Output of metal-processing industry

Hoffmann Year	Official based	Hoffmann
1913	100.0	100.0
1925	88.9	131.4
1926	77.6	103.9
1927	103.1	142.6
1928	120.4	163.5
1929	125.6	170.3
1930	97.2	156.9
1931	71.0	120.3
1932	48.8	84.2
1933	57.3	91.6
1934	80.6	125.5
1935	107.8	163.9
1936	127.4	202.6
1937	148.4	239.7
1938	177.7	281.1

NOTES

1. See Mitchell (1975) and Maddison (1982,1991,1995).
2. The main references are Falkus (1975) and Balderston (1974, 1977). A recent reappraisal is Balderston (1993).
3. The concept is from Maier (1976).
4. A recent survey of productivity and labor cost estimates in English is Spoerer (1994).
5. Results are presented in detail in Ritschl (1996).
6. This work starts with Statistisches Reichsamt (1932) and is continued in the statistical yearbooks through 1941–2. Data to 1944–5 are compiled in a statistical handbook compiled after the war (Länderrat, 1949).
7. Lack of balance of payment data for the late 1930s induces Hoffmann (1965) to present two different versions of his expenditure estimates. See pp. 95–100 for details.
8. A counterexample is provided by Feinstein's (1972) estimates of British national product, where the income tax based estimate is consistently above the output-based figures.
9. For investment, see Ehrlicher (1956) and, above all, Gehrig (1961). Public spending is recalculated in Erbe (1958). An almost complete expenditure account is given in Klein (1959).
10. The historical background is provided in James (1985, 1986).
11. A subtle point which emerges from archival evidence not accessible at the time is the precise timing of armament bonds flotation. As noted in Ritschl (1996), some parts of the existing circulation were bought back during 1935 and 1936 and later recycled into the market. This explains some of the deviations between Hoffmann's public consumption figures and my own recalculations for the mid-1930s.
12. See, for example, Kroll (1958); Erbe (1958); Klein (1959); and, more recently, Overy (1982); James (1986).

PART II

Phillips Curves and Labor Markets:
Macro versus Micro Views

5. The labor market a hundred years ago: new, micro-level evidence on long-term change from the depression of 1893–4

Susan Carter and Richard Sutch*

INTRODUCTION

The apparent increasing stability of the economy and growing rigidity of nominal wages over time pose a puzzle for macroeconomists. Wage stickiness is supposed to *reduce* stability. The profession's response to this apparent contradiction between theory and evidence has taken three forms. Some have reconsidered the theory, proposing new theoretical links between price rigidities and economic stability (DeLong and Summers, 1986b; Grey and Kandil, 1991; Tobin, 1993). Others have looked for change in some other factor, especially shocks (Taylor, 1986). A third response has been to reconsider 'the facts' (Romer, 1986b; Allen, 1992; Weir, 1992). Our chapter is a contribution to this third response.

'The facts' in question are the annual unemployment rate series developed by Stanley Lebergott (1964) and the average hourly earnings series developed by Albert Rees (1961). These series have been considered the standard since their creation in the early 1960s and form the evidentiary basis for all analyses of long-term change in the stability of employment and wages (Sachs, 1980; Gordon, 1982b; DeLong and Summers, 1986a; Taylor, 1986). Recently, Christina Romer (1986b), Steven Allen (1992), and David Weir (1992) have raised objections to the methods used to produce these series. Recomputing the

* We are grateful to George Akerlof, Gary Solon, and participants at the McGill University Conference on Labour Market Evolution, February 1991, for valuable comments and suggestions that were influential in revising this chapter. Eric Bales and Brian A'Hearn assisted in the collection of the data. Financial support for this work was provided by the National Science Foundation; the Institute of Industrial Relations and the Institute of Business and Economic Research, both at the University of California, Berkeley; and the Academic Senate, University of California, Riverside. The data are available through the Historical Labor Statistics Project, Institute of Business and Economic Research, University of California, Berkeley 94720.

underlying evidence has generated new, alternative annual estimates. Our tack is different. We begin by noting that the data upon which the well-known time series are based are but a small fraction of the data collected by state labor bureaus in the late nineteenth and early twentieth centuries.[1] We analyze new, heretofore unused micro-level evidence on the response of manufacturing firms to the deep depression of 1893–4.[2] Whereas previous revisions to the annual series on unemployment and average hourly earnings seem to suggest that macroeconomic labor market outcomes have been remarkably uniform over the past hundred years, our evidence reveals significant differences between then and now.

THE CONNECTICUT DEPRESSION SURVEYS

Our data come from two large-scale surveys of manufacturing firms in Connecticut conducted by that state's Bureau of Labor Statistics in order to ascertain the effects of the industrial depression of 1893–4.[3] The first survey, undertaken in September 1894, was an attempt to measure the severity of the decline. The Connecticut Bureau sent questionnaires to 500 large firms in 27 separate industries, requesting detailed information on employment, wage payments, the value of production, days in operation, and hours per day for 1892; average monthly output and days in operation over the period June 1893–August 1894, and monthly data on employment, hours, and wages for each of the 15 months in the depression period. Firms were also asked to report changes in wage rates between June 1, 1893 and August 31, 1894. The survey was limited to large establishments which, 'because of their size, were presumed to have accounts which would facilitate the filling out of the schedule.'[4]

Altogether, firms employing approximately half of the state's industrial labor force were included.

An overriding concern for accuracy is evident in the Bureau's discussions of questionnaire design, sample selection, and tabulation. The introduction to the first survey noted:

> Monthly conditions were asked, rather than a general statement, in the belief that thereby a closer approach to accuracy could be made. The mental depression caused by the industrial depression might unconsciously result in exaggerated conclusions ... But a statement of monthly conditions demanded care, attention and an examination of accounts. (Connecticut Bureau of Labor Statistics, 1894: 168)

Returns containing 'irremedial defects in the schedules' were omitted; 378 were published by the Bureau.

The second survey, begun in July 1895, focused on the recovery. Firms were asked to report employment on July 1 for the years 1892, 1894, and

1895, and any wage rate changes in fiscal 1895, especially the *restoration* of wage rates cut during the depression. The second questionnaire was simpler than the first, and an effort was made to contact more firms. The schedule was mailed together with a prepaid return envelope. Bureau agents contacted firms which did not respond promptly. Schedules which were 'evidently the result of estimate' were excluded from the published tabulations. 'Nothing appears in the report of the accuracy of which there is the slightest doubt,' the Bureau bragged (Connecticut Bureau of Labor Statistics, 1895: 133–4). One thousand schedules from the 1895 survey were published. These schedules came from firms in 26 separate industries (including a miscellaneous category) and employed approximately three-fourths of the state's industrial labor force. A fuller description of both surveys, together with a discussion of their coverage, representativeness, and bias is provided in the Appendix to this chapter.

THE DEPRESSION OF 1893–4

Table 5.1, based on the first of the two surveys, reveals the seriousness of the depression of 1893–4. The decline in the nominal value of output averaged 20.5 per cent for the Connecticut firms included in the 1894 sample. This is very similar to the 19 per cent drop in the nominal value of industrial production at the national level between 1892 and the period June 1893 through August 1894, although smaller than the collapse of industrial production between 1920 and 1921 and between 1929 and 1933.[5]

The reduction in labor input was even greater than the decline in nominal output. Total hours worked fell 31.4 per cent. This reduction was accomplished through a 14.8 per cent reduction in employment, a 14.9 per cent reduction in days worked per worker, and a 4.3 per cent reduction in the length of the average working day. The magnitude of the employment reduction is confirmed by the 1895 survey which recorded employment on July 1, 1892 and July 1, 1894. Weighted by the 1892 employment, the average decline in employment reported was also 14.8 per cent.

Three phenomena revealed in Table 5.1 are noteworthy; indeed, they are surprising, given the empirical regularities in the modern labor market and recent theoretical debates on labor market dynamics:

1. the Connecticut figures indicate that employment decline was responsible for only one-half of the increase in idleness. Temporary plant closures of less than a week were an equally important source of lost time. Today, by contrast, short weeks are rarely employed to reduce labor inputs;

2. output per worker hour *increased* 15.9 per cent in the depression. Productivity increased! This is the opposite of the modern pattern. Today, productivity falls during recessions;
3. nominal average hourly wages *rose* by 12.3 per cent. Since prices were falling, real wages rose even more. Today, real wages are acyclical. The counter-cyclical pattern of nominal hourly wages in the 1890s is especially startling since wage *rates* fell.

Each of these findings has important implications for the estimation of annual series on employment and wages and for the evaluation of long-term change in labor market dynamics. We discuss them in turn.

Table 5.1   How bad was the depression of 1893–4? Percentage change in the annual rate of output, labor inputs, and wages between calendar year 1892 and the period spanning June 1893 through August 1894 for 348 Connecticut manufacturing firms

	Average percentage change	
	Average across firms	Average across employees
Value of output	−20.5	−22.3
Total hours worked	−29.9	−31.4
employment	−15.0	−14.8
days per worker	−13.7	−14.9
hours per day	−2.9	−4.3
Wages per worker	−9.2	−10.8
Output per worker	−5.2	−7.7
Hours per worker	−17.4	−19.4
Wages per hour	+11.5	+12.3
Output per hour	+16.6	+15.9
Markup on unit labor cost	+5.2	+4.0

Note: The percentage changes are calculated for all firms that reported all the variables required to calculate this table. The number of employees in 1892 was used to calculate the weighted averages in the second column of figures.

Sources: Connecticut Bureau of Labor Statistics (1894) and Carter *et al.* (1993).

SHORT WEEKS

The Connecticut data indicate that temporary plant shutdowns of less than a week accounted for half the reductions in labor inputs in the depression of 1893–4. In the modern era plant shutdowns to accommodate reductions in demand are

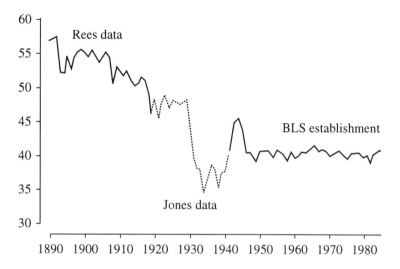

Figure 5.1 Average hours worked per week in manufacturing, 1890–1990

rare (Lilien and Hall, 1986: 1006; Kniesner and Goldsmith, 1987: 1244).[6]
Information on hours per week collected since 1955 as part of the Current
Population Survey suggest that idle days forced upon full-time workers in

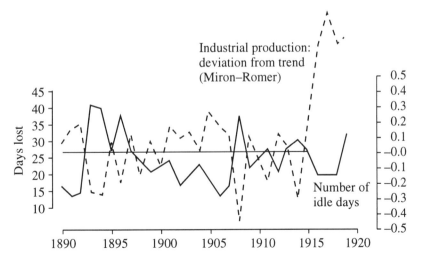

*Figure 5.2 Days lost from industrial suspensions and the index of industrial
production, 1890–1920*

Table 5.2   Industrial suspensions (number of idle days) in US manufacturing, 1890–1919

Year	Days idle	Year	Days idle
1890	12	1905	14
1891	10	1906	9
1892	12	1907	12
1893	35	1908	33
1894	34	1909	18
1895	22	1910	21
1896	33	1911	22
1897	23	1912	17
1898	19	1913	23
1899	16	1914	26
1900	17	1915	23
1901	19	1916	15
1902	12	1917	15
1903	16	1918	15
1904	20	1919	27

Notes: Our calculations begin with the estimates of days in operation constructed by Albert Rees from data reported for Massachusetts, New Jersey, and Pennsylvania. Idle days are the days lost due to industrial suspensions. They are computed by subtracting days in operation from our estimate of the full-time year which, in turn, was calculated as the number of days in the year minus the number of Sundays and holidays that fell on days other than Sunday. Frequent testimony suggests that there were between five and nine recognized work holidays per year in this period. Both the Massachusetts and New Jersey reports explicitly state that the full year was 306 days long (Massachusetts 1890: 231; New Jersey 1901: 25). This suggests seven holidays in most years. Roy Rosenzweig (1983: 180) says that the number of legal holidays in Massachusetts rose from five in 1870 to nine in 1920 (one of those added was Labor Day, established in 1887). We considered New Year's Day, George Washington's Birthday, Good Friday, July 4, Labor Day, Thanksgiving, and Christmas to be holidays for the purposes of calculating the nominal number of full-time days. Curiously, Rees declared that a full-time year was '312 days – 365 minus 52 Sundays and one holiday' (1961: 34).

Source: Rees (1961: Table 10, 33–4; and 1960: Table 8, 19).

non-agricultural establishments amounted to an average of less than two per year.[7] The deviation in idle days from peak to trough is less than one-half day. Data on the average number of hours worked in manufacturing displayed in Figure 5.1 suggest that the use of idle days was abruptly abandoned about the end of the Great Depression.[8]

Prior to the Great Depression, however, the temporary suspension of business operations was a widespread practice. Firms of that era often closed, idling their entire workforce. Judging from the Connecticut returns, the shutdowns lasted from a single day to several months but were usually less than a week. Table 5.2 presents evidence on industrial suspensions from 1890 through 1919 derived by Albert Rees (1960, 1961) from reports published by the Massachusetts, Pennsylvania, and New Jersey bureaus of labor statistics. Rees' figures show that in the year of most continuous operation, 1906, establishments were closed for an average of one and one-half weeks.[9] In 1893 average downtime was nearly six weeks. Figure 5.2 plots the number of days lost from industrial suspensions against an index of industrial production for the years 1890 through to 1920. Temporary plant closures appear to have been an important mechanism for reducing labor inputs in the face of a fall in demand for the firm's product.[10]

Why Suspend Operations?

We can infer some firms' motives for suspending operations from Table 5.3. This table tabulates in a two-way layout the 328 Connecticut firms that did not increase output during the depression period. The rows of the table divide the firms into three groups based on the number of idle days reported during the 15 months covered by the survey. The columns of the table distribute the firms by the percentage decline in employment. Table 5.3 indicates that 240 of the 328 firms, 73 per cent, reported more than 15 idle days during the 15-month period; 15 days in 15 months represents approximately 12 per year or about the average number of idle days reported in boom years (see Table 5.2). Among these Connecticut firms, just as in the more broadly representative evidence discussed above, suspensions of operations appear to have been a response to depression-

Table 5.3   Use of short weeks and employment layoffs during the depression of 1893–4: 328 Connecticut manufacturing firms that did not increase output

| No. of idle days reported | Decline in employment (%) | | | |
	Zero	8% or less	Greater than 8%	Total
0	13	7	33	53
1–15	5	4	26	35
16+	32	42	166	240
Total	50	53	225	328

Note: Fifteen idle days per year is approximately the rate of days idle during boom times. The number of idle days was inferred from the published data, which give idle days as a percentage of the number of days at full time. Inspection reveals that 385 days was the standard for full-time operation for the 15 months covered by the survey. This total represents a six-day week with seven days of vacation (New Years, July 4 (twice), Christmas, and three others).

Sources: Connecticut Bureau of Labor Statistics (1894); Carter *et al.* (1993).

induced reductions in demand. Within the sample, each unit reduction in the output index was associated with a 0.277 unit rise in the index of days idle.[11]

Suspensions of operations seem to have been used in conjunction with, rather than as a substitute for, employment reductions. Even those firms that reduced employment sharply (by more than 8 per cent) relied heavily upon short weeks to further reduce their labor inputs (166 firms out of 225 did so – 74 per cent). A somewhat greater number of firms resorted to frequent suspensions while resisting employment cuts (79 firms below the diagonal of the matrix displayed in Table 5.3) than cut employment without imposing an extensive number of idle days (66 firms above the diagonal). But the most striking feature of Table 5.3 is that about half of the firms (166) cut *both* employment *and* days of operation significantly.

Short Weeks and the Stylized Facts

The widespread use of industrial suspensions in the pre-World War I era raises questions about comparisons of lost time between that period and the present. First, it suggests that the modern definition of unemployment may be inappropriate for the measurement of lost time in the past. The modern, official statistics on unemployment do not include unemployment that takes the form of time lost due to suspensions of less than a week or to reductions in the length of the work shift (US Bureau of Labor Statistics, 1988: 3–5). The failure to include this form of lost time does not seriously bias the unemployment measures in the post-World War II period because short weeks are relatively infrequent. When the modern definitions are pushed back to the pre-World War I era, however, the neglect of short weeks and short days leads to a serious understatement of the extent of lost time and to distortions in the pattern of unemployment over the cycle. For meaningful historical comparisons, either the modern definition of unemployment would need to be replaced with a new one that incorporates time lost due to short weeks and days[12] or a new companion series measuring short time would have to be developed.[13]

Irrespective of which course is taken, our discovery of the heavy reliance on short weeks to reduce labor inputs in the past means that existing estimates of unemployment for years prior to 1940 are in need of adjustment. When he initially developed his unemployment series, Lebergott intended it to embody the same concepts of labor force, employment, and unemployment used by the Bureau of Labor Statistics since its introduction in 1940.[14] In fact, however, Lebergott's application of the modern concept to his construction of the data series is inconsistent. He derived estimates of the number of persons unemployed by subtracting estimates of annual employment from estimates of the labor force. Intercensal estimates of employment and labor force were interpolated between benchmarks based upon occupational data reported in the decennial censuses

(Lebergott, 1964: 403). Of the various steps in this procedure, the modern concept of unemployment is embodied only in the intercensal estimates. The census benchmark figures embody the modern concept *plus* loss due to short weeks. Romer's (1986a) and Weir's (1992) revised unemployment series accept Lebergott's benchmarks so their estimates also involve an inconsistency between census year and intercensal figures.[15]

Third, the heavy use of industrial suspensions suggests a new explanation for the measured homogeneity of unemployment and the relative brevity of unemployment spells in the late nineteenth century. In contrast to the modern labor market, where the burden of unemployment falls on a relatively small proportion of the labor force who are out of work a long time (Clark and Summers, 1979: 14; Murphy and Topel, 1987: 13), unemployment in the late nineteenth century has been shown to have been more widely shared and of briefer duration (Bolino, 1966; Keyssar, 1986: 82; Sutch, 1988; Margo, 1990a, b; Hatton and Williamson, 1990a, b). Since heterogeneity and long duration of unemployment in the modern era are commonly attributed to labor market structure, the homogeneity and brief duration of turn-of-the-century unemployment appear to imply that such structure was absent. The Connecticut data suggest another explanation for the patterns from the early period. A century ago, a large fraction of all unemployment took the form of short weeks. These *are* brief spells of unemployment, but they are unlike the unemployment spells in a modern labor market. Idle days did not deprive the worker of a job. The worker would experience 'days lost,' and report them to the census taker, but would consider his or her tenure with the employer to have continued. It is certainly too soon to conclude that unemployment was largely frictional or that the labor market was a spot market in the 1890s.

COUNTERCYCLICAL PRODUCTIVITY

A surprising feature of the Connecticut experience is that the total number of hours worked fell by more than output declined: total hours declined by 31.9 per cent while the nominal value of output declined by 23.1 per cent. This means that average productivity per worker hour actually rose by 16.2 per cent. Since prices were falling, real output per hour increased even more.[16] This is precisely the opposite of what is seen in modern data. The short-run cyclical production function estimated with data from the 1920s and later consistently reveals *decreasing* productivity per worker hour when firms reduce total hours (Hultgren, 1960; Fair, 1969; Bernanke and Powell, 1986; Bernanke and Parkinson, 1991). Our findings imply that this well-known macroeconomic labor market outcome first appeared some time after the 1890s.

The accepted explanations for the present-day phenomenon are that, first, some workers represent 'overhead' laborers who cannot be easily laid off and, second, some production-line labor is 'hoarded' by employers during temporary downturns. 'Labor hoarding' occurs when production workers are retained on the payroll despite the fact that their labor is not fully required, given the level of production. It is usually suggested that this practice minimizes costs over the business cycle since some of the unemployed workers would find other jobs if laid off and would be expensive to replace when output returns to full capacity. Presumably such workers possess hard-to-replace skills or valuable firm-specific knowledge (Fay and Medoff, 1985; Bernanke and Parkinson, 1991).

Whatever the force of these two factors in Connecticut manufacturing during the 1890s, however, it was overwhelmed by some productivity-enhancing effect. Among most firms in the Connecticut survey, productivity rose when output was reduced.

Why Did Productivity Rise?

We have considered three reasons why labor productivity rose during the depression of 1893–94. For brevity we refer to them as: the reduction-of-fatigue effect; the selective-retention effect; and the extra-effort effect.

Reduction of fatigue
It is often asserted that 'long' working hours produce fatigue and drive down the marginal product of hours worked.[17] During the depression of the 1890s many workers experienced a reduction in the length of their work week. Perhaps the shorter work week allowed them to be more productive during the hours at which they were employed.[18]

Selective retention
The increase in average product we have observed in the Connecticut data might have been induced by discrimination against less-productive workers.[19] Carroll Wright, US Commissioner of Labor, commented on this possibility in 1904:

> Where the employer is perfectly free, as he usually is in a non-union establishment, to 'take on' or 'let go' his men without notice, he is able to select the speediest men, giving to them the steadier jobs and leaving the irregular and seasonal work to the slower men. (Wright, 1904: 20).[20]

Extra effort
The third possibility is that workers, observing employers selectively dismissing the less diligent, would put forth an extra effort during times of employment insecurity to protect their own jobs.[21] Carroll Wright argued that this extra-effort effect was another force operating in the turn-of-the-century labor market:

(I)t is also asserted by practically every person interviewed, both employers and workmen, that the men will not work as hard when they can get work in other establishments as when they feel that their chances for other employment are slim. (Ibid.: 21–2).

The Connecticut data can be used to discriminate among these three possibilities and to measure their relative strength. The reduction-of-fatigue effect, for example, would come into play when workers were retained *and* worked fewer days or fewer hours per day. It should not be present when labor input is reduced solely through employment reductions. On the other hand, the selective-retention effect can only be produced by dismissing low-productivity workers. Complete plant shutdowns, cutting everyone back equally, could not produce the selective-retention effect. The extra-effort hypothesis makes sense only within firms that practice (or are likely to practice) discrimination based on productivity.[22]

Table 5.4 presents ordinary least-squares estimates of the short-run cyclical production function of Connecticut manufacturing firms during the depression of 1893–4. Equation 1 and Figure 5.3 display an estimate of the standard Cobb–Douglas elasticity of output with respect to total hours worked. The estimated value of 0.682 indicates that output fell less than total labor hours – in other words, productivity rose. Equation 2 re-estimates the short-run production function but decomposes total hours worked into three components: an index of

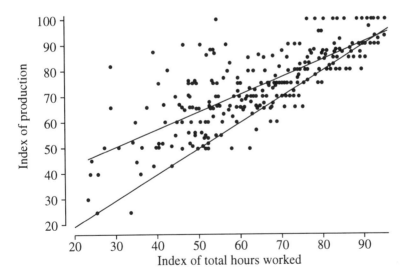

Figure 5.3   Short-run production function, Connecticut manufacturing during the depression of 1893–4

the number employed, an index of the number of days in operation, and an index of the number of hours per day. The estimated elasticities associated with the three variables are all less than one. This suggests that all three effects – reduction-of-fatigue, selective-retention, and extra-effort – raised productivity during the depression of 1893–4. The smaller coefficients on hours per day and days in operation relative to the coefficient on employment suggests that short time raised productivity more than employment reductions.[23] Recall that productivity rises with short time because of the reduction-of-fatigue effect. The low-valued coefficients on our short-time measures suggest that the reduction-of-fatigue effect was the most powerful force responsible for raising output in the depression and that the fatigue effect is about the same whether work was reduced through shortening hours per day or shortening the number of days per week.[24] Since the average work week today is only about half as long as it was in the 1890s, it is not surprising that the reduction-of-fatigue effect is no longer prominent.

Table 5.4   Why did productivity rise when output fell? Log-linear OLS estimates of the short-run cyclical production function, Cobb-Douglas elasticities and their standard errors for 276 Connecticut manufacturing firms that reduced output and employment [a]

	(1)	(2)
Total hours worked	0.682	
	(0.016)	
Employment		0.735
		(0.033)
Days in operation		0.618
		(0.045)
Hours per day		0.580
		(0.064)
adjusted R^2		
Log linear	0.873	0.874
Cobb–Douglas	0.985	0.985

Notes:
[a]   Dependent variable is output; standard errors in parentheses.
Includes all firms that reduced both output and employment between 1892 and the depression period spanning June 1893 through August 1894 and that reported the average wage of workers in 1892. All variables are the logarithms of index numbers with 1892 = 1. Since the constant is suppressed in these regressions, the surface that minimizes the sum of squared residuals passes through the point defined for 1892. The first of each pair of adjusted R^2 statistics is for the logarithmic form of the dependent variable. The second is for the index number form of the dependent variable.

Sources: Connecticut Bureau of Labor Statistics (1894); Carter *et al.* (1993).

Countercyclical Productivity and the Stylized Facts

Countercyclical productivity in the 1890s has implications for the estimation of unemployment in this period. Lebergott calculated unemployment by subtracting an estimate of employment from an estimate of the labor force. The employment estimates were based on real output assuming that output and employment moved proportionately. Implicitly Lebergott's methods assumed that labor productivity was insensitive to the cycle. Since in modern data productivity is *pro*cyclical, Romer proposed that this procyclical relationship held in the prewar era as well (Romer 1986b: 27–8). Her argument implies that employment should not swing as widely as output, therefore unemployment should be less volatile than in Lebergott's estimates. The Connecticut data implies yet a different relationship between employment and output. By our measurements, labor productivity was *counter*cyclical during the depression of 1893–4. If this finding can be confirmed, Lebergott's implicit productivity assumptions contributed too little, not too much, volatility to his unemployment estimates.[25]

Our evidence on the selective retention of more-productive workers during the depression also bears on debates about the nature of the employment relation in that era. Selective retention would make no sense if labor's wages were determined in a spot market. Workers would be paid their marginal product and the employer would be indifferent between the choice of dismissing a 'speedy' man highly paid because of his productivity or the less-productive but low-paid man. The narrative evidence offered by contemporaries and the statistical evidence on selective retention presented here suggest that even in this early period wages did more than simply equilibrate supply and demand.

COUNTERCYCLICAL AVERAGE HOURLY WAGES

Nominal average hourly wages at firms in the 1894 sample *rose* 11.3 per cent between 1892 and the 15-month depression period. Since prices were falling, real wages rose even more. This pattern is different from the acyclical behavior of real average hourly wages in the post-World War II period.[26] It is also at odds with the common characterization of pre-World War I wages as flexible and *pro*cyclical (Sachs, 1980; Gordon, 1982; DeLong and Summers, 1986a; Taylor, 1986).[27]

As we show below, average hourly earnings rose during the 1893–4 depression because a disproportionate share of low-paid workers lost their jobs. The effect on average hourly earnings of this shift in the skill mix of employment was noted by contemporaries. Typical is a comment offered by a New Jersey manufacturer interviewed during an investigation of the effects of the 1893 depression in his state:

> The average amount paid per man during June, 1893, shows a decided increase over June, 1892, ... an increase of about 25%. This apparent inconsistency is explained in a measure by the fact that in periods of depression the higher-priced men are retained, while the helpers and other low-priced hands are laid off – with the peculiar result that when business is at the lowest point, the average wages paid per hour is apt to be highest. (New Jersey Bureau of Statistics of Labor and Industries, 1894 (published 1895): 11–12)

Compositional effects have been noted in modern data as well, but their effects work in the opposite direction. Michael Keane, Robert Moffitt, and David Runkle (1988) find that workers with *high* wages are more likely to lose their jobs today. Compositional effects bias modern data toward procyclicality.

Wage Rates

The Connecticut surveys also provide direct evidence on wage *rates*. These are summarized in Table 5.5. The reports from 1894 are remarkable. Despite the severity of the depression, 44.5 per cent of firms that did not increase output made no change in their wage rates whatsoever. Over 40 per cent of workers received their old rate of pay. It would appear that wage rates were very sticky.

Table 5.5   Were wage rates sticky? Proportion of firms instituting wage rate changes and percentage of employees affected between calendar year 1892 and the period spanning June 1893 through August 1894 for 328 Connecticut manufacturing firms that did not increase output

Factors/reported	No. of firms	% of firms	% of employees affected
General wage rate increase	2	0.1	0.8
Partial wage rate increase	7	2.1	0.9
No wage rate changes	146	44.5	42.2
Partial wage rate cut	67	20.4	8.5
General wage rate cut	118	36.0	39.0

Note: A general wage cut affected all employees. A partial wage cut affected only a fraction of the firms' employees. The number of employees in 1892 was used to calculate the weighted averages in the third column of figures. Number of firms does not total to 328 and percentage of firms and percentage of employees affected do not total to 100 because some firms followed more than one strategy.

Sources: Connecticut Bureau of Labor Statistics (1894); Carter *et al.* (1993).

Table 5.6   How big were the wage rate cuts? 328 Connecticut manufacturing firms that did not increase output

Wage rate cut (%)	General wage rate cut		Partial wage rate cut	
	No. of firms instituting	% of employees affected	No. of firms instituting	% of employees affected
No change or increase	210	61.0	261	91.5
2.5			1	0.0
4.25			1	0.1
5.0	4	2.0	6	0.3
5.5	5	1.6	1	0.1
6.25			1	0.2
6.5			1	0.0
7.0	1	0.2		
7.5	5	1.4	2	0.2
8.0			2	0.0
8.5	2	0.4	2	0.3
8.75	1	0.4	1	0.6
9.0			1	0.9
10.0	47	17.3	32	3.5
11.25			1	0.1
12.0	1	0.3	1	1.1
12.5	17	5.8	2	0.2
13.0	1	2.5		
13.5	1	0.2		
15.0	14	3.0	4	0.5
17.0	1	0.1		
17.5	5	1.0	3	0.1
18.0	3	0.7		
20.0	2	0.3	2	0.2
25.0	3	0.9	3	0.5
29.15	1	0.1		
30.0	2	1.0		
33.33	1	0.1		
40.0	1	0.1		
Total	328	100.0	328	100.0

Sources: Connecticut Bureau of Labor Statistics (1894); Carter *et al.* (1993).

This quantitative evidence of wage rate stickiness is confirmed by descriptive evidence from the period. For example, the owner of a lime plant located in Maine responded in July 1894 to an inquiry from that state's Commissioner of Labor:

> The working force has been reduced 70 per cent on account of no demand for lime, with no prospect of returning to full capacity at present. What men are retained are paid the old rate of wages, yet it would be easy to hire a crew at much lower rates (Maine Bureau of Industrial and Labor Statistics 1895: 30)

Of course, the glass that is half full is also half empty. In this case, over half of the firms *cut* wages. Another surprising discovery, however, is that the overwhelming majority of wage rate cuts affected *all* of the workers in a firm and were clustered at exactly 10 per cent. Table 5.5 shows that 39 per cent of all employees received a firm-wide wage rate cut, compared with 8.5 per cent of workers who suffered a cut that was not firm-wide. Table 5.6 distributes firms according to the character and magnitude of their wage cuts. Column 2 shows that 40 per cent of the firms which issued general wage rate cuts $(47/(328-210))$ cut wages by exactly 10 per cent.[28] Such clustering suggests the influence of social norms.

Table 5.7   Wage rate restorations: proportion of firms instituting general wage rate changes and percentage of employees affected, year ending July 1, 1895, Connecticut manufacturing

	Firms instituting (%)	Employees affected (%)
General wage rate increases	3.3	2.3
Restoration of wage rate cuts	10.6	18.0
General wage rate reductions	1.6	1.3
No wage rate changes	84.5	78.4
	100.0	100.0

Sources: Connecticut Bureau of Labor Statistics (1895); Carter *et al.* (1993).

The 1895 survey of post-depression conditions among Connecticut manufacturers provides further evidence that late nineteenth-century wage rates were sticky and regulated by notions of a customary standard. The 1895 survey collected information on general wage rate changes. The results are shown in Table 5.7. The responses indicate that the most common reason for changing wage rates in that year was to *restore* cuts made during the depression. Eleven per cent of firms issued wage cut restorations affecting 18 per cent of manufacturing employees. Restorations were instituted even though prices and employment remained below their 1892 level. Only 3.3 per cent of firms issued wage rate increases that were not wage cut restorations. Only 1.6 per cent of firms cut the wage rate. It appears that when firms did cut wage rates during the depression, it was understood that they would be restored as soon as 'normal conditions of business' returned. Reports of strikes in 1895 repeatedly emphasize workers' view that they were entitled to maintain their 'customary' wage. When employers took exception it was not to the notion that workers be paid their customary standard but to workers' claim that the depression was over.[29,30]

Which Firms Cut Wage Rates?

Of the 328 Connecticut firms that did not increase output, 118 instituted general wage rate cuts, while 210 did not. What, if anything, distinguished the firms that chose to issue general wage rate cuts? To explore that question we performed a series of probit experiments. The results are reported in Table 5.8. The dependent variable takes the value of '1' for firms that issued general wage rate cuts and 0 otherwise. The independent variables include three index numbers

Table 5.8   Estimated probability of a general wage rate cut: 328 Connecticut manufacturing firms that did not increase output, 1892–94, Probit Estimates

	Coefficients	*t*-statistics	Mean of independent variable
Output index	0.0086	1.275	74.44
Employment index	−0.0153*	−3.098	80.00
Days in operation index	−0.0074	−1.245	85.66
Average wage, 1892	−0.0142*	−2.061	38.92
Log of firm size, 1892	0.1468	1.837	4.826
Constant	0.6894	0.959	1
Mean of dependent variable	0.360		
Log likelihood	−202.4400		
Number of observations	328		

Note: Includes all firms that did not increase output between 1892 and the depression period spanning June 1893 through August 1894 and that reported the average wage of workers in 1892 (seven firms did not report this statistic). The dependent variable takes the value of 1 for firms instituting a general wage rate reduction and 0 otherwise. The first of the three independent variables are index numbers with the 1892 value set equal to 100. Firm size in 1892 was measured by employment in 1892.

Sources: Connecticut Bureau of Labor Statistics (1894); Carter *et al.* (1993).

(for output, employment, and days in operation) as well as a measure of the firm's average weekly wage and its number of employees. The coefficients on the three index numbers need to be considered as a group. The negative coefficients on employment and days in operation suggest that firms which cut labor inputs (given the decline in output) were *more* likely to cut wage rates than firms which retained their workers. The magnitude of the effect is shown in Table 5.9.[31] For firms which retained all their employees, the probability of a wage rate cut was 26.7 per cent. Employment reductions of 25 and 50 per cent raised the probability of a wage rate cut to 39.0 and 52.6 per cent respectively. Perhaps wage rate cuts provoked less agitation when they were accompanied by draconian employment cuts. Perhaps the circumstances that led employers to dismiss their staffs in downturns also led them to feel they could cut wage rates. In any case, wage rate cuts certainly did not preserve jobs.

We also find that wage rate cutting was more common at large, low-pay establishments. Predicted probabilities in Table 5.9 indicate that a firm employing

Table 5.9   Predicted probabilities of general wage rate reduction: Connecticut manufacturing firms, 1893–4

Level of independent variable	Predicted probability of a General wage rate cut
Employment index	
100	0.267
75	0.390
50	0.526
Average wage in 1892 ($)	
20	0.445
40	0.339
60	0.245
Firm size	
20	0.259
200	0.373
2,000	0.499
Predicted probability at sample means	0.349
Actual probability at sample means	0.360

Note: Based on the probit coefficients reported in Table 5.8.

Source: Connecticut Bureau of Labor Statistics (1894), Carter *et al.* (1993).

2000 workers was almost twice as likely to cut wage rates as one employing 20. A firm with an average weekly wage of $20 was almost twice as likely to cut wage rates as one paying $60. Ironically, it would seem that wage-cutting was most pronounced in the large-scale, modern enterprises. The small, artisanal shops were the ones with the sticky wage rates.[32]

Countercyclical Average Hourly Earnings and the Stylized Facts

Annual data on average hourly earnings over the past century have been used to infer changes in the sensitivity of the wage *rate* to the cycle (Sachs, 1980; Gordon, 1982b; DeLong and Summers, 1986a; Taylor, 1986; Allen, 1992). Our analysis of the Connecticut data suggests that this procedure is inappropriate. In the 1890s changes in the composition of the labor force over the cycle imparted a countercyclical bias to average hourly earnings. In fact, countercyclical compositional effects were so large that average hourly earnings rose even though workers who retained their jobs experienced, on average, a 5 per cent *cut* in their wage rate.[33] Today the bias imparted by compositional effects is procyclical. Because the cyclical relationship between average hourly earnings and the wage rate has changed over time, it is hazardous to use average hourly earnings to infer long-term change in wage rate flexibility. In fact, our evidence suggests that this approach should be abandoned altogether.

Our finding of sticky wage rates is also important. It is further evidence against a spot-market characterization of the labor market in this period. Wage rates were reduced at some firms during the depression of 1893–4, but less than half of all workers were affected and wage rate cuts were heavily clustered at exactly 10 per cent across the board. Social considerations seem to have played an important role in wage-setting, even in this early period.

CONCLUSIONS

In this chapter we used newly coded, micro-level data collected in Connecticut during the deep depression of 1893–4 to assess long-term change in the operation of the labor market. We discovered that since the 1890s: (a) the importance of short time in accounting for reductions in labor inputs has been radically reduced; (b) labor productivity has shifted from a pro- to a countercyclical pattern; and (c) cyclical employment compositional effects have become muted. We also discovered one thing that appears *not* to have changed: wage rates in the 1890s were remarkably sticky.

Our new evidence implies that the standard long-term historical series on unemployment and average hourly earnings are flawed. The neglect of time lost due to short weeks and the assumption of an acyclical relationship between employment and output make the standard unemployment rate series (Lebergott, 1964) excessively stable over the cycle. The neglect of cyclical employment composition effects makes the standard average annual earnings series (Rees, 1961) excessively countercyclical. Since recent proposed revisions to these series (Romer, 1986; Allen, 1992) assume macroeconomic regularities characteristic of the *modern* labor market, our findings imply that these are off the mark as well.

Our findings also hint at the kind of research needed to produce annual unemployment and wage series that would more accurately reflect long-term change. To capture shifts in the importance of short time, a consistent, annual, long-term series on hours of work needs to be developed. To infer employment from output series for the early period, more and better estimates of the cyclical behavior of labor productivity are required. To assess long-term change in the cyclical behavior of wage rates, micro-level data uncontaminated by compositional effects must be used. Fortunately the recent appearance in machine-readable form of labor market survey data from the late nineteenth and early twentieth centuries makes each of these research projects feasible (Carter *et al.* 1991, 1993).

APPENDIX

Much of the empirical work in this chapter is based on data collected by the Connecticut Bureau of Labor Statistics in two investigations of the industrial depression of 1894–5.[34] The first investigation was conducted in September 1894 and netted responses from 500 firms, of which 378 were published. The second took place in July 1895 and elicited replies from 1000 firms, all of which were published. In its two reports, the Bureau took pains to emphasize the accuracy of the underlying firm records and the fidelity of its own reporting. We describe these assurances in the body of the chapter. Here we assess the representativeness of the surveys and relate the questions asked in the investigations to modern labor economics concepts.

Representativeness of the Connecticut Surveys

The numbers of firms and workers, by industry, in the 1894 and 1895 surveys are presented in Table A5.1. The 378 firms in the published returns from the first survey are drawn from 27 different industries. While these firms accounted for only 5.5 per cent of the state's manufacturing establishments, they employed 73 804 workers, or fully half of the state's manufacturing labor force (Connecticut Bureau of Labor Statistics, 1894: 169). The 1000 published returns from the 1895 survey were drawn from 25 different industries plus a miscellaneous category.

The firms accounted for 15 per cent of the state's manufacturing establishments and employed 115 139, or three-fourths, of the state's industrial labor force.

Table A5.1   Firms and number of workers by industry, Connecticut BLS surveys, 1894 and 1895

Industry	1894 survey		1895 survey	
	Firms	Workers	Firms	Workers
Boots and shoes	7	640	12	584
Leather goods	—	—	15	679
Brass and brass goods	30	8 790	80	16 749
Brick	—	—	17	613
Buttons, buckles, and pins	9	1 100	19	1 726
Carriages and carriage parts	17	1 138	38	1 455
Cast iron and forgings	23	3 738	44	5 086
Clocks	3	1 368	—	—
Corsets	9	4 040	13	4 698
Cotton	39	9 351	26	7 255
Cutlery and tools	12	1 626	48	3 931
Firearms	3	426	10	3 668
Hardware	38	6 894	79	10 671
Hats	14	1 782	46	5 656
Hosiery and knit goods	16	2 883	26	3 595
Machine shops	34	5 850	76	5 785
Manufactures of cotton goods	6	1 339	37	6 365
Musical instruments and parts	4	778	10	1 104
Paper mills	7	451	76	3 455
Paper boxes and envelopes	7	980	—	—
Printing and book binding	6	429	—	—
Rubber and elastic goods	11	4 396	18	5 620
Silk	12	3 736	25	5 329
Silver-plated ware	19	4 021	35	5 297
Stone cutting	10	1 483	19	1 003
Twine	4	175	—	
Wire and wire goods	3	208	22	1 003
Woodworking	5	648	57	1 954
Woolen goods	30	5 535	51	8 435
Miscellaneous	—	—	101	3 423
All industries	378	73 804	1 000	115 139

In terms of their size, the *firms* included in the surveys are atypically large. The average firm in the sample employed 195 workers; the average industrial firm in the state employed only 20.

Fortunately, for our purposes, this bias toward big firms is not a problem. Our interest is not in the firms *per se*, but in the experience of industrial workers. The typical *worker* was employed by an atypical (that is, especially large) firm. Since the surveys include half or three-fourths of the state's industrial workers, it describes the experience of a significant fraction of those workers.

Table A5.2   Distribution of employment by industry category, Connecticut BLS surveys 1894 and 1895 and the US manufacturing census of 1889 with totals for Connecticut and the nation

Industrial category	Connecticut Bureau of Labor Statistics		US Census of Manufactures, 1889	
	1894	1895	Conn.	US
Food	0.0	0.0	1.8	5.4
Textiles	39.1	35.9	34.4	19.1
Iron and steel	25.4	26.2	18.6	8.5
Lumber and its remanufactures	0.9	1.7	2.1	12.5
Leather and products	0.9	1.1	1.9	5.9
Paper and printing	2.5	3.0	4.0	6.2
Liquors and beverages	0.0	0.0	0.3	1.2
Chemicals and allied products	0.0	0.0	0.9	1.8
Clay, glass and stone products	2.0	1.4	1.3	7.8
Metals other than iron	19.2	19.1	14.1	2.9
Tobacco	0.0	0.0	0.5	2.9
Vehicles for land transportation	1.5	1.3	2.4	5.0
Shipbuilding	0.0	0.0	0.4	0.6
Miscellaneous industries	8.5	7.3	12.2	9.5
Hand trades	0.0	0.0	4.8	10.7
Uncategorized	—	3.0	—	—
Total	100.0	100.0	100.0	100.0

Sources: 1894 survey: Connecticut Bureau of Labor Statistics, *Tenth Annual Report for the Year Ending November 30, 1894*. Meriden, CT, 1894. 1895 survey: Connecticut Bureau of Labor Statistics, *Eleventh Annual Report for the Year Ending November 30, 1895*. Meriden, CT, 1895. Connecticut and US: US Department of the Interior, Census Office, *Report on Manufacturing Industries in the United States at the Eleventh Census: 1890. Part 1: Totals for States and Industries*. Washington, DC: Government Printing Office, 1895. Industry categories from *Twelfth Census*.

To assess the representativeness of the survey in another dimension, we categorized the industries according to the industrial classification used in the Census of Manufactures of 1889. We then calculated the distribution of employment in the surveys and compared it with the distribution of industrial employment in the State of Connecticut and in the United States a few years earlier. The results are reported in Table A5.2. Our calculations suggest that the industrial distribution of employment in the two surveys accurately reflects the industrial distribution of employment for the State of Connecticut as a whole. In the surveys approximately 35 per cent of employment is in textiles; in the state as a whole the comparable figure is 34.4 per cent. In the surveys one-fourth of employment is in iron and steel production and another fifth is in the production of other metals, chiefly brass. Comparable figures for the state are 19 and 14 per cent, respectively. Food; lumber; leather; paper; liquors; chemicals; clay, glass, and stone; tobacco; land vehicles; shipbuilding; and the hand trades account for only about 8 per cent of employment in the surveys and 14.5 per cent in the state.

The industrial distribution of Connecticut employment did differ from that in the country as a whole, however. In the nation, only about a fifth of the labor force was employed in textiles and 11 per cent in the production of metals. Almost half (47.9 per cent) were engaged in industries such as food, lumber, and so on, that were virtually absent from the Connecticut industrial scene. The Connecticut data thus provide a window on employment dynamics for about half of industrial employment nationwide.

Survey Questions, Modern Labor Force Concepts, and Coding Protocol

In its 1894 survey, the Connecticut Bureau requested information on employment, wages paid, the value of production, days in operation, and hours per day for 1892; average monthly output and days in operation over the period June 1893 to August 1894, and employment, hours, and wages by month for each of the 15 months of the depression period. Firms were also asked to report changes in wage rates between June 1, 1893 and August 31, 1894. Responses to the 1894 survey were tabulated in three separate tables. The first provided firm-level data for the average number employed in 1892 and average monthly wage payments in 1892, together with indexes showing total hours, employment, and monthly wage payments during the 15-month depression period as a proportion of the corresponding values in 1892. A code number for each firm was also given. The second table reported hours worked, number employed, and wages paid as a percentage of the corresponding value for full time for each of the 15 months of the depression as *industry averages*. The third table returned to a reporting of firm-level data, describing indexes on days idle as a fraction of working days, production in fiscal year 1893–4 as a fraction of production in 1892, and wage rate changes.

In its 1895 survey, firms were asked to report employment on July 1 for the years 1892, 1894, and 1895, and any wage rate changes in fiscal 1895. A specific question asked whether any wage rate change was a restoration of a wage rate cut made during the depression. Responses to the second survey were reported in a single table, by industry, by firm. We assume that many firms included in the first survey were also in the second. Because none of the questions asked on the first survey were repeated on the second, however, it was not possible to match firms' responses in the two sets of questions.

The questions asked, in the exact words used in the report, are listed in Table A5.3. The table also indicates the level to which each response was aggregated in the published report.

Table A5.3   Responses reported by degree of aggregation and report: Connecticut BLS surveys, 1894 and 1895

1894 survey, firm-level data
Number of establishments
Industry
Percentage hours worked of full-time
Average number employed in 1892
Average number employed June 1893 to August 1894
Average monthly payment in wages in 1892
Average monthly payment in wages, June 1893 to August 1894
Percent number idle days of working days
Percent production in last fiscal year of that in 1892
General reduction in wage rate, percentage
Partial reduction in wage rates, percentage
Percentage of employees affected by partial wage reduction
General increase in all wage rates, percentage
Partial increase in wage rates, percentage
Percentage of employees affected by partial wage increase

1894 survey, industry-level data
Industry
Percent hours worked of full-time, June 1893
Percent hours worked of full-time, July 1893
Percent hours worked of full-time, August 1893
Percent hours worked of full-time, September 1893
Percent hours worked of full-time, October 1893
Percent hours worked of full-time, November 1893

Table A5.3   continued

Percent hours worked of full-time, December 1893
Percent hours worked of full-time, January 1894
Percent hours worked of full-time, February 1894
Percent hours worked of full-time, March 1894
Percent hours worked of full-time, April 1894
Percent hours worked of full-time, May 1894
Percent hours worked of full-time, June 1894
Percent hours worked of full-time, July 1894
Percent hours worked of full-time, August 1894
Percent number employed of average number in 1892, June 1893
Percent number employed of average number in 1892, July 1893
Percent number employed of average number in 1892, August 1893
Percent number employed of average number in 1892, September 1893
Percent number employed of average number in 1892, October 1893
Percent number employed of average number in 1892, November 1893
Percent number employed of average number in 1892, December 1893
Percent number employed of average number in 1892, January 1894
Percent number employed of average number in 1892, February 1894
Percent number employed of average number in 1892, March 1894
Percent number employed of average number in 1892, April 1894
Percent number employed of average number in 1892, May 1894
Percent number employed of average number in 1892, June 1894
Percent number employed of average number in 1892, July 1894
Percent number employed of average number in 1892, August 1894
Percent wages paid of average monthly payments in 1892, June 1893
Percent wages paid of average monthly payments in 1892, July 1893
Percent wages paid of average monthly payments in 1892, August 1893
Percent wages paid of average monthly payments in 1892, September 1893
Percent wages paid of average monthly payments in 1892, October 1893
Percent wages paid of average monthly payments in 1892, November 1893
Percent wages paid of average monthly payments in 1892, December 1893
Percent wages paid of average monthly payments in 1892, January 1894
Percent wages paid of average monthly payments in 1892, February 1894
Percent wages paid of average monthly payments in 1892, March 1894
Percent wages paid of average monthly payments in 1892, April 1894
Percent wages paid of average monthly payments in 1892, May 1894
Percent wages paid of average monthly payments in 1892, June 1894
Percent wages paid of average monthly payments in 1892, July 1894
Percent wages paid of average monthly payments in 1892, August 1894

1895 survey, firm-level data (answers pertain to conditions in July 1895)
Establishment number
Industry
Number employed, July 1 1892
Number employed, July 1 1894
Number employed, July 1 1895
Average weekly hours of labor
Number of days closed
Percent wages advanced since July 1894
Percent wages restored since July 1894
Percent wages reduced since July 1894

Sources: 1894 survey: Connecticut Bureau of Labor Statistics, *Tenth Annual Report for the Year Ending November 30, 1894*. Meriden, CT, 1894. 1895 survey: Connecticut Bureau of Labor Statistics, *Eleventh Annual Report for the Year Ending November 30, 1895*. Meriden, CT, 1895.

The methods used to calculate the values in our tables from the original returns are self-explanatory. It is worth noting a particular advantage of the Connecticut data: the explicit description of the variables and the provision of three different measures of labor input completely eliminate any ambiguity regarding the possible double-counting of labor inputs. The possibility of double-counting was raised by Steven Allen (1992: 127) in his discussion of Albert Rees' (1961) nominal average wage series for the period. In historical data, the reduction in total labor input during a downturn is typically computed from evidence on the reduction in days in operation and the reduction in employment. Allen noted that if employment were reported as zero when the plant was closed, then the standard technique for computing total labor input would overstate the reduction since the same reduction (in days in operation) would, in effect, be counted twice. The detail of the Connecticut data make it possible to state without ambiguity that the measure of total labor input involves no double counting. The Connecticut BLS survey provided an explicit measure of the overall reduction in labor inputs, 'percent hours worked of full time.' This variable is explicitly defined as the reduction in *total* labor input, whether achieved through a reduction in hours worked per worker or through a reduction in the number of workers. To clarify their use of the term 'percent hours worked of full time,' the Connecticut BLS offered an extended discussion of its statistics of a firm in the brass industry:

> This establishment employed in 1892 an average of 200 people, who worked fifty-nine and one-half hours weekly, or ten hours daily on five days of the week and nine and one-half hours on Saturday. If that number of people had worked full time in June, 1893, each of them would have worked 258 hours, and the total of hours worked would be 200 times 258 hours, or 51,600 hours. During that month 195 people were employed at fifty-nine and one-half hours weekly, so that the hours worked were 50,310, and the percent. hours worked of full time for that establishment in June, 1893, was

97.50. This calculation was made for each month for each establishment. (Connecticut Bureau of Labor Statistics 1894: 183)

Some corroborative evidence that also argues against the double-counting hypothesis is presented in Table 5.2 of our text. Here we display the decline in total labor input as measured by 'percent hours worked of full-time' and compare it with the value of two components of total hours reduction: employment reduction and days per worker (computed from 'percent number idle days of working days'). The value of total labor input reduction obtained from the components is *slightly less* than the value of total labor input directly measured (the residual is the reduction in hours per day). If the employment and days per worker measures duplicated one another, their combined effect would have been greater than the explicit measure of total labor input.

NOTES

1. See Carter *et al.* (1991) for a description of these state labor bureaus data and the circumstances that led to their collection.
2. Some summary statistics computed from these data were presented in Carter and Sutch (1990).
3. Connecticut Bureau of Labor Statistics (1894 and 1895). There are several other state surveys that also deal with the impact of the depression of 1893–4. The most detailed are Maine Bureau of Industrial and Labor Statistics (1895), New Jersey Bureau of Statistics of Labor and Industries (1894 and 1895), and New York Bureau of Statistics of Labor (1894). See John A. James' (Chapter 8 in this volume) for an analysis of the New Jersey data.
4. Connecticut Bureau of Labor Statistics (1894: 168). The average firm in the sample employed 195 workers, over nine times the state-wide average.
5. The real value of industrial production by month is from Miron and Romer (1990). Price deflators are from US Bureau of the Census (1975, Series B62).
6. The reluctance of US employers in the post-World War II economy to reduce labor inputs by shortening the work week is sometimes attributed to certain institutional features of the US unemployment benefits system. For a discussion of the asymmetry of the treatment of unemployment and idle days in the US unemployment benefits system, which is different in this regard than that of Europe, see Becker (1972) and Burdett and Wright (1989). Also see Feldstein (1976). For empirical work on the impact of unemployment insurance on the hours–employment tradeoff see Topel (1983) and FitzRoy and Hart (1985). The role of collective bargaining in establishing rules that favor employment reductions rather than hours reductions is noted by Feldstein (1976: 938) and discussed at length by Medoff (1979).
7. US Bureau of Labor Statistics (1982: Tables A-18 and A-19, 386–9). We have derived the number of idle days from the BLS data on the average number of hours for workers on part-time schedules for economic reasons who usually work full time. 'Economic reasons' seem to be reasonably close to the concept we have called industrial suspensions; however, they are more inclusive. Officially, economic reasons include shortage of raw materials, slack work, and repairs to plant and equipment – all of which coincide with our notion of suspension of operations – and start or termination of a job during the week and inability to find full-time employment – which do not. The BLS also estimates the number of individuals forced to work part time (that is, less than 35 hours) for economic reasons. To calculate idle days, we follow the BLS procedure and assume that persons working part-time only because full-time work

was not available would have worked 37.5 hours per week had there been no idle days. See US Bureau of Labor Statistics (1982: 782–3).

8. The average hours worked per week comes from Rees (1960: Table 8; and 1961: Table 10) for 1890–1919; Jones (1963: Table 1) for 1919–41; and the US Bureau of Labor Statistics (1985: 58) for 1942–1987. When interpreting the chart, it is helpful to know that the Fair Labor Standards Act of 1938 established the 40-hour week (effective in late 1940 following a transitional 44-hour week in 1939 and a 42-hour week in 1940) with premium pay required for overtime. The act was suspended early in 1943 for the duration of World War II. Beginning early in 1943 a 48-hour week *minimum* was established (Wood, 1944: 845, 849–51). For general discussions of the decline in the American work week see Hunnicutt (1988), Owen (1989), Roediger and Foner (1989), and Whaples (1990).

9. The standard full-time work week was six days long; Connecticut Bureau of Labor Statistics (1894: 307–8).

10. The results of OLS regression analysis are consistent with this conclusion. Let the dependent variable be the detrended series on industrial suspensions shown in Table 5.2. Let the independent variable be the Miron–Romer industrial production index (Miron and Romer, 1990), detrended. The results of OLS regression (standard errors in parentheses) are:

$$\text{Industrial suspensions} = 1.395 - (0.209 * \text{Production index}) \qquad R^2 = 0.1125$$
$$(1.2665)\ (0.111)$$

11. The regression is:

$$\text{Days idle} = 35.195 - (0.277 * \text{Production index}) \qquad R^2 = 0.174$$
$$(2.54)\quad (0.031)$$

12. The Bureau of Labor Statistics does calculate a measure of labor time lost based on the Current Population Survey. This data is available covering the period since 1955. Labor time lost is expressed as a percentage of potentially available aggregate hours. Potential hours are calculated by assuming (a) that employed persons who worked more than 35 hours during the survey week were working 'full-time,' (b) that unemployed members of the labor force looking for 'full-time' jobs and persons working part-time only because full-time work was not available would have worked 37.5 hours per week were they full time, and (c) that unemployed persons looking for part-time work would have worked the same number of hours that voluntary part-time workers reported during the survey week.

13. The prevalence of plant suspensions in the prewar era also explains the otherwise puzzling fact that unemployment measures based on payroll statistics are considerably lower than those based on self-reported 'days lost' in worker surveys or 'months unemployed' in the US Censuses. The payroll employment measure refers to the number of names on payrolls when manufacturing firms were in operation and thus excludes time lost due to suspensions (US Census Office, 1895: 14).

14. Lebergott (1964: 356, 403–8). Also see Lebergott (1957). For a history of the development of labor force statistics, see President's Committee to Appraise Employment and Unemployment Statistics (1962) and Durand (1957).

15. For an effort to gauge the magnitude of these effects for the period 1890 through 1905, see Carter and Sutch (1992).

16. Layer (1955: 29) also reports an increase in output per worker during nineteenth-century depressions in the cotton textile firms he studied.

17. Atack and Bateman (1989) identified the presence of a fatigue effect from working a long day using data drawn from the manufacturing census of 1880. These findings were not included in the published version of the paper, however (Atack and Bateman, 1992).

18. While this seems plausible, we know of no statistical work on fatigue and productivity change induced by changes in the length of the work week. The Connecticut Bureau of Labor Statistics, however, in the same volume that reported the results of the 1894 survey on the effects of the industrial depression, printed a long article on the 'Effect of Reduced Working Time on Production.' Much of the article was given to a discussion of the productivity-

enhancing effects of a reduction in the number of hours per day and a series of experiments with an eight-hour day conducted in England. In addition it contained a discussion of the experience of about 100 Connecticut manufactures with the practice of closing at noon on Saturdays, particularly in the summer months. A half-day off may not have the same qualitative impact on productivity as an idle day. The results are, however, at least, suggestive. 'It was found, upon inquiry,' stated the report speaking of firms that had introduced the half Saturday, that:

> In many establishments there had been no reduction in production, and in others the reduction in product was not commensurate with the reduction in working time. There was also noted, in several establishments, a saving in incidental expense and an economy in the operation, caused by the lessening of irregular absenteeism. (Connecticut Bureau of Labor Statistics, 1894: 308)

In short, productivity increased.

19. Interestingly, when Akerlof and Yellen explored the consequences of their fair wage-effort model in a system with two labor groups, both of which behave according to the hypothesis, they found that unemployment will fall on the group with the lower wage: the less skilled (see Akerlof and Yellen, 1990: 269, 272–6).

20. Further testimony in support of this view can be found in an investigation of the depression conducted by the Maine Bureau of Industrial and Labor Statistics:

> A furniture manufacturer in Maine explained his view in the midst of the depression of 1893–94:
> Last year, at this time, we had orders for about 14,000 chairs at good prices, and now we have only about 3,000 chairs ordered on which there is really no profit, even when running at reduced wages. Our only object in running today is to keep our best help together, hoping sometime to be able to get more profitable work to do. (Maine Bureau of Industrial and Labor Statistics, 1894 (published 1895): 39)

21. As described, this mechanism requires that individual productivity be observed by the employer. We might still observe the extra-effort effect even if this were not so, but in that case the workers would put forth the extra effort collectively (perhaps monitored by each other, if that were possible) to assist the firm's survival in the face of a decline in demand.

22. Suspensions of operations might in some circumstances induce the extra-effort effect. If suspensions lead to employment cuts, as we suggest above, then the imposition of idle days might send a signal to workers that layoffs were coming. This might intensify the 'competition of the men among themselves' referred to by Wright, thereby forcing up 'the speed of all.'

23. The coefficients on hours per day and days in operation are not significantly different. The F-test that they are equal ($F(1,273) = 0.26$) cannot be rejected.

24. The productivity-enhancing effects of shorter hours were well known at the time. See the review of this literature in Atack and Bateman (1991). Moreover, workers put shorter hours at the top of their list of labor demands. Just why employers insisted on these seemingly longer-than-optimal hours is one of the great unresolved questions in the economic history of the late nineteenth and early twentieth centuries. See Shiells (1987), Hunnicutt (1988), Owen (1989), Roediger and Foner (1989), and Whaples (1990).

25. Weir (1986) has also noted that the correctness of Romer's revision of Lebergott depends on her assumption that labor productivity has always been procyclical. Weir questions this assumption. He reports that the 'elasticity of (manufacturing) employment on output was not significantly different from one over the period 1890–1909' (361–4).

26. In the *General Theory* Keynes predicted countercyclical real wages. Most studies using post-World War II data do not find this pattern. See Bodkin (1969); Keane *et al.* (1988); and Solon *et al.* (1994). It is interesting that data from the earlier period are consistent with Keynes' prediction.

27. The average hourly wage series developed by Rees (1961) also rises between 1892 and 1893 and is out of phase in the 1890s and, indeed, throughout most of the period before the Great

Depression. The only major exception is the World War I boom (1914–18) when nominal average hourly earnings grew 32.4 per cent. O'Brien (1985) drew attention to the fact that Sachs' conclusions regarding increasing wage stickiness over time depend crucially upon his dating the peaks and troughs of business cycles with reference to the price and wage rather than output series (Sachs, 1980: 80). For the post-World War II period the price, wage and output series are nearly perfectly in phase (Bemanke and Powell, 1986). But in the pre-World War I period, dating cycles by the peak of prices and wages means calling 1893 a peak. According to Miron and Romer (1990: 336), industrial production in 1893 was down 13.8 per cent from the previous year. Allen (1990) noted that Sachs' conclusions regarding the flexibility of pre-World War II wages are extremely sensitive to the inclusion of data from the World War I period.

28. Other investigators have reported similar findings. Only 22 per cent of workers in the Ohio sample analyzed by Sundstrom (1990) experienced wage rate cuts during the depression of 1893–4. One possible explanation for the smaller extent of wage rate cutting in Sundstrom's sample may be that his data was collected in the year 1893 only. An investigation in New Jersey during the 1893 depression shows that wage rate cutting did not begin until rather late in the downturn. Of firms that cut wage rates at some point in the 12-month period June 1893 through May 1894, only 60 per cent had instituted their cuts by December 1893 (New Jersey Bureau of Statistics of Labor and Industries, 1894: 8). For additional statistical evidence of sticky wages in the nineteenth century, see DeCanio and Mokyr (1977), Goldin and Margo (1989), Hanes (1992), and Sundstrom (1992).

29. Our evidence that late nineteenth-century wages were sticky is consistent with the views of contemporaries. The great supply-and-demand economist, Alfred Marshall, made this observation about wages in England, but that should not make his observation irrelevant:

> The basis of the notion that there should be given 'a fair day's wage for a fair day's work' is that every man who is up to the usual standard of efficiency of his trade in his own neighborhood, and exerts himself honestly, ought to be paid for his work at the usual rate for his trade and neighborhood; so that he may be able to live in that way to which he and his neighbors in his rank of life have been accustomed. And further, the popular notion of fairness demands that he should be paid this rate ungrudgingly. (Quoted in Solow, 1990: 16–17)

Similar observations were made of the American economy. Wright concluded his study of the Aldrich reports as follows:

> Whenever prices of commodities rise, they rise higher, relatively, than does the price of labor, and … when prices go down they go down much lower, relatively, than does the price of labor, which remains ordinarily very nearly at its inflated price. (Wright, 1893: 228)

Mitchell (1908) felt that nominal wages were rigid because of the prevalence of paying 'conventional sums.' DeCanio and Mokyr (1977: 327) support Mitchell's conclusion with modern econometric analysis. Wright (1988) has called attention to the stickiness of nineteenth-century American wages as well.

30. For numerous, detailed descriptions of firms' hesitancy at cutting wage rates, see Connecticut Bureau of Labor Statistics (1895: 202, 205–6 and 208–9).

31. We assume that all other values in the probit equation are at their mean sample values.

32. One way to make sense of these results is to suggest that there were two types of firms. First, there might be firms that subscribed to nineteenth-century notions of fairness. In the face of an output decline they tried to hold wages constant and minimize the reduction in employment. These firms were also more likely to be small and pay higher-than-average wages. Second, there could have been firms with a more capitalistic orientation that responded to the decline in business, not with fairness, but with self-protective strategies that pushed as much of the cost of the depression on to the workers as possible. These firms cut wages and reduced both employment and the number of days in operation. Such firms were more likely to be large. The first type of firms got the benefit of bigger productivity increases, as Akerlof and Yellen

(1990) suggest. The second type did not. Ironically, the first type of firm was hit harder by the depression of 1893–4 than the second. This might help explain why the concepts of fairness influencing labor markets in the 1890 were eroded away. Firms that could institute more impersonal, 'scientific' methods of personnel management were better able to survive industrial depressions and to prosper.

33. We constructed this wage rate index by setting the value of wage change in firms with no wage rate change equal to 100; in firms which issued general wage cuts of 10 per cent at 90; in firms which issued wage cuts of 10 per cent to half of all workers at 95, and so on. The average of this index across firms is 94.7.

34. Connecticut Bureau of Labour Statistics (1894, 1895).

6. Phillips curves under the gold standard regime: Canada and the United States compared

Trevor J.O. Dick[*]

INTRODUCTION

Canadian economic growth has been accompanied by macroeconomic fluctuations commonly patterned on the fluctuations of her two principal trading partners, Great Britain and the United States, and more closely on the latter than the former (Chambers, 1964; Hay, 1966, 1967). Economic historians have portrayed the pre-1914 period as distinctive. In this gold standard era, it is alleged that prices fluctuated less violently, expectations were relatively static, and the Fisher equation underlying the Gibson paradox broke down (Floyd, 1985; Sargent, 1973).[1] Canada, in common with her trading partners after 1879, remained committed to the gold standard while international capital mobility had major implications for how the balance of payments adjusted to the capital inflow attracted by Canadian opportunities, an important shock to the small open-economy equilibrium (Dick and Floyd, 1991, 1992). In this chapter we ask whether price and output behavior in Canada and the United States had distinguishing characteristics before 1914 and what implications these may have for the understanding of business cycle activity. It is particularly appropriate to re-examine these questions using recently revised macroeconomic time series data available for both countries, and to assess how sensitive the answers are to data reconstruction.

The Canadian story of price and output adjustment in the short run over the 1870–1914 period is of particular interest, not only for comparison with later periods and with the experience of other countries over the same period, but also

[*] The author acknowledges the helpful comments of Charles Calomiris, Michael Edelstein, Barry Eichengreen, John Floyd, Joseph Haubrich, John James, Robert Lucas, Marvin McInnis, Angela Redish, Richard Sutch, Mac Urquhart, Gavin Wright, Timothy Hatton and participants at the 17th Conference on the Use of Quantitative Methods in Canadian Economic History, the Stanford Social Science History Seminar, the University of California at Berkeley Economic History Seminar and the Eleventh International Economic History Congress.

for whether or not the adjustment process in Canada underwent any changes over the gold standard years. Economic historians have long regarded the mid-1890s as an important turning point in Canada's economic growth process (Urquhart, 1986; Inwood and Stengos, 1991). Was there also a change in the short-run adjustment process? While some historians have emphasized institutional persistence, others point to evidence of changes in the structure and operation of markets (Easterbrook and Aitken, 1956; Scott, 1958; Shearer *et al.*, 1984). While Canada became progressively more integrated into world markets for goods and assets, many activities, including banking, became more highly concentrated thereby reducing competition. While Canada and the United States shared contemporaneously in some of these changes, fundamental structural changes associated with industrialization occurred earlier in the United States (Lithwick, 1970). Canada also received massive net capital inflow after 1900 while the United States showed little dependence on foreign capital after 1870. In addition, the years before the 1890s were years of generally falling prices while the later years were generally inflationary. Were short-run fluctuations influenced by the pattern of these longer-term changes?

To begin the investigation of these issues it is useful to look for simple regularities and patterns in the aggregate data with the aid of some simple macroeconomic frameworks. In this chapter we examine annual data on price levels and output for Canada and the United States before 1914. The basic framework is neo-Keynesian and allows us to test for the presence of gradual price adjustment to nominal demand shocks (Gordon, 1982a, 1990b). In this modern Phillips curve analysis, inflation has three determinants: demand, supply, and inertia. Such a framework, of course, does not identify the specific microeconomic components of price and quantity interaction that undoubtedly helped to determine the macroeconomic outcomes. It is merely a first step in charting the landscape and pointing to features of that landscape that need to be explored in further work.

The next section of the chapter provides a brief theoretical overview of the macroeconomic framework used. The third and fourth sections discuss the data and present the empirical results. A final section interprets these results and suggests areas for possible further work.

OUTPUT FLUCTUATIONS AND PRICE ADJUSTMENT

While the Phillips curve was originally developed as an association between the change in nominal wage rates and the level of unemployment, it has become common to use the Phillips-curve terminology to label any relation between the rate of change of nominal prices or wages and the level of a utilization variable like the unemployment rate or detrended output (Phillips, 1958; Gordon, 1990b: 1122).

The critical issue we wish to investigate is *how quickly short-run changes in nominal demand are reflected in price level changes.* In the long run there is widespread agreement that changes in nominal demand, that is, changes in monetary growth, are reflected in the rate of inflation (Schwartz, 1987). In the shorter run, it is extreme to argue that fully anticipated changes in nominal aggregate demand can have no effect on output, but only on prices (Lucas, 1973). If prices adjust more gradually in the short run, even anticipated changes in nominal demand will be temporarily absorbed partly in an altered inflation rate and partly in some departure of real output from its long-run equilibrium level. Such short-run behavior might be the result of adjustment costs, of long-term contracts, or of imperfect competition or decision-making.

The framework chosen to begin the investigation of such issues at a macro level, therefore, must accommodate a variable speed of adjustment of prices to nominal demand shocks. For this reason, we put aside the more restrictive models that take output as a choice variable and imply instantaneous adjustment (Blanchard and Fischer, 1989: ch. 7; Lucas, 1973). A useful alternative is provided by neo-Keynesians who focus on price stickiness as a consequence of imperfectly competitive behavior (Blanchard and Fischer, 1989; ch. 8; Ball *et al.*, 1988). In this framework, price rather than quantity becomes the choice variable. This approach to exploring price–quantity interaction at the macro level has already begun to be applied to historical contexts including the United States, but not yet Canada, with interesting comparative results.[2] The present study may be viewed as an extension of this approach emphasizing the pre-1914 period and drawing Canadian experience into the comparisons. The essential feature of this approach is to show how nominal demand shocks are absorbed in the short run partly by prices and partly by output, while in the longer run they are absorbed entirely by price change.

To fix ideas, we consider some fundamental identities (Gordon, 1981), and add to these the hypothesis of variable speeds of price accommodation to nominal demand shocks (Gordon, 1982a):

$$Y \equiv P + Q \qquad (6.1)$$

where Y, P and Q (upper case) are the log of nominal income, the price level and real GNP respectively. Taking derivatives (lower case) with respect to time, that is, percentage rates of change:

$$y \equiv p + q$$

$$p \equiv y - q \qquad (6.2)$$

The change in nominal income is divided between a change in the price level and a change in real output. Subtracting the 'natural' or trend rate of real output growth (q^*) from either side of (6.2) leaves:

$$y - q^* \equiv p + (q - q^*)$$

$$\hat{y} \equiv p + \hat{q}$$

$$p \equiv \hat{y} - \hat{q}$$

$$p_t \equiv \hat{y} - (\hat{Q}_t - \hat{Q}_{t-1}) \tag{6.3}$$

where $\hat{y}$ and $\hat{q}$ indicate y and q net of trend. Hence any change in $\hat{y}$ (excess nominal income growth) must be some combination of inflation (p_t) and a deviation of real output growth from trend $(\hat{q}_t)$. This deviation is defined as the change in the log 'output ratio,' $\hat{q}_t \equiv (\hat{Q}_t - \hat{Q}_{t-1})$, where $\hat{Q}_t = Q_t - Q_t^*$ (real output gap), and Q_t^* is the log of 'natural' output. Hence, if $\hat{y} = p$, then $\hat{q} = 0$, and there is no price inertia. To allow for price inertia requires the introduction of an adjustment parameter (α):

$$p = \alpha \hat{y}$$

$$\hat{q} = \hat{y} - p$$

$$= \hat{y} - \alpha \hat{y}$$

$$= (1 - \alpha)\,\hat{y} \tag{6.4}$$

Then for α between 0 and 1, any $\hat{y}$ will be partly absorbed in p and partly in $\hat{q}$, some deviation of q from trend. Only if $\alpha = 1$ does an expected change in Y go fully into p and leave no effect on q. The Lucas (1973) proposition, therefore, amounts to $\alpha = 1$.

Following Gordon (1982a) and James (1989), (6.4) can be elaborated by specifying price change (p) to deviate less than instantaneously from past p in response to both demand and supply shocks. Demand is felt by the level of and change in the output ratio, and supply by the rate of change of agricultural prices relative to all prices. North American economies were predominantly agricultural and vulnerable to external market conditions. The influence of past prices is captured by a distributed lag $a(L)$.

$$p_t = a(L)p_{t-1} + b_0\hat{Q}_t + b_1\Delta\hat{Q}_t + b_2 z_t + e_t \tag{6.5}$$

where Δ is the change in a variable and e_t are serially independent with mean 0. Rewriting (6.5), making use of (6.3), and breaking $\hat{y}_t$ into its expected $(E\hat{y}_t)$ and unexpected (Uy_t) components, yields the price equation, an augmented Phillips curve:

$$p_t = c(L)p_{t-1} + d_0 E\hat{y}_t + d_1 Uy_t + d_2 \hat{Q}_{t-1} + d_3 z_t + u_t \qquad (6.6)$$

Under instantaneous price adjustment, $d_0 = 1$. Also, d_1 is less than 1 whether or not there is instantaneous price adjustment. Equation (6.6) is also consistent with long-run neutrality of money. Now taking (6.3) and the right-hand side of (6.6) to eliminate p_t yields the output equation, the dual of the Phillips curve:

$$\hat{Q}_t = -c(L)p_{t-1} + (1-d_0)E\hat{y}_t + (1-d_1)Uy_t + (1-d_2)\hat{Q}_{t-1} - d_3 z_t - u_t \quad (6.7)$$

Under instantaneous price adjustment, $1-d_0 = 0$ and the coefficients associated with $-c(L)$ are also zero.[3] The Lucas equations, therefore, can be nested within (6.6) and (6.7):

$$p_t = E\hat{y}_t + d_1 Uy_t + d_2 \hat{Q}_{t-1} + d_3 z_t + v_t \qquad (6.6')$$

$$\hat{Q}_t = (1-d_1)Uy_t + (1-d_2)\hat{Q}_{t-1} - d_3 z_t - \xi_t \qquad (6.7')$$

Our econometric strategy is to implement equations (6.6) and (6.7) to determine whether their estimated coefficients are more consistent with gradual or instantaneous price adjustment.[4] To do this requires the decomposition of nominal demand change into expected and unexpected components. First, net potential GNP is obtained as the fitted values from a regression of real GNP on time trend.[5] The real output gap is then the difference between real GNP and these fitted values. The change in nominal demand must be estimated using the real output gap as one of the right-hand side variables (see equation (6.14) below). The residuals and fitted values from this estimation proxy the unexpected (Uy_t) and expected $(E\hat{y}_t)$ changes in nominal demand respectively to be used in estimating equations (6.6) and (6.7).[6]

To reveal the Phillips curve still more directly as a relationship between changes in prices and the level of demand, the more traditional formulation, we explicitly model all three dimensions of price stickiness: (a) price inertia, (b) rate of change effects, and (c) level effects (Gordon, 1990b). The Phillips curve relation based on level effects (γ) may be written:

$$p_t = \gamma \hat{Q}_t + z_t \qquad (6.8)$$

This says simply that the rate of price change depends on the level of the output ratio $\hat{Q}$ and a supply shock. Adding the idea of price inertia (λ) gives:

$$p_t = \lambda p_{t-1} + \gamma \hat{Q}_t + z_t \tag{6.9}$$

where λ is the coefficient on price lagged one period. Finally, adding $\hat{y}$ from (6.4) for rate of change effects (α) gives:

$$p_t = \lambda p_{t-1} + \alpha \hat{y}_t + \gamma \hat{Q}_t + z_t \tag{6.10}$$

As Gordon (1982a, 1990b) has shown, moving from (6.8) to (6.10) is not an *ad hoc* matter but follows from the theory embedded in equations (6.4) to (6.5) used to arrive at equations (6.6) and (6.7). Equation (6.10) is the fundamental structural equation of the theoretical development of the present chapter; it is not an identity, but differs from equation (6.3) by the inclusion of p_{t-1} and the exclusion of $\hat{Q}_{t-1}$ (Gordon, 1990b: 1163–4). To investigate the Phillips curve, therefore, we need a γ that gives simultaneous recognition to λ and α. All three are in fact recognized by (6.6) and (6.7): λ is recognized by $c(L)$, α implicitly by d_0 and d_1, and γ by b_0, and implicitly by b_1 and d_2.[7] Stickiness is implied by high λ and low α and γ. $\alpha = 0$ implies a Phillips curve world with a level effect and no hysteresis; $\gamma = 0$ implies hysteresis with no level effect and no Phillips curve. If there were no business cycle and if prices quickly mimicked nominal demand changes, we would find $\alpha = 1$ (no rate of change effect) and $\lambda = \gamma = 0$ (no inertia or Phillips curve level effect).

For econometric purposes, the identity (6.3) may be used with the adjustment theory in (6.10) to yield:

$$p_t = (1/(1 + \gamma))(\lambda p_{t-1} + (\alpha + \gamma)\hat{y}_t + \gamma \hat{Q}_{t-1} + z_t) \tag{6.11}$$

Equation (6.11) makes $\hat{Q}_t$ a residual given the structure embodied in (6.11) to determine p_t. Estimating (6.11), however, encounters a significant problem due to the endogeneity of $\hat{y}$. We follow Gordon (1990b), who attempts a solution by bracketing the α parameter with estimates obtained first from using (6.11), and second from using (6.12) obtained below from (6.10) and (6.3) to eliminate $\hat{y}$ rather than $\hat{q}$:[8]

$$p_t = (1/(1 - \alpha))(\lambda p_{t-1} + (\alpha + \gamma)\hat{q}_t + \gamma \hat{Q}_{t-1} + z_t) \tag{6.12}$$

From (6.11) and (6.12) estimates of λ, α, and γ can be readily recovered and the relative importance of the three elements of price stickiness assessed.

THE DATA

This study uses annual data for both Canada and the United States over the period 1871–1913.[9] The principal series are for nominal output and the price level and have recently been revised for both countries.

The original output series for Canada are due to O.J. Firestone and his precursors (Firestone, 1958, 1969). These data are based on the value-added technique of reconstruction applied to census benchmarks interpolated with a wide variety of other annual time series. Uncertainties about the details of construction of many of these series make it difficult to evaluate their usefulness as indicators of output variability.

The revised series are due to Urquhart (1986), and also rest on the interpolation of census-based value-added data. Although these estimates are more reliable than earlier estimates and differ significantly from Firestone's estimates (Green and Urquhart, 1987), they do make extensive use of commodity output interpolators that possibly affect the volatility and behavior of the estimates over the business cycle.[10] To the extent that reliance on commodity data for interpolation may be disproportionate, these data are subject to the same exaggerated volatility bias recently uncovered in the Kuznets data for the United States (Romer, 1988, 1989; Balke and Gordon, 1989). While the most important interpolators appear to be commodity based (Urquhart, 1986: 69–70, 74–5), lack of inventory data imparts a partially offsetting bias.[11]

The standard real output series for the United States are due to Kuznets (1961) and Gallman (1966) as modified by Friedman and Schwartz (1982). These data suffer from the same shortage of inventory data as the Canadian data. To some extent the bias toward understatement of volatility due to incomplete inventory data is offset by the disproportionate use of commodity-based data as interpolators between census benchmarks. Romer (1988, 1989) corrects for the latter deficiency by allowing changes in economic structure over time to influence the extent of reliance on commodity output series for interpolation. While Romer relies on regression relationships between commodity output and GNP to revise the older estimates, Balke and Gordon (1989) go further in this direction by decomposing construction, transportation and communications output into commodity and non-commodity components to modify the older interpolation procedures that gave an upward bias to volatility.[12]

Several different Canadian price series are available, both wholesale indexes and GNP deflators. Wholesale price series are more volatile than retail and their coverage is frequently limited to traded goods, only one component of the output typically incorporated in nominal GNP measures. Some categories of output, particularly investment goods like housing, and services like transportation, trade and finance, are not usually included. A further problem is that Toronto and Montreal prices are typically overrepresented in available wholesale price series. Western wholesale markets appear to have started before 1900 (Careless, 1970; Kerr, 1977; McCann, 1978). The official wholesale price index due to the Dominion Bureau of Statistics probably exaggerates the relevant price variability.[13]

Firestone (1958, 1969) was the first to construct an implicit price deflator as the result of separately deflating the main components of his nominal GNP estimates and recombining them to obtain a constant dollar series. His index is the quotient of current divided by constant dollar aggregate GNP. While this index, in principle, meets the requirements of our study, it is not known exactly what series Firestone used for sectoral deflators.

Urquhart (1986) constructs a GNP deflator as the combination of a cost-of-living index for household expenditure and other price series prepared by Statistics Canada to apply to capital formation. Largely retail price movement is measured by the cost-of-living index and is derived from a splicing together of Kingston retail prices of food, fuel, light and an average all-Canada rent index for all of the years before 1900, and a revised Department of Labour index of retail prices for all Canada for the post-1900 years, interpolating a few gaps early in the twentieth century with wholesale price movement (Urquhart, 1986: app. 5). This cost-of-living index is then combined with historical capital stock price indexes. While the retail price coverage might be improved, the movement of the deflator overall may be quite well suited for the task at hand.

Altman (1992a) approaches the construction of a GNP deflator by relying on the wholesale price movement of components of value added on the production side of the accounts. To the extent that wholesale and retail price movements differ, as is widely acknowledged (David and Solar, 1977), the Altman index differs in concept from that used by Urquhart, and differs in actual calculation quite substantially in the 1870s (Altman, 1992a: 460). While the Altman index offers another view of price movement, it draws attention to an unconventional measure by failing to recognize that value added is a conceptually equivalent proxy for expenditure for which Urquhart adopts a conventional measure of price change (Urquhart, 1994).

All of the United States output estimates have accompanying implicit price deflators constructed from taking the ratio of current to constant dollar aggregate output where the latter is the sum of the appropriately deflated nominal output components. We use the Friedman and Schwartz (1982) implicit price deflator, which is a minor revision of the Gallman–Kuznets series in line with the revision of output data produced by Friedman and Schwartz. Both Romer (1989) and Balke and Gordon (1989) develop implicit price deflators that are in principle faithful to the revised output measures they construct. While Romer reworks the data used to deflate earlier output estimates, Balke and Gordon (1989) go further to incorporate consumer retail price series prepared by Hoover

(1960) and Rees (1961) not previously used in the context of real output estimation.

Since much of the motivation for data revision has been to improve the understanding of business cycle behavior from the point of view of how data reconstruction affects volatility, it is important to understand how volatility is related to the task at hand in the present chapter. Although it is of some interest to note the extent of volatility in the various available measures of output and the price level, *volatility alone implies little about the speed of price level adjustment* analyzed in the previous section. The significance of price flexibility to this adjustment can only be understood in the context of a suitable macroeconomic framework. There are two main volatility issues: (a) how should volatility be measured and what changes in volatility may have occurred across historical time? and (b) do changes in volatility have any direct implications for the shape of the Phillips curve?

On the first issue, volatility is typically measured by some definition of the variance, and is often found to change with the passage of time and with the way in which the series are constructed. In the case of output gap, volatility is further dependent on the method of detrending. In addition, the observation of variability may differ depending on the level of aggregation. Aggregate data tends to 'wash away' individual non-linearities (Stoker, 1986: 780). Micro data, therefore, may present a different picture, particularly when representative agent theory is applied to macro data in isolation.

On the second issue, it is often casually assumed that less variability or volatility means more price stickiness, when in fact the two are separate phenomena. Macro views have commonly concluded, especially in the case of the United States, that there has been increasing price rigidity with the passage of time, suggesting to some that the Phillips curve has flattened with time (Sachs, 1980; Taylor, 1986). Micro views, on the other hand, have indicated otherwise with evidence of early price and wage stickiness (Sundstrom, 1990, 1992; Carter and Sutch, 1991). The suggestion that rigidity was an early phenomenon implies only that spells of unemployment were likely to have occurred, and not that the economy experienced more volatility. In fact, Romer (1986, 1989, 1991) and Balke and Gordon (1989) have shown that volatility in these same times may have been exaggerated. It is not entirely clear, moreover, that price stickiness always translates into poorer macro performance meaning a flatter Phillips curve (Akerlof and Yellen, 1985; Blanchard and Fischer, 1989: ch. 8; Hahn and Solow, 1986). The primary issue in the present study is whether price change mimics excess nominal income growth, and not why prices are sticky or volatile (Gordon, 1981: 496). From a Keynesian perspective, it would seem possible to proceed as Sims has suggested without an elaborate rationalization of nominal rigidities (in Ball *et al.*, 1988: 75–6).[14]

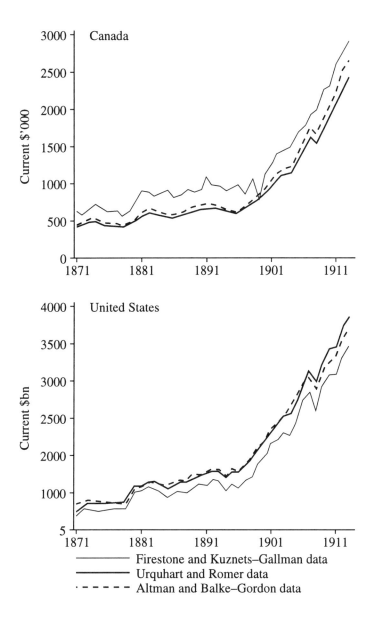

Sources: Canada: Firestone (1958, 1969); Urquhart (1986); Altman (1989). United States: Friedman and Schwartz (1982); Romer (1989); Balke and Gordon (1989).

Figure 6.1 Nominal GNP, 1871–1913

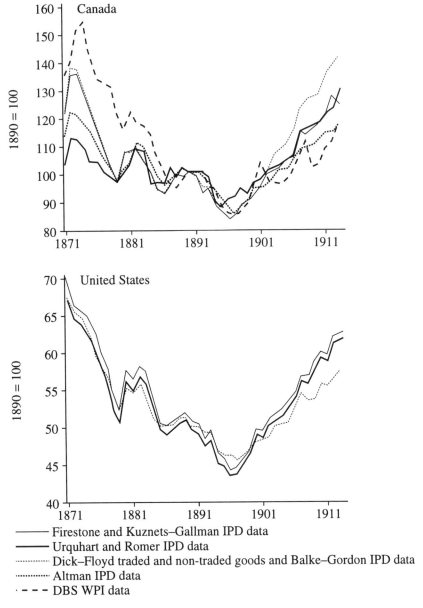

Sources: Canada: Firestone (1958, 1969); Urquhart (1986); Altman (1989); Dick and Floyd (1992); Urquhart and Buckley (1965). United States: Friedman and Schwartz (1982); Romer (1989); Balke and Gordon (1989).

Figure 6.2 Price level movement, 1871–1913

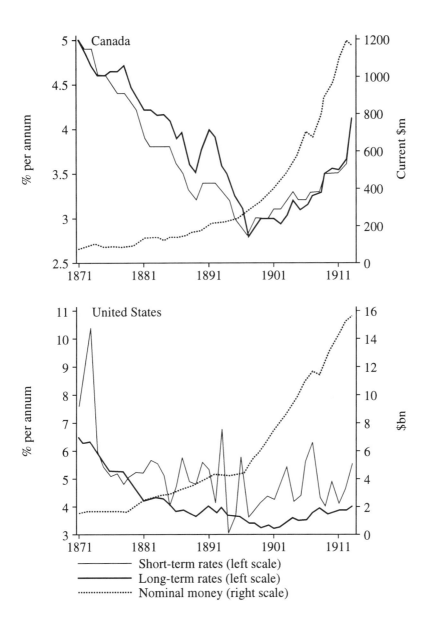

Sources: Canada: Rich (1988); Neufeld (1972). United States: Friedman and Schwartz (1982).

Figure 6.3   Interest rates and money, 1871–1913

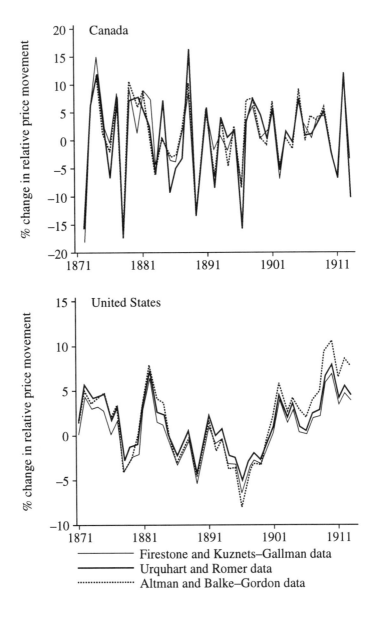

Sources: Canada: Firestone (1958, 1969); Urquhart (1986); Altman (1989). United States: Friedman and Schwartz (1982); Romer (1989); Balke and Gordon (1989).

Figure 6.4   Supply shocks (relative movement of agricultural prices), 1871–1913

Finally, implementing the theory of the previous section requires other suitable predetermined variables for the first stage regressions and, of course, an appropriate proxy for supply-side shocks in this period. For Canada, two alternative interest rate series and one money stock series were tried in the first stage regressions. Rich (1988) provides an implicit yield in London on Dominion, Provincial and municipal bonds, and Neufeld (1972) provides an interest rate on Canada's long-term borrowing. The nominal money stock used is the sum of chartered bank deposits held by the public, Dominion notes held by the public, and chartered banknotes held by the public and by the government computed by Rich (1988) largely from the several components of the money supply reported by Urquhart and Buckley (1965: series H-15, H-19, and H-20). For the United States, we use Friedman and Schwartz's (1982) short-term commercial paper rate and the yield on high-grade corporate bonds plus their money stock that equals currency held by the public plus commercial bank deposits.

Supply shocks in agriculture are considered likely to have been important, given the importance of the agricultural sector in both countries (James, 1989; Gordon, 1982a). Accordingly, a wholesale food price index was chosen from Urquhart and Buckley (1965: series J-165) that is the unweighted average movement of the wholesale prices of 15 foodstuffs, first computed by Michell (1931). Warren and Pearson (1933) provide a similar series for the United States. The shock is measured by the change in the movement of prices in this sector relative to total price movement.

The paths of these data over time are revealed in Figures 6.1–6.4. Nominal GNP rose steadily over the period, showing a somewhat sharper rate of increase after 1900 in both countries (Figure 6.1). The price level generally fell before 1900 and rose thereafter to about the same level by 1914 as in 1870 in both countries (Figure 6.2). Interest rates in Canada and the United States fell before the 1890s and rose moderately thereafter. Both the Canadian and United States money stocks rose steadily and more sharply after 1900 than earlier (Figure 6.3). Supply shocks are notably more severe for Canada than for the United States (Figure 6.4).

STATISTICAL RESULTS AND THEIR INTERPRETATION

The first regressions were run to determine the real output gap.[15] The log of real output was run on a time trend and a dummy variable:

$$Q_t = k_0 + k_1 T + k_2 DT + \varepsilon \qquad (6.13)$$

where T is trend, D is a dummy variable taking the value 1 for 1871–95 and 0 for 1896–1913, and ε is a random error.[16] Trend was statistically significant at the 0.01 level in all cases, and the dummy was significant at the 5 per cent level in most cases, particularly for Canada. Experimenting with the Hodrick–Prescott (1980) technique based on a smoothing parameter of 400 indicated a similar change in trend. Since there are theoretical reasons to believe that the growth component of estimates based on economic time series vary smoothly over time, the Hodrick–Prescott trends (rather than estimates based on equation (6.13)) were adopted to derive output gaps.[17] The real output gap was computed, using the Firestone, Urquhart, and Altman data for Canada and the Friedman and Schwartz (Kuznets–Gallman), Romer, and Balke and Gordon data for the United States, as the difference between the actual and trend values (Figure 6.5). A positive (negative) gap means output was above (below) its natural level. The real output gap (difference between the log of actual and trend) varied between + 0.14 for 1885 and –0.30 for 1899 in Canada and between + 0.11 for 1880 and –0.10 for 1894 in the United States using the Friedman and Schwartz data. As Figure 6.5 reveals, these fluctuations were less extreme using the Romer or Balke and Gordon series, and less extreme in the United States than in Canada.

The next task was to decompose the change in nominal demand into its expected and unexpected components. Using the nominal GNP estimates provided by Firestone, Urquhart, and Altman, first stage regressions were run on identical specifications for changes in nominal income (y) and money (m) that included on the right-hand side two lags of changes in nominal GNP (y_{t-1}, y_{t-2}), and one lag of the money supply (m_{t-1}), interest rate (r_{t-1}), rate of price level change (p_{t-1}), and real output gap ($\hat{Q}_{t-1}$), the supply shock – the relative rate of food price change (z_t), and the dummy D used in (6.13).

$$
\left.\begin{array}{c} y_t \\ m_t \end{array}\right\} = f_0 + f_1 y_{t-1} + f_2 y_{t-2} + f_3 m_{t-1} + f_4 r_{t-1} + f_5 p_{t-1} + f_6 \hat{Q}_{t-1} + f_7 z_t + f_8 D + v
$$

$$(6.14)$$

where v is a random error. These regressions performed reasonably well. Similar results were obtained for the United States using the Friedman and Schwartz, Romer, and Balke and Gordon data sets.

Table 6.1 displays the means and standard deviations of the various rate-of-change variables to emerge from the data and the first-stage regressions.[18] Although the variability of individual series alone do not establish the strength of the price inertia hypothesis, some regularities are worth noting. The Firestone data, for whatever reason, often behave with greater volatility, while the Romer and Balke and Gordon series, as expected, are less volatile than the Friedman and Schwartz version of the Kuznets–Gallman data. There appears to be some fall in the variability of prices and nominal income over time in both Canada

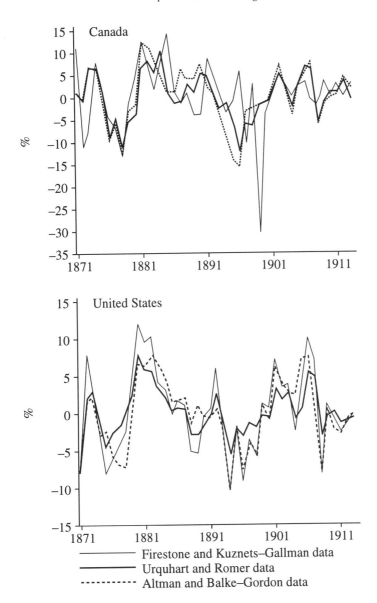

Note: Output ratio = [log (actual output) – log ('natural' output)] × 100%.

Sources: Canada: Firestone (1958, 1969); Urquhart (1986); Altman (1989). United States: Friedman and Schwartz (1982); Romer (1989); Balke and Gordon (1989).

Figure 6.5   Real output gap, 1871–1913

and the United States. Price-level variability after 1895 is only about half what it was in the earlier period. Some, though by no means all, of this drop is reflected in a fall in the variability of nominal income. Money drops somewhat in variability. Nominal income displays about the same level of variability throughout the overall period. The variability of expected nominal income shows some tendency to exceed that of prices but by much less than the variability of nominal income exceeds that of prices.

Table 6.1 Mean and standard deviation of key variables: Canada and the United States, 1874–1913

	$\hat{y}$	$E\hat{y}$	Uy	$\hat{m}$	$E\hat{m}$	Um	p	$\hat{q}$
Canada								
(1) Firestone	2.1						−1.2	−4.8
	(9 3)	(7.5)	(7.2)				(4.9)	(8.4)
(1) Urquhart	1.9			4.8			−0.6	0.3
	(6.6)	(4.1)	(5.4)	(7.7)	(4.5)	(5.4)	(4.4)	(5.2)
(1) Altman	1.8						−0.6	0.7
	(7.5)	(5.5)	(5.0)				(3.9)	(5.8)
(2) Firestone	7.6						2.1	0.2
	(13.0)	(10.0)	(6.7)				(2.6)	(12.1)
(2) Urquhart	8.3			9.4			2.2	0.3
	(5.0)	(3.5)	(3.1)	(5.5)	(3.1)	(5.9)	(2.0)	(4.6)
(2) Altman	8.8						1.5	0.9
	(5.7)	(5.2)	(3.1)				(2.1)	(5.7)
(3) Firestone	4.5						0.2	0.2
	(11.2)	(9.0)	(6.9)				(4 4)	(10.0)
(3) Urquhart	4.7			6.9			0.6	0.7
	(6.7)	(5.2)	(4.4)	(6.9)	(4.4)	(5.6)	(3.8)	(4.9)
(3) Altman	4.8						0.3	0.01
	(7.6)	(6.6)	(3.9)				(3.3)	(5.8)
United States								
(1) Kuznets–Gallman	2.1						−1.5	−0.02
	(7.4)	(4.8)	(6.5)				(3.9)	(5.1)
(1) Romer	2.2			4.9			−1.5	−0.02
	(5.4)	(2.7)	(4.9)	(6.6)	(3.8)	(5.3)	(3.8)	(2.6)
(1) Balke–Gordon	2.2						−1.5	−0.02
	(5.6)	(3.5)	(4.6)				(2.6)	(3.7)
(2) Kuznets–Gallman	6.1						1.8	0.1
	(7.2)	(3.8)	(5.2)				(2.1)	(6.2)

Table 6.1   continued

	$\hat{y}$	$E\hat{y}$	Uy	$\hat{m}$	$E\hat{m}$	Um	p	$\hat{q}$
(2) Romer	5.8			7.4			1.8	0.1
	(4.0)	(2.2)	(3.3)	(4.6)	(2.3)	(4.2)	(2.1)	(2.8)
(2) Balke–Gordon	5.4						1.2	0.1
	(5.0)	(2.9)	(3.9)				(1.7)	(4.7)
(3) Kuznets–Gallman	3.9						–0.04	–0.1
	(7.5)	(4.8)	(6.2)				(3.6)	(5.5)
(3) Romer	3.8			6.0			–0.02	–0.07
	(5.1)	(3.0)	(4.4)	(5.8)	(3.4)	(4.7)	(3.6)	(2.6)
(3) Balke–Gordon	3.7						–0.3	–0.06
	(5.5)	(3.6)	(4.4)				(2.6)	(4.1)

Note: All data pertain to annual percentage rates of change over periods (1) 1874–95, (2) 1896–1913, (3) 1874–1913. See text for variable definitions.

Sources: Canada: Firestone (1958, 1969); Urquhart (1986); Altman (1989). United States: Friedman and Schwartz (1982); Romer (1989); Balke and Gordon (1989).

Chow tests were performed on the subperiods 1874–95 and 1896–1913 for possible regime changes that might facilitate subsequent testing to discriminate between alternative theories and reduce the problem of observational equivalence (Sargent, 1976). Over 1874–1913, on the basis of the most recent GNP estimates, there is little evidence of any regime change for the United States (Table 6.2).[19] For Canada, however, the Urquhart and Altman data do hint at some change around 1895, but there was no important change in the money supply process before 1914. The money supply remained endogenous and was driven by the balance of payments and a commitment to the gold standard throughout the overall period.[20] Putting together the results of Tables 6.1 and 6.2, the evidence is thin for arguing that there was a major regime change in macroeconomic experience around the turn of the century.

The regression results for estimating equations (6.6) and (6.7) are reported in Tables 6.3 and 6.4 respectively for the alternative sets of Canadian and United States data. The coefficients of $E\hat{y}_t$ and Uy_t are positive and statistically significant at the 5 per cent level in 21 out of 24 cases, demonstrating the sensitivity of both the output ratio and the rate of price change to changes in nominal demand. Increases in nominal demand clearly increase output. The reported F-ratios confirm that the Ey_t coefficients differ from zero in the output ratio equation and from unity in the price change equation, consistent with gradual price adjustment. These coefficients are all positive and less than unity. Likewise, the coefficient of the lagged output ratio in the output ratio equation is also less than one and statistically significant at the 5 per cent level. The influence of past inflation rates on the current rate, however, is not typically discernible from these regressions. Lagged inflation rates do not appear to be statistically significant in more than half the cases. Possibly their correlation is so high that their coefficients cannot be distinguished. In any event, it appears that rate of change effects may dominate inertia in explaining price stickiness. A dummy variable was used to break the period at 1895, and was statistically significant at the 5 per cent level in 10 out of 12 cases.

Table 6.2   Chow tests for regime changes: Canada and the United States, 1874–1913

	y	m
Canada		
Firestone	2.67	
Urquhart	1.90	
Altman	3 94	
Rich		1.85
United States		
Kuznets–Gallman	1.10	
Romer	1.19	
Balke–Gordon	1.02	
Friedman–Schwartz		1.09

Notes:
1. Subperiods analysed: 1874–95, 1896–1913.
2. The table numbers are $F(8, 24)$ statistics obtained from estimating equation (6.14).
3. $F(8, 24) = 1.94$ at the 10 per cent significance level.

Sources: Canada: Firestone (1958, 1969); Urquhart (1986); Altman (1989); Rich (1988). United States: Friedman and Schwartz (1982); Romer (1989); Balke and Gordon (1989).

The supply shock proxied by the relative rate of food price change performs somewhat indifferently. Since food includes a major export, one would expect the output gap to rise with relative food price rises (equation (6.7), data sets (2) and (3)). But since food prices dominated traded goods' prices, a fall in these prices relative to all prices could well have been associated with a rise in non-traded goods' prices sufficient to cause a rise in prices overall (equation (6.6), data set (2)). These scenarios are consistent with only half the results that typically seem to demonstrate weak and inconsistent effects from this variable.[21]

Table 6.3 Price level change regressions – equation (6.6): Canada and the United States, 1873–1913

	Canada			United States		
	(1)	(2)	(3)	(4)	(5)	(6)
Constant	0.01	0.001	0.01	−0.05	−0.03	−0.05
	(0.72)	(0.06)	(0.61)	(−4.7)	(−3.3)	(−7.24)
p_{t-1}	−0.10	0.10	−0.07	0.21	0.11	0.24
	(−0.64)	(0.80)	(−0.45)	(1.56)	(1.18)	(2.03)
p_{t-2}	0.08	−0.07	−0.18	0.10	0.03	0.29
	(0.62)	(−0.54)	(−1.29)	(0.75)	(0.33)	(2.65)
$E\hat{y}_t$	0.08	0.15	0.09	0.63	0.42	0.68
	(1.07)	(1.15)	(0.92)	(4.09)	(2.96)	(6.59)
Uy_t	0.40	0.44	0.28	0.63	0.40	0.69
	(3.77)	(4.38)	(2.65)	(9.61)	(5.96)	(12.8)
$\hat{Q}_{t-1}$	0.29	0.21	0.41	0.67	0.61	0.69
	(2.86)	(1.99)	(4.22)	(6.60)	(5.89)	(11.12)
z_t	0.17	−0.15	0.03	−0.05	−0.04	−0.06
	(1.69)	(−2.16)	(0.43)	(0.59)	(−0.81)	(−1.54)
Dummy	−0.02	−0.01	−0.01	0.05	0.03	0.04
	(−1.89)	(−0.44)	(−1.29)	(4.35)	(3.16)	(6.50)
Observations	40	40	40	40	40	40
R^2	0.52	0.57	0.56	0.85	0.74	0.92
Standard error	0.031	0.026	0.024	0.023	0.017	0.013
Durbin–Watson	1.89	2.21	1.79	2.05	1.93	2.27
$F(1, 32)$	172.59	37.36	95.5	16.76	8.74	43.42

Notes:
1. Dummy = 1 for 1873–95 and = 0 for 1896–1913.
2. T-ratios are in parentheses below the estimated coefficients.
3. $T(32) = 1.6$ at the 5 per cent level, and = 2.4 at the 1 per cent level. $F(1, 32) = 4.17$ at the 5 per cent level, and = 7.56 at the 1 per cent level testing the null hypothesis $E\hat{y}_t = 1$.

Sources: Col. (1) Firestone (1958, 1969); col. (2) Urquhart (1986); col. (3) Altman (1989); col. (4) Friedman and Schwartz (1982); col. (5) Romer (1989); col. (6) Balke and Gordon (1989).

To further investigate these findings and to reveal more explicitly the Phillips curve relationship, estimation of equations (6.11) and (6.12) was attempted. These generalizations identify the three types of price stickiness summarized by equation (6.10). These estimation results are reported in Tables 6.5, 6.6 and 6.7, the latter showing the implied estimates for α, λ and γ for the time period as a whole and for the two subperiods on either side of 1895. The estimated equations are not as well fitting as (6.6) and (6.7), and equation (6.11) performs better than (6.12).[22] The inertia effect, measured by the coefficient λ, continues to be statistically insignificant, and the rate of change effect, measured by α, tends to dominate in magnitude and statistical significance, at least in equation (6.11).[23] The α and λ coefficients tend to fall over time in both countries.

Table 6.4 Output gap regressions – equation (6.7): Canada and the United States, 1873–1913

	Canada			United States		
	(1)	(2)	(3)	(4)	(5)	(6)
Constant	−0.08	−0.07	−0.08	−0.05	−0.03	−0.05
	(−10.5)	(−7.45)	(−13.5)	(−4.70)	(−3.3)	(−7.24)
P_{t-1}	0.24	0.18	0.31	0.21	0.12	0.24
	(1.75)	(1.55)	(3.50)	(1.56)	(1.18)	(2.03)
P_{t-2}	0.02	0.22	0.12	0.10	0.03	0.29
	(0.18)	(2.26)	(1.37)	(0.74)	(0.33)	(2.65)
$E\hat{y}_t$	0.89	0.70	0.76	0.63	0.42	0.68
	(14.9)	(6.68)	(13.43)	(4.09)	(2.96)	(6.59)
Uy_t	0.46	0.34	0.46	0.63	0.40	0.69
	(5.08)	(4.43)	(7.03)	(9.61)	(5.96)	(12.8)
$\hat{Q}_{t-1}$	0.72	0.65	0.59	0.67	0.61	0.69
	(8.30)	(8.28)	(10.2)	(6.60)	(5.89)	(11.12)
z_t	−0.20	0.09	0.03	−0.05	−0.04	−0.06
	(−2.39)	(1.77)	(0.60)	(−0.59)	(−0.82)	(−1.54)
Dummy	0.09	0.07	0.08	0.05	0.03	0.04
	(8.29)	(6.79)	(11.53)	(4.35)	(3.16)	(6.51)
Observations	40	40	40	40	40	40
R^2	0.89	0.88	0.96	0.85	0.74	0.92
Standard error	0.026	0.02	0.02	0.024	0.017	0.014
Durbin–Watson	1.71	2.18	1.86	2.05	1.93	2.27
$F(1, 32)$	220.9	44.68	180.46	16.76	8.74	43.42

Notes and Sources: As for Table 6.3.

Of particular interest is the tendency for asymmetric behavior of the estimated Phillips curve coefficient, γ, over time across the two countries. For Canada, the Firestone and Altman data sets show γ falling (less price stickiness and hysteresis) by the average of results using equations (6.11) and (6.12), and falling dramatically by the statistically significant results using equation (6.11). The apparently exceptional behavior of the Urquhart data set is associated with the statistical insignificance of equation (6.12) estimates and a mildly opposing tendency in the result using equation (6.11). For the United States, the Balke and Gordon data set show γ clearly rising (more price stickiness and hysteresis) by the average of results using equations (6.11) and (6.12), and the Romer data set shows γ rising by the statistically significant results using equation (6.11). The apparently exceptional behavior of the Kuznets–Gallman data may be due to poorer data, while the opposing tendency of the Romer data using equation (6.12) is associated with statistical insignificance. There seems little doubt from these results that the Phillips curve relationships were unstable over the 1871–1913 period in both countries. A further more tentative conclusion is that the Phillips curve tended to become steeper in Canada and flatter in the United States.[24]

Table 6.5   Phillips curve regressions – equation (6.11): Canada and the United States, 1873–1913

	Constant (a_2)	p_{t-1} (a_1)	$\hat{y}_t$ (a_3)	$\hat{Q}_{t-1}$	z_t	NOBS	RSQ	DW
Canada								
F1	−0.01	0.20	0.23	0.18	−0.01	41	0.33	1.93
	(−1.92)	(1.54)	(3.34)	(1.92)	(−0.06)			
F2	−0.03	0.05	0.40	0.20	−0.18	23	0.48	1.91
	(−3.38)	(0.33)	(3.67)	(1.77)	(−1.29)			
F3	0.02	−0.16	0.08	0.09	0.19	18	0.22	2.04
	(1.79)	(−0.61)	(1.06)	(0.72)	(1.47)			
U1	−0.02	−0.08	0.45	0.16	−0.20	41	0.62	2.19
	(−3.40)	(−0.75)	(6.97)	(2.15)	(−3.79)			
U2	−0.02	−0.26	0.60	0.18	−0.21	23	0.70	2.28
	(−3.80)	(−1.77)	(5.96)	(1.70)	(−3.12)			
U3	0.02	−0.36	0.11	0.21	−0.06	18	0.51	1.95
	(1.85)	(−1.42)	(1.18)	(2.53)	(−0.79)			
A1	−0.01	−0.12	0.32	0.28	−0.09	41	0.60	1.96
	(−3.20)	(−0.99)	(6.00)	(4.70)	(−1.65)			
A2	−0.02	−0.25	0.38	0.32	−0.10	23	0.62	1.88
	(−3.47)	(−1.58)	(4.36)	(3.59)	(−1.24)			
A3	0.01	−0.11	0.13	0.28	−0.06	18	0.61	1.69
	(1.15)	(−0.55)	(1.84)	(3.80)	(−0 97)			

Table 6.5   continued

	Constant (a₂)	p_{t-1} (a₁)	$\hat{y}_t$ (a₃)	$\hat{Q}_{t-1}$	z_t	NOBS	RSQ	DW
United States								
KG1	−0.01	0.11	0.35	0.22	6.86	40	0.61	2.03
	(−3.24)	(0.96)	(6.03)	(2.82)	(1.00)			
KG2	−0.02	0.70	0.40	0.24	0.02	22	0.66	1.71
	(−3.79)	(0.41)	(4.83)	(2.24)	(0.20)			
KG3	0.01	−0.16	0.18	0.20	0.13	18	0.57	2.20
	(1.44)	(−0.77)	(2.57)	(2.00)	(1.61)			
R1	−0.02	0.12	0.58	0.24	5.44	40	0.78	1.78
	(−6.42)	(1.44)	(9.89)	(2.33)	(1.11)			
R2	−0.03	0.08	0.60	0.23	0.04	22	0.79	1.46
	(−5.79)	(0.70)	(7.15)	(1.62)	(0.52)			
R3	−0.004	−0.08	0.40	0.30	0.08	18	0.70	2.08
	(−0.72)	(−0.49)	(4.34)	(1.96)	(1.33)			
BG1	−0.01	0.19	0.31	0.20	0.04	40	0.60	2.10
	(−3.99)	(1.59)	(5.56)	(2.79)	(0.92)			
BG2	−0.02	0.10	0.35	0.16	0.06	22	0.72	1.81
	(−5.02)	(0.66)	(5.12)	(1.80)	(1.12)			
BG3	0.01	−0.26	0.13	0.27	−0.01	18	0.46	2.01
	(1.39)	(−1.26)	(1.67)	(3.13)	(−0.15)			

Note: F1 = Firestone data (1873–1913), F2 = Firestone data (1873–1895), F3 = Firestone data (1896–1913), and so on, T-ratios are in parentheses below the coefficients.

Sources: As in Tables 6.1, 6.3, and 6.4.

Table 6.6   Phillips curve regressions – equation (6.12): Canada and the United States, 1873–1913

	Constant (b₂)	p_{t-1} (b₁)	$\hat{q}_t$ (b₃)	$\hat{Q}_{t-1}$	z_t	NOBS	RSQ	DW
Canada								
F1	−0.003	0.28	−0.01	−0.03	0.08	41	0.12	1.84
	(−0.42)	(1.95)	(−0.16)	(−0.29)	(−0.73)			
F2	−0.02	0.18	0.05	0.04	0.07	23	0.09	1.92
	(−1.78)	(0.92)	(0.26)	(0.24)	(0.37)			
F3	0.02	−0.19	−0.02	−0.03	0.19	18	0.16	2.04
	(2.74)	(−0.73)	(−0.22)	(−0.28)	(1.42)			

Table 6.6   continued

	Constant (b_2)	p_{t-1} (b_1)	$\hat{q}_t$ (b_3)	$\hat{Q}_{t-1}$	z_t	NOBS	RSQ	DW
U1	0.004	0.23	0.03	0.02	−0.17	41	0.12	1.85
	(0.63)	(1.34)	(0.18)	(0.36)	(−1.97)			
U2	−0.01	0.12	0.08	−0.02	−0.19	23	0.11	1.91
	(−0.93)	(0.44)	(0.35)	(−0.13)	(−1.37)			
U3	0.03	−0.52	−0.02	0.20	−0.01	18	0.45	2.02
	(5.46)	(−2.09)	(−0.14)	(2.14)	(−0.13)			
A1	0.001	0.16	0.14	0.22	−0.01	40	0.25	1.79
	(0.30)	(0.91)	(1.23)	(2.32)	(−0.08)			
A2	−0.01	−0.07	0.18	0.31	0.01	22	0.28	1.70
	(−1.45)	(−0.24)	(1.02)	(2.13)	(0.06)			
A3	0.02	−0.15	0.08	0.30	−0.04	18	0.53	1.72
	(3.97)	(−0.66)	(0.83)	(3.32)	(−0 61)			
United States								
KG1	−0.001	0.14	0.19	0.16	0.18	40	0.26	2.16
	(−0.15)	(0.92)	(1.70)	(1.34)	(2.02)			
KG2	−0.02	−0.08	0.24	0.27	0.12	22	0.25	2.11
	(−1.78)	(−0.32)	(1.24)	(1.60)	(0.92)			
KG3	0.02	−0.09	0.12	0.15	0.20	18	0.43	2.11
	(2.75)	(0.40)	(1.23)	(1.19)	(2.19)			
R1	−0.07	0.18	0.44	0.24	0.17	40	0.26	2.16
	(−0.13)	(1.17)	(2.00)	(1.13)	(2.07)			
R2	−0.02	−0.07	0.44	0.41	0.14	22	0.24	2.14
	(−1.79)	(−0.29)	(1.26)	(1.44)	(1.11)			
R3	0.02	−0.01	0.28	0.20	0.18	18	0.35	2.09
	(2.55)	(−0.03)	(1.32)	(0.80)	(2.04)			
BG1	0.002	0.24	0.19	0.17	0.11	40	0.30	2.04
	(−0.62)	(1.50)	(1.82)	(1.73)	(1.89)			
BG2	−0.01	0.08	0.33	0.17	0.13	22	0.45	2.16
	(−2.25)	(0.38)	(2.25)	(1.33)	(1.90)			
BG3	0.02	−0.33	0.05	0.26	0.002	18	0.36	2.04
	(3.40)	(−1.45)	(0.51)	(2.45)	(0.02)			

Note: F1 = Firestone data (1873–1913), F2 = Firestone data (1873–1895), F3 = Firestone data (1896–1913), and so on, T-ratios are in parentheses below the coefficients.

Sources: As in Tables 6.1, 6.3, and 6.4.

Table 6.7   Coefficients of price stickiness: Canada and the United States,
1873–1913

	Eqn (6.11)			Eqn (6.12)			Average		
	α	γ	λ	α	γ	λ	α	γ	λ
Canada									
F1	0.05	0.22	0.24	0.02	–0.03	0.27	0.03	0.10	0.26
F2	0.20	0.25	0.06	0.01	0.04	0.18	0.10	0.14	0.12
F3	–0.01	0.10	0.18	0.05	–0.03	–0.09	0.02	0.04	–0.13
U1	0.29	0.19	–0.95	–0.05	–0.02	0.24	0.12	0.11	–0.36
U2	0.42	0.22	–0.32	0.09	–0.02	0.11	0.26	0.10	–0.10
U3	–0.10	0.27	–0.46	–0.28	0.26	–0.41	–0.19	0.26	–0.43
A1	0.04	0.39	–0.17	–0.09	0.24	0.17	–0.02	0.31	0.004
A2	0.06	0.47	–0.37	–0.15	0.36	–0.08	–0.04	0.41	–0.22
A3	–0.15	0.39	–0.15	–0.28	0.38	–0.19	–0.22	0.39	–0.17
United States									
KG1	0.13	0.28	0.14	0.03	0.16	0.14	0.08	0.22	0.14
KG2	0.16	0.32	0.92	–0.03	0.28	–0.08	0.06	0.30	0.42
KG3	–0.02	0.25	–0.20	–0.03	0.15	–0.09	–0.03	0.20	–0.15
R1	0.34	0.32	0.16	0.17	0.20	0.15	0.25	0.26	0.15
R2	0.37	0.30	0.10	0.03	0.40	–0.07	0.20	0.35	0.02
R3	0.10	0.43	–0.11	0.07	0.19	–0.01	0.09	0.31	–0.06
BG1	0.11	0.25	0.24	0.02	0.17	0.24	0.06	0.21	0.24
BG2	0.19	0.19	0.12	0.14	0.15	0.07	0.16	0.17	0.09
BG3	–0.14	0.37	–0.36	–0.27	0.33	–0.42	–0.20	0.35	–0.39

Note: For equation (6.11), $\alpha = a_1 - \gamma(1 - a_1)$, $\gamma = a_3/(1 - a_3)$, and $\lambda = a_2(1 + \gamma)$. For equation (6.12), $\alpha = (b_1 - b_3)/(1 + b_1 - b_3)$, $\gamma = b_3(1 - \alpha)$, and $\lambda = b_2(1 - \alpha)$. F1 = Firestone data (1873–1913), F2 = Firestone data (1873–1895), F3 = Firestone data (1896–1913), and so on.

Sources: As in Tables 6.5 and 6.6.

A graphical impression of the data characteristics that lie behind the overall results of this study can be obtained by plotting the growth rates of excess nominal GNP and its deflator for the two countries. Graphs are presented only for the Romer and Urquhart data, but the results are similar for the other data sets.[25] For the United States, the GNP deflator appears to mimic excess nominal income growth a bit more loosely later in the period than earlier (Figure 6.6), yet the cycles of real output (Figure 6.5) are not of greater amplitude than those in nominal income. α and λ both fall, and γ increases using the average measure with the Balke–Gordon data or using equation (6.11) with the Romer data

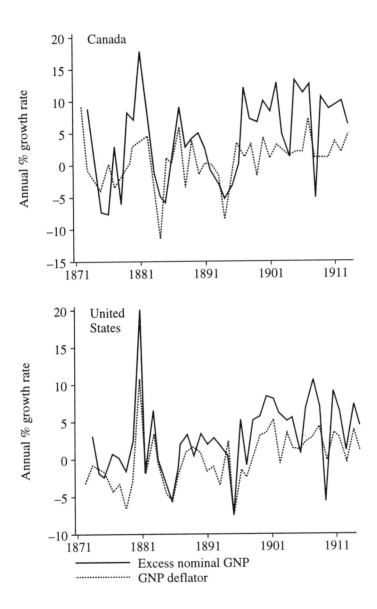

Sources: Canada: Urquhart (1986). United States: Romer (1989).

Figure 6.6   Nominal GNP and prices, 1871–1913

(Table 6.7). For Canada, the GNP deflator appears to mimic excess nominal income growth poorly throughout. Many parameters of price stickiness are lower in Canada than in the United States (Table 6.7). Fluctuations in real output (Figure 6.5) are smaller later in the period, and smaller in amplitude than fluctuations in excess nominal income (Figure 6.6). The tentative conclusion made above from the regression analysis is evident from Figures 6.5 and 6.6. After 1900, although prices appear to mimic nominal GNP poorly in both countries (Figure 6.6), the output ratio sustains smaller disturbances in Canada than in the United States (Figure 6.5).

Figure 6.6 also reveals some important characteristics of historical episodes. The final years of the greenback era in the United States prior to the resumption of 1879 generated sharply deflationary expectations (Calomiris, 1988, 1994). The 'Crime of 1873' is clearly evident in the abrupt negative movement in nominal GNP and its deflator after 1879 (Friedman, 1992: ch. 3). But the un-Friedmanlike poor mimicking of one by the other in the years leading up to this event is also evident (Calomiris, 1994: 93). Final rejection of silver in the 1890s reaffirmed these deflationary expectations and, for a brief interval, brought excess nominal GNP and its deflator into closer alignment. In the period following World War I, expectations underwent a dramatic revision anticipating the possible collapse of the gold standard and a release from its monetary discipline (Calomiris, 1994). Associated with inflationary expectations in both Canada and the United States was a much weaker mimicking of prices by excess nominal GNP. The linkage of the Canadian to the United States economy is seen in the remarkably corresponding movements of Canadian and American nominal GNP (Chambers, 1964). It is particularly notable in the case of the 1907 depression (Rich, 1989; Dick and Floyd, 1994).

CONCLUSION

Two principal conclusions emerge from this preliminary excursus into macroeconomic behavior in North America during the late nineteenth and early twentieth centuries. First, in both Canada and the United States, there was price stickiness predominantly explained by the rate of change in excess nominal income. The pre-World War I price stickiness finding harmonizes with recent findings from other data sources that conflict with the view that price adjustment to nominal demand shocks was instantaneous.[26] Second, the Phillips curve relationship measured by level effects (γ) was not stable over the 1871–1913 period; in these terms, output in Canada became less sensitive over time to nominal demand changes while in the United States this sensitivity appears to have increased.

In the United States, these results are not necessarily inconsistent with James (1989) that finds relative stability in the Phillips curve relationship over the nineteenth century alone. They are consistent with James (1993) that uses VARs to show increased sensitivity of the American economy to monetary shocks in the twentieth century. They are also consistent with the rate of change (α) and level (γ) effects obtained by Gordon (1990b). They are also consistent with the Hanes (1993) finding of decreased wage flexibility toward the end of the nineteenth century.

In Canada, the results may appear to be associated with the increasingly more perfect operation of markets as transportation and transactions costs fell, whereas in the United States it has been traditionally observed that industry became increasingly concentrated as the period progressed. But these explanations are too simplistic and implausible since such institutional changes were common to both countries over the period examined. In preliminary experimentation with VARs along the lines of James (1993) using Canadian data, decreased sensitivity of real output over time to nominal demand shocks is a tentative finding, in harmony with the results of this study, and in contrast to the United States results both here and in James (1993).[27] Following the lead of Calomiris and Hubbard (1987), also using VARs, there is a suggestion in the Canadian data that changes in the innovations may have mitigated the impact on real output (steepening the Phillips curve relative to what it might have been without these changes). A major consideration here may have been the increased role played by international capital mobility in Canadian development after 1895 facilitated by the more stable banking system in Canada (Dick and Floyd, 1994; Calomiris, 1992: 33–8). This role dramatically distinguished Canada from the United States at the same time as it caused Canadian fluctuations to mimic more closely American fluctuations (Chambers, 1964). Much more of the price adjustment mechanism operated through the medium of international trade in the Canadian case than in the American case. The larger extent to which Canada participated in world markets as a price taker may have accelerated the absorption of nominal shocks into price level changes relative to the American experience.[28]

Finally, it may be asked how these results and the conjectures based upon them are affected by the refinements to the data sets that have taken place in recent years. There are two levels at which an answer may be given based on the present investigation and the work of others. At one level, it is reassuring that the central result of price stickiness is robust for virtually all data sets, both the macro data sets explored in this chapter and the micro data sets that others have begun to explore in recent years. This implies that the volatility issue is not crucial to the overall hypothesis of price stickiness investigated here, a hardly surprising conclusion. This in no way comments on the merits or demerits of alternative data sets for the somewhat different volatility measures their reconstruction has generated (Romer 1988, 1989, 1991; Altman, 1992a). It simply argues that all these series make the central point of this chapter. At another level, the results regarding the various specific hypotheses about price stickiness are sensitive to the particular data set chosen. This implies that some criteria must be found to discriminate among series – criteria that are independent of the hypotheses being examined with these series. The conclusion, therefore, is that there is always the possibility that explicit data refinements can improve our understanding of intertemporal processes, but that these refinements must stand on their own merits without regard for their consequences in testing interesting historical hypotheses (Lebergott, 1986, 1992).

NOTES

1. It has been pointed out, however, that there was probably too little variation in expected inflation before 1913 to provide significant evidence against the Fisher hypothesis (Barsky, 1987). The Gibson Paradox correlation between nominal interest and price is subsequently shown to depend on the relative importance of gold discoveries and shocks to the real interest rate (Barsky and Summers, 1988). Calomiris (1994) presents a further contrasting view.

2. Gordon (1981, 1982a, 1990b) rejects the Lucas hypothesis for the United States 1890–1980, and James (1989) rejects it for the United States 1837–1909. Gordon (1981, 1982a), however, notes the potential for cross-country variety; Easton (1984) and Dwyer (1985) concur. James (1989) finds remarkable stability in the American experience over time, while Gordon (1981) notes rapid price response during and after World War I and little price response to high unemployment in the 1930–40 and 1970–71 subperiods.

3. For a full development of the theoretical background to equations (6.6) and (6.7), see Gordon (1981, 1982a). The Phillips curve used here differs from the original conception of this curve by the deliberate omission of expectations, unemployment and wages (Gordon, 1990a). Price inertia need not be in conflict with rational expectations because agents can, in principle, instantaneously form rational expectations about a slowly adjusting price level. Indeed, while changing expectations are not explicitly modelled in equations (6.6) and (6.7), their influence is indirectly felt. For cyclical analysis, capacity utilization is more relevant than unemployment because the latter confounds cyclical and structural components of aggregate activity. These difficulties, circumvented in the present study, are evident in the controversy over the volatility implied by alternative United States unemployment series (Romer, 1986; Weir, 1986, 1992; Lebergott, 1986, 1992; Carter and Sutch, 1992; Hanes, 1993). And wages are separated from prices by a markup implicit in the share of labor income, known to be unstable over the cycle (Gordon, 1988). The modern Phillips curve used in this chapter underlines the gap between macroeconomic observation and microeconomic theory inherent in the neo-Keynesian approach that challenges us to explain the reality of inflation inertia. For an example of the more traditional approach, see Alogoskoufis and Smith (1989). In another approach, Calomiris (1994) uses financial data to establish that expectations associated with monetary regime change were not static during the gold standard era and had a significant impact on Phillips curve relationships.

4. It may be noted that equations (6.6) and (6.7) exclude lagged demand innovations. This is done to avoid observational equivalence between the Lucas hypothesis and the hypothesis of price inertia (Gordon, 1982a: 1095–6). An alternative approach would be to constrain particular variables to influence monetary growth, but not affect output directly (Barro, 1977, 1978). Wogin (1980) has applied this approach to Canadian data in a later time period.

5. While it is controversial how much bias any one particular method of detrending imparts to the results of the analysis, it is unclear which of any of a number of alternative methods is the most historically meaningful and the least statistically misleading method to use. Gordon (1993:

app. C) generates subperiod trends using geometric interpolations between 'full employment' benchmarks. Other methods based on recursive residuals for detecting changes in trend do not offer powerful tests (Alogoskoufis and Smith, 1989; Brown *et al.*, 1975). While Nelson and Plosser (1982) cast doubt on the existence of deterministic trend, Stock (1990) has noted the wide confidence intervals associated with this result. After experimenting with an historically meaningful dummy (see pp. 157–70), we adopted the Hodrick–Prescott (1980) time-varying trend using a value of 400 for the smoothing parameter based on their analysis of United States data with a Kalman filter (Harvey, 1989).

6. To keep the estimation consistent, it is necessary to ensure that all predetermined variables in (6.6) and (6.7) are included in the estimation of nominal demand change. Lagged innovations in nominal demand are excluded and only lagged predetermined variables are included. This ensures that Uy_t is orthogonal to the other predetermined variables in (6.6) and (6.7). This does not, unfortunately, overcome the potential problem of estimating the coefficients from observations made after anticipations were formed, but this appears to be less of a problem in practice than in principle (Gordon, 1982a: 1096–7). See the Chow tests (pp. 157–70) for further discussion.

7. This has been labelled the 'triangle model' of inflation (Gordon, 1990a: 1).

8. Treating $\hat{y}$ as exogeneous in (6.11) ignores any feedback from prices to nominal GNP, potentially biasing the coefficient of $\hat{y}$ away from 0 and γ toward 0, although the presence of supply shock variables tends to mitigate the problem. The procedure invoked here achieves an identification in the spirit of the rational expectations monetarist identification of Phillips curves advocated by King and Watson (1994: 180, and fn. 14), and described by Gordon as 'mainstream.'

9. There is some potential for developing more fully quarterly data (already available for the United States: Gordon, 1993) for Canada, and the author is currently engaged in pursuing this possibility. Some of the series are now available on a monthly and/or quarterly basis (Chambers, 1964). While James (1989) used annual data for the nineteenth-century United States, Gordon (1982a) used quarterly United States data for a somewhat later period. Quarterly data would enrich the study of price–quantity variability and substantially lengthen the available times series. At the present stage of investigation, for example, it was not found feasible to investigate properly with annual data the direct impact of anticipated vs. unanticipated changes in money as an alternative avenue for discriminating between the neoclassical and the neo-Keynesian models of price–quantity interaction (Barro, 1978; Mishkin, 1982).

10. Linear interpolation was made between base years for the manufacturing data (Urquhart, 1986: 85; 1993: 242, 360–87). The interpolator series were used to construct interpolator ratios between the interpolator and the incomplete series for the base years. These ratios were then linearly interpolated and used to calculate the missing values. This interpolation method, however, is a purely arbitrary noncorrelation method with unknown error (Friedman, 1962). It corresponds to method 6a discussed by Friedman (ibid.: 735).

11. Recently Altman (1989, 1992a) has attempted to correct for this bias. It would be surprising if the Urquhart series for Canada resolved these matters in a fundamentally different way to the resolution provided by the United States data generated by Kuzuets and Gallman using similar types of data and methods. Yet the volatility of Canadian GNP is not much affected by this revision of the Urquhart data (Altman, 1992b: 260–66). This result, however, may be misleading since the Altman estimates are conceptually faulted by the application of inappropriate price indices (Urquhart, 1994).

12. There can be little doubt that volatility is sensitive to data reconstruction, and in particular to which series are used (Zarnowitz, 1992: 78; Calomiris and Hanes, 1994).

13. Altman (1987, 1989) uses sectoral price series as a basis for his deflator, but misses the appropriate price variation by relying exclusively on wholesale price movement. Dick and Floyd (1991, 1992) construct an index designed to decompose price movement into traded and non-traded goods' price components. Although it is more broadly based than the typical wholesale price index, it is not really appropriate in the present context since wholesale prices dominate traded goods' prices.

14. The approach followed in the present study, however, should be distinguished from 'atheoretical' macroeconomics of the Sims variety that uses VARs as a starting point, with or without

extending to a structural VAR analysis. Examples of related relevant contributions in this alternative mode of analysis include Eichengreen (1983), Gordon and King (1982), Calomiris and Hubbard (1987), Catao and Solomou (1993), and James (1993). The present chapter, by contrast, takes theory as a starting point and formulates econometric exercises to discriminate between competing hypotheses (Gordon, 1981).

15. All regressions in this paper were run using RATS386 version 3.11. All graphs were produced using Quattro Pro for DOS version 4.0 and imported as PCX files into the manuscript processed with the VTEX version of TEX.

16. Most authors have taken 1896 as a breaking point for Canada (Rostow, 1978: ch. 36; Urquhart, 1986; Inwood and Stengos, 1991). This also appears a suitable breaking point for the United States (Figure 6.1).

17. Gordon (1982a: app.) argues strenuously for using multiple time trends where the growth rate of natural GNP has varied over long periods. It is observed that Gordon's work is concerned with much longer periods than is the present study, and uses quarterly data (not available to us) to compensate for the loss of degrees of freedom that accompanies dividing the sample into subperiods.

18. The estimated coefficients are not reported since they play no role in subsequent analysis.

19. While this may seem to argue for the importance in further work of extending the time period of the analysis to include regime changes as a way of reducing the problem of observational equivalence, analysis of United States data over longer periods covering more obvious regime changes has failed to discover instability (Gordon, 1982a: 1101–2). This suggests that there is little evidence that the critical invariance assumption is not met.

20. Rich (1988) has nonetheless argued that the early period should be characterized somewhat differently due to the presence of a minor amount of 'uncovered issue.' It seems doubtful that this gave much scope for monetary policy before the mid-1880s. There is perhaps less doubt that capital inflow assumed a much larger magnitude after 1896 than before, helping to affirm the mechanism of adjustment that precluded any effective monetary policy (Dick and Floyd, 1991, 1992, 1994).

21. The results here may be quite sensitive to the particular price series used. Although James (1989) did not find this to be the case, his supply shock proxy also performed rather indifferently.

22. The result for Canada can be given a Ball *et al.* (1988) interpretation since the data show that the mean rate of nominal income growth rose with time as the economy moved from deflation to inflation in the longer term, while the variance of nominal income growth (demand) barely changed (Table 6.1). The variance drops only slightly in both Canada and the United States over the period studied. This is precisely the type of evidence Ball *et al.* (1988: 32) require to distinguish their Keynesian view of nominal rigidities from the Lucas (1973) view based on imperfect information. While Ball *et al.* have to control in their empirical analysis for the influence of changing (rising) variance to isolate the effect of average inflation, the Canadian data used here appear to manifest this effect more directly, simplifying a pro-Keynesian interpretation. In the framework of this chapter, means count for the slope of the Phillips curve, whereas in Lucas (1973) only variances count.

23. Dominance of α is also obtained with United States data over the 1890–1978 period (Gordon, 1980).

24. At this stage of the analysis, it is difficult to assess the statistical significance of intertemporal differences in the magnitudes of individual coefficients. This is because the parameters of theoretical interest are complex combinations of those actually estimated (to allow for feedback), making the relevant distributions for testing somewhat problematic. The results of estimating equations (6.6) and (6.7), however, already indicate that a modern Phillips curve relationship did shift over time in both countries. Given this, those instances of rather large differences in parameter estimates found over time from estimating equations (6.11) and (6.12) cannot be lightly discounted. Using a VAR approach, Neely and Wood (1995) also find some evidence of asymmetric dynamic relationships between price changes and output growth across subperiods of the 1870–1913 period.

25. Pictorial representations of Phillips curves are not presented. The effects identified by the 'triangular' approach developed here translate into conventional diagrams (plotting inflation rates against output gaps) that display various sorts of loops that are not easily interpretable

(Gordon, 1990b: 1023–4). Partial scatters of the estimated equations based on (6.10) only provide a visualization of goodness of fit.

26. Neely and Wood (1995), using a VAR approach, find clear evidence of interaction between prices and output growth during the gold standard for a number of countries including Canada and the United States.

27. Hay (1967) also found some difficulties in replicating United States experience with Canadian data with respect to the relation between nominal shocks and the business cycle. In particular, he found that Canada–United States ties were stronger during contractions than expansions, implying that Canada was less sensitive to nominal shocks emanating from the United States during upswings.

28. In principle, the results of Dick and Floyd (1991, 1992) regarding the operation of mechanisms of adjustment in the balance of payments should not be affected by this issue. Empirically, however, the findings there are influenced in one aspect by the extent of price adjustments completed within a year, the periodicity of the data. Price stickiness is an unavoidable characteristic of the data set when viewed through the window of the model of the present chapter. It manifests itself in the balance of payments study in the reduced form errors that mask unidentified intertemporal processes. While the *timing* of adjustments is obviously affected by price stickiness, the power of the non-nested tests to discriminate between competing hypotheses in Dick and Floyd (1991, 1992) is not. Hence, the results of Dick and Floyd (1991, 1992) are consistent with the present finding of price stickiness, while neither study makes direct inferences about the results of the other.

7. Consistent wholesale price series for the United States, 1860–1990

Christopher Hanes

INTRODUCTION

To compare the cyclical behavior of variables across historical periods, it is necessary to have data that are consistent across those periods, in the sense that the variables measured by the data do not change from one period to the next and the cyclical biases in the data as measures of the 'true' variables of interest hold stable. Christina Romer (1986a, 1989) showed that the historical employment and output series used by nearly all studies failed this test, casting doubt on many common observations about the history of business cycles. Steven Allen (1992) did the same for historical data on average hourly earnings. In this chapter I point out a similar problem for measures of the price level. Historical indices of wholesale prices and GNP deflators put much more weight on prices of raw materials and intermediate goods than do postwar series. That affects the cyclical behavior of the price indices, and comparisons with behavior of postwar series, because prices of less-finished goods are more flexible than prices of more-finished goods.

I present wholesale price series for the years 1914–40 and 1947–90 designed to match the series constructed by Warren and Pearson (1932) for the 1870s through 1890. The goods in the basket for these newly constructed series are, as far as possible, identical to the goods in the Warren and Pearson series. Together with the matching series for 1890–1914 presented in Hanes (1992), the series given here make a consistent price index for the United States that covers the entire period from the end of the War Between the States through 1990, excluding only the early 1940s. I compare the cyclical behavior of this series to that of the standard wholesale price index.

CHANGES IN THE CYCLICAL BEHAVIOR OF STANDARD HISTORICAL PRICE SERIES

The Bureau of Labor Statistics has collected data on wholesale prices since the 1890s and publishes several indices derived from these data. One series, the 'all-items' index, stretches from 1890 up to the present. This series is often linked to the wholesale price index constructed by Warren and Pearson for the years before 1890. There are several GNP deflators for prewar years that have been compared to the post-war deflators in the National Income and Product Accounts. Milton Friedman and Anna Schwartz (1982) present a series originally

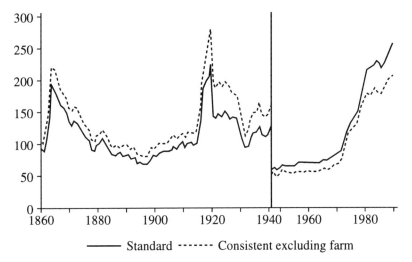

——— Standard ------ Consistent excluding farm

Figure 7.1a Wholesale price indices: standard series and consistent series excluding farm products, 1860–1990

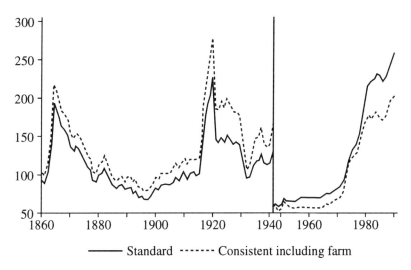

——— Standard ------ Consistent including farm

Figure 7.1b Wholesale price indices: standard series and consistent series including farm products, 1860–1990

constructed by Kuznets, modified by Robert Gallman, John Kendrick, and Friedman and Schwartz. Nathan Balke and Robert Gordon (1989) point out problems with this series and present their own. Christina Romer (1989) presents yet another. A number of studies have compared the cyclical behavior of prices in the period before World War I with the behavior of prices in the post-war period using these wholesale price indices and GNP deflators. Nearly all find that inflation has become more 'persistent.' Many find that prices have become less 'flexible' across cycles (see, for example, Cagan, 1975; Sachs, 1980; Schultz, 1981; DeLong and Summers, 1986b; Gordon, 1990b).

Table 7.1 present results of similar comparisons between the period before World War I and the twentieth-century post-war period. Several studies have suggested that price behavior was very unusual in the oil shock of the early 1970s, so I also present results excluding 1974. I use the Warren and Pearson index linked to the BLS all-items WPI (PPI) and some simple descriptions of cyclical price behavior: 'expectations-augmented' Phillips curves with the level of real economic activity indicated by the deviation from trend in output. Output is measured by the Frickey index of manufacturing production for years through 1914 and the Federal Reserve Board Materials production index for postwar years. (Romer, 1986, explains why these series are comparable.) The trend in output is defined to be the Hodrick–Prescott trend at conventional parameter values.[1] I have excluded the interwar period from consideration here because the 1930s present unique problems associated with the effects of the National Industrial Recovery Act (Weinstein, 1980). More importantly, there is no consistent output or employment series that stretches across the years before 1914, the interwar period, and the postwar period, unless a choice is made between the two sets of real GNP series constructed by Romer (1989) and by Balke and Gordon (1989). As Trevor Dick (Chapter 6 in this volume) shows, those two series give different results in an exercise such as this.

Specification (1) is a regression of current inflation – the rate of change in the price index from the previous year – on the current year's deviation from trend in output and inflation in the previous year. Specification (2) replaces last year's inflation rate with a weighted average of inflation rates in the past four years. Weights were estimated along with the coefficient on the weighted average; I report only the coefficient on the weighted average. Specification (3) adds the rate of change of output, that is, the change in the output deviation from the previous year, to specification (1).

The results replicate those in most other studies. In specifications (1) and (2) – the more conventional versions of the Phillips curve – the coefficient on past inflation is larger in the postwar period: inflation is more 'persistent.' The coefficient on output is smaller in the postwar period or about the same in both periods. In specification (3), adding the rate of change in output, the coefficient on past inflation is again larger in the postwar period; the coefficient on the output level increases, and that on the change in output decreases.

Table 7.1   Historical changes in price behavior: standard WPI (Warren and Pearson linked to BLS)

Specifications

(1)   One lag of inflation

$$(p_t - p_{t-1}) - \alpha + \beta(y_t - \hat{y}_t) + \gamma(p_{t-1} - p_{t-2})$$

(2)   Four lags of inflation

$$(p_t - p_{t-1}) = \alpha + \beta(y_t - \hat{y}_t) + \gamma \sum_{i=4}^{i=1} c_t (p_{t-1} - p_{t-i-1})$$

(3)   Output level and growth rate

$$(p_t - p_{t-1}) - \alpha + \beta(y_t - \hat{y}_t) + \beta_\Delta[(y_t - \hat{y}_t) - (y_{t-1} - \hat{y}_{t-1}] + \gamma(p_{t-1} - p_{t-2})$$

(1)			(2)		
	β	γ		β	γ
1869–1914	0.3501	0.0987		0.3452	0.1167
	(3.630)	(0.738)		(3.488)	(0.531)
1949–1990	0.3516	0.5790	1952–1990	0.2847	0.709
	(3.998)	(5.065)		(3.049)	(4.635)
Excluding 1974					
1949–1990	0.3189	0.4932	1952–1990	0.2536	0.6437
	(3.790)	(4.336)		(2.974)	(4.585)

(3)			
	β	β_Δ	γ
1869–1914	0.1914	0.2313	0.2334
	(1.553)	(2.077)	(1.599)
1949–1990	0.3176	0.0540	0.6095
	(2.877)	(0.519)	(4.708)
Excluding 1974			
1949–1990	0.2698	0.0763	0.5336
	(2.555)	(0.777)	(4.248)

Notes:
All variables in logs
p Wholesale price index
y Industrial production
      1869–1914 Frickey manufacturing output
      1949–1990 FRB materials production
$\hat{x}$ Hodrick–Prescott trend in variable

Gordon (1990) notes that the increase in the persistence of price inflation, like that shown in Table 7.1, is larger than the increase in the persistence of wage inflation across the same historical periods indicated by standard measures of hourly earnings: 'inertia in price change seems to have increased more than for wage change' (ibid.: 1130). Allen (1992: 137) shows that more consistent measures of hourly earnings display a decrease in the coefficient on output from the prewar to the postwar period, unlike the increase or lack of change in the output coefficient for price inflation shown in Table 7.1. Thus, the results in Table 7.1, like those in other studies of standard price series, suggest that the historical change in the cyclical behavior of prices was different from that in wages.

DIFFERENCES IN THE CYCLICAL BEHAVIOR OF MORE- AND LESS-FINISHED GOODS

However, there is good reason to doubt the results in Table 7.1 and the studies referred to above. The basket of goods covered by the Warren and Pearson wholesale price index and the BLS WPI for years around the turn of the century is very different from that making up the postwar price index. The BLS has revised the WPI many times and with each revision it has changed the composition of goods covered by the all-items index and its components to cover more goods, add services, and increase the weight on finished goods, as opposed to raw materials and intermediate products. This is true for GNP deflators as well. Balke and Gordon (1989: 86) note that the Kuznets–Gallman–Kendrick deflator for prewar years was 'based entirely on components of the wholesale price index and, going back in time, becomes more and more dependent on the prices of crude and intermediate goods.' Balke and Gordon attempt to improve the Kuznets–Gallman–Kendrick deflator by averaging it with CPIs and a series for construction costs. One may doubt this helps much, if only because the CPIs are heavily weighted toward food prices (which appear elsewhere in the deflators). More importantly, over the 1880s the 'CPI' used by Balke and Gordon is not a CPI at all. It is constructed from wholesale food and clothing prices plus an assumption that nominal house rents were absolutely fixed from one year to the next (Hoover, 1960: 162–3). In fact, there are no time series of consumer prices over the 1880s from which a CPI could be constructed.

The increasing importance of more-finished goods in the composition of these price indices affects their cyclical behavior. Since the 1930s at least it has been noted that prices of raw materials and intermediate products are more 'flexible' than prices of finished goods (Means, 1935; Gordon, 1990), in that the relative prices of less-finished goods are strongly procyclical (Rotemberg

Table 7.2 Differences in price behavior: goods at different stages of production (BLS Producer Price Indices)

Specifications

(1) $(p_t - p_{t-1}) = \alpha + \beta(y_t - \hat{y}_t) + \gamma(p_{t-1} - p_{t-2})$

(2) $(p_t - p_{t-1}) = \alpha + \beta(y_t - \hat{y}_t) + \gamma \sum_{i=4}^{i=1} c_t(p_{t-1} - p_{t-i-1})$

(3) $(p_t - p_{t-1}) = \alpha + \beta(y_t - \hat{y}_t) + \beta_\Delta[(y_t - \hat{y}_t) - (y_{t-1} - \hat{y}_{t-1}] + \gamma(p_{t-1} - p_{t-2})$

(1) 1949–1990	β	γ	(2) 1952–1990 β	γ
Crude	0.5723	0.2626	0.4814	0.5015
	(3.257)	(1.944)	(2.469)	(2.230)
Intermediate	0.3795	0.5610	0.3161	0.6671
	(3.901)	(4.720)	(2.964)	(3.961)
Finished	0.2732	0.6755	0.2048	0.7517
	(3.860)	(6.182)	(2.741)	(5.428)
Excluding 1974				
Crude	0.5746	0.2759	0.4841	0.5214
	(3.216)	(1.670)	(2.443)	(2.111)
Intermediate	0.3274	0.4627	0.2623	0.5965
	(3.927)	(4.472)	(3.090)	(4.463)
Finished	0.2458	0.6127	0.1787	0.7121
	(3.654)	(5.809)	(2.643)	(5.697)
(3)	β	β_Δ	γ	
Crude	0.3885	0.2556	0.3491	
	(1.695)	(1.236)	(2.306)	
Intermediate	0.3477	0.0517	0.5887	
	(2.869)	(0.450)	(4.361)	
Finished	0.3028	−0.0481	0.6480	
	(3.494)	(−0.602)	(5.435)	
Excluding 1974				
Crude	0.3902	0.2579	0.3692	
	(1.679)	(1.230)	(2.042)	
Intermediate	0.2607	0.1051	0.5156	
	(2.521)	(1.085)	(4.517)	
Finished	0.2594	−0.0213	0 6016	
	(3.104)	(−0.280)	(5.281)	

Notes:
All variables in logs
p Wholesale price index
y FRB materials production
$\hat{x}$ Hodrick–Prescott trend in variable

and Woodford, 1991) and their inflation rates are less persistent (McAllister, 1961). McAllister (1961), Cagan (1975), Sachs (1980) and Schultz (1981) all note that this poses a problem for comparisons of price behavior between periods. Schultz (1981: 538) judged that the differences between periods in the goods covered by the index meant that 'To some extent the reduction in wholesale price flexibility may be a statistical mirage.' Balke and Gordon (1989: 80) observe that the Kuznets–Gallman–Kendrick GNP deflators are 'too volatile since they are based on an overrepresentation of crude and intermediate goods prices.'

To guess how important this problem might be, I applied the same specifications used in Table 7.2 to postwar BLS price indices for goods at different stages of production: crude, intermediate, and finished. Results are shown in Table 7.2. In the conventional Phillips curve specifications, coefficients on both output and lagged inflation vary with stage of processing. Passing from less-finished to more-finished goods, the coefficient on output decreases and the coefficient on lagged inflation increases. In the specification including the rate of change of output, the coefficient on lagged inflation is also larger for more-finished goods; the coefficient on the output level is smaller, and the coefficient on the rate of change of output is much smaller. Thus, the difference between less- and more-finished goods in the postwar period resembles the difference between periods shown in Table 7.1.

CONSISTENT WHOLESALE PRICE SERIES

A price index based on a fixed, unchanging set of goods would allow changes in the cyclical behavior of prices to be distinguished from changes in the composition of goods. I constructed a set of wholesale price series for 1890–1990 to match the Warren and Pearson series for the 1880s. Because the bundle of goods in the Warren and Pearson series is almost fixed from the late 1860s on, this gives a consistent price index for the entire 1860–1990 period.

Warren and Pearson constructed their series on the 'fixed-weight relative' method, as it was known at the time. Each good's price was converted into an index based to its average price over 1876–91. Weights were applied to these indices to construct composite indices for groups of goods such as 'farm products,' 'food,' 'textiles,' and 'metals and metal products.' Groups were chosen to correspond to the categories in the BLS wholesale price index for the early twentieth century, though the goods and weights in each group did not match the BLS series exactly. Another set of weights was applied to the group series (based to the average price 1876–91) to create the 'total' or 'all-items' index that has been used in most studies. The weights for the standard series vary over time, but Warren and Pearson (1933: 69) also constructed a version of the series with fixed weights. Within the total index a weight of 25 per cent was given to farm products, in addition to the weight given farm products in the food group. Warren and Pearson present the group and all-items indices rebased to the average over 1910–14, to match the BLS series of their time.

I matched the goods in the Warren and Pearson bundle in 1889 to the same goods, similar goods, or small groups of goods in BLS price records for the years 1890–1990. The present-day BLS would classify most of the goods as intermediate or raw materials. Sources were:

1890–1914: Hanes (1993).

1914–28: prices of individual goods collected by the BLS over this period are given in US Bureau of Labor Statistics (1929). Price series were converted to indices with the base set to the average value over the period covered by the source (in this case 1913–28) and these indices were averaged with the weights in Warren and Pearson's Table 51 (p. 121) for 1889. The resulting group indices were weighted as above to give the fixed-weight WPI for this period.

1928–41: BLS individual-good price series for this period appear in two BLS publications: *Wholesale Prices of Commodities*, through February 1932, and *Wholesale Prices* thereafter. The same scheme that was applied to the 1914–28 data was applied to these series.

1947–90: individual goods' prices over this period are recorded in the US Bureau of Labor Statistics computer database, kindly provided by the Bureau. In some cases Warren and Pearson goods were matched to BLS subgroup indices rather than individual goods. Otherwise the same scheme was followed as for preceding periods.

The Appendix lists the specific goods or BLS group indices matched to the set of Warren and Pearson goods in the set of years covered by each source.

I constructed separate price indices for each set of years separately, and then linked them to the Warren and Pearson series and to each other. For example, for the period 1890–1914 I converted each individual good's price series to an index with the base set to the average value over 1890–1914. To these indices I applied the 1889 weights in Warren and Pearson's Table 51 (p. 121). That gave group indices based to the average over 1890–1914. I did this for all groups except farm products, since its BLS price index has remained at about the same stage of processing as the Warren and Pearson index. The series for that group were taken from US Bureau of the Census (1975: series E42 and E25), and US Council of Economic Advisors (1993). For the farm group I took the BLS series and rebased it to the average value for 1890–1914. To combine the group indices into totals, I applied Warren and Pearson's group weights for 1889 (and their constant-weight index). I constructed two total indices. One includes farm products, and thus matches Warren and Pearson's total index; the other excludes farm products (but it includes foods).

This process was repeated for each period 1914–28, 1928–41, and 1947–90. I then linked the group and total indices to each other, and to the Warren and Pearson series. To construct a total index excluding farm products for the years covered by Warren and Pearson, I converted the series they give in Tables 36 through 45 (pp. 86–11) back to the 1876–91 base and applied the group weights excluding farm products.

Within each period some of the goods in the Warren and Pearson series could not be matched. The weight for such goods was allocated to the other goods in the same group.

Though the Warren and Pearson series and most of the BLS series are presented with a monthly frequency, not all the component goods were marketed every month, and it is not clear whether Warren and Pearson's method for interpolating between observations matches that of the BLS. The price series was therefore constructed with an annual frequency only.

The graph shows the standard series – the Warren and Pearson total index linked to the BLS all-items index – along with the two consistent indices I constructed, including and excluding farm products.

Annual values for the group and total indices are given in Table A7.1 in the Appendix. They are given with the base set to the average value over 1890–1914, to match the series in Hanes (1992).

CHANGES IN THE CYCLICAL BEHAVIOR OF THE CONSISTENT WHOLESALE PRICE INDEX

Table 7.3 repeats the measures of Table 7.1 on the consistent (fixed-bundle) price index, including and excluding farm products. Results are as expected, given the patterns for less- versus more-finished goods that appear in Table 7.2. In the two standard Phillips-curve specifications (1) and (2), replacing the standard price series with the consistent series increases the postwar coefficient on output and decreases the postwar coefficient on lagged inflation. In specification (1) there is a considerable increase in the coefficient on output, whether or not farm products are included in the index. In specification (3), including the rate of growth of output, the consistent series give a smaller increase from the prewar to postwar period in the coefficient on the output level, and a smaller decrease in the coefficient on output growth, as well as a smaller increase in the coefficient on lagged inflation.

Table 7.3   Historical changes in price behavior: consistent WPI (fixed weight)

Specifications

(1) $(p_t - p_{t-1}) = \alpha + \beta(y_t - \hat{y}_t) + \gamma(p_{t-1} - p_{t-2})$

(2) $(p_t - p_{t-1}) = \alpha + \beta(y_t - \hat{y}_t) + \gamma \sum_{i=4}^{i=1} c_t(p_{t-1} - p_{t-i-1})$

(3) $(p_t - p_{t-1}) = \alpha + \beta(y_t - \hat{y}_t) + \beta_\Delta[(y_t - \hat{y}_t) - (y_{t-1} - \hat{y}_{t-1}] + \gamma(p_{t-1} - p_{t-2})$

Including farm products

(1)   (2)

	β	γ		β	γ
1869–1914	0.3477	0.0962		0.3361	0.1064
	(3.499)	(0.707)		(3.295)	(0.494)
1949–1990	0.4493	0.3561	1952–1990	0.3362	0.6179
	(3.419)	(2.735)		(2.529)	(3.236)
Excluding 1974					
1949–1990	0.4301	0.2576	1952–1990	0.3161	0.5158
	(3.287)	(1.739)		(2.414)	(2.600)

(3)

	β	β_Δ	γ
1869–1914	0.2330	0.1654	0.1890
	(1.783)	(1.438)	(1.253)
1949–1990	0.2798	0.2406	0.4631
	(1.659)	(1.561)	(3.193)
Excluding 1974			
1949–1990	0.2632	0.2374	0.3649
	(1.573)	(1.557)	(2.267)

Excluding farm products

(1)   (2)

	β	γ		β	γ
1869–1914	0.3282	0.1317		0.3264	0.1626
	(3.678)	(0.991)		(3.531)	(0.785)
1949–1990	0.4393	0.4028	1952–1990	0.3374	0.6640
	(3.583)	(3.162)		(2.768)	(3.689)
Excluding 1974					
1949–1990	0.3987	0.2652	1952–1990	0.2898	0.5211
	(3.489)	(2.075)		(2.692)	(3.193)

Table 7.3   continued

(3)			
	β	β_Δ	γ
1869–1914	0.2091	0.1780	0.2302
	(1.723)	(1.672)	(1.533)
1949–1990	0.2729	0.2438	0.5185
	(1.762)	(1.694)	(3.653)
Excluding 1974			
1949–1990	0.2200	0.2601	0.3846
	(1.546)	(1.981)	(2.805)

Notes:
All variables in logs
p Wholesale price index
y Industrial production
      1869–1914 Frickey manufacturing output
      1949–1990 FRB materials production
$\hat{x}$ Hodrick–Prescott trend in variable

In general, relative to standard price series, the consistent (fixed-bundle) price index shows a smaller increase in the 'persistence' of price inflation and a smaller decrease in the coefficient on output. In most cases, the consistent price series show an increase in the coefficient on output from the prewar period to the postwar period. Thus, the historical changes in the cyclical behavior of price inflation indicated by the consistent price index are closer to those in the cyclical behavior of wage inflation.

CONCLUSION

The historical change in the cyclical behavior of the consistent (fixed-bundle) price index presented in this chapter differs from that shown by standard indices of wholesale prices or GNP deflators. In terms of a standard Phillips curve specification, the consistent price index shows a smaller increase in the coefficient on lagged inflation, and an increase rather than a decrease (or no change) in the coefficient on output. That is closer to the historical change in the cyclical behavior of wage rates shown in other studies.

Of course, one may ask whether a fixed-bundle price index is appropriate to indicate changes in the cyclical behavior of the 'price level.' After all, from the late nineteenth to the late twentieth centuries, the output produced by firms and consumed by households has shifted toward more-finished goods. Given the increasing importance of finished goods in final output, a wholesale price index or GNP deflator based on a basket of goods and services that changes over time to reflect the changing mix of output in the economy might be preferable. Unfortunately, such a price index does not exist and cannot be constructed. At the turn of the century the BLS made little effort to survey all sectors of the economy, much less all stages of production. It collected the prices that were easy to get. That excluded prices of most of the finished goods of the day. Warren and Pearson could certainly do no better when constructing historical series. They had to rely on what history had left behind: prices in newspapers and the odd government report. Thus, the difference between standard prewar and postwar WPIs greatly exaggerates the increased importance of finished goods in the economy.

Until the BLS finds a way to send agents into the past we will always lack records of prices of most finished goods and of nearly all services for prewar years. That means that any attempt to construct a comprehensive WPI or GNP deflator for the prewar period must rely on questionable assumptions. All that can be said with reasonable certainty is that the historical change in the cyclical behavior of the overall price level was a combination of the change in the behavior of prices of given goods indicated by Table 7.3 and a shift toward more finished goods with effects indicated by Table 7.2.

One lesson is clear: historical studies of cyclical price behavior should pay attention to the difference between more- and less-finished goods, not only in the construction of data, but in the interpretation of empirical patterns. That will require macroeconomic models which take account of production in different stages, and describe what happens to an economy as the composition of output changes across historical periods.

APPENDIX: GOODS IN CONSISTENT WHOLESALE PRICE INDEX

Group

Warren and Pearson good (weight within group sums to one)
Period   Matched good (code in BLS database, if available)

Foods

Beans (.01)
1914–1928:   Beans, medium, choice.
1928–1941:   Beans, medium, choice.
1947–1990:   Beans, dried (WPU01130101).

Bread, crackers (.025)
1914–1928:   Average of crackers, pound, New York, oyster and soda, plain.
1928–1941:   Crackers, soda, New York.
1947–1983:   Crackers (WPU02112104).
1983–1990:   Crackers, etc. (WPU02112104).

Bread, Navy (.025)
1914–1928:   Average of crackers, pound, New York, oyster and soda, plain.
1928–1941:   Crackers, soda, New York.
1947–1983:   Crackers (WPU02112104).
1983–1990:   Crackers, etc. (WPU02112104).

Butter (.08)
1914–1928:   Average of Boston, extra, firsts, seconds; Chicago, firsts, extra, extra firsts; New Orleans, fancy, choice; New York, extra, firsts, seconds; Philadelphia, extra, extra firsts; San Francisco, extra, firsts.
1928–1941:   Average of Boston, extra; Boston, firsts; Chicago, extra; Chicago, extra, firsts; Chicago, firsts; Cincinnati, as to score; New Orleans, fancy; New Orleans, choice; New York, extra; New York, firsts; New York, seconds; Philadelphia, extra; Philadelphia, extra firsts; Philadelphia, firsts; St Louis, extra; San Francisco, extra; San Francisco, firsts.
1947–1990:   Butter (WPU0232).

Cheese (.02)
1914–1928:   Average of whole milk, pound, Chicago, American twins; New York, colored, average run; San Francisco, California fats, fancy.
1928–1941:   Average of whole milk, Chicago and whole milk, San Francisco.
1947–1990:   Natural, etc. cheese (WPU0233).

Coffee (.03)
1914–1928:   Average of Brazilian grades, per pound, New York, Rio No. 7 and Santos, No. 4.
1928–1941:   Average of Brazilian grades, per pound, New York, Rio No. 7 and Santos, No. 4.
1947–1963:   Average of green coffee, Santos No. 4 (WPU01910101) and Colombian, Manizales (WPU01910111).
1963–1971:   Green coffee, cocoa beans and tea (WPU0191).
1971–1974:   Average of green coffee, Santos No. 4 (WPU01910101) and Colombian, Manizales (WPU01910111).

1974–1979:   Green coffee (WPU019101).

1979–1985:   Average of green coffee, Santos No. 4 (WPU01910101) and Colombian, Manizales (WPU01910111).

1985–1990:   Other farm products (WPU019).

Eggs (.03)

1914–1927:   Average of firsts, Boston; firsts, Chicago; extra firsts, Cincinnati; western, candled, New Orleans; firsts, New York; extra first, Philadelphia; No. 1, extras, San Francisco.

1928–1941:   Average of firsts, western Boston; firsts, Chicago; extra firsts, Cincinnati; candled, New Orleans; firsts, New York; extra firsts, Philadelphia; extras, San Francisco.

1947–1990:   Eggs (WPU017).

Fish (.01)

1914–1928:   Average of cod, cured, Gloucester and mackerel, salt, Boston.

1928–1941:   Average of cod, pickled, Gloucester and mackerel, New York, pickled, salt.

1947–1990:   Canned and cured seafood (WPU022304).

Flour (.145)

1914–1928:   Weighted average of rye, Minneapolis and wheat, hard winter, Buffalo, first clears; winter, Kansas City, straights; Minneapolis, second patents; patents, Portland; soft winter, St Louis, straights; soft winter patents, Toledo.

1928–1941:   Weighted average of rye, white, Minneapolis and wheat, Buffalo hard winter; Buffalo, hard winter, first clears; Kansas City, winter, straight patents; Kansas City, winter, straights; Minneapolis, standard patents; Minneapolis, second patents; Portland, patents; St Louis, soft winter, patents; St Louis, soft winter straights; Toledo, soft winter, patents.

1947–1990:   Flour (WPU021203).

Fruit (.039)

1914–1928:   Weighted average of apples, Baldwins, Chicago and New York, Winesaps, Portland; currants uncleaned and cleaned, dried, New York; California prunes, 60–70s, dried, New York; raisins, London layered and coast, seeded, dried, New York.

1928–1941:   Weighted average of apples, Baldwins, Chicago and New York, medium grade, Portland and Seattle; California prunes, dried, New York; raisins, seeded, dried, New York; currants, cleaned, New York; raisins substitute for currants 1940, 1941.

1947–1990:   Fresh fruits (WPU0111).

Cornmeal (.03)

1914–1928:   Average of fine white, mill and fine, yellow and fancy yellow.
1928–1941:   Average of white, mill and yellow, fancy, Philadelphia.
1947–1973:   Other cereals (WPU0214).
1973–1983:   Corn meal, white (WPU02140103).
1983–1990:   Cornmeal, grits, hominy (WPU02140106).

Lard (.05)

1914–1928:   Lard, prime, contract, New York.
1928–1941:   Lard, prime, New York.
1947–1990:   Animal fats and oils (WPU0271).

Hams (.04)

1914–1928:   Hams, cured, pound, Chicago.
1928–1941:   Pork, cured, hams, Chicago.
1947–1988:   Hams (WPU02210423).
1988–1990:   Hams and picnics (WPU02210432).

Pork, mess (.05)

1914–1928:   Pork, mess, barrel, New York.
1928–1941:   Pork, cured, mess, New York.
1947–1990:   Pork (WPU022104).

Pork, prime (.03)

1914–1928:   Hogs, dressed, fresh, pound, Chicago.
1928–1941:   Pork, fresh, Chicago.
1947–1990:   Pork (WPU022104).

Beef (.14)

1914–1928:   Average of New York, salt, mess; New York, native sides; New York, western dressed, native.
1928–1941:   Beef, cured, New York family except 1940 when mutton substitutes.
1947–1990:   Beef and veal (WPU022101).

Tallow (.01)

1914–1928:   Tallow, edible, Chicago.
1928–1941:   Tallow, edible, Chicago.
1947–1990:   Animal fats and oils (WPU0271).

Milk (.034)

1914–1928:   Average of New York, Chicago, San Francisco, fluid, fresh, 100 pounds.

1928–1941:   Average of New York, and San Francisco, fluid.
1947–1990:   Fluid milk products (WPU0231).

Molasses (.01)
1914–1928:   Molasses, New Orleans, open kettle.
1928–1941:   Molasses, New Orleans, fancy.
1947–1985:   Sugar and confectionery (WPU025).
1985–1990:   Sweetening syrups and molasses (WPU025504).

Rice (.005)
1914–1928:   Honduras rice, head, clean, medium to choice, New York.
1928–1941:   Average of New Orleans head, clean Edith and Blue Rose.
1947–1990:   Milled rice (WPU0213).

Salt (.01)
1914–1928:   Average of salt, Chicago, American medium and granulated, bulk.
1928–1941:   Salt, Chicago, American, medium.
1947–1973:   Salt, rock (WPU06110369).
1973–1984:   Basic inorganic chemicals (WPU0613).
1984–1990:   Rock salt (WPU06130271).

Pepper (.001)
1914–1928:   Black pepper, New York.
1928–1941:   Pepper, black, New York.
1947–1985:   Pepper, whole black (WPU02890131).
1985–1990:   Other misc. processed foods (WPU0289).

Olive oil (.001)
1914–1928:   Olive oil, New York.
1928–1941:   Olive oil, New York.
1947–1990:   Shortening and cooking oil (WPU0276).

Nutmeg (.001)
1914–1928:   No data available.
1928–1941:   No data available.
1947–1990:   No data available.

Sugar (.08)
1914–1928:   Sugar, granulated, New York.
1928–1941:   Sugar, granulated, New York.
1947–1982:   Granulated cane sugar in bags (WPU02530201).
1982–1990:   Granulated sugar (WPU025303).

Tea (.01)

1914–1928:	Tea, Formosa, fine, New York.
1928–1941:	Tea, Formosa, fine, New York, except coffee 1939–41.
1947–1990:	Tea (WPU026303).

Mutton (.02)

1914–1928:	Mutton, dressed, pound, New York.
1928–1941:	Mutton, cured, New York, dressed.
1947–1980:	USDA prime and choice lamb (WPU02210315).
1980–1990:	Meats (WPU0221).

Potatoes (.06)

1914–1928:	Average of Boston, Chicago, New York, Portland, white, 100 pounds and Philadelphia, sweet Jersey.
1928–1941:	Average of white potatoes, Boston, Chicago, New York, Portland and sweet potatoes, Philadelphia.
1947–1990:	White potatoes (WPU011304).

Hides and leather

Hides (.30)

1914–1928:	Average of hides, Chicago, country cows, No. 1, heavy and steers, heavy, native and Texas.
1928–1941:	Average of hides, Chicago, country cows; hides, packers, heavy native steers; hides, packers, heavy Texas steers.
1947–1981:	Hides and skins (WPU041).
1981–1988:	Leather (WPU042).
1988–1990:	Hides and skins (WPU041).

Leather (.70)

1914–1928:	Average of chrome calf, Boston, glazed kid, Boston, harness California oak No. 1; side, black chromed, Boston; sole, Boston; sole, oak scoured, Boston; sole, union backs, New York.
1928–1941:	Average of leather, glazed kid, top grade; leather, harness, California oak; leather, side, B grade, black chrome; leather, Boston, sole oak, in sides; leather, Boston, sole oak, scoured backs; leather, sole, New York, union backs.
1947–1990:	Leather (WPU042).

Textiles

Shawls (.05)
1914–1928:   Blankets, wool.
1928–1941:   Blankets, wool.
1947–1990:   Women's apparel (WPU038101).

Furs, beaver (.03)
1914–1928:   No data available.
1928–1941:   No data available.
1947–1990:   No data available.

Carpets (.15)
1914–1928:   Average of Axminster, Wilton, Brussels.
1928–1940:   Average of Brussels and Wilton.
1940–1941:   Wilton
1947–1990:   Soft surface floor covering (WPU1231).

Whalebone, slab (.01)
1914–1928:   No data available.
1928–1941:   No data available.
1947–1990:   No data available.

Cordage, domestic and foreign (.02)
1914–1928:   Weighted average of binder twine; rope, Manila.
1928–1941:   Average of binder twine and rope, pure Manila, New York.
1947–1985:   Cordage, twine, rope (WPU03830322)
1985–1990:   Soft fiber cordage and twins (WPU03830324)

Silk, tsatlee (.10)
1914–1928:   Average of raw silk, China canton, and China steam filature;
               Japanese, filature; silk, gray, spun, domestic and imported.
1928–1939:   Silk and rayon index.
1939–1940:   Average of silk, raw, Japan and silk, raw, special crack.
1940–1941:   Average of rayon, visc., 100 denier and 150 denier.
1947–1963:   Silk, raw.
1963–1990:   Plant and animal fibers (WPU015)

Cassimeres (.05)
1914–1928:   Women's Dress Goods: broadcloth, worsted and wool index.
1928–1941:   Woolen and worsted index.
1947–1975:   Broadwoven goods (WPU0312).
1975–1990:   Broadwovens (WPU0337).

Satinets (.10)
1914–1928:   Cotton textiles index number.
1928–1932:   Cotton goods index number.
1932–1941:   Sateen
1947–1975:   Broadwoven goods (WPU0312).
1975–1990:   Broadwovens (WPU0337).

Sheeting (.14)
1914–1928:   Weighted average of bleached 10-4, Pepperell; bleached, 10-4, Wamsutta; brown, 4-4 Indian Head; brown, 4-4, Pepperell; brown, 4-4, Trion.
1928–1941:   Average of sheeting, bleached, Pequot; sheeting, brown, Indian Head, Pepperell, Trion.
1947–1975:   Broadwoven goods (WPU0312).
1975–1990:   Broadwovens (WPU0337).

Ducks (.07)
1914–1928:   Average of duck, yard, Army, 8oz. and wide, No. 8.
1928–1941:   Average of duck, mill, Army, 8oz. and duck, mill, wide, 36 inch.
1947–1975:   Broadwoven goods (WPU0312).
1975–1990:   Broadwovens (WPU0337).

Gingham (.07)
1914–1928:   Average of ginghams, Amoskeag, Lancaster, and Security.
1928–1941:   Gingham, Amoskeag.
1947–1975:   Broadwoven goods (WPU0312).
1975–1990:   Broadwovens (WPU0337).

Prints (.07)
1914–1928:   Average of print cloth, 27 inch and $38\frac{1}{2}$ inch.
1928–1941:   Average of print cloth, 27 inch and $38\frac{1}{2}$ inch.
1947–1975:   Broadwoven goods (WPU0312).
1975–1990:   Broadwovens (WPU0337).

Drills (.07)
1914–1928:   Average of drillings, brown, Massachusetts, 30 inch and Pepperell, 29 inch.
1928–1941:   Cotton goods index.
1947–1975:   Broadwoven goods (WPU0312).
1975–1990:   Broadwovens (WPU0337).

Tickings (.07)

1914–1928:   Tickings, Amoskeag, A.C.A.

1928–1941:   Tickings, mill, Amoskeag.

1947–1975:   Broadwoven goods (WPU0312).

1975–1990:   Broadwovens (WPU0337).

Fuel and lighting

Coal, anthracite (.34)

1914–1928:   Average of anthracite, broken and anthracite, chestnut, egg, stove.

1928–1941:   Average of anthracite coal, chestnut, egg, pea.

1947–1990:   Anthracite (WPU0511).

Coal, bituminous (.50)

1914–1928:   Average of bituminous, mine run; bituminous, prepared sizes; bituminous, screenings.

1928–1941:   Average of bituminous, mine run; bituminous, prepared sizes; bituminous, screenings.

1947–1990:   Bituminous coal (WPU0512).

Candles, sperm (.015)

1914–1928:   No data available.

1928–1941:   No data available.

1947–1985:   No data available.

1985–1990:   Candles (WPU159AO1).

Candles, adamantine (.015)

1914–1928:   No data available.

1928–1941:   No data available.

1947–1985:   No data available.

1985–1990:   Candles (WPU159A01).

Oil, whale (.02)

1914–1928:   No data available.

1928–1941:   No data available.

1947–1970:   Fish and marine animal oil (WPU06410121).

1970–1970:   Fats and oils, inedible (WPU064).

1970–1974:   Fish and marine animal oil (WPU06410121).

1974–1974:   Fats and oils, inedible (WPU064).

1974–1977:   Fish and marine animal oil (WPU06410121).

1977–1977:   Fats and oils, inedible (WPU064).
1977–1979:   Fish and marine animal oil (WPU06410121).
1979–1979:   Fats and oils, inedible (WPU064).
1979–1980:   Fish and marine animal oil (WPU06410121).
1980–1980:   Fats and oils, inedible (WPU064).
1980–1983:   Fish and marine animal oil (WPU06410121).
1983–1983:   Fats and oils, inedible (WPU064).
1983–1984:   Fish and marine animal oil (WPU06410121).
1984–1984:   Fats and oils, inedible (WPU064).
1984–1990:   Fish and marine animal oil (WPU06410121).

Petroleum (.10)
1914–1928:   Average of fuel oil, refinery, Oklahoma and refinery, Philadelphia.
1928–1941:   Fuel oil, refinery, Pennsylvania.
1947–1990:   Crude petroleum (domestic production) (WPU0561).

Matches (.01)
1914–1928:   No data available.
1928–1931:   No data available.
1932–1941:   Matches, factory, average of regular and safety.
1947–1990:   Matches (WPU1592).

Metals and metal products

Pig iron (.17)
1914–1928:   Average of basic, furnace; Bessemer, Pittsburgh; foundry No. 2, Northern, Pittsburgh; foundry No. 2, Southern, Birmingham and Cincinnati, ferromanganese, furnace; Spiegeleisen, furnace.
1928–1941:   Average of basic, furnace; Bessemer, Pittsburgh, foundry No. 2, Northern, Pittsburgh; foundry No. 2, Southern, Birmingham; ferromanganese, furnace; Spiegeleisen, furnace.
1947–1982:   Pig iron, basic (WPU10160101).
1982–1986:   Pig iron (WPU10160291).
1986–1990:   Blast furnace products (WPU101601).

Sheet iron (.21)
1914–1928:   Sheet steel, box annealed.
1928–1941:   Sheet steel, box annealed.
1947–1990:   Sheets, C.R., carbon (WPU10170711).

Nails (.10)
1914–1928:   Nails, wire.
1928–1941:   Nails, wire, Pittsburgh.
1947–1989:   Bright nails (WPU10880211).
1989–1990:   Steel nails and spikes (WPU108802).

Copper, sheathing (.10)
1914–1928:   Copper sheet, hot rolled (base sizes).
1928–1941:   Copper sheet, New York, hot rolled.
1947–1990:   Copper-base alloy strip (WPU10250231).

Copper, pig (.05)
1914–1928:   Ingot, electrolytic.
1928–1941:   Copper ingot, refinery, electrolytic.
1947–1990:   Domestic copper cathode (WPU10220123).

Lead, pig (.04)
1914–1928:   Lead, pig, desilverized.
1928–1941:   Lead, pig, New York, desilverized.
1947–1990:   Lead, pig, common (WPU10220127).

Shot (.02)
1914–1928:   Lead pipe.
1928–1941:   Lead pipe.
1947–1990:   Non-ferrous mill shapes (WPU1025).

Quicksilver (.01)
1914–1928:   Quicksilver, flask.
1928–1941:   Quicksilver, New York.
1947–1987:   Mercury 761b. flask (WPU10220146).
1987–1990:   Primary non-ferrous metals (WPU10220132).

Zinc (.05)
1914–1928:   Zinc, sheet, La Salle, Ill.
1928–1941:   Zinc, sheet, La Salle, Ill.
1947–1990:   Zinc, slab, Prime Western (WPU10220132).

Tin, pig (.05)
1914–1928:   Tin, pig.
1928–1941:   Tin, pig, straits, New York.
1947–1985:   Tin, pig, grade A (WPU10220126).
1985–1990:   Primary non-ferrous metals (WPU102201).

Butts (.02)
1914–1928:   Butts, loose-pin, wrought steel.
1928–1932:   Nails, wire.
1932–1941:   Butts.
1947–1990:   Steel mill products (WPU1017).

Spelter (.03)
1914–1928:   Zinc, pig, slab, New York.
1928–1941:   Zinc, pig, slab, New York.
1947–1990:   Zinc, slab, Prime Western (WPU10220132).

Wood screws (.05)
1914–1928:   Wood screws, 1 inch, No. 10, flathead.
1928–1932:   Nails, wire.
1932–1941:   Wood screws
1947–1972:   Wood screws (WPU10810126).
1972–1990:   Bolts, nuts, screws, rivets and washers (WPU1081).

Shovels (.05)
1914–1928:   Shovels, Ames, No. 2.
1928–1932:   Plow, walking, one-horse.
1932–1941:   Shovels exe. 1939, spades.
1947–1983:   Shovel (WPU10420156).
1983–1990:   Hand and edge tools (WPU1042).

Iron wire (.05)
1914–1928:   Wire, fence annealed plain.
1928–1941:   Wire, fence annealed plain.
1947–1990:   Plain wire, carbon steel (WPU10170511).

Building materials

North River white pine (.24)
1914–1928:   Average of white pine, No. 2 barn, Buffalo and New York.
1928–1941:   White pine, No. 2, Buffalo.
1947–1990:   Lumber (WPU081).

Georgia yellow pine (.08)
1914–1928:   Average of yellow pine boards, flooring, siding.
1928–1941:   Pine, yellow flooring, mill.
1947–1990:   Lumber (WPU081).

Oak timber (.10)
1914–1928:   Average of white oak, plain and white oak, quartered.
1928–1941:   Oak, plain, No. 1, white, Cincinnati.
1947–1990:   Lumber (WPU081).

Spruce boards (.05)
1914–1928:   Spruce, eastern.
1928–1941:   Spruce, Boston, Eastern.
1947–1990:   Lumber (WPU081).

Pine shingles (.12)
1914–1928:   Average of shingles, cypress and shingles, red cedar.
1928–1939:   Shingles, mill, cypress.
1939–1941:   Shingles, mill, cedar, red.
1947–1990:   Lumber (WPU081).

Staves (.14)
1914–1928:   No data available.
1928–1941:   No data available.
1947–1990:   Lumber (WPU081).

White oak headings (.03)
1914–1928:   No data available.
1928–1941:   No data available.
1947–1990:   Lumber (WPU081).

Linseed oil (.02)
1914–1928:   Linseed oil, raw, New York.
1928–1941:   Linseed oil, raw, New York.
1947–1986:   Linseed oil (WPU06220136).
1986–1990:   Paint materials (WPU0622).

Lead (.04)
1914–1928:   Weighted average of red lead, dry, New York, and carbonate of
              white lead, American, in oil, New York.
1928–1941:   Weighted average of red lead, dry, New York, and white lead,
              in oil, New York.
1947–1990:   Paint materials (WPU0622).

Turpentine (.004)
1914–1928:   Turpentine, Southern.
1928–1941:   Turpentine, Southern, New York.

1947–1973:   Turpentine (WPU06120486).
1973–1990:   Other basic organics (WPU061403).

Glass (.03)
1914–1928:   Average of plate glass, polished 3 to 5 square feet and 5 to 10
               square feet and window glass, American, grade A and grade B.
1928–1941:   Average of plate glass, 3 to 5 square feet and 5 to 10 square feet
               and window glass, works, single A and single B.
1947–1966:   Flat glass (WPU131).
1966–1990:   Glass (WPU1311).

Bricks (.05)
1914–1928:   Average of common building, salmon, red (Cincinnati), red
               (New York).
1928–1941:   Average of bricks, common building and bricks, common (red),
               domestic, New York.
1947–1984:   Building brick (WPU13410101).
1984–1990:   Brick, except ceramic (WPU134201).

Lime (.05)
1914–1928:   Lime, common, lump.
1928–1941:   Average of lime, common building and lime, hydrated.
1947–1985:   Building lime (WPU1391).
1985–1990:   Other non-metallic minerals (WPU139).

Cement (.02)
1914–1928:   Average of Portland cement, Buffington, Ind., Northampton, Pa.,
               San Francisco, Ca.
1928–1941:   Average of Portland cement, Buffington, Ind. and Northampton,
               Pa.
1947–1989:   Portland cement (WPU13220131).
1989–1990:   Cement (WPU1322).

Tar (.005)
1914–1918:   No data available.
1918–1928:   Asphalt, bulk
1928–1932:   Asphalt, bulk.
1932–1941:   Tar, pine.
1947–1973:   Crudes (WPU061201).
1973–1990:   Primary crudes (WPU061401).

Putty (.001)
1914–1928:   Putty, commercial, New York.
1928–1941:   Putty, commercial, New York.
1947–1983:   Paint materials (WPU0622).
1983–1988:   Putty and putty products (WPU06230102).
1988–1990:   Misc. products, including putty (WPU06230113).

Nails, cut (.02)
1914–1928:   Nails, wire.
1928–1941:   Nails, wire, Pittsburgh.
1947–1989:   Bright nails (WPU10880211).
1989–1990:   Steel nails and spikes (WPU108802).

Drugs and chemicals

Alum (.20)
1914–1928:   Alum, lump, New York.
1928–1941:   Aluminum sulphate, commercial, New York.

Blue vitriol (.20)
1914–1928:   Copper sulphate, crystals, New York.
1928–1941:   Copper sulphate, New York.
1947–1973:   Inorganic chemicals (WPU0611).
1973–1990:   Basic inorganic chemicals (WPU0613).

Copperas (.20)
1914–1928:   Copperas, bulk.
1928–1941:   Copperas, works.
1947–1973:   Inorganic chemicals (WPU0611).
1973–1990:   Basic inorganic chemicals (WPU0613).

Indigo (.20)
1914–1928:   Coal tar colors, indigo, 20% paste.
1928–1941:   Coal tar colors, New York, indigo paste.
1947–1973:   Inorganic chemicals (WPU0611).
1973–1990:   Basic inorganic chemicals (WPU0613).

Sulfuric acid (.20)
1914–1928:   Sulfuric acid, 66 degree.
1928–1941:   Sulfuric acid, New York.
1947–1973:   Sulfuric acid (WPU06110335).
1973–1990:   Basic inorganic chemicals (WPU0613).

House furnishings

Carpets, ingrain (.10)
1914–1928:   Average of Axminster, Brussels, Wilton.
1928–1941:   Average of Axminster and Wilton.
1947–1990:   Soft surface floor coverings (WPU1231).

Earthenware, plates (.10)
1914–1928:   Plates, white granite.
1928–1941:   Plates, white granite.
1947–1990:   Stoneware and earthenware tableware (WPU12610111)

Earthenware, teacups and chambers (.20)
1914–1928:   Teacups and saucers, white granite.
1928–1941:   Teacups and saucers, white granite.
1947–1990:   Stoneware and earthenware tableware (WPU12610111)

Kitchen chairs (.10)
1914–1928:   Kitchen chairs.
1928–1929:   Furniture index.
1930–1941:   Furniture, kitchen chair.
1947–1990:   Wood household furniture (WPU1212).

Wooden pails (.10)
1914–1928:   Pails, galvanized iron.
1928–1938:   Pails, galvanized iron.
1938–1941:   Furnishings index.
1947–1990:   Wood household furniture (WPU1212).

Wooden tubs (.10)
1914–1928:   Tubs, galvanized iron.
1928–1941:   Tubs, factory, galvanized iron.
1947–1990:   Wood household furniture (WPU1212).

Bedroom chairs (.10)
1914–1928:   Furniture, bedroom chairs.
1928–1929:   Furniture, factory, index.
1930–1941:   Furniture, bedroom chairs.
1947–1990:   Wood household furniture (WPU1212).

Feathers (.10)
1914–1928:   No data available.

1928–1941:   No data available.
1947–1990:   No data available.

Sheeting, brown (.10)
1914–1928:   Average of brown, 4-4, Indian Head; brown, 4-4 Pepperell; brown, 4-4, Trion.
1928–1941:   Average of Indian Head, Pepperell, Trion.
1947–1975:   Broadwoven goods (WPU0312).
1975–1990:   Broadwovens (WPU0337).

Spirits

Alcohol (1.0)
1914–1928:   Alcohol, grain, New York.
1928–1941:   Alcohol, grain, New York.
1947–1963:   Ethyl alcohol
1963–1971:   Organic chemicals
1971–1973:   Other basic organics
1973–1988:   Ethyl alcohol
1988–1990:   Basic organics (WPU0614)

Miscellaneous

Gunpowder, rifle (.30)
1914–1928:   Chemicals index number.
1928–1941:   Chemicals index number.
1947–1973:   Inorganic chemicals (WPU0611).
1973–1990:   Basic inorganic chemicals (WPU0613).

Rubber (.10)
1914–1928:   Average of rubber Para Island and rubber, plantation.
1928–1941:   Average of rubber, crude, New York, amber No. 3; rubber, crude, latex crepe; rubber, crude, plantation, ribbed, smoked sheets.
1947–1985:   Natural rubber (WPU071101).
1985–1990:   Synthetic rubber (WPU071102).

Soap, Castile (.30)
1914–1928:   Average of soap, laundry, Cincinnati and Philadelphia.
1928–1932:   Average of soap, laundry, Cincinnati and Philadelphia.

1932–1941:   Soap, toilet, New York.
1947–1983:   Soaps (WPU067101).
1983–1990:   Household soaps (WPU06710403).

Ashes, pearl (.20)
1914–1928:   Average of potash, muriate and potash, sulfate.
1928–1941:   Average of potash, muriate and potash, sulfate
1947–1984:   Potash (WPU065203).
1984–1990:   Fertilizer materials (WPU0652).

Starch (.10)
1914–1928:   Starch, laundry, New York.
1928–1941:   Starch, laundry, New York.
1947–1990:   No data available.

NOTE

1. See Kydland and Prescott (1990). For a time-series variable x, the Hodrick–Prescott trend $\hat{x}$ is the solution to

$$\min_{\hat{x}_t} \sum_{t_0}^{t_1} \left(x_t - \hat{x}_t\right)^2 + \mu \sum_{t_0+1}^{t_1-1} \left[\left(\hat{x}_{t+1} - \hat{x}_t\right) - \left(\hat{x}_t - \hat{x}_{t-1}\right)\right]^2$$

with μ set at 1600 for quarterly data, 400 for annual.

Table A7.1   Consistent wholesale price series, 1860–1990: group and total indices

Year	Farm products (from BLS)	Foods	Hides and leather	Textiles	Fuel and lighting	Metals and metal products	Building materials	Drugs and chemicals	House furnishings	Spirits	Misc.	Total inc. farm products	Total exc. farm products
(Base: average 1890–1914 = 100)													
1860	97.519	110.437	116.746	122.342	119.930	138.140	68.643	177.664	130.280	29.458	100.110	105.428	108.106
1861	94.986	102.384	103.011	123.370	97.902	140.921	66.531	176.649	122.486	26.897	100.110	99.977	101.615
1862	108.917	123.091	123.614	151.128	106.469	166.880	72.868	209.136	138.075	35.862	124.626	116.863	119.536
1863	143.112	141.497	152.228	211.785	152.972	218.798	92.933	237.562	183.729	57.635	149.143	150.246	152.577
1864	205.170	217.422	187.710	271.413	241.084	328.198	120.390	301.521	247.199	135.763	193.068	217.608	221.740
1865	187.439	207.069	173.975	273.470	261.888	283.696	124.614	304.567	238.290	192.118	178.767	210.433	218.364
1866	177.307	199.016	167.107	251.880	195.804	257.737	135.175	287.308	244.971	197.241	173.659	195.944	202.333
1867	168.442	192.114	151.083	226.178	176.224	229.924	126.726	232.486	218.247	186.995	165.487	182.411	187.146
1868	174.774	196.715	144.216	202.532	182.343	208.600	122.502	207.106	198.204	149.852	156.294	179.382	180.761
1869	162.109	177.159	153.372	199.448	203.147	210.454	116.166	230.456	198.204	110.148	138.928	171.623	174.775
1870	141.846	159.903	146.505	184.027	163.986	185.422	106.661	202.029	182.615	99.901	130.755	152.316	155.840
1871	129.181	149.550	144.216	174.774	186.014	188.204	107.717	179.695	171.480	94.778	122.583	147.567	153.939
1872	136.780	139.196	148.794	181.970	187.238	238.268	112.997	177.664	177.048	93.497	127.691	153.008	158.599
1873	130.447	140.347	151.083	179.914	181.119	225.288	111.941	183.755	178.161	96.059	117.476	149.670	156.340
1874	129.181	144.948	146.505	155.240	165.210	179.860	106.661	178.679	165.913	99.901	113.389	141.784	146.090
1875	125.381	138.046	140.782	144.959	156.643	162.245	95.045	151.268	149.210	112.709	100.110	133.980	136.861
1876	112.717	129.993	119.035	141.875	155.420	145.557	88.708	142.131	136.961	110.148	100.110	124.986	129.199
1877	112.717	132.294	124.758	128.510	132.168	130.723	84.484	138.070	131.394	110.148	97.045	120.260	122.783
1878	91.186	106.986	108.734	118.229	113.811	116.816	76.036	128.933	121.372	105.025	89.894	102.392	106.256
1879	91.186	103.534	114.457	117.201	97.902	124.233	78.148	121.827	116.918	105.025	91.937	100.872	104.194
1880	101.318	110.437	129.337	131.594	112.587	153.901	85.540	121.827	130.280	106.305	92.959	112.202	115.937
1881	112.717	121.941	124.758	122.342	111.364	139.067	87.652	121.827	121.372	103.744	91.937	115.680	116.566
1882	125.381	131.144	123.614	122.342	112.587	145.557	92.933	115.735	121.372	102.463	95.002	122.485	121.258
1883	110.184	118.489	122.469	119.257	108.916	133.504	89.764	111.675	122.486	106.305	95.002	113.375	114.347

Table A7.1   continued

Year (from BLS)	Farm products	Foods	Hides and leather	Textiles	Fuel and lighting	Metals and metal products	Building materials	Drugs and chemicals	House furnishings	Spirits	Misc.	Total inc. farm products	Total exc. farm products
1884	103.851	106.986	127.047	112.061	94.231	114.962	88.708	106.598	116.918	103.744	79.679	104.858	105.058
1885	91.186	96.632	120.180	107.949	88.112	101.055	85.540	101.522	110.237	101.182	79.679	95.983	97.558
1886	86.121	89.730	115.602	102.808	85.664	101.982	86.596	100.507	104.670	101.182	75.593	92.184	94.219
1887	89.920	98.933	105.301	100.752	85.664	110.326	85.540	98.477	102.443	98.621	76.614	95.326	97.120
1888	94.986	98.933	98.433	100.752	88.112	112.181	84.484	104.568	104.670	102.463	74.571	96.859	97.383
1889	84.854	90.880	91.566	101.780	86.888	107.545	85.540	102.538	104.670	94.778	81.722	91.508	93.756
1890	89.920	98.933	84.698	105.892	88.112	114.035	88.708	91.370	101.329	84.455	90.916	95.646	97.554
1891	96.250	102.186	85.340	101.414	96.282	102.405	85.399	82.834	99.257	88.604	95.322	97.005	97.257
1892	87.390	90.696	80.990	99.889	95.148	95.291	83.994	93.847	94.654	86.207	90.372	90.568	91.628
1893	91.190	98.488	78.000	101.333	95.444	89.859	84.183	88.037	93.994	85.930	90.015	92.920	93.497
1894	79.790	87.556	72.109	87.696	82.921	78.161	79.744	79.713	88.611	90.817	86.676	82.848	83.867
1895	78.520	83.508	91.597	85.564	79.209	80.841	78.567	75.695	83.764	97.086	80.675	81.903	83.031
1896	70.920	74.830	78.487	84.640	82.170	86.108	77.377	74.360	83.878	96.441	78.558	77.868	80.184
1897	75.990	78.315	83.431	82.845	81.730	73.918	74.119	91.858	82.311	94.874	81.571	78.578	79.441
1898	79.790	85.098	92.287	82.358	79.926	74.693	76.936	102.588	84.590	98.008	85.015	81.967	82.693
1899	81.050	84.350	97.309	89.919	77.928	111.739	84.690	107.276	89.739	99.576	87.153	87.499	89.649
1900	89.920	88.466	98.764	96.982	97.580	116.410	91.477	108.631	100.911	99.945	93.938	94.825	96.460
1901	93.720	90.725	98.286	90.845	100.021	103.071	91.949	114.207	100.137	103.079	96.200	94.829	95.199
1902	103.850	99.776	101.878	93.693	104.005	106.251	96.780	120.606	100.973	105.384	99.289	101.425	100.616
1903	98.780	92.294	97.423	99.598	119.388	105.942	99.797	117.119	103.070	102.711	101.318	100.434	100.986
1904	103.850	97.535	95.191	100.915	114.151	93.140	101.571	118.147	103.504	101.789	100.776	101.410	100.596
1905	100.050	96.855	103.725	100.705	109.391	103.531	105.886	116.517	101.059	101.143	102.112	101.558	102.060
1906	101.320	96.839	111.536	108.083	109.034	117.548	118.251	102.109	104.068	103.264	103.565	105.488	106.878
1907	110.180	101.343	111.719	121.257	111.590	130.212	125.362	102.109	112.067	105.292	104.321	112.535	113.320
1908	110.180	107.251	105.917	103.920	113.471	100.456	116.229	102.750	110.974	108.796	104.473	108.448	107.871

206

Year													
1909	124.110	115.409	117.851	107.155	109.284	101.130	119.878	101.835	108.278	108.888	147.722	115.183	112.208
1910	131.710	118.317	114.460	113.117	107.650	104.780	124.243	100.794	109.368	106.214	148.539	118.838	114.547
1911	119.050	113.568	110.214	109.890	108.001	98.623	123.764	100.794	108.217	107.228	116.768	113.066	111.071
1912	129.180	124.823	122.192	108.493	110.141	108.345	124.543	100.794	108.895	109.072	109.455	120.004	116.946
1913	126.650	121.274	130.053	113.577	113.869	107.709	125.244	100.794	112.925	105.569	103.957	119.567	117.206
1914	126.650	125.219	136.542	109.861	113.553	95.802	121.305	105.216	113.430	109.626	101.294	118.969	116.409
1915	127.184	126.724	149.371	105.360	110.500	94.695	119.902	146.444	119.821	110.042	145.076	120.214	117.887
1916	150.130	148.909	182.531	138.688	132.448	105.634	133.754	259.226	143.339	114.419	208.748	143.137	140.796
1917	229.464	214.748	236.778	202.704	178.477	135.570	171.659	230.273	196.128	162.146	217.371	200.631	191.084
1918	263.261	224.922	219.523	282.329	187.319	161.454	204.150	253.843	270.226	212.791	222.575	227.391	215.520
1919	280.338	258.946	291.105	292.503	187.796	193.397	244.540	176.207	270.357	208.414	192.748	250.080	240.052
1920	268.064	258.906	263.154	352.534	265.274	262.576	332.014	210.064	352.249	226.963	202.658	276.539	279.257
1921	157.245	169.473	145.345	199.716	224.401	192.413	243.296	146.738	260.919	204.871	130.528	184.419	193.318
1922	166.851	161.900	148.494	207.372	236.496	182.827	231.175	135.456	224.536	201.953	102.203	183.768	189.289
1923	175.389	169.398	145.308	238.225	225.378	194.997	246.564	117.449	246.849	203.620	106.611	192.199	197.683
1924	177.879	174.366	134.413	223.854	213.659	181.304	229.250	108.223	241.792	206.121	106.773	187.961	191.231
1925	195.311	196.813	145.620	221.667	213.270	176.419	223.073	95.656	229.586	208.622	122.203	197.012	197.520
1926	177.879	192.880	134.776	199.728	218.948	170.281	215.312	97.700	223.691	208.414	115.338	188.396	191.809
1927	176.812	182.754	160.332	193.542	212.250	161.870	204.676	99.934	219.388	160.687	110.562	181.901	183.529
1928	188.374	188.429	192.668	197.586	178.539	158.790	200.782	101.726	211.207	115.878	108.262	182.413	180.402
1929	186.595	181.372	156.900	193.069	174.683	167.138	205.422	104.788	206.146	117.754	108.307	178.853	176.180
1930	157.067	158.223	131.864	168.212	169.121	143.280	191.901	97.581	198.233	113.586	100.954	157.009	157.153
1931	115.266	120.516	102.322	134.010	159.877	125.419	171.635	90.098	180.261	107.333	88.840	126.515	130.807
1932	85.738	98.611	79.284	108.179	157.225	114.802	151.109	86.732	164.986	107.125	81.401	106.110	113.753
1933	91.430	106.059	94.414	128.172	154.902	122.596	160.576	90.378	167.100	107.125	76.003	113.521	121.807
1934	116.155	126.528	93.040	148.680	169.246	135.572	176.808	93.306	181.690	184.029	78.255	133.339	139.832
1935	140.169	150.068	105.935	147.377	171.784	135.758	174.517	93.430	176.519	193.408	80.467	146.704	149.275
1936	143.904	148.128	113.307	144.006	173.858	138.442	179.216	94.010	194.466	193.825	87.057	148.323	150.113
1937	153.688	155.698	134.736	157.004	174.960	169.092	200.455	99.391	198.964	195.909	94.047	160.288	162.897
1938	121.847	133.101	105.416	131.255	174.744	154.570	189.339	96.277	187.150	200.494	80.227	139.390	146.022
1939	116.155	123.881	111.598	138.474	170.994	155.125	188.530	97.508	187.636	205.496	81.373	136.304	143.897

Table A7.1 continued

Year	Farm products (from BLS)	Foods	Hides and leather	Textiles	Fuel and lighting	Metals and metal products	Building materials	Drugs and chemicals	House furnishings	Spirits	Misc.	Total inc. farm products	Total exc. farm products
1940	120.424	124.535	115.665	148.400	172.450	156.517	188.728	98.144	192.168	229.880	84.483	139.775	147.076
1941	146.572	148.236	129.986	180.682	187.645	172.665	211.907	99.241	218.225	283.651	88.765	163.130	169.423

(Base: average 1947–1990 = 100)

Year	Farm products (from BLS)	Foods	Hides and leather	Textiles	Fuel and lighting	Metals and metal products	Building materials	Drugs and chemicals	House furnishings	Spirits	Misc.	Total inc. farm products	Total exc. farm products
1947	70.263	63.548	57.616	68.247	29.932	30.911	41.051	35.486	44.928	81.554	53.302	56.555	51.986
1948	75.465	66.205	54.486	66.348	35.126	36.213	45.280	37.492	47.470	73.940	54.424	59.506	54.186
1949	65.253	58.625	49.367	59.800	33.638	36.333	42.178	39.578	47.154	33.226	50.144	52.505	48.255
1950	68.529	59.625	56.883	66.907	34.271	38.192	46.835	41.016	50.387	46.692	57.647	55.826	51.591
1951	79.768	66.859	65.975	77.151	36.464	44.141	51.022	44.989	56.835	78.974	67.330	64.234	59.056
1952	75.273	66.280	42.941	68.548	35.720	43.954	49.476	45.036	53.424	60.159	58.796	60.253	55.246
1953	68.208	62.703	45.249	66.828	37.554	43.785	49.181	47.358	53.931	49.146	55.064	57.310	53.678
1954	67.244	63.877	39.902	63.537	35.842	44.125	48.700	49.327	54.005	45.748	57.150	56.574	53.017
1955	63.070	60.208	39.948	64.499	35.202	47.780	51.115	49.846	54.622	45.371	61.948	55.302	52.713
1956	62.235	60.079	42.734	65.441	37.365	51.409	52.678	51.025	56.999	50.971	60.702	56.193	54.180
1957	63.905	61.106	41.614	64.476	40.718	50.900	50.564	51.733	58.200	53.677	60.269	56.895	54.559
1958	66.731	62.949	42.756	61.885	40.289	50.388	50.238	52.299	58.229	54.684	59.562	57.752	54.758
1959	62.620	59.294	56.010	63.986	40.128	52.182	53.112	52.582	58.998	57.830	63.161	57.142	55.316
1960	62.428	60.881	47.943	66.335	39.653	53.055	51.374	53.007	60.161	57.830	64.136	57.294	55.583
1961	61.849	60.009	49.862	64.387	38.883	52.125	49.448	53.243	60.065	57.830	62.824	56.440	54.636
1962	62.941	61.345	50.432	65.685	38.097	52.210	50.040	53.243	60.758	57.830	63.178	57.199	55.284
1963	61.657	60.779	45.290	66.503	38.575	52.286	50.758	53.149	60.891	57.830	62.815	56.736	55.096
1964	60.758	62.097	46.090	66.741	39.384	55.110	51.729	53.526	61.669	56.932	62.857	57.342	56.204
1965	63.391	65.487	51.004	66.041	38.908	58.182	52.183	54.669	61.854	57.060	64.475	59.313	57.953
1966	68.015	68.378	59.368	65.927	39.284	57.735	54.711	56.023	63.785	57.188	64.040	61.793	59.719
1967	64.226	65.678	49.402	64.885	40.079	58.386	54.963	58.945	65.518	57.445	62.231	59.873	58.423

1968	65.831	66.355	50.978	66.013	41.332	60.289	62.387	62.420	67.848	57.188	61.668	61.723	60.353
1969	69.878	70.946	55.663	66.911	44.669	64.172	68.604	63.304	70.132	55.584	61.021	65.480	64.014
1970	71.291	73.658	52.758	67.423	55.194	68.838	61.741	63.116	72.235	56.290	64.398	67.353	66.041
1971	72.536	73.796	56.003	68.689	64.690	69.939	71.469	63.978	75.993	56.412	66.044	70.054	69.227
1972	80.319	78.402	78.742	74.934	67.691	73.668	81.432	64.450	80.420	54.835	66.718	76.363	75.045
1973	113.162	99.354	91.057	90.530	76.076	79.506	101.158	66.820	85.139	55.010	74.172	95.410	89.493
1974	120.478	123.967	81.591	105.349	116.741	110.840	108.377	82.772	94.885	86.480	90.602	113.783	111.551
1975	119.856	127.795	77.818	102.111	144.501	123.780	105.367	116.135	104.751	123.848	107.021	119.596	119.509
1976	122.657	116.943	101.878	122.324	141.384	127.497	122.390	125.003	111.115	133.233	113.199	122.825	122.881
1977	123.591	118.368	110.286	120.033	147.403	137.084	142.223	129.015	116.315	136.803	115.409	127.287	128.519
1978	136.511	132.762	133.407	131.121	158.599	146.711	162.965	133.449	125.730	131.563	123.625	140.369	141.655
1979	155.034	145.708	199.059	139.734	168.424	167.730	180.076	140.629	134.853	149.988	139.743	157.396	158.184
1980	160.171	163.044	161.213	155.070	186.081	175.569	172.258	163.856	156.471	203.765	160.594	167.072	169.373
1981	163.751	165.450	164.391	162.568	218.089	182.811	175.004	196.585	166.764	218.332	175.849	174.665	178.303
1982	155.657	163.747	160.069	159.120	229.803	180.824	169.999	211.154	173.286	198.813	179.751	171.834	177.227
1983	159.392	163.535	169.994	163.187	225.550	185.147	188.278	200.808	183.482	193.573	179.116	175.189	180.455
1984	164.218	170.807	191.443	163.280	227.326	190.664	188.737	199.118	192.203	196.740	186.767	180.698	186.191
1985	148.029	161.978	181.518	165.164	224.932	186.056	185.709	204.186	193.090	188.737	186.351	172.447	180.586
1986	144.605	160.893	196.725	163.778	214.389	181.229	186.196	201.230	193.790	178.949	182.056	169.942	178.388
1987	148.652	165.134	225.538	171.719	213.050	193.165	196.422	199.541	198.307	179.726	183.727	176.111	185.264
1988	163.284	169.861	268.116	180.428	210.338	220.318	203.331	213.055	207.796	177.141	197.728	186.952	194.842
1989	172.623	183.122	272.758	182.987	215.367	233.766	209.835	229.947	218.196	190.238	207.369	196.304	204.198
1990	174.647	188.363	284.123	187.370	223.258	230.995	209.407	235.859	227.410	184.836	211.017	199.508	207.795

8. The cyclical adjustment of hours and employment in the prewar United States: evidence from the depression of 1893–4

John A. James[*]

INTRODUCTION

Has the character of American business cycles changed over the last century? The institutional framework of the labor market, first of all, changed dramatically in the second quarter of the twentieth century as unions, firm-specific capital, and long-term relationships between employers and workers became significant influences. Such factors have been thought in turn to have reduced the flexibility of the labor market in adjusting to shocks or disturbances in the post-World War II period relative to pre-World War II and, *a fortiori*, pre-World War I periods.

Bernanke and Powell (1986), examining monthly US manufacturing data covering the 1923–39 and 1954–82 periods, find that postwar employers were more inclined to reduce labor inputs during downturns by layoffs than by shorter work weeks. During the Great Depression labor input declined by 43 per cent: in manufacturing from the peak (1929: 3) to the trough (1933: 1). Employment in manufacturing fell by 28 per cent, while work hours per week fell by 21 per cent. In other words, reduction in hours accounted for about one-third of the fall in labor input. In contrast, it was responsible for less than 10 per cent of the decline in labor input during the 1981–2 downturn (ibid.: 625).

Pressing further back in time, into the period before World War I, the use of hours reduction as a means of adjustment has been seen as even more important. In his influential study of unemployment in Massachusetts before World War I, Keyssar (1986) notes that hours reduction was a common means of reducing labor input during times of slack demand. This could have taken the form either of shutting the plant completely for periods of days, weeks, or months,

---

[*] I would like to acknowledge the comments of Mark Thomas, Susan Carter, and Richard Sutch, and my discussant, Tim Hatton, although responsibility for errors must still fall on the author.

or of running the establishment on 'short time' by limiting the hours per day or days per week that each employee worked. He observes: 'During depressions factories often operated three or four days a week, with everyone working a few days less than usual' (ibid.: 49). Examining Connecticut data over the 1893–4 period, Carter and Sutch (1991, 1994) also emphasize the role of shutdowns in cyclical adjustment on the basis of Connecticut data from 1893–4.

Such a view implies that in the industrial labor market of earlier times the burden of reducing labor input during downturns was distributed among workers more widely (or more fairly in Carter and Sutch's term) than it is in the contemporary one. Rather than relying primarily or exclusively on selective layoffs or dismissals, nineteenth- and early twentieth-century firms often used instead hours reduction or work-sharing arrangements through temporary plant shutdowns or short time. The burdens of depressions then were spread more widely and consequently were less severe on some than they would have been under the present system in which adjustment comes primarily through changes in employment.

I would like to argue here that the use of cyclical hours adjustment in the period before World War I may well have been overstated. This in turn suggests that the trend away from shutdowns and short time toward layoffs and dismissals as methods of cyclical adjustment before World War II was weaker than otherwise would be implied. Although hours changes played a larger role in labor input adjustment before World War II than after, the contrast should not be exaggerated. The evidence to be presented here suggests that although reductions in hours, as opposed to in employment, were more prevalent during the late nineteenth century than today, it was not in fact the generally dominant practice. Firm-level micro data show that in late nineteenth-century downturns the majority of the fall in labor input was, as now, accomplished through decreases in the level of employment, a practice which seems to have been an enduring characteristic of American labor markets over the last century. Furthermore, the decline in the use of hours reduction as a cyclical response that did occur must have come primarily quite abruptly around World War II, since there seems to have been only a slight downward trend in their use between the 1890s, based on my data here, and the 1930s, based on Bernanke and Powell (1986).

To study the adjustment process in prewar downturns, I examine the depression of 1893–4, one of the most serious in American history. The output gap (the percentage deviation of real output from long-term trend) fell by more than 11 percentage points from peak to trough of the cycle (James, 1985). Lebergott (1964: 522) calculated that the unemployment rate rose from 3.0 per cent in 1892 to 18.4 per cent in 1894, a remarkable rise in view of the fact that agriculture still constituted 43 per cent of the labor force in 1890. Over the course of the downturn there were more than 600 bank failures (about 5 per cent of US banks) and over 15 000 commercial bankruptcies (Mishkin, 1991: 87).

It was most probably the most severe downturn the United States had ever experienced up to that time, and more data were collected than ever before on its course and severity by state bureaux of labor statistics. In this chapter I use monthly data compiled by the New Jersey Bureau of Labor Statistics to examine the course of adjustment of hours and employment in manufacturing over the downturn. These results in turn will be compared with data covering the same period collected by the State of Connecticut.

The data are described in the Appendix. The next section briefly recounts the course of the 1893–4 depression. This is followed by an examination of the nature and magnitude of the cyclical movement in labor input in New Jersey firms, and subsequently by a comparison of those results with ones from Connecticut. The final section summarizes and concludes.

THE COURSE OF THE 1893–4 DOWNTURN

Chronology

The peak of the business cycle is identified by the National Bureau of Economic Research (NBER) as falling in January 1893. The first half of 1893 witnessed a wave of bankruptcies, initiated by the failure of the Reading Railroad on February 26. Early in May the announcement of the failure of the National Cordage Co., said to have been the result of an inability to secure working capital, led to a stock market collapse. On the financial front, in April the gold reserve of the Treasury fell below $100 million, which obliged the Secretary of the Treasury to discontinue the issuance of gold certificates. This in turn caused a 'semi-panic' and a sharp increase in gold exports.

The May stock market plunge, however, was not the proximate cause of the summer's financial instability. Rather, it had its immediate origins in public doubts about the solvency of banks. Friedman and Schwartz (1963: 108) suggest that the commercial failures of the winter and spring created doubts about the soundness of bank loans and hence bank portfolios. Nineteen interior national banks, along with substantial numbers of state and private banks, failed in May and June in the west and south. Beginning in early June, country banks started to draw down their deposits with New York banks in order to bolster their reserve positions at home. The normal seasonal inflow of cash into New York was reversed, resulting in a substantial drain of funds to the interior. During the third week of June pressure on interior banks, and hence the withdrawal of funds from New York, intensified.

Finally, at the beginning of August banks in New York suspended or restricted cash payments, and those in other parts of the country followed; that is, banks in concert refused to convert deposits into currency (specie) on demand. One dollar in deposits was no longer redeemable for a dollar in specie. Instead, a premium on currency developed, usually ranging between 1 and 2 per cent; reaching a maximum of 4 per cent (Sprague 1910: 187). The suspension was caused most directly by the internal drain, which added to the strains caused by the earlier international drain. In fact, the gold outflow had stopped by June 6, and after that date gold was actually flowing into the country. By early September, after the public's desire for a higher currency–deposit ratio had ebbed and reserves had been enhanced by gold inflows, the currency premium had disappeared and banks removed their restrictions on currency payments.[1]

The Timing of the Decline in Labor Input

Monthly levels of labor input in the sample of New Jersey manufacturing firms between June 1893 and May 1894 are shown in Figure 8.1. They are measured relative to the level of June 1892, which is taken to have been a normal period (see the Appendix). The horizontal line (at 1) therefore represents the labor input of average employment levels working full time. Note, first of all, that even though the downturn began in January there probably had been little impact on labor input in New Jersey manufacturing over the first half of year since by June labor input was not lower and indeed a bit higher than it had been a year earlier in June 1892 (by 0.23 per cent on average) – with 63 firms (out of 252) showing decreases in employment in the interim, while 62 showed increases.

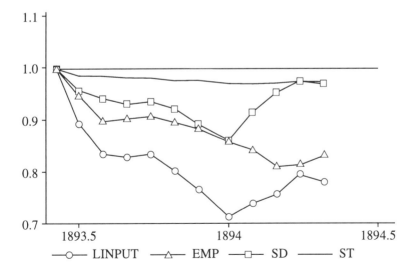

Figure 8.1   New Jersey labor input, June 1893–May 1894

In the summer, however, labor input fell sharply, declining by 11.4 per cent on average between June and July and by a further 9.1 per cent between July and August. Labor use in New Jersey manufacturing then stabilized between August and October at a level about 20 per cent below the June figure before declining again to a low in January almost 30 per cent below the June level.[2] Sundstrom (1992: 435), in his study of wage rigidity during the 1893 depression, based on data from Cincinnati manufacturing firms, finds a similar pattern for male workers: employment declines by almost 20 per cent between June and August and then roughly stabilizes.[3] While the NBER dates the cyclical trough as June 1894, Fels (1959: 189) argues that is misleading because contractionary forces had ebbed by the summer of 1893. The period after September 1893 therefore should be viewed as a transitional one. The data in Figure 8.1 would generally support this view, although there is an additional (seasonal?) fall in labor input at the end of the year.

COMPOSITION AND MAGNITUDE OF THE DECLINE IN LABOR INPUT

Changes in Average Wages and Labor Input

Market adjustment to the adverse shock initiating the 1893 downturn was primarily through decreases in labor inputs rather than through reductions in the real wage. Nominal full-time monthly earnings among the New Jersey firms in the sample declined by almost 10 per cent between June and October 1893 and thereafter began to rise, regaining their original level by the spring of 1894. A 10 per cent wholesale price decline between October and March reinforced this rising trend so that by spring 1894 real full-time monthly earnings were almost 10 per cent above their level in the 'normal' times of June 1892 (and June 1893). In contrast, the decline in labor input was substantial, falling by about one-third over the last six months of 1893.

Consider again Figure 8.1, which shows the course of average labor input and its decomposition between June 1893 and May 1894 for all manufacturing firms in the New Jersey sample measured relative to June 1892 levels (see the Appendix). The 'EMP' line represents what would have been the course of labor input if employment changes had proceeded as they actually did but there had been no reductions in hours.[4] Hours, as noted earlier, could have been reduced by shutting the plant down completely for periods of time or by limiting the number of hours an employee could work in a given week (short time).[5] The 'SD' line shows what would have happened to labor input if employment had remained fixed at its initial level but the actual course of shutdowns had occurred, while for the 'ST' line employment and shutdowns are fixed at initial levels and the actual course of short time is followed.[6] Thus, the level of labor input for firm i in month t is measured as:

$$\text{LINPUT}_{it} = \text{EMP}_{it} \times \text{SD}_{it} \times \text{ST}_{it}$$

where SD is, for example, 1 if the firm does not shut down in the given month and 0 if it is shut down completely for the full month.

Reductions in employment account for the majority of the reduction in labor input over the year (about 60 per cent). Only in the winter months of December and January does the contribution of shutdowns to reducing labor input approach that due to declines in employment. In Figure 8.2 the variables are weighted by firm size, as measured by the June 1892 employment level. Here reductions in employment were clearly the principal means by which reductions in labor input were accomplished during downturns. Thus, larger firms were more likely to cut employment and less likely to cut hours, other things being equal.

The relative importance of employment cuts versus shutdowns in reducing labor input varied across industries. In Figures 8.3–8.5 we see the change in labor input after June 1893 and its decomposition for three major New Jersey industries: metalworking, textiles and textile products, leather and leather products. In metals (Figure 8.3) cuts in employment clearly dominated, accounting for more than two-thirds of the decline in labor input. In textiles (Figure 8.4) employment cuts were relatively less important but still represented

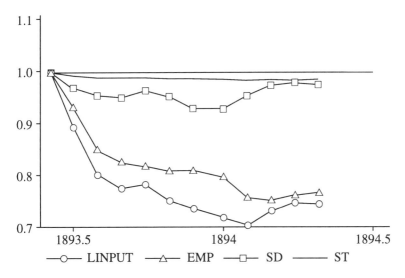

Figure 8.2   New Jersey labor input weighted by firm size, June 1893–May 1894

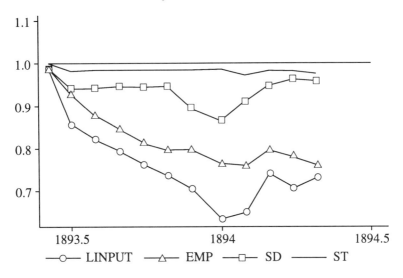

Figure 8.3   New Jersey metalworking labor input, June 1893–May 1894

more than half (58 per cent) of labor input reductions over the course of the year, with shutdowns playing a major role in the winter. In leather (Figure 8.5) employment cuts also accounted for about 58 per cent of labor input cuts over the year, with shutdowns having been particularly important in January 1894.

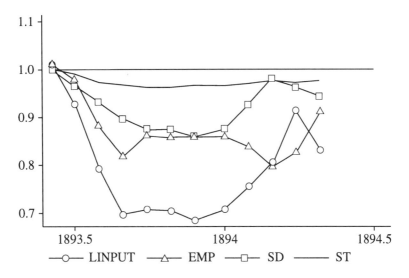

Figure 8.4   New Jersey textiles labor input, June 1893–May 1894

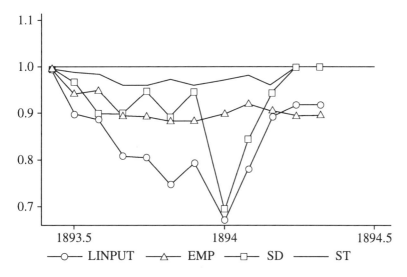

Figure 8.5   New Jersey leather labor input, June 1893–May 1894

One feature common to all the industries pictured in Figures 8.3–8.5 (as well as Figure 8.1) is the quantitative unimportance of short time in reducing labor input. In none of the three industries would short time alone, *ceteris paribus*, have reduced the level of labor inputs at any time by more than 4.1 per cent. To the extent that firms chose to reduce hours of work rather than employment, the method was primarily through plant closures rather than direct hours reductions. I now turn, therefore, to the pattern of shutdowns in more detail.

Shutdowns

Under what circumstances did New Jersey firms choose to shut down? Figure 8.6 shows the number of firms (out of 252) by month which reported some period of shutdown or short time. Rather than being at their highest levels in the initial stages of the downturn, the incidence of both shutdowns and short time rises fairly steadily over the last half of 1893, reaching a peak in the winter. At that time around 15 per cent of firms in the sample reported some shutdown period, while about 10 per cent reported short time. The data in Figure 8.6 represent responses to both cyclical and seasonal conditions. Since shutdowns were also well-known seasonal phenomena, these figures overstate (to an unknown extent) the use of shutdowns as a response to cyclical declines in demand and thus make it even less likely that they were the major form of cyclical adjustment in labor input. Indeed, the pattern, with a winter peak in shutdowns (and also in short time), suggests that seasonal influences may well have been

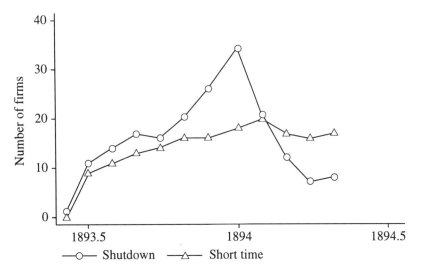

Figure 8.6   New Jersey shutdowns and short time, June 1893–May 1894

quite significant. However, since I am unable to separate seasonal from cyclical responses here, for my purposes in the following discussion I view the decision to shut down as a response to the economic downturn, which of course overstates the use of shutdowns as a cyclical response.

The first column of Table 8.1 shows the results of a probit regression examining factors influencing the decision to suspend operations. The dependent variable equals 1 if a firm reported having shut down at least part of the time in a given month and had been in full-time operation the month before, and equals 0 if operation over the month was full time. Months in which the period of suspension continued are excluded from the sample. The magnitude of the prior decline in labor input was an important element in the decision to shut down. The coefficient of the total decline in labor input up until the given month (DLABTOT, measured as positive numbers) is relatively large, of the expected sign, and statistically significantly different from zero in both specifications based on the reported z statistics in parentheses. Similarly, a larger decline in employment in the previous month (DEMP measured as positive) also increased the likelihood (statistically significantly) of suspension this month. Larger intraindustry firm size (measured by June 1892 employment) and greater industry capital intensity (measured at essentially the four-digit industry level from the 1890 Census of Manufactures) are negatively associated with shutdowns, other things being equal, but not quite statistically significantly so.

Table 8.1   Estimated timing of shutdowns and determinants of the mix of
labor input reduction

	(1) Probit	(2) OLS	(3) OLS
Dependent variable	BEGINSD	Ln((l–SD)/ (l–LINPUT))	Ln((1–EMP)/ l(–LINPUT))
Independent variables			
DEMP	0.3577		
	(2.04)		
DLABTOT	3.2164	0.08684	–0.08997
	(7.44)	(5.49)	(–6.36)
Size	–0.0017	0.00007	0.0000006
	(–1.60)	(0.47)	(0.04)
KLRATIO	–0.0004	–0.00004	0.00004
	(–1.57)	(–3.88)	(4.34)
Metal	6.5413	0.09809	–0.09553
	(15.23)	(3.93)	(–4.28)
Textile	6.4073	0.13940	–0.13660
	(14.55)	(5.71)	(–6.26)
Leather	7.1056	0.08463	–0.08071
	(20.29)	(2.99)	(–3.19)
Stone	6.1030	0.15826	–0.11040
	(12.93)	(5.76)	(–4.48)
Rubber	6.0876	0.14992	–0.14708
	(9.95)	(5.00)	(–5.49)
July		0.05342	–0.05194
		(1.73)	(–1.89)
August		0.04341	–0.04148
		(1.44)	(–1.54)
September		–0.00285	0.00362
		(–0.10)	(0.14)
October		0.09018	–0.08942
		(2.93)	(–3.25)
November		–0.01028	0.00861
		(–0.25)	(0.23)
December		0.09634	–0.09504
		(3.18)	(–3.51)
January		0.06573	–0.05487
		(2.37)	(–2.21)
February		0.04044	–0.02878
		(1.45)	(–1.15)

Table 8.1   continued

	(1) Probit	(2) OLS	(3) OLS
March		−0.08023	0.09042
		(−1.92)	(2.42)
April		0.04521	−0.03375
		(1.52)	(−1.26)
May		−0.04722	0.05597
		(−1.19)	(1.58)
Constant	−9.5460	−0.05810	0.74527
		(−1.91)	(27.36)
NOB	1888	1634	1629
Adj R^2		0.0638	0.0701
Cases correct	1870		

The results from the regression reported in the second and third columns reinforce those from the probit regression. In the second the dependent variable is the logarithm of the ratio of the reduction of labor input due to shutdowns (1−SD) to the total fall in labor input (1−LINPUT) for a given firm in a given month plus one, while in the third it is a similar ratio for cuts in employment (1−EMP). Although similar, they are not precisely the same thing as their shares in labor input declines. In column one, the magnitude of the fall in labor input (DLABTOT) had a significantly positive relation to the decision to shut down – the larger the decline in labor input, the more important shutdowns were in accomplishing it, other things being equal. In columns (2) and (3) we see that the more labor input declines, the larger the share of shutdowns and the smaller the share of employment reductions were in total labor input decline, *ceteris paribus*. As in the probit regression in column (1), the estimated coefficients of firm size were not statistically significant in either equation. But in the case of the capital–labor ratio, although the signs are consistent across the regressions, in the least-squares regressions the estimated coefficient is statistically significantly different from zero. The estimated positive coefficient in column (3) is consonant with more capital-intensive firms having higher ratios of fixed to total costs and thus being more likely to cut employment and less likely to close down in the face of a given fall in demand.[7] Industry and month dummy variables are also included.

Carter and Sutch (1991:11) have also argued that in the face of a decrease in demand in the depression of 1893 firms, influenced by considerations of fairness, first tried hours reduction policies. Only if the downturn was severe and prolonged would employers then resort to layoffs and dismissals. The

New Jersey data, however, do not support this argument. In fact, they suggest exactly the opposite. Firms generally turned to shutdowns to reduce labor inputs after, rather than before, substantial cuts in total employment and/or large recent declines. Rather than a first resort, shutdowns seemed to have been more of a last resort. This pattern might suggest that employers were influenced by considerations of minimum efficient scale in their labor input decisions. Complementarities among jobs may have limited the extent to which the level of employment could be reduced. Beyond that point, resulting inefficiencies would have caused costs to rise dramatically. Thus to reduce labor input even further, firms then might have had to reduce hours of all employed (for example, through shutdowns) rather than by continuing to cut employment.

Cyclical Movements in Labor Productivity

The New Jersey Bureau of Labor Statistics also reported figures on the changes in price and quantity of output over the June 1893–May 1894 period relative to the previous year for 78 of the 252 firms. These data combined with the figures on labor input (from which I compute an annual average for each firm) allow me to calculate the relative change in labor productivity over the year of the 1893–4 downturn. To be sure, the sample is rather limited, and there is considerable variation within it. Nevertheless, the results are rather interesting. On average, firm-level labor productivity rose by 0.56 per cent over the 1893 downturn as compared to the previous year. In other words, there was a very slight countercyclical movement in labor productivity in New Jersey manufacturing, but in view of the possible measurement errors involved it seems more prudent to regard it as acyclical.

Consider now the regressions reported in Table 8.2, which attempt to sort out some factors underlying the calculated productivity change. With the industry dummies I had hoped to capture differences in productivity change between industries more reliant on skilled labor (metals) and those less reliant (textiles). While the more-skilled industries did show slower productivity growth (more labor hoarding), the estimates are sufficiently imprecise to render the difference is not statistically significant. Greater capital intensity had a negative (but not significantly so) influence on productivity growth, while greater power intensity, HPWRKR, horsepower per (June 1892) worker, measured again at the four-digit industry level from the 1890 Census, had a positive effect. The influence of firm size (June 1892 employment level) was insignificant, but the effect of declines in labor input (DLABOR) was strongly significant. The larger the fall in labor input (more positive value), the larger the increase in labor productivity, other things being equal. This result fits with the expected effects of an increase in the effective capital–labor ratio as employment is cut back over the business cycle.

*Table 8.2   Estimated influences on labor productivity change (*t *statistics in parentheses)*

Independent variables	(1)	(2)	(3)
KLRATIO	–0.0110	–0.01269	–0.0110
	(–1.59)	(–1.87)	(–1.59)
HPWRKR	8.0604	8.6021	7.9812
	(1.90)	(2.01)	(1.85)
Size	–0.0047	–0.0043	–0.0048
	(–0.91)	(–0.83)	(–0.91)
DLABOR	–1.0370	–1.0325	–1.0384
	(–21.97)	(–21.73)	(–21.92)
MAXSD	–8.7152		
	(–1.19)		
MAXST		–13.6664	
		(–0.60)	
MAXHRS			–7.7116
			(–1.21)
Metal	–0.5606	0.3907	–0.7888
	(–0.08)	(0.05)	(–0.11)
Textile	13.5386	12.3049	12.9173
	(1.86)	(1.63)	(1.77)
Leather	12.5352	10.3051	11.9446
	(1.34)	(1.09)	(1.29)
Constant	–15.8151	–15.0977	–15.3276
	(–2.49)	(–2.30)	(–2.41)
NOB	78	78	78
$\bar{R}^2$	0.8722	0.8703	0.8723

Carter and Sutch (1991: 13–19; 1994), however, find that such a relationship held generally in the Connecticut data (*mutatis mutandis* rather than *ceteris paribus*). In other words, they calculate observed average labor productivity to have moved countercyclically, rather than essentially acyclically as reported here, and attribute this computed rise in productivity primarily to the productivity-enhancing effects of hours reduction. Reduction of fatigue is said to have been the most important factor behind productivity increases, with selective retention (the better workers kept on during cutbacks) and extra effort playing lesser roles.

To test whether the manner in which labor input was reduced, that is, by hours reductions, had an independent effect on productivity change, I include three such measures in the equation specification: the maximum decline in labor input for the firm over the course of the year due to shutdowns (MAXSD), The maximum decline in labor input over the year due to short time (MAXST), and their sum (MAXHRS). None of the estimated coefficients for these three variables is close to statistical significance. Among New Jersey firms there seems to be no evidence that the degree of hours reduction, given the overall fall in labor input, increased labor productivity.

THE CONNECTICUT DATA

Now consider the information collected by the Connecticut Bureau of Labor Statistics (1894) on the course of the 1893–4 depression. Five hundred relatively large establishments 'which, because of their size, were presumed to have accounts which would facilitate the filling out of the schedule' were contacted by the Bureau, and usable monthly reports on employment, lost time, and wages paid from June 1893 to August 1894 were received from 378 establishments (ibid.: 167–8). The published version in the 1894 *Annual Report*, however, reports only averages at the establishment level – average number employed and monthly wages paid in 1892 as compared with the June 1893–August 1894 period, along with 'per cent hours worked of full time,' the percentage of hours worked of full time if the average number employed in 1892 had been maintained in the latter period, in other words, a measure of the decline in labor input. Monthly data on deviations of hours, employment, and wages paid from the 1892 level are available only at the industry level, while in the New Jersey survey monthly observations at the firm level are reported.

For purposes of comparison, the appropriate more-detailed (four-digit) Connecticut industry groupings are combined unweighted, as I did for New Jersey, into the metals and metalworking and the textiles and textiles products industries. The courses of monthly movements in the level of labor input and employment are shown in Figures 8.7 and 8.8. Note, first, that the decline in labor input is both much larger and more rapid for the Connecticut industries than for their New Jersey counterparts (Figures 8.3 and 8.4). Labor input falls by about 60 per cent and more than 50 per cent in Connecticut metals and textiles in contrast with a decline of less than one-third in New Jersey. In Connecticut the trough is reached in only four months (September), while in New Jersey it usually came around January. More important, however, is the fact that in the Connecticut cases employment fell not nearly as dramatically as labor input did. Hours reduction, particularly through shutdowns, appears to have been a major means by which labor inputs were reduced there.

Could the different conclusions be due to differences in the two samples? The Connecticut survey made a point of contacting relatively large firms, and average employment in June 1893 among them was double that for the firms

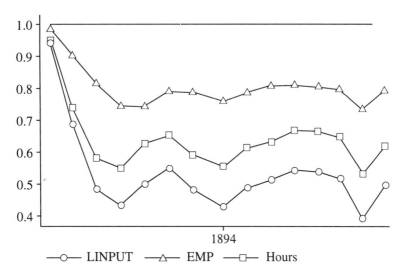

Figure 8.7   Connecticut metalworking labor input, June 1893–May 1894

in the New Jersey sample (330 versus 162). However, Figure 8.2 suggests firm size in New Jersey at least was negatively, rather than positively, associated with the use of shutdowns in reducing labor input. Moreover, Figures 8.3, 8.4, 8.7, and 8.8 compare similar industries, metalworking and textiles, in the two

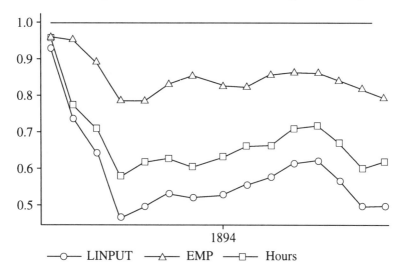

Figure 8.8   Connecticut textiles labor input, June 1893–May 1894

states. Differences in the implied relative importance of shutdowns between the New Jersey and Connecticut data therefore must not have been simply due to compositional effects in which the mix of industries in the former used shutdowns less frequently than those in the latter.

Another sample difference is that the reporting Connecticut firms all survived the depression, while some of the New Jersey firms apparently did not – or at least they reported no production by the end of the period (May 1894). Could the presence of failed firms (ones in which labor input went to zero and stayed there) in the New Jersey sample have understated the importance of the strategy of shutdowns and short time among survivors?[8] To examine such a possibility, I excluded from the New Jersey sample all firms which had zero labor input in May 1894 or in the previous three months and then recalculated the course of labor input and the effects of employment changes over the year. While the declines in labor input and employment appear somewhat less severe among surviving firms, the relationship between them remains essentially unchanged. Reductions in employment still account for the great majority of the declines in labor input among firms which did not fail.

The differing responses in the composition of labor input over the last half of 1893 and the first half of 1894 in Connecticut and New Jersey, therefore, might suggest more fundamental differences in the nature of manufacturing between the two states rather than just sampling differences. One important difference was in the source of power used in manufacturing. The significant reliance on water power in Connecticut manufacturing raises doubts that those data were representative of the adjustment of American manufacturing in general to demand shocks. In 1890 almost 40 per cent of the horsepower generated in Connecticut manufacturing was from water power as compared with about 20 per cent in the United States as a whole (US Census Office, 1895: 754–6). Seasonal variations or irregularities in stream flow made water power a rather unreliable power source. Shutdowns or slowdowns were not uncommon events due to periods of low water (or winter ice). Before the Civil War water-powered factories were often idle for three or four months per year. After the war the use of storage reservoirs by some of the larger firms mitigated, but did not entirely alleviate, the problem (Hunter, 1979: 504–16). So Connecticut (and New England more generally) manufacturing was more vulnerable to work interruptions and shut downs than manufacturing in the country as a whole and in New Jersey in particular. The 1905 Census of Manufactures, for example, in its study of days in operation lists New Jersey as one of the states in which more than half the factories operated full time over the course of the year, but not Connecticut.

The summer of 1893, moreover, was quite a dry one in Connecticut. Rainfall in Hartford during June and July, for example, was 3.7 inches in contrast to a 7.68 inches average for the period between 1895 and 1917, or 1.5 standard deviations below the mean (US Department of Agriculture, 1894: 200; Weather Disk Associates, 1990). It would seem plausible therefore that some part of the sharp increase in shutdowns during the early months of the downturn was due to dry weather rather than to considerations of fairness. In New Jersey, on the other hand, water supplied only 10 per cent of power generated in manufacturing, so we can be more confident that observed changes in labor input levels represented responses to the economic downturn.[9]

One other noteworthy feature of the Connecticut data is shown in Figures 8.9 and 8.10 which compare the movements in average full-time monthly earnings in the two industries, metalworking and textiles, between New Jersey and Connecticut. In Connecticut the movement in nominal average earnings is clearly upward (except perhaps for February 1894 in textiles) in spite of great downward pressure from unemployment and deflation. Taking the price decline into account, the upward trend in Connecticut real wages is even more pronounced: about a 20 per cent rise in metalworking. In contrast the New Jersey data all show an initial decline in nominal average wages and then a subsequent recovery back toward 'normal' (or initial) levels over the course of the year (except for the anomalous observation of January 1894 in textiles).

It is on the basis of such data that Carter and Sutch (1991, 1994) argue that average hourly earnings in manufacturing moved countercyclically in the pre-World War I period. They find that for the Connecticut sample as a whole nominal average hourly earnings rose by more than 11 per cent over the period even though no firms reported increasing wages and attribute it primarily to selective

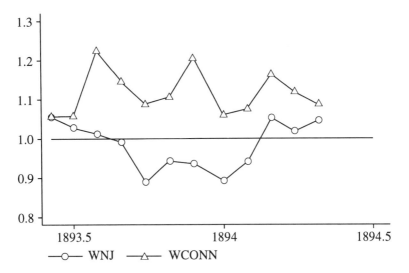

Figure 8.9   Metalworking average wages, June 1893–May 1894

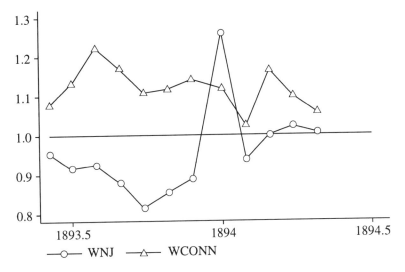

Figure 8.10   Textiles average wages, June 1893–May 1894

retention (higher-paid, more valuable workers are retained during employment cuts) (Carter and Sutch, 1991: 21–3; 1994).

It is possible that massive selective retention could have caused such a countercyclical pattern in average earnings. The surveyed Connecticut metalworking firms had on average twice as many employees as those in the New Jersey sample and thus may have had more latitude in selective layoffs. More research work is clearly needed to identify the sources of the differences implied by the New Jersey and Connecticut data. Nevertheless, a pattern such as that pictured in Figures 8.9 and 8.10, however, inclines me to be suspicious of the Connecticut data. Other studies of cyclical movements in average hourly earnings over this period have found no evidence of a countercyclical pattern. Sundstrom (1990), for example, in his study of wage adjustment in Ohio manufacturing during the 1907–8 downturn, also using micro-level data, finds a fall in average hourly earnings with the onset of the downturn. In 1908 average earnings began to rise even as the depression continued, as the New Jersey data show in Figures 8.9 and 8.10.[10] Although they were sticky, nominal average wages seemed to move procyclically rather than countercyclically.[11]

SUMMARY AND CONCLUSIONS

Data on labor adjustments by New Jersey firms in response to the 1893–4 depression suggest that employment cuts were the principal means by which labor input was reduced. There seems, therefore, to have been relatively little fundamental change in the way in which firms primarily responded to decreases in demand over the last century.[12] Layoffs and dismissals then, that is before World War I, as now were the most important means used by firms to reduce hours of work. As in the case of wage rigidity (see James, 1995), here in the nature of quantity adjustments as well, the nineteenth-century labor market appears to have been less flexible and less different from the 'modern' labor market than might have been supposed.

This is not to deny that hours reductions through shutdowns or short time were more prevalent before the 1940s than after. Rees (1961: 33) estimated that manufacturing establishments were closed 25 days a year on average between 1890 and 1914, although we do not know how many of these closures were the consequence of the power technology, either because of low water or the central character of steam power, or vacations, or whatever. Days in operation did move procyclically. Nevertheless, the use of shutdowns did not seem, based on the evidence presented here, to have been the major method of adjusting labor input during cyclical downturns, and they usually seem to have been rather a last resort, coming only after substantial falls in employment. Moreover, there does not seem to have been a strong trend toward an increasing use of layoffs or dismissals in the early twentieth century. The slight increase that may have occurred could have been due simply to increases in firm size.

APPENDIX

The course of the 1893–4 depression has probably been better documented than any other downturn in the United States before the Great Depression through the efforts of state bureaux of labor statistics (see Carter and Sutch, 1990, 1991; Sundstrom 1990, 1992). The data collected by the New Jersey Bureau of Labor Statistics, in particular, are especially valuable, not only for their detail but also for their representativeness. The Bureau collected and published data from individual New Jersey manufacturing firms on wages paid and employment by month over the first year of the downturn ('the period of greatest industrial inactivity'). Moreover, the experience of New Jersey, the sixth largest manufacturing state in 1890 by value of output, I would argue, is quite likely to be representative of that of manufacturing in the country as a whole because of its central location, its product mix, and its reliance on steam power (see pp. 223–7).

The report presented returns from 252 establishments, of which 88 were from the metals and metallic products industries and 61 were from textiles. The remaining were drawn from industries including leather, rubber, pottery, bricks, glass, and clothing. The data were displayed in tabular form. Entries for the average number of hands employed by month were presented for each firm in a row, with deviations from full utilization of workers by a given firm in a given month marked by special symbols such as asterisks, daggers, and so on. These referred to the bottom of the page, where the nature of the deviation in the given month was identified: 'shut down,' 'half time,' 'five days per week,' 'shut down two weeks,' and so forth. Total wages paid per month by firm were presented in a similar table.

The distribution of firm size in the sample, as measured by the logarithm of June 1892 employment levels, is shown in Figure A8.1. It seems to be satisfyingly close to lognormal. The mean number of employees in the New Jersey sample of firms is 162, however, as compared with 13.3 in all US manufacturing and 20.3 in all New Jersey in 1890. While this sample clearly misses many artisanal shops, the average size would not seem out of line for factories.[13]

As noted above, the New Jersey survey reports figures on wages paid and employment for June 1892. I, as the collectors of the data undoubtedly did, take this to represent a 'normal' period, one of mid-expansion in the business cycle, falling about midway between the NBER-dated trough of May 1891 and peak of January 1893 (Burns and Mitchell, 1946: 78). Subsequent levels of wages and labor input, therefore, are measured relative to the June 1892 benchmark.

In addition to monthly firm employment levels, the report also notes variations in the utilization rate, such as if workers put in only 30 hours per week during part or all of the month or if the plant was shut down for two weeks during that month. I use this information to calculate the reduction in labor input due to short

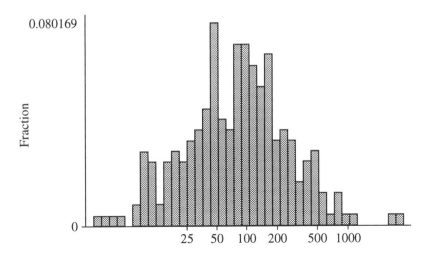

Figure A8.1   New Jersey firm size distribution

time (reduced work weeks) and shutdowns (plant closures). While, to be sure, it is not possible to be too precise about distinguishing between these two effects (a reported 50 per cent reduction in hours worked may have been accomplished by a shutdown, for example), the combined influence of short time and shutdowns should nevertheless give us a clear picture of the magnitude of hours reduction. I take EMP, the relative employment level, during a month in which the firm was shut as equal to the level of employment in the month before the shutdown. Full-time employment is taken as 10 hours per day, 60 hours per week (Atack and Bateman, 1992; Rees, 1961: 27, 33, 37; Long, 1960: 47).[14] Labor input then is measured as monthly employment adjusted for hours reductions (by short time or shutdowns).

I calculate the index, relative to June 1892, of nominal full-time monthly earnings by firm by dividing wages paid by the labor input index. In turn, the nominal wage index is adjusted for price changes using the (monthly) Warren–Pearson (1933) wholesale price index to come up with a real wage series.

NOTES

1. For a detailed description of the course of the panic and downturn, see Sprague (1910: 153–215). See also Fels (1959: 184–8), Friedman and Schwartz (1963: 107–11), and Mishkin (1991: 86–7).
2. O.M.W. Sprague, the most famous contemporary student of American financial crises, viewed suspensions or restrictions of cash payments by banks as little short of disastrous. He argued that suspension was in fact a 'potent factor' in accentuating depression through its effect on expectations and, more tangibly, by making money for payrolls difficult to obtain. As a case in point, he points to a large number of factory shutdowns in August 1893 which are said to have resulted from the inability to find cash to meet payrolls (Sprague, 1910: 199–203). In a well-known discussion in their *Monetary History of the United States*, Friedman and Schwartz (1963: 167–8) turn this argument on its head. Rather than exacerbating the downturn, they claim, suspension of cash payments was actually a mitigating force. Restriction of payments halted the failures of fundamentally sound, but temporarily illiquid, banks. It allowed time for the panic desire to convert deposits to cash to ebb and for banks to build up their reserves. By allowing the price of currency in terms of deposits to vary (through the currency premium), further adjustments in the quantity of money adjustments were precluded.
    The evidence on average labor input in Figure 8.1 is clearly consistent with the Friedman and Schwartz position. Rather than intensifying under suspension, the mid-summer plunge in labor input levels virtually stopped cold in August. Certainly, this is *post hoc, propter hoc*, but the contractionary impulse did stall in August. Furthermore, after the restriction of cash payments was ended in September, the decline in the level of labor input recommenced, albeit at a slower rate than in the summer. This is true even after allowing for seasonal fluctuations. Estimates of the seasonal pattern in New Jersey manufacturing employment based on a panel data set over the 1895–1917 period show an average decline between October and January of 5.1 per cent, while in 1893 the decline in labor input was more than double.
3. The Miron–Romer monthly industrial production index also shows a sharp decline after June. While the index fell by only 3.5 per cent between January and June, it plunged 19.2 per cent between June and August and another 4.2 per cent between August and September. However, unlike our labor input measure, production rebounded sharply (rising by 13.2 per

cent) between September and October before drifting down slightly again in early 1894 (1990).

4. A value of 1 therefore indicates no change in employment and, by the same token, labor input from June 1892 levels.
5. The line between shutdowns and short time is poorly defined, as suggested in the Appendix. I take firms reporting, say, 'forty hours per week,' but not explicitly saying that they were partially closed or shut down, as operating on short time. Even if my method of differentiation may be in error at times, it makes little difference to the tenor of the results discussed in the chapter. Labor input reductions by whichever means, shutdowns or short time, were small relative to those resulting from employment cuts; hours reductions resulting from short time were small relative to those due to shutdowns.
6. Note that these simulations overstate the actual contributions of shut downs and short time to reducing labor input. If there had already been significant reductions in the workforce, then cutting hours might well have only a small effect in reducing further actual labor inputs relative to full employment levels. On the other hand, here I apply the shutdown or short time to the original employment level so that their impact is magnified. The initial level of shutdowns for every firm in the sample, incidentally, was zero.
7. Carter and Sutch (1991: 10) find in their study based on 1893 Connecticut data, on the other hand, that 'the more capital intensive the industry, the larger the reduction in days reported.'
8. See Carter and Sutch (1992: 356–61).
9. Steam power was, of course, also a central power source, so any power interruptions would immobilize the factory. Shutdowns occurred due to the power technology of steam as well (although to a lesser degree). It might be expected, therefore, that there would be a fall in the number of shutdowns following the switch to electric unit drive in US manufacturing in the 1920s (Devine, 1983). No longer were all plant operations dependent on the functioning of the central steam engine.
10. Other studies of cyclical movements in average hourly earnings over this period based on more aggregated data (Rees, 1961; Allen, 1992) similarly find no evidence of a countercyclical pattern.
11. As for the associated finding of countercyclical productivity, if productivity rose in times of depression because of decreased worker fatigue, then accounting for the very slow rate of decline in hours worked per day in manufacturing becomes quite problematical in view of the substantial gains in profits and wages that were being forgone (see Rees, 1961: 33).
12. The data here, of course, compound the effects of seasonal and cyclical variation, and thus the decomposition depends on whether employment or shutdowns were more seasonally variable. In view of the often-argued seasonality of shutdowns, it seems more likely that layoffs and dismissals were the more likely method of reducing cyclical labor input, but more research on this question is clearly needed.
13. Data on manufacturing firms for this period by other states, notably Ohio and Connecticut, also concentrate on large firms (Connecticut Bureau of Labor Statistics, 1894: 168; Sundstrom, 1992: 434).
14. If workers put in less than a full day on Saturday, then the reduction in labor input here as a result of reported short time (for example, 'forty hours per week') will be exaggerated.

9. Central bank behavior, the exchange rate regime, and the persistence of inflation in historical perspective

Pierre L. Siklos and Richard C.K. Burdekin*

INTRODUCTION

Analysis of business cycle fluctuations has, until recently, focused primarily on post-World War II data. There is, however, increasing appreciation of the importance of long series of historical data. Such earlier data series can help us understand the evolution of business cycles in industrialized economies, notwith-standing the difficulties and controversies surrounding the measurement of prewar business cycles. If, for example, an analysis of the behaviour of inflation were restricted to the postwar era then the richness of exchange rate and central banking regimes would be severely curtailed. The recent surge of interest in the connection between the type of monetary regime and inflation has been fuelled, in part, by the fact that inflation performance through both the nineteenth and twentieth centuries has varied a great deal. Only an examination of the long historical record of inflation and business cycle activity in general can begin to help us place in proper historical perspective the role of institutions and of monetary regimes in influencing economic performance.

The present study, then, has two objectives. We are interested in how inflation has evolved since the late 1800s and we wish also to quantify the impact of various important economic and institutional events on the development of inflation. Moreover, precisely because there is much debate about the relative performance of economies is the prewar and postwar periods, we are also

* The first author thanks the Social Sciences and Humanities Research Council of Canada (under grant 410-93-1409) and Wilfrid Laurier University for financial support. The first author is also grateful to UC-San Diego where he was a Visiting Professor while some portions of this chapter were written. A previous version of the paper was presented at the Quantitative Economic History Conference (Cambridge, England), and the Eleventh International Congress of the International Economic History Association (Milan, Italy). We are grateful to Tim Hatton and Trevor Dick for comments on previous drafts, to Catherine Timko for excellent research assistance, and to Lars Jonung for providing Swedish data. Results not presented in the main body of the chapter are relegated to an appendix in the working paper version.

interested in evaluating how our interpretation of the facts may be influenced by the methods used to construct some of the key aggregate data.

As with Alogoskoufis and Smith (1991), we represent inflation, and business cycle fluctuations more generally, in terms of the Phillips curve. However, not only do we examine a variety of different specifications, but we believe that the basic specifications need to be augmented to recognize significant economic and institutional changes that have taken place over time. The reasons are that, as far as we are aware, there exists no 'consensus' model of inflation. Moreover, by examining several specifications we are not only able to compare our results with those in the existing literature but we can also point out more clearly why certain specifications appear to perform better than others based on statistical and other criteria. A novel feature of our analysis is that we pool data from four industrialized countries: Canada, Sweden, the United Kingdom, and the United States. This approach allows us to test whether these countries form an integrated 'block.' We conclude that they do.

We also explore various statistical means of extracting the cyclical component in the data and consider how different 'filtering' techniques affect our interpretation of the amplitude and volatility of business cycles. Finally, we examine how data reconstructed in light of recent research would alter our conclusions based on the use of 'standard' time series. The chapter ends with a summary and some suggestions for further extensions.

Briefly, our findings suggest that the persistence of inflation over the last century or more of data[1] is quite sensitive with respect both to the source of data and the method used to extract the cyclical component of the data. More importantly, however, we conclude that inflation persistence is considerably reduced if allowance is made for large, unusual events in economic history, such as wars and oil price shocks, as well as changes in government–central-bank relations. Exchange rate regimes matter less, in our opinion, than the previous literature seems to have suggested. Of course, as with all techniques, there are limitations to our analysis. In particular, while we consider different economic models, cyclical extraction techniques, and sources of data, our ability to model institutional change and significant events is rather crude largely because of data limitations (although our approach remains well within existing practice).

METHODOLOGY

We wish to examine how the persistence of inflation, and the Phillips curve, is affected by the method used to model the cyclical component of the time series under study. We also consider whether our inferences are affected by different ways of constructing some of the key macroeconomic aggregates. We will return to the data issue below. Given that the variety of data series available is relatively small if we wish to go back in history as far as possible, we have opted to model the relationships of interest via various augmented versions of fairly standard Phillips curve type relationships.

We first begin by exploring some of the basic features of the individual time series for each country. However, unlike previous analyses of the kind performed here, we model each relevant econometric relationship in a pooled cross-section format. That is, the time series under consideration are stacked and each Phillips curve representation is estimated for the various countries in our sample as if they formed a single unit. In other words, a particular time series for each individual country is placed on top of the same time series for the other countries to form a single time series in a pooled time series format. We then investigate whether some of the country differences can be attributed to the exchange rate regime or to certain aspects of central bank behavior, and also whether there are any cross-country differences in the persistence of inflation. The panel data approach permits us to analyze directly whether particular aspects of business cycle activity differ across countries that have experienced reasonably similar financial development, at least since the 1870s (see Bordo and Jonung, 1987; Siklos, 1993; and Bordo *et al.*, 1997).

Alogoskoufis and Smith (1991) hypothesize that the persistence of inflation, and thus the Phillips curve, changes under different external regimes such as the gold standard and the Bretton Woods agreement. Alogoskoufis and Smith find evidence suggesting that the degree of inertia in price movements increased in 1914, at the end of the gold standard, and increased again after the 1967 devaluation of sterling near the end of the Bretton Woods era. The finding of a similar upward shift in the coefficient on lagged inflation in their wage equation implied that this increased inflation persistence led to a corresponding shift in the behaviour of wage-setters and an upward shift in the Phillips trade-off. The notion of a postwar rise in inflation persistence is also suggested by Gordon (1986). However, he attributes the postwar shift not only to shifts in wage-setting behavior but also to the willingness and ability of governments to engage actively in stabilization policies.

In previous work (Burdekin and Siklos, 1996) we offer support for Alogoskoufis and Smith's emphasis on the gold standard. However, we find that individual time series data on Canada, Sweden, the United Kingdom, and the United States offer very little support for a shift at the end of the Bretton Woods period. Rather, any increase in inflation persistence appears to be delayed until after the first OPEC oil price shock in 1973–4. The apparently lesser importance of the exchange rate regime *per se* is implied also by Emery's (1994) recent finding of a downward shift in US inflation persistence after 1981. While our own data set does not include a sufficient number of post-1981 observations to test effectively for this break, it is interesting that, despite no formal change in international exchange rate relationships, 'recent movements in inflation closely resemble the behaviour of inflation during the US gold standard' (ibid.: 151).

In order to model more accurately the effects of such worldwide shocks as the gold standard, oil price hikes, and wars, we use panel data on four countries to assess the implications for the Phillips curve. This approach also permits us to determine whether there exists, in effect, a 'global' Phillips curve and, if not, whether one source of cross-country differences in inflation and output performance may lie in selected institutional features of the central banks in the countries we consider. The respective nationalizations of the Bank of Canada and the Bank of England in 1935 and 1945, the creation of the US Federal Reserve system in 1914, and the 'Coyne Affair' in Canada in 1960[2] represent illustrations of country-specific central bank institutional features. Sweden, as a country where no major changes in the status of the central bank took place over our sample, provides us with a control for whether institutional change affects the delineation of monetary regimes.

Another key issue is whether our interpretation of business cycles for over a century of data, as reflected here by an analysis of inflation persistence and the slope of the Phillips curve, is subject to neat demarcation lines such as the oft-discussed prewar versus postwar distinction popular in the literature. DeLong and Summers (1986b), for example, find that pre- and post-World War II cycles in the United States differ from each other, and attribute this in part to more widespread use of interventionist monetary and fiscal policies on the part of governments since 1945. To the extent that cycles in the United Kingdom, the United States, and perhaps other countries mirror each other (Friedman and Schwartz, 1982; Backus and Kehoe, 1992; Backus *et al.*, 1993), and that there are notable common features in the financial development of industrialized countries (Bordo and Jonung, 1987), we would expect some commonality in the degree of inflation persistence across countries. Moreover, many major external shocks, such as wars or oil price rises, have impacted the full set of industrialized countries. Where these countries may also differ is in some of the institutional developments, particularly the role and independence of their respective central banks.

There is now widespread belief that the more independent central banks can deliver lower average inflation rates. Prior to World War II, however, many countries were still linked via some version of the gold standard, while in other countries central banks did not even exist until well into the twentieth century. The US Federal Reserve System was created in 1914 while the Bank of Canada began operations only in 1935. Amongst our sample, only Sweden and the United Kingdom had central banks in the nineteenth century and, in the UK case, the nature of central bank–government relations has changed over time, as noted previously. Could differences in central bank institutions account for some of the differences in, say, inflation persistence across countries? An important complication, as noted by Capie *et al.* (1994), among others, is that a change in the regime governing central bank actions is rarely exogenous to the economic history which precedes the change. While we are unable to model such changes explicitly, our use of a panel data set at least indirectly captures, or partially controls for, effects on the central banking institution that may have originated abroad. Few, other than Capie, *et al.* (1994), have explicitly considered the importance in this context of the role played by central banking institutions.[3]

In a separate set of tests, we are interested in determining whether cross-country differences are, in retrospect, significantly influenced by changes in the way in which some of the aggregate data have been reconstructed. Thus, again for the United States, there has been much discussion about whether differences in the measured amplitude of business cycles are due to the way in which some of the aggregate data, particularly unemployment and GDP, are constructed. Similar considerations have prompted researchers in the other countries considered in this study to reconsider the construction of key macroeconomic aggregates. Romer (1986a, 1988), for example, concludes that the relatively smoother business cycles found in post-1945 US data are an illusion when she reconstructs pre-1945 US unemployment rate and GNP data series, among others. The data appendix in this study lists the various data sources used for each of the four countries we examine. It provides a basic introduction to the different data sets that are compiled and used in the estimation phase of this study. We turn to this after a further discussion about the measurement of the cyclical component of the time series under study.

The specific versions of the Phillips curve that we consider in our empirical work (before augmentation to account for the institutional features described above) are as follows:

$$\Delta p_{it} = \alpha_0 + \alpha_1 \Delta p_{i,t-1} + \alpha_2 p_{i,t-1} + \alpha_3 \tau_i + \varepsilon_{1,it} \tag{9.1}$$

$$\Delta p_{it} = \beta_0 + \beta_1 \Delta p_{i,t-1} + \varepsilon_{2,it} \tag{9.2}$$

$$\Delta w_{it} = \gamma_0 + \gamma_1 \Delta p_{i,t-1} + \gamma_2 \Delta u_{it} + \gamma_3 u_{i,t-1} + \varepsilon_{3,it} \tag{9.3}$$

$$\Delta p_t = \theta_0 + \theta_1 \Delta y_{i,t-1} + \theta_2 y_{i,t-1} + \varepsilon_{4,it} \tag{9.4}$$

where:

p_t is the log of the consumer price index;
w_t is the log of nominal wages;
u_t is the unemployment rate;
τ is a time trend,

y_t is the log of an aggregate income measure;
Δ is the difference operator; and
$\varepsilon_j, j = 1, 2, 3, 4$ are error terms.

The foregoing variable definitions are maintained throughout. Equations (9.1) to (9.3) represent different versions of the so-called expectations-augmented Phillips curve as employed, for example, by Alogoskoufis and Smith (1991). Equations (9.1) and (9.2) are identical except for the presence of the lagged price-level term in (9.1) to capture its autoregressive behaviour. Equation (9.3) is the version of the Phillips curve that comes closest to Phillips' original specification in representing the trade-off between changes in wages and the change in the unemployment rate. The final equation (equation (9.4)) is a version of the Phillips curve, specified in terms of output as opposed to unemployment,[4] popularized by Lucas (1973) and implemented by many since, albeit with mixed success (Siklos, 1988, briefly reviews the empirical evidence, but see Ericsson and Irons, 1995, for a comprehensive bibliographic reference). It should be emphasized that the Phillips curve models represented by equations (9.1)–(9.4) represent a starting point in our analysis. Each equation is, of course, estimated separately, depending upon econometric considerations, data availability, and the method of data construction or source. In the econometric aspects of this study, our concern is to rely on inferences based on an estimated model which successfully passes a minimum set of diagnostic tests. At the same time, the four specifications considered usefully characterize most economists' views about the nature of inflation – unemployment (or output) trade-offs.

TESTING FOR UNIT ROOTS AND COINTEGRATION

Specifications (9.1)–(9.4) above implicitly assume that there is a unit root in the log of prices, wages, unemployment, and output. If, for each country and time series, we utilized the longest available sample, then tests for a unit root, based on the augmented Dickey–Fuller procedure,[5] reveal that for virtually all the series and all the countries the null hypothesis of a unit root cannot be rejected at conventional significance levels of 1 to 10 per cent. The exceptions are: nominal wages for Canada, and the unemployment rate for the United Kingdom and United States. However, it must be pointed out that the test results for these particular cases are sensitive to assumptions made about whether or not the series contain a time trend, as well as depending upon how one specifies the test equation regarding the order of the autoregressive correction factor in the test equation for the presence of a unit root. We also tested for higher-order unit roots, but implementation of the Dickey–Pantula (1987) procedure confirmed that none of the series used in this chapter has two unit roots.

As argued by Perron (1989), the test statistics used here to detect the presence of a unit root may be biased if the data contain any 'structural breaks.' Clearly, when an annual data set as long as that here is considered, such breaks are to be expected. Zivot and Andrews (1992) and Perron and Vogelsang (1992) suggest methods for selecting break-points that are endogenous to the behavior of the time series in question. Using the Perron–Vogelsang method,[6] we now find that the unemployment and wage series each possess a unit root with at least one break-point. It is possible that output for Sweden, the United Kingdom, and the United States may itself be best described as trend-stationary with a break-point – but these results are sensitive to whether one or more break-points are permitted.[7] In any event, as we shall see, our findings about the slope of the Phillips curve and the degree of inflation persistence are significantly influenced by whether we wish to worry about trend-stationarity versus difference-stationarity considerations, let alone how we transform the data.

Table 9.1   Cointegrating regressions

Country	Regression
Canada	$W_t = -14.3302 - 0.1085 \text{ trend} + 0.3516\, P_t + 0.0549\, U_t$
US	$W_t = -6.995 - 0.0556 \text{ trend} + 0.4981\, P_t - 0.0188\, U_t$
UK	No cointegration found
Sweden	$W_t = -0.65423 - 0.0788 \text{ trend} + 0.0278\, U_t$
	$P_t = -5.0056 - 0.0655 \text{ trend} + 0.1255\, U_t$

Note: Estimated via Johansen's Maximum Likelihood method. The coefficient estimates are normalized on the left-hand side variables. W, P, and U are (log) wage, (log) price and unemployment *levels*, respectively. The sample period is governed by data availability; for Canada: 1926–93; US: 1890–1993; UK: 1855–1993; Sweden: 1929–93.

Of somewhat more importance in the modeling process is the long-run relationship between the time series in each of the equations (9.1)–(9.4). It is, by now, well known that if the variables in a model are all difference-stationary – that is, integrated of order 1 or I(1) – then there exists the possibility that they share the same common trend. In other words, the series in question may be cointegrated. Failure to test for cointegration will mean that any long-run equilibrium conditions present in the data will not be imposed.[8] Table 9.1 shows that there is evidence of some cointegration in the data, especially between wages, prices, and the unemployment rate, and the relevant equilibrium or long-run relationships between the series that were found to be cointegrated are laid out there. No cointegration was found in any of the specifications using UK data, however.[9] In each of the other countries in our sample, nominal wages and prices were found to be positively related to each other in the long run. In the US case, a negative long-run relationship between wages and the unemployment rate is also detected. In contrast, the sign of the wage–unemployment relationship is positive for Canada and Sweden. These results may reflect the fact that the US labour market has been much more flexible than the Swedish and Canadian labour markets. The latter have traditionally been more heavily regulated and the degree of union membership has been relatively greater than in the United States, thereby perhaps allowing wages to rise with unemployment and limiting the role of unemployment in disciplining wage claims (on the potential importance of this issue, see, for example, Burdekin and Burkett, 1996). The finding of cointegration suggests, however, that equation (9.3), at least, may need to be augmented with an error correction term.[10] We shall, therefore, also consider how our results are affected by these considerations.

OTHER APPROACHES TO THE EXTRACTION OF THE CYCLICAL COMPONENT OF TIME SERIES

As noted previously, the issue of differencing versus detrending, with or without breaks, has preoccupied a significant portion of the literature which deals with the modeling of macroeconomic relationships. But there are at least two other techniques that are widely used to extract the cyclical portion of a time series. One is the Hodrick–Prescott (1980; hereafter H–P) filter which assumes that the series are trend-stationary but where the trend is modeled in a more complicated fashion than in the case of a simple time trend. A second device used by many researchers is the Beveridge–Nelson (1981; hereafter B–N) decomposition, in which the (non-stationary) time series under study are modeled as an autoregressive integrated moving average process, better known as an ARIMA model. Here, the *permanent* component of the time series is a random walk (perhaps with a drift) while the cyclical component is then essentially the residual of the process viewed in this fashion.

In the H–P approach, assume that a time series is decomposed into trend and stationary components as follows:

$$x_t = \mu_t + \kappa_t, \tag{9.5}$$

where x is the time series under investigation, μ is the trend component and κ is the cyclical component. It can be shown (see Mills and Wood, 1993) that the trend portion can be expressed as an infinite moving average. H–P provide an algorithm that approximates this process and extracts the cyclical component.[11]

In the case of the B–N decomposition, we begin by assuming that the time series x_t is generated by an ARIMA(p, 1, q), where the terms in parenthesis represent the autoregressive order of the process (here p), the order of differencing (here 1), and the moving average portion (here of order q). Let:

$$w_t = z_t - z_{t-1} \tag{9.6}$$

where z_t is the series generated by an ARIMA model and $w_t = \theta(B)\varepsilon_t$. If the permanent component of z, z^*, follows a random walk, then:

$$c_t = z^*_t - z_t \tag{9.7}$$

is the cyclical component of the time series. B–N (1981), Miller (1988), and Newbold (1990) show how, by using the coefficients on the MA and AR components in the ARIMA process as fixed weights, the cyclical component, c_t, can be generated.

To illustrate the consequences of these different methods of generating the cyclical component of time series, consider Figures 9.1–9.4. Figure 9.1 shows

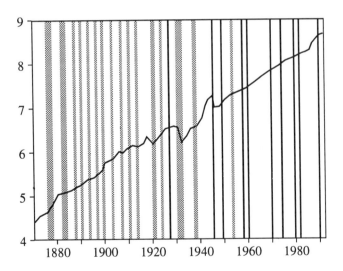

Note: The shaded areas and the vertical lines represent the national Bureau of Economic Research's dates for recessions.

Source: Series US2 (see Appendix).

Figure 9.1   The logarithm of US real GNP (1929 $)

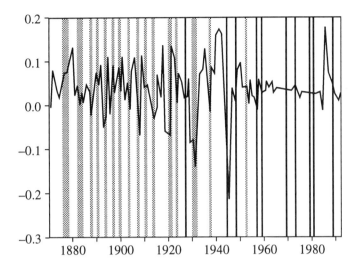

Note: Growth is evaluated as the first difference in the logarithm of real GNP.

Source: Series US3 (see Appendix).

Figure 9.2   The growth rate of US real GNP

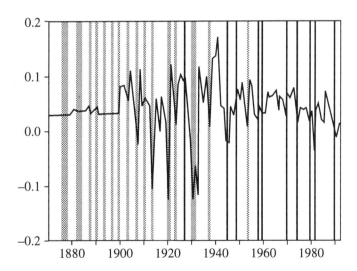

Note: See pp. 239–40 for a description of the filter; see also Mills and Wood (1993).

Source: Series US3 (see Appendix).

Figure 9.3   Cyclical real US GNP generated via the Hodrick–Prescott filter

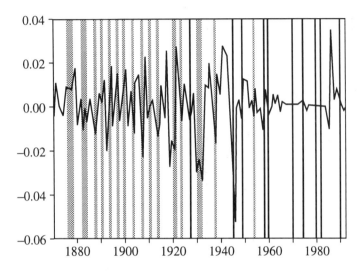

Note: See p. 240 for a description of the Beveridge–Nelson decomposition.

Source: Series US3 (see Appendix).

Figure 9.4   Cyclical real US GNP generated via the Beveridge–Nelson decomposition

the logarithm of US real GNP since 1870. The shaded bars and vertical lines in the figure represent the NBER recession dates. These were added to illustrate further the connection between different measures of business cycle activity.[12] Figure 9.2 plots the first log difference in US real GNP. The connection between troughs and the NBER dates seems fairly strong, at least based on a visual inspection of the data, while the volatility of the series clearly appears to have fallen since the end of World War II. For the purposes of the data reported in Figures 9.1–9.4 we utilized series US2 listed in the Appendix; it is also used by, among others, Bordo and Jonung (1987), Siklos (1993), and Bordo *et al.* (1996). Table 9.2 gives details of the series used for all the other cases considered. Romer's (1986a, 1988) revised GNP and unemployment data (not shown) reveal less-pronounced differences in volatility in the prewar versus postwar samples. Figure 9.3 plots the cyclical portion of US real GNP after extracting the trend using the H–P filter. Again, pre-1945 (and as far back as 1900) volatility appears to be greater than in the postwar period, but the postwar data also appear to be more volatile than in the differenced specification. The H–P filtered series appears to reveal more business cycle fluctuations than in the differenced data.

Table 9.2   The size of the cyclical component[a]

Series	Canada	US	UK	Sweden
Price level	3.46	0.27	0.58	0.07
	1882–1993[C1]	1815–1993[US1]	1786–1993[UK1]	1831–1993[S1]
Real income	0.66	0.05	0.05	1.15
	1875–1993[C3]	1871–1993[US3]	1873–1993[UK2]	1879–1993[S2]
Money supply	0.48	1.09	0.18	0.09
	1875–1993[C6]	1880–1993[US5]	1877–1993[UK4]	1873–1993[S5]
Wages	0.79	2.94	0.47	0.29
	1928–1993[C8]	1902–1993[US9]	1815–1993[UK7]	1865–1993[S8]
Unemployment rate	0.41	0.70	0.52	0.13
	1923–1993[C7]	1891–1993[US8]	1891–1993[UK6]	1936–1993[S7]

[a]   Based on the Beveridge–Nelson (1981) decomposition as simplified by Miller (1988) with additional remarks by Newbold (1990). The figures shown are the $\text{Var}(c_t)/\text{Var}(z_t)$, where c is the cyclical component and z is the original series. Data sources are given in brackets based on the series name labels described in the Appendix.

Interestingly, we find that for most samples the cyclical components of prices and output are positively correlated – with the highest correlation for US data (0.56; 1801–1993) and the smallest correlation obtained for UK data (0.26; 1782–1993). Moreover, we find that these correlations are much higher in most cases for the post-World War II period than for earlier samples. Only in the US case are the differences small, with a 0.52 correlation for pre-1945 data and 0.58 for the postwar period. By contrast, the correlation between detrended prices and output is 0.13 for prewar Swedish data, for example, but rises to 0.76 for postwar data. The only negative correlation found was for UK data for the 1900–1946 sample. Our results, therefore, differ from those reported by Backus and Kehoe (1992), and Cooley and Ohanian (1991), but are consistent with the notion that inflation shocks have positively contributed to output shocks. Cogley and Nason (1995) argue that the H–P filter may indeed create periodicities in the data when there is none in the underlying series.

Finally, Figure 9.4 displays the cyclical portion of US real GNP as derived from the application of the B–N decomposition. The resulting series resemble the differenced series although the amplitude of the series seems relatively larger. Note that the B–N methodology is applied to the individual time series under study. Evans and Reichlin (1994) point out that, since the information set used to produce the GNP series shown in Figure 9.1 consists of a simultaneous relationship with other series, the B–N decomposition should reflect the influence of structural relationships between related time series.[13]

One way to summarize neatly both the impact of a particular decomposition as well the significance of business cycles over time is to evaluate how large are cyclical shocks relative to the variation in the time series under consideration. Table 9.2 shows the size of the cyclical component as a ratio of the variance of the cyclical component to the variance of the trend component for a selection of the time series used in this study. Note the wide variety of experiences across the four countries considered. For example, the cyclical component is very large for Canadian real GNP but is comparatively small for Sweden, at least when viewed through the B–N decomposition. Nor can it be said that the same series are the most or least volatile across the four countries. Thus, cyclical variations in prices are relatively volatile for Canada and the United Kingdom, real income volatility is lowest for the United Kingdom and United States, while the cyclical component of money supply volatility ranks low for all countries except the United States. Based on these results, either the macroeconomic experiences of these four countries are different in appearance or the construction of the series itself is partly to blame. Alternatively, the univariate nature of the analysis is the possible source of our results so far – which is an important consideration, we believe.

Viewed individually, then, the business cycle experiences of the four countries considered appears quite varied and our interpretation of their amplitude and volatility is clearly influenced by how we believe the business cycle should be modelled in a time series sense. However useful such an exercise may be, it is nevertheless incomplete. The role of institutions and of monetary regimes in business cycles, in particular, can only really be understood in the context of some underlying relationship which characterizes business cycle movements, such as the one summarized in the various Phillips curve specifications detailed above. It is to this type of empirical evidence that we now turn.

EMPIRICAL RESULTS

Tests Based on the Original Specifications

Table 9.3 gives the regression results for equations (9.1)–(9.4), each estimated individually in a panel. The data were 'stacked' in the following order: Canada, the United States, the United Kingdom, and Sweden. As is clear from the tables and the Appendix, given that the time series for some countries in our sample are longer than for others, the resulting panel is 'unbalanced.' The series used are untransformed, that is, they enter precisely in the manner in which they were originally defined (see pp. 236–7). In the estimation phase, specifications (9.1)–(9.4) were individually augmented with a set of dummy variables. Some of these capture shocks which are common to all countries:[14] World Wars I and II (WW12), the gold standard (GOLD), and oil price shocks

(OIL). Other dummy variables capture individual influences on each country, particularly those having to do with the structure or role of the central bank, such as the nationalization of the Bank of England (BOE), the creation of the Bank of Canada (BOC), the Coyne Affair (COYNE), a dummy for the formation of the European Union (EUNION), a dummy for the European Community (EC), plus dummies for each country, and an extra war dummy that adds, as well as the two World Wars, the Korean and Vietnam wars affecting the United States (USWARS).[15] A time trend (trend) is also included throughout. The precise definition of these and other dummies is provided in the notes to Table 9.3 but all are of the [0,1] variety.

Table 9.3   Results based on specifications (9.1)–(9.4) with common and idiosyncratic shocks

Independent variables	Dependent variables (equation)			
	Inflation (9.1)	Inflation (9.2)	Wage (9.3)	Inflation (9.4)
Constant	−17.63 (16.08)	−20.06 (15.98)	45.71 (35.79)	−124.53 (43.69)[*]
Δp (−1)	0.33 (0.04)[*]	0.32 (0.04)[*]	0.56 (0.06)[*]	—
p(−1)	−0.66 (0.52)	—	—	—
Δu	—	—	−0.85(0.12)[*]	—
u(−1)	—	—	−0.15(0.07)[†]	—
$\hat{y}$(−1)	—	—	—	0.06 (0.04)
Step dummy variables				
BOE	1.18 (1.31)	1.29 (1.31)	2.36 (1.28)[‡]	1.32 (1.82)
COYNE	2.26 (1.62)	1.62 (1.54)	0.01 (1.43)	1.10 (2.09)
BOC	0.45 (1.78)	0.37 (1.78)	7.87 (2.14)[*]	0.65 (2.39)
EUNION	1.88 (0.90)[†]	1.20 (0.72)[‡]	0.63 (0.78)	0.87 (0.99)
EC	0.01 (0.01)	0.01 (0.06)	−0.28 (0.67)	0.06 (0.08)
GOLD	0.40 (1.02)	−0.15 (0.92)	2.37 (1.25)[†]	−1.70 (1.46)
OIL	4.49 (1.42)[*]	4.47 (1.42)[*]	1.28 (1.16)	2.17 (1.21)[‡]
USWARS	1.01 (0.90)	1.13 (0.90)	1.89 (0.81)[†]	0.52 (0.98)
WW12	3.18 (1.25)[*]	3.40 (1.24)[*]	−1.16 (1.19)	3.66 (1.41)[*]
Country step dummies				
CANADA	−1.17 (0.98)	−0.60 (0.87)	−9.73 (12.51)	−0.45 (1.33)
US	−0.87 (0.83)	−0.29 (0.69)	−1.47 (3.14)	−0.63 (1.23)
UK	−0.23 (0.70)	−0.40 (0.68)	1.02 (6.51)	−1.21 (1.27)
Trend	0.01 (0.01)	0.01 (0.01)	−0.02 (0.02)	0.07 (0.02)[*]
Summary statistics				
Observations	652	652	381	453
R^2 adj.	0.31	0.31	0.55	0.46
SEE[a]	5.14	5.14	4.10	4.10
AR(1)[b]	0.09 (2.44)[†]	0.09 (2.45)[*]	0.16 (3.11)[*]	0.50 (12.95)[*]
Log. lik.(deg. fr.)[c]	(2) 2.12	(1) 2.21	(1) 7.24[*]	(1) 126.08[*]

Table 9.3   continued

Notes:
Estimated vis OLS with AR(I) serial correlation connection factor estimated by maximum likelihood.
BOE = Bank of England nationalization ($t < 1945 = 0$, $t > = 1945=1$), C0YNE = Coyne Affair (t
$< 1960 = 0$, $t > = 1960 = 1$), BOC = Bank of Canada formation ($t < 1935 = 0$, $t > = 1935 = 1$),
EUNION = European Community, EMS ($t < 1959 = 0$, $t > 1959 = 1$, $t > = 1979$ and $< = 1991 = 2$,
$> = 1991 = 1$), EC = European Community dummy ($t < 1959 = 0$, $t > = 1959 = I$ times inflation),
GOLD = gold standard ($t < 1914 = 0$, $t > = 1914 = 1$), OIL = oil price shocks ($t < 1972 = 0$, $t > =$
1972 and $t < = 1974$, $t > = 1979$ and $t < = 1980 = 1$, $t > 1980 = 0$), USWARS = World Wars, Korean
and Vietnam wars(= WW12, and $t > = 1950$ and $< = 1951$ and $> = 1964$ and $< = 1973 = 1$; $= 0$
otherwise), WW12 = World Wars ($t > = 1914$ and $t < = 1918 = 1$, $t > = 1939$ and $t < = 1945 = 1$,
0 otherwise), CANADA, US, UK, are country dummies. All other variables defined in equations
(9.1)–(9.4), with $\Delta p = 100$ times the first log difference in consumer prices (P), UN = unemployment
rate (per cent), = difference operator, $y = 100$ times first log difference in GNP or GDP, Δ = difference
operator. Series used were C3, US2, UK2, and S2. The same data were also in producing the results
presented in Tables 9.4 to 9.6. The number of observations are before differencing or other transformations and lags. See Table 9.2 for the list of series used (as well as the Appendix). Variables
are defined on pp. 255–6.
[a]   Standard error of the estimates.
[b]   AR(I) serial correlation adjustment factor of the first order.
[c]   Test of the AR(I) versus no serial correlation correction model.
*   statistically significant at the 1% level.
†   statistically significant at the 5%, level.
‡   statistically significant at the 10% level.

The results in Table 9.3 reveal that, when equations (9.1)–(9.4) are conditioned on the dummies described above, the degree of inflation persistence is considerably lower than the estimates presented by Alogoskoufis and Smith (1991), who also neglected to test properly for serial correlation (see Burdekin and Siklos, 1996).[16] Moreover, only the wage equation reveals a statistically significant rise in the degree of inflation persistence in the post-gold-standard period as a result of the positive coefficient on the GOLD dummy. Wars exert a positive effect on inflation persistence, but not on wages. The lack of effect on wages may be due to the imposition of controls, the omission of which likely biases the results. Oil price shocks also have a large positive impact on inflation in all but the wage specification. On the other hand, institutional characteristics of the central banks in our sample are seen to affect inflation only in the wage equation. The nationalization of the Bank of England and the creation of the Bank of Canada are both associated with higher than average wage growth. Finally, the EUNION dummy is found to have a positive effect on the average inflation rate in equation (9.1), suggesting that any disinflationary effects on the member countries did not 'spill over' to the four countries considered here (the United Kingdom's European Monetary System (EMS) membership lasted less than two years).

Turning to the Lucas version of the Phillips curve (equation (9.4)), the insignificance of the output series is consistent with the neutrality of output predicted in the classical model. In general, then, and other than for some important institutional effects associated with two of the central banks in our study, there appears to be a great deal of commonality in inflation persistence. The apparently common features in business cycles reported here are akin to the evidence reported by Backus and Kehoe (1992) and Backus *et al.* (1993) in their descriptive comparison of international business cycles with long annual data. The shift points seem more attributable to supply shocks and *domestic* monetary institutions than to the exchange rate regime, however, and give little support for the idea that fixed exchange rates have been effective historically in disciplining inflation (see also Burdekin *et al.*, forthcoming).[17]

The estimates given in Table 9.3 so far assume that the same specifications are valid for all the countries in our sample (see also Alogoskoufis and Smith, 1991, and Burdekin and Siklos, 1996). There is also the possibility that the error terms in specifications (9.1)–(9.3) are correlated with the lagged dependent variable in the equation. As a result, instrumental variable estimation was also tried and found to have little quantitative or qualitative impact on the conclusions and is, therefore, not discussed any further.[18] Finally, instead of estimating each equation in a panel, we could have estimated the equation separately for each country (see Burdekin and Siklos, 1996). This is the typical approach followed in the literature, but it has the disadvantage of not recognizing interdependencies which must surely exist among the countries in our sample. An alternative, which recognizes such interdependencies, is to estimate equations (9.1)–(9.4) separately for each country in a system. The technique of seemingly unrelated regressions (SUR) is well-suited to deal with the econometric issues just raised. Accordingly, we also reproduced the estimates of Table 9.3 via SUR estimation (results not shown). The results for specifications (9.1)–(9.3) are broadly similar to the ones presented in Table 9.3, except that the degree of persistence is now slightly higher than the previous estimates given. The impact of WW12 now disappears but the oil shocks and the impact of the nationalization of the Bank of England and the formation of the Bank of Canada remain. At the same time, output effects on inflation (equation (9.4)) no longer appear to be neutral when the SUR estimates are considered; output growth and inflation are positively correlated in all four countries.

In Table 9.4 we repeat the estimation conducted in Table 9.3, except that we now explicitly account for country-specific responses using the structural breaks uncovered in the tests discussed earlier. In Table 9.4, we consider how our estimates of inflation persistence would be affected by assuming that structural breaks in inflation are known. That is, we use information uncovered from the univariate tests for detecting structural breaks in the data to further augment specifications (9.1)–(9.4). Therefore, in addition to the dummies used to augment the original specifications as shown in Table 9.5, we now add both step and interaction dummies. The former are the usual [0, 1] type dummy variables. The latter dummies recognize that trends in inflation change following

Table 9.4 Specifications (9.1)–(9.4) augmented with country-specific 'structural' breaks

Independent variables	Dependent variables (equation)			
	Inflation (9.1)	Inflation (9.2)	Wage (9.3)	Inflation *(9.4)*
Constant	–8.15 (15.64)	–15.17 (15.74)	41.57 (31.95)	–21.45 (26.52)
Δp (–1)	–0.01 (0.02)	–0.03 (0.02)	0.12 (0.04)	—
p(–1)	–1.45 (0.40)	—	—	—
Δu	—	—	–0.39 (0.07)*	—
u (–1)	—	—	–0.10 (0.07)	—
$\dot{y}$(–1)	—	—	—	0.04 (0.02)
Country break dummies				
Step dummies				
Canada	–6.05 (2.73)[†]	–6.57 (2.76)[†]	3.12 (1.81)[‡]	–5.85 (2.27)*
US	–1.55 (0.82)[‡]	–1.86 (0.83)[†]	0.00002 (0.00002)	–3.85 (1.09)*
UK	–3.00 (1.36)[†]	–2.72 (1.37)[†]	–0.28 (0.69)	3.32 (1.14)*
Sweden	–2.44 (1.33)[‡]	–2.97 (1.34)[†]	–1.09 (1.20)	3.72 (1.16)
Interactive dummies				
Canada	0.10 (0.08)	0.10 (0.08)	—	0.10 (0.06)[‡]
US	0.62 (0.04)*	0.60 (0.04)*	0.82 (0.06)*	0.56 (0.03)*
UK	0.76 (0.03)	0.76 (0.03)*	0.48 (0.02)*	0.56 (0.03)*
Sweden	1.02 (0.07)*	1.02 (0.07)*	0.98 (0.06)*	1.00 (0.79)
Summary statistics				
Observations	652	652	381	453
R^2 adj.	0.75	0.75	0.85	0.82
SEE	3.08	3.11	2.40	2.37
AR(I)	0.37 (10.23)*	0.37 (10.34)*	0.61 (14.81)*	0.39 (9.36)*
Log lik.	(1) 62.88*	(1) 65.54*	(1) 123.38*	(1) 68.77*

Notes:
1. See Tables 9.2 and 9.3 for variable and series definitions. The regressions include the same set of variables as in Table 9.3 but only the coefficient estimates on the break dummies are shown, to conserve space. That is, the variables under the heading 'Dummy variables' in Table 9.3 were estimated but coefficient estimates are not shown.
2. Estimated via OLS with an AR(I) serial correlation correction factor estimated by maximum likelihood. The 'break-points' are (with the year in parentheses): p (1925), y (1918), w (1972), u (1950) for Canada; p (1863), y (1929), w (1919), u (1937) for the US; p (1799), y (1917), w (1917), u (1871) for the UK; and p (1914), y (1915), w (1917), u (1992) for Sweden. Thus, p (1925) for Canada means that the dummy takes on a value of 1 beginning in 1925 until the end of the sample (1993). If the dummy is interactive then the game dummy is multiplied by Δp or inflation. The same principle applies to the other dummies and series.

a structural break. This is accomplished by multiplying the [0, 1] dummy by the relevant dependent variable where the dummy is active in the year the break is assumed to take place and the years following the break. The break points were estimated for each country and variable separately so that changes in inflation trends are permitted to differ across the four countries in our panel. One limitation of the analysis is that only one break was estimated for each series. Nevertheless, for the panel as a whole there are effectively four breaks considered (one for each country). To conserve space, only the coefficients and test statistics for the additional break dummies that interact with output are shown in Table 9.4. However, the set of dummy variables introduced in Table 9.3 were also included in producing the results shown in Table 9.4.

Table 9.5   Estimates of (9.1)–(9.4) based on Hodrick–Prescott filtered data

Independent variables	Dependent variables (equation)			
	Inflation (9.1)	Inflation (9.1)	Wage (9.3)	Inflation (9.4)
Constant	0.65 (0.30)†	0.46 (0.31)	–3.53 (3.77)	3.57 (1.06)*
Δp (–1)	0.60 (0.03)*	0.59 (0.03)*	0.56 (0.16)*	—
p (–1)	–0.05 (0.01)	—	—	—
Δu	—	—	–0.04 (0.02)‡	—
$u(-1)$	—	—	0.0003 (0.007)	—
$\hat{y}(-1)$	—	—	—	0.15 (0.04)$\dagger$
Dummy variables				
BOE	0.03 (0.02)	0.04 (0.02)	–0.13 (0.16)	–0.02 (0.06)
COYNE	0.08 (0.03)*	0.04 (0.03)	–0.08 (0.16)	0.02 (0.06)
BOC	0.07 (0.03)*	0.07 (0.03)*	0.06 (0.19)	0.09 (0.06)
EUNION	0.01 (0.02)	0.04 (0.01)*	–0.10 (0.07)	0.007 (0.03)
GOLD	0.10 (0.02)	0.06 (0.02)*	0.15 (0.17)	0.005 (0.04)
OIL	0.03 (0.02)	0.03 (0.02)	0.01 (0.06)	–0.02 (0.02)
USWARS	0.02 (0.02)	0.02 (0.02)	0.01 (0.01)	–0.05 (0.02)*
WW12	–0.005 (0.02)	0.01 (0.02)	–0.12 (0.09)*	0.03 (0.02)
Country dummies				
CANADA	0.30 (0.03)*	0.34 (0.04)*	–0.82 (0.26)*	0.96 (0.14)*
US	0.05 (0.02)*	0.09 (0.02)*	–0.12 (0.14)	0.06 (0.10)
UK	0.10 (0.02)*	0.09 (0.02)*	–0.17 (0.15)	0.18 (0.08)†
Trend	–0.0003 (0.0002)†	–0.0003 (0.0002)‡	0.002 (0.002)	–0.002 (0.0006)*
Summary statistics				
Observations	652	652	381	453
R^2 adj.	0.96	0.95	0.48	0.98
SEE	0.08	0.08	0.22	0.06
AR(I)	0.31 (8.56)*	0.34 (9.58)*	0.70 (17.75)*	0.95 (68.83)
Log. lik.	(1) 37.91*	(1) 42.48*	(1) 162.36*	(1) 539.79*

Note: Estimated via OLS, with AR(I) serial correlation correction factor estimated by maximum likelihood. The regressions are the same as in Table 9.3 except that the series of interest are filtered via the H–P filter instead of first differencing. The H–P filter is described on pp. 239–40. See Tables 9.2 and 9.3 for other details of variable definitions (and also the Appendix).

The impact on the results of including the additional break dummies is quite dramatic. Inflation persistence disappears in specifications (9.1) and (9.2) and is considerably reduced in the wage equation. For the most part, the hypothesized breaks are significant, particularly the interactive dummies, which suggests not only higher average persistence of inflation during the twentieth century but also a rising level of persistence over time. However, the rising inflation persistence following the termination of the classical gold standard in the United States, the United Kingdom, and Sweden reflects a structural break that is most accurately dated at 1917. Accordingly, the break may have less to do with the ending of the gold standard than a combination of the ending of this regime and the onset of World War I. 'Forcing' the change in inflation persistence to coincide with the end of the gold standard, as in Alogoskoufis and Smith (1991), may not be entirely accurate, therefore, and our analysis reveals the potential pitfalls of exogenously assigning 'break-points' in the data. These results may also explain the poor performance of the GOLD dummy dated at 1914 that was included in the earlier estimates.

We also repeated the regressions reported in Table 9.4 using the SUR estimation technique (results not shown). Here, there is more evidence of significant persistence in the presence of structural breaks than in Table 9.4, but the coefficient estimates remain considerably lower than when such breaks are ignored. Again, we can draw the conclusion that common shocks must be modeled, as well as domestically generated shocks, in order to properly model inflation. Otherwise the results mirror those reported in Table 9.4.

Tests based on different data filters

To summarize, the progression of results from Tables 9.3–9.4 clearly illustrates the importance, first, of economic shocks common to the four countries and, second, the role of institutional factors and supply shocks in the inflation process. So far, however, we have imposed the difference operator to model the cyclical component of the time series being studied. Tables 9.5 and 9.6 repeat the results reported in Table 9.3, except that the relevant series are now replaced with their filtered values either via the H–P filter, in Table 9.5, or the B–N method, regulated to Table 9.6. Application of the H–P technique produces an increase in the degree of inflation persistence relative to the original specifications by a wide margin. Moreover, we can no longer reject non-neutrality since output is found to influence inflation significantly and positively. Moreover, the significance of the trend term suggests that interdependence between these economies may well have been significant in accounting for the rising inflation rates seen over more than a century of data. These results are broadly in line with what one would expect based on the reported 'biases' created when applying the H–P filter, including the enhancement of the amplitude of fluctuations in inflation relative to the original model and the importance of the trend factor in explaining inflation. The latter results are also consistent with rising persistence over the twentieth century. Otherwise, the results are broadly similar to the ones reported in the earlier tables.

Table 9.6   Estimates of (9.1)–(9.4) based on Beveridge–Nelson decomposition

Independent variables	Dependent variables (equations)			
	Inflation (9.1)	Inflation (9.2)	Wage (9.3)	Inflation (9.4)
Constant	0.06 (0.08)	0.05 (0.08)	−1.93(0.61)*	−0.23 (0.44)
Δp (−1)	0.74 (0.03)*	0.74 (0.03)*	0.01(0.08)	
p (−1)	−0.01 (0.03)	—		—
u	—	—	0.007(0.002)*	
Δu	—	—	0.0006(0.001)	—
$\hat{y}(-1)$	—	—	—	−0.008 (0.08)
Dummy variables				
BOE	0.01 (0.006)†	0.02 (0.006)*	−0.03 (0.02)	0.03 (0.02)
COYNE	0.03 (0.008)*	0.03 (0.008)	−0.03 (0.02)	0.06 (0.02)*
BOC	0.01 (0.007)	0.009 (0.007)*	0.03 (0.03)	0.03 (0.02)
EUNION	0.007 (0.004)	0.001 (0.003)	−0.02 (0.01)	0.004 (0.01)
GOLD	0.004 (0.005)	0.0002 (0.004)	0.05 (0.02)†	0.002 (0.02)
OIL	0.02 (0.008)†	0.02 (0.008)†	0.008 (0.01)	0.005 (0.01)
USWARS	0.002 (0.005)	0.003 (0.005)	0.007 (0.01)	0.01 (0.008)
WW12	0.01 (0.006)‡	0.01 (0.006)†	0.01 (0.02)	−0.005 (0.01)
CANADA	−0.02 (0.005)*	−0.01 (0.005)†	−0.03 (0.03)	−0.05 (0.02)*
US	−0.004 (0.004)	0.0004 (0.003)	−0.01 (0.02)	0.008 (0.02)
UK	−0.002 (0.003)	−0.003 (0.003)	0.04 (0.02)†	−0.001 (0.02)
Trend	−0.00002 (0.00004)	−0.00002 (0.00004)	0.0009 (0.0003)*	0.0001 (0.0002)
Summary statistics				
Observations	652	652	381	453
R^2 adj	0.55	0.55	0.42	0.67
SEE	0.03	0.03	0.05	0.03
AR(I)	−0.32 (−8.74)*	−0.32 (−8.54)*	0.40 (7.85)*	0.73 (22.97)*
Log. lik.	(1) 41.12*	(1) 38.87*	(1) 47.20 (0.00)*	(1) 311.11*

Note   Estimated via OLS, with AR(I) serial combination correction factor estimated by maximum likelihood. Here the series are filtered according to the B–N decomposition; otherwise the regressions are as in Table 9.3. The B–N decomposition is described on p. 240. See Tables 9.2 and 9.3 and the Appendix for other details about variable definitions.

Inflation persistence is even higher when the cyclical component of the time series is extracted via the B–N technique, as shown in Table 9.6 (with the possible exception of the wage equation).[19] We did not consider 'breaks' in the H–P or B–N decompositions because the statistical testing for such breaks has not, to our knowledge, been developed.

Tests based on the construction of the data

Clearly, our interpretation of business cycles can be influenced by how the data are constructed, as noted previously. Controversies surrounding pre-1945 business cycles have been especially important in the existing literature. Table 9.7 presents estimates of the slope of the Phillips curve based on equation

Table 9.7   The Phillips curve by type of income or unemployment measure

(A) Income	(1)	(2)	(3)	(4)	(5)	(6)	(7)	(8)
Constant	−100.78	−155.64	−115.48	−100.78	−144.96	−114.95	−125.87	−140.96
	(33.91)	(27.58)*	(30.60)*	(33.91)*	(33.36)	(29.17)*	(26.91)*	(30.40)*
Income (−1)	0.16	0.27	0.17	0.16	0.24	0.17	0.18	0.26
	(0.08)‡	(0.07)*	(0.07)†	(0.08)‡	(0.08)*	(0.08)†	(0.07)*	(0.09)*
Trend	0.05	0.08	0.06	0.05	0.08	0.06	0.07	0.07
	(0.02)*	(0.01)*	(0.02)*	(0.02)*	(0.02)*	(0.02)	(0.01)*	(0.02)
Canada	0.12	−1.79	0.23	0.12	0.64	−1.27	−1.55	−1.88
	(1.07)	(0.91)†	(1.01)	(1.07)	(1.59)	(1.17)	(1.10)	(0.96)†
US	0.80	0.57	−0.24	0.80	0.11	0.87	0.11	0.94
	(1.50)	(1.36)	(1.02)	(1.50)	(1.55)	(1.38)	(0.96)	(1.55)
UK	−0.38	0.30	−0.36	−0.38	−0.04	−0.36	−0.33	−0.14
	(0.93)	(1.18)	(0.88)	(0.93)	(1.36)	(0.88)	(0.83)	(1.28)
Summary statistics								
R^2	0.06	0.26	0.07	0.06	0.21	0.10	0.12	0.22
SEE	6.10	4.55	5.77	6.10	4.97	5.74	5.45	4.84
Observations	259	307	292	268	240	335	359	283

(B) Unemployment	Dependent variable: wage	
	Original	Romer
Constant	−38.57 (15.86)†	−55.52 (18.82)*
Infl (−1)	0.65 (0.05)*	0.64 (0.06)*
ΔU	−0.92 (0.12)*	−0.96 (0.16)*
UNEM (−1)	−0.15 (0.06)*	−0.28 (0.07)*
Trend	0.02 (0.008)*	0.03 (0.01)*
Canada	2.23 (0.76)*	2.29 (0.78)*
US	−0.40 (0.71)	0.22 (1.00)
UK	−0.46 (0.70)	−0.21 (0.74)
Summary statistics		
R^2	0.50	0.51
SEE	4.35	4.48
Observations	381	308

Notes:
1. Income is defined as follows: col. (1) sources are: C4, US3, UK3, S3; col. (2) C3, US4, UK3, S4; col. (3): C4, US4, UK3, S3; col. (4): C4, US3, UK3, S3; col. (5): C4, US4, UK3, S4; col. (6): C3, US3, UK3, S3; col. (7): C3, US4, UK3, S3; col. (8): C3, US3, UK3, S4. Standard errors are given in parenthesis.
2. * = statistically significant at 1% level.
   † = statistically significant at 5% level.
   ‡ = statistically significant at 10% level.
3. Observation numbers are before differencing and lags.

(9.4), where these were generated by utilizing *different* estimates for real GNP or GDP levels. The resulting findings are shown in part (A) of the table. Part (B) provides estimates for the wage equation when Romer's revised unemployment rate estimates are entered in place of those used in Tables 9.3–9.6. To facilitate comparison across different data sources, results based on the revised data are shown alongside estimates with the original data. In all cases the full set of variables used to generate the results in Table 9.3 was included in the regression. Moreover, only the original version of equation (9.4) is estimated without allowance for breaks. To conserve space, only the coefficients for the country dummies are shown.

Because it is unclear how long historical series from different sources should be put together, the results in Table 9.7 proceed by combining different samples for the four countries considered. Such an approach produced eight different combinations or panels. Obviously, this implies some loss of information relative to full sample estimation, but this was thought to be preferable to splitting different data sources in some *ad hoc* fashion. Our objective here, therefore, is not to compare estimates across the various panels considered but rather to determine the sensitivity of Phillips curve slope estimates relative to the 'standard' data series employed in the relevant empirical literature.

No matter how the revised output data are entered, neutrality between output fluctuations and inflation is decisively rejected for every combination tested. Moreover, the impact of output on inflation is almost twice as large as the estimates reported earlier and, in some cases, almost three times as large as the coefficient based on the earlier versions of the data considered. However, the previously reported result, namely that there are few country-specific effects (as evidenced by the insignificance of the country dummies usually) continues to hold. Clearly, the Lucas version of the Phillips curve is generally 'steeper' with revised data than with the data originally used in earlier tables. This may mean that post-World War II business cycles are not different from prewar cycles. More testing along the lines indicated earlier in the chapter is necessary, however, before we can reach a definite conclusion. Finally, when the Romer unemployment rate data are used, we find little change in the degree of inflation persistence, as shown in part (B) of Table 9.7. In addition, there is little or no change in the interpretation of results. It remains possible, however, that if unemployment rate estimates for the other countries were revised, the results could change.[20]

CONCLUSIONS

This chapter has considered institutional and economic determinants of the degree of inflation persistence and Phillips curve slopes in four industrialized countries for over a century of data. Apart from the World Wars and the two oil price shocks, institutional features of central banks in some of the countries considered were the only other statistically significant influences on the degree of inflation persistence. Exchange rate regimes, thought by some to be important demarcation points in the history of inflation, appear to be somewhat less important than the other shocks or events considered. An explanation lies in the fact that the dating of exchange rate regimes is often closely related to other significant events in the economic history of a country that could be 'causal' (although the present study makes no claim to have uncovered new evidence about the causality between economic history and the behaviour of the Phillips curve). It is also quite noteworthy that we find the degree of inflation persistence to be markedly lower when 'breaks' are incorporated as separate determinants of price inflation or wage inflation. Indeed, the dating of these breaks helps confirm the reduced significance of exchange rate regimes. Finally, aside from the influence of changes in central banking structure in the individual countries considered, the behaviour of the Phillips curve is similar in all four countries – as well as yielding evidence of significant transmission of inflationary disturbances across countries. Since a different conclusion would have been reached based on a univariate analysis, the present study reinforces the view that too much reliance should not be placed on the statistical behavior of individual time series in isolation.

We were also interested in whether inferences about the nature of the Phillips curve trade-off are influenced by how the cyclical portion of the time series of interest was extracted. We find that the interpretation of the degree of inflation persistence is, in fact, quite sensitive to the filter used to generate stationarity. We did not, however, investigate whether the substantial reduction in inflation persistence in the presence of economic 'shocks' is replicated when different filters are utilized.

We also considered whether the evidence about the neutrality of output effects on inflation might be a figment of the particular data series commonly used in prior studies with long samples of annual data. In this regard, our results suggest that inflation is more responsive to output when recently revised pre-World War II data are employed in the empirical analysis. There are several other avenues open to further investigation. For example, we estimated the different specifications as a panel, but we could have estimated the various versions of the Phillips curve considered in this study separately for prewar and postwar samples. Alternatively, the general approach followed in this chapter could be used to focus on the potential importance of whether the countries in question were under a commodity standard or a fiat standard (as in Rolnick and Weber, 1994). Finally, given the apparent statistical importance of shocks to inflation that are common to the four countries in our sample, another step would be to model the specifications considered as VARs.

Nevertheless, our study as it stands suggests that major economic events such as wars and oil shocks and certain institutional features of central bank arrangement account for much of the inflation persistence experienced over the last 150 years or so of available data.

APPENDIX: SAMPLES AND SOURCES

		Country		
Series	Canada	United States	United Kingdom	Sweden
		Sample/source		
Price level	1913–93/C1	1800–1993/US1	1781–1993/UK1	1830–1993/S1
	1870–1926/C2			
Real income	1870–1993/C3	1870–1993/US2	1870–1993 /UK2	1870–1993/S2
	1870–1926/C4	1909–1929/US3	1870–1955/UK3	1861–1955/S3
	1926–93/C5	1875–1928/US4		1950–92/S4
Money supply	1870–1993/C6	1870–1993/US5	1871–1993/UK4	1871–1993/S5
		1875–1992/US6	1871–1969/UK5	1871–1990/S6
Unemployment rate	1921–92/C7	1885–1993/US7	1855–1993/UK6	1929–93/S7
		1890–1930/US8		
Wage	1926–93/C8	1890–1993/US9	1809–1993/UK7	1861–1993/S8

Sources

Canada
C1. Urquhart and Buckley (1965), Bank of Canada Review, 1949 = 100, Consumer Price Index.
C2. Urquhart (1993), 1900= 100, Implicit Price Deflator.
C3. Bordo and Jonung (1987) and Bank of Canada Review, 1949 dollars, GNP.
C4. Urquhart (1993), 1900 dollars, GNP.
C5. Cansim, series D14442, 1987 dollars, GDP.
C6. Bordo and Jonung (1987), Bank of Canada Review, millions of dollars, M2.
C7. Urquhart and Buckley (1965), Bank of Canada Review, percent of the labour force.
C8. Urquhart and Buckley (1965), Bank of Canada Review, total labour income (wages, salaries, and supplementary labor income), CANSIM series D20002, billions of dollars.

United States
US1. Bureau of the Census (1975), Economic Indicators, Survey of Current Business, 1967 = 100, Consumer Price Index.
US2. Bordo and Jonung (1987), Survey of Current Business, 1929 dollars, net national product.
US3. Romer (1988), 1982 dollars, GNP.
US4. Balke and Gordon (1989), 1987 dollars, GNP.
US5. Bordo and Jonung (1987), International Financial Statistics (based on mean growth rate of Ml (line 59 mb) and M2 (line 59 ma) for 1991–3).
US6. Gordon (1993), billions of dollars, M2.
US7. Economic Report of the President, January 1993, and Survey of Current Business (March 1994, pp. 5–10), percent of the civilian labour force.
US8. Romer (1986), as in US7.

US9.   Same as US1 (March 1994, pp. 5–10), hourly average earnings in manufacturing, in dollars.

United Kingdom   UK1.   Bordo and Jonung (1987), and International Financial Statistics, line 64, 1912 = 100, Consumer Price Index.

UK2.   Bordo and Jonung (1987), National Institute Economic Review, Table 1 (2/1994), Statistical Appendix, millions of 1970 pounds, net national product and GNP applied after 1985.

UK3.   Capie and Webber (1985), millions of 1913 pounds, GNP.

UK4.   Bordon and Jonung (1987), International Financial Statistics (based on mean growth rate of lines 50 mc and 59 md for 1991–3), millions of pounds, M2.

UK5.   Capie and Webber (1985), millions of pounds. The authors call their money supply definition M3.

UK6.   Mitchell (1992), Economic Trends, and National Institute Economic Review (2/1994), Statistical Appendix, Table 5, percent of the labour force.

UK7.   Mitchell (1992) and International Financial Statistics, line 65 .. i, wages in industry, 1909 = 100.

Sweden   S1.   Mitchell (1992), OECD Main Economic Indicators and International Financial Statistics, line 64, 1913 = 100, Consumer Price Index.

S2.   Bordo and Jonung (1987), International Financial Statistics, line 99'bp, 1913 prices, millions kronor, GDP.

S3.   1913 prices, Östen Johanson, *The Gross Domestic Product of Sweden and Its Composition 1861–1955*, Stockholm, 1967 (millions kronor).

S4.   1985 prices, Swedish Bureau of Statistics (millions kronor).

S5.   Bordo and Jonung (1987), International Financial Statistics, line 38n, broad money, national definition, M2, millions kronor).

S6.   Yearly averages of the sum of notes held by the public and time and demand deposits of commercial banks. Computed by Jonung (million, kronor), M2.

S7.   OECD Main Economic Indicators, International Financial Statistics, percent of the labour force.

S8.   Mitchell (1992), OECD Main Economic Indicators and International Financial Statistics, line 65, wages in industry, 1900–1901 = 100.

NOTES

1. For the United Kingdom, the data employed in the chapter go back to the eighteenth century. Otherwise, much of the sample begins in the second half of the nineteenth century or the early part of the twentieth century. (See the Appendix.)
2. Toward the end of the 1950s, James Coyne, Governor of the Bank of Canada, chose to follow a restrictive monetary policy at a time of recession even though Conservative prime minister, John Diefenbaker, demanded a more expansionary policy. When the governor refused to change course the government introduced a bill to declare vacant the post of

Governor. The Senate (Canada has a bi-cameral system of government) did not pass the bill. Feeling vindicated, Coyne resigned soon after.

3. Capie *et al.* (1994) examine the evolution of inflation in a non-parametric setting and do not directly test for cross-country differences. However, their sample consists of more countries than does ours.

4. Sheffrin (1983) gives an excellent discussion of the reasoning and assumptions made by Lucas and others in redefining the Phillips curve in terms of output as opposed to unemployment.

5. Though by no means the only available procedure, it seems to be the method preferred by most researchers for a variety of reasons. Campbell and Perron (1991) provide a survey of the existing techniques and their relative advantages and disadvantages.

6. The authors are grateful to Pierre Perron for a copy of a RATS program which was used to produce the test results.

7. Generally, the tests for a unit root that we consider allow for only one break in the sample – even though there is, of course, the possibility of several breaks in the data. One problem, however, is that the distribution of the test statistics will also be affected by the number of breaks permitted in the data. An additional, but neglected problem, is that the finding of a break will be affected by the length of the sample initially chosen by the researcher. Thus, for example, if, in the empirical exercise which follows, we restricted ourselves only to data from, say, 1870, our unit root findings (with or without breaks) and the timing of any break would be affected. Thus, for the United States, we initially found a break in the log of prices in 1863 but upon re-estimation with data starting in 1870 we now find the break to be in 1950. Since unit root costs ignore the more interesting question of the joint relationship between different time series, we have chosen only to discuss our findings as a means of describing some of the general features of the data, not as an end in itself.

8. Alogoskoufis and Smith (1991), in estimating (9.1)–(9.3), did not test for cointegration (as well as being subject to the other caveats discussed in Burdekin and Siklos, 1996).

9. In testing for cointegration we used Johansen's method (see Banerjee *et al.*, 1993, for a description).

10. Engle and Granger (1987) show the connection between cointegration and the modeling of cyclical relationships via the addition of an error correction term, which restricts the relevant variables to be related to each other in the long run.

11. Applying the filter $\alpha(B)y_t$ produces an estimate of μ which is 'optimal' in a particular sense only (see Mills and Wood, 1993: 20), where $\alpha(B) = [\lambda(1 - B)^2(1 - B^{-1})^2 + 1]^{-1}$, and where B is the backward shift operator such that $Bx_t = x_{t-1}$. The cyclical component is then just calculated from $\kappa = x_t - \mu_t$.

12. Notice that the duration of recessions is longer in the pre-1945 period than in subsequent years. As pointed out by Watson (1994), this may be due to biases in the construction of the NBER reference dates rather than to inherently longer recessions before 1945.

13. They also argue that a multivariate approach to the estimation of c_t yields a series that is positively correlated with the NBER reference cycles in contrast with the univariate approach. While the findings for US data suggest a negative correlation between c_t and the NBER dates, this result is sample sensitive – at least in our data set.

14. The error correction term was added to the wage equation but it proved to be statistically insignificant and so was dropped from the final specification. Its lack of significance is probably due in part to the absence of cointegration in the UK wage equation, which takes up a sizeable portion of the sample.

15. We also originally considered adding a Bretton Woods dummy, but this proved to be insignificant, as was a dummy capturing the entire period of the Fed's existence. For additional analysis of this period, see Burdekin and Siklos (1996). Naturally, inclusion of dummies idiosyncratic to each country implies that they take on a zero value for other countries. This means that in the case of the Coyne affair, for example, this dummy has a value of zero for the UK, the US, and Sweden – in effect implying the commonsense conclusion that there was a Coyne affair only for Canada.

16. As is clear from Table 9.3, we have relied on a fixed effects model. Implementing Hausman's (1978) test rejects the null hypothesis that the individual effects are uncorrelated with the other regressors, at least for model (9.2), and as assumed in the random effects model. We, therefore,

maintain the assumption that differences between the countries in our study are viewed as parametric shifts.

17. Differencing may account for the fact that the country dummies are statistically insignificant. However, it must also be remembered that few series have an exact unit root and that the power of such tests is relatively low.

18. Where the instruments were the constant, trend, and dummies, and lagged values of money supply growth.

19. The results for the wage equation may be partly explained by problems in filtering the data appropriately. It proved difficult to extract sensible (as in, for example, Figure 9.4) cyclical data due to difficulties in fitting an appropriate ARIMA model for the unemployment rate, especially for Sweden and the United Kingdom.

20. While there have been some revisions of implicit price deflators for GNP and GDP, we found little in the way of revisions of consumer prices and, hence, we are unable to re-estimate (9.1) and (9.2) with 'new' data. Hanes (1994) considers the impact, stemming from the incompatibility of the pre- and post-World War II price indexes, of existing differences in estimates of inflation persistence based on wage and price formulations of the Phillips curve for US data (that is, versions of equations (9.1)–(9.3) in this chapter). He also argues that an index of manufacturing production is a better measure of output than existing variants of US real GNP series.

References

Akerlof, G.A. and Yellen, J.L. (1985), 'A near-rational model of the business cycle, with wage and price inertia', *Quarterly Journal of Economics*, 100 (Supplement): 823–38.

Akerlof, G.A., and Yellen, J.L. (1900), 'The fair wage–effort hypothesis and unemployment', *Quarterly Journal of Economics*, 105: 255–83.

Aldcroft, D.H. and Fearon, P. (1972), 'Introduction', in D.H. Aldcroft and P. Fearon (eds), *British Economic Fluctuations, 1790–1939*, London: Macmillan.

Allen, S.G. (1990), 'Changes in the cyclical sensitivity of wages in the United States, 1891–1987', North Carolina State University and National Bureau of Economics Research, mimeo.

Allen, S.G. (1992), 'Changes in the cyclical sensitivity of wages in the United States, 1891–1987', *American Economic Review*, 82: 122–40.

Alogoskoufis, G.S. and Smith, R. (1989), 'The Phillips curve and the Lucas critique: some historical evidence', Discussion Paper no. 321, London: Centre for Economic Policy Research.

Alogoskoufis, G.S. and Smith, R. (1991), 'The Phillips curve, the persistence of inflation, and the Lucas critique: evidence from exchange-rate regimes', *American Economic Review*, 81: 1254–75.

Altman, M. (1987), 'A revision of Canadian economic growth: 1870–1910: a challenge to the gradualist interpretation', *Canadian Journal of Economics*, 20(1): 86–113.

Altman, M. (1989), *Revised Estimates of Real Canadian GNP and Growth and the Pre and Post World War Two Volatility of the Canadian Business with Some Comparisons to the American Record*, Working Paper no. 89-06, Saskatoon: Department of Economics, University of Saskatchewan.

Altman, M. (1992a), 'Business cycle volatility in developed market economies, 1870–1986: revisions and conjectures', *Eastern Economic Journal*, 18(3): 259–75.

Altman, M. (1992b), 'Revised real Canadian GNP estimates and Canadian economic growth, 1870–1926', *Review of Income and Wealth*, 38(4): 455–73.

American Iron and Steel Association (1917), *Annual Statistical Report for 1895*, New York: AISA, 1896.

Arndt, H.W. (1944), *The Economic Lessons of the Nineteen-thirties*. Oxford: Oxford University Press.

Asakura, K. and Nishiyama, C. (1974), *Nihon Keizai no Kaheiteki Bunseki*. [English: Monetary Analysis of Japanese Economy 1868-1970], Tokyo: Sobunsha.

Atack, J. and Bateman, F. (1989), 'How long did people work in 1880?', paper presented at the NBER Summer Institute on the Development of the American Economy, Cambridge, Mass.

Atack, J. and Bateman, F. (1991), 'Louis Brandeis, work and fatigue at the start of the twentieth century: prelude to Oregon's Hours Limitation Law', unpublished paper, University of Indiana.

Atack, J. and Bateman, F. (1992), 'How long was the workday in 1880?', *Journal of Economic History*, 52(1): 129–60.

Backus, D.K. and Kehoe, P.J. (1992), 'International evidence on the historical properties of business cycles', *American Economic Review*, 82(4): 864–88.

Backus, D.K., Kehoe, P.J. and Kydland, F.E. (1993), 'International business cycles: theory vs. evidence', *Quarterly Review of the Federal Reserve Bank of Minneapolis*, 17(4): 14–29.

Balderston, T. (1974), 'Statistical sources on German investment, 1924–1929', in H. Mommsen, D. Petzina and B. Weisbrod (eds), *Industrielles System und politische Entwicklung in der Weimarer Republik*, Düsseldorf: Droste.

Balderston, T. (1977), 'The German business cycle in the 1920s: a comment', *Economic History Review*, 30: 159–61.

Balderston, T. (1993), *The Origins and Course of the German Economic Crisis, 1924–1933*, Berlin: Haude & Spener.

Balke, N.S. and Gordon, R.J. (1989), 'The estimation of prewar gross national product: methodology and new evidence', *Journal of Political Economy*, 97: 38–92.

Ball, L., Mankiw, N.G. and Romer, D. (1988), 'The new Keynesian economics and the output–inflation trade-off', *Brookings Papers on Economic Activity*, 1: 1–82.

Banerjee, A., Dolado, J., Galbraith, J.W. and Hendry, D.F. (1993), *Co-integration, Error Correction, and the Econometric Analysis of Non-stationary Data*, Oxford and New York: Oxford University Press.

Barkai, A. (1990), *Nazi Economics: Ideology, theory, and policy*, Oxford: Berg.

Barro, R.J. (1977), 'Unanticipated money growth and unemployment in the United States', *American Economic Review*, 67(1): 101–15.

Barro, R.J. (1978), 'Unanticipated money, output, and the price level in the United States', *Journal of Political Economy*, 86(4): 549–80.

Barsky, R.B. (1987), 'The Fisher hypothesis and the forecastability and persistence of inflation', *Journal of Monetary Economics*, 19(1): 3–24.

Barsky, R.B. and Summers, L.H. (1988), 'Gibson's paradox and the gold standard', *Journal of Political Economy*, 96(3): 528–50.

Baxter, M. and King, R.G. (1995), 'Measuring business cycles: approximate band-pass filters for economic time series', NBER Working Paper no. 5022, Cambridge: NBER.

Becker, J.M. (1972), *Experience Rating in Unemployment Insurance: An Experiment in Competitive Socialism*, Baltimore, MD: Johns Hopkins University Press.

Bernanke, B.S. and Parkinson, M.L. (1991), 'Procyclical labor productivity and competing theories of the business cycle: some evidence from interwar US manufacturing industries', *Journal of Political Economy*, 99: 439–59.

Bernanke, B.S. and Powell, J.L. (1986), 'The cyclical behavior of industrial labor markets: a comparison of the prewar and postwar eras', in R. Gordon (ed.), *The American Business Cycle: Continuity and Change*, National Bureau of Economic Research Studies in Business Cycles, 25, Chicago: University of Chicago Press, 583-637.

Berry, T.S. (1968), *Estimated Annual Variations in Gross National Product, 1789 to 1909*, Bostwick Paper no. 1, Richmond, Va: Bostwick Press.

Berry, T.S. (1988), *Production and Population since 1789: Revised GNP series in constant dollars*, Bostwick Paper no. 6, Richmond, Va: Bostwick Press.

Beveridge, S. and Nelson, C.R. (1981), 'A new approach to decomposition of economic times series into permanent and transitory components with particular attention to measurement of the business cycle', *Journal of Monetary Economics*, 7: 151–74.

Beveridge, W.H. (1944), *Full Employment in a Free Society*, London: Liberal Publications Dept.

Bils, M.J. (1985), 'Real wages over the business cycle: evidence from panel data', *Journal of Political Economy*, 93(4): 666–89.

Blackburn, K. and Ravn, M.O. (1992), 'Business cycles in the United Kingdom: facts and fictions', *Economica*, 59: 383–401.

Blanchard, O.J. and Fischer, S. (1989), *Lectures on Macroeconomics*, Cambridge, Mass.: MIT Press.

Bodkin, R.G. (1969), 'Real wages and cyclical variations in employment', *Canadian Journal of Economics*, 2: 353–74.

Bolino, A.C. (1966), 'The duration of unemployment: some tentative historical comparisons', *Quarterly Journal of Economics and Business*, 6: 31–49.

Borchardt, J. ([1979] 1991), 'Constraints and room of manoeuvre in the economic policies of the early 1930s', in his *Perspectives on Modern German Economic History and Policy*, Cambridge: Cambridge University Press.

Borchardt, K. (1990), 'A Decade of Debate about Bruening's Economic Policy', in J. von Kruedener (ed.), *Economic Crisis and Political Collapse. The Weimar Republic 1924–33*, Oxford: Berg, 99–151.

Bordo, M.D. and Jonung, L. (1987), *The Long-run Behavior of the Velocity of Circulation*, Cambridge: Cambridge University Press.

Bordo, M.D., Jonung, L. and Siklos, P. (1994), 'The common development of institutional change as measured by income velocity of circulation: a century of evidence from industrialized countries', Wilfrid Laurier University, unpublished paper.

Bordo, M.D., Jonung, L. and Siklos, P. (1997), 'Institutional change and the velocity of money: a century of evidence', *Economic Inquiry*, 35: 710–24.

Bowley, A.L. (1900), *Wages in the United Kingdom in the Nineteenth Century*, Cambridge: Cambridge University Press.

Bowley, A.L. and Wood, G.H. (1906), 'The statistics of wages in the United Kingdom during the last hundred years, Part XIV: Engineering and shipbuilding. E: Averages, index numbers and general results', *Journal of the Statistical Society*, LXIX: 142-92.

Broadberry, S.N. and Ritschl, L. (1994), 'The iron twenties: wages, productivity, and the lack of prosperity in Britain and Germany before the Great Depression', in C. Buchheim, M. Hutter and H. James (eds), *Zerrissene Zwischenkriegszeit, Festschrift Knut Borchardt*, Baden-Baden: Nomos.

Broadberry, S.N. and Ritschl, L. (1995), 'Real wages, productivity, and unemployment in Britain and Germany during the 1920s', *Explorations in Economic History*, 32: 327–49.

Brown, R.L., Durbin, J. and Evans, J.M. (1975), 'Techniques for testing the constancy of regression relationships over time', *Journal of the Royal Statistical Society*, 37: 146–92.

Bry, G. and Boschan, C. (1971), *Cyclical Analysis of Time Series: Selected procedures and computer programs*, National Bureau of Economic Research Technical Paper 20, New York: Columbia University Press, for NBER.

Burdekin, R.C.K. and Burkett, P. (1996), *Distributional Conflict and Inflation: Theoretical and historical perspectives*, London: Macmillan.

Burdekin, R.C.K. and Siklos, P. (1994), 'Exchange rate regimes and inflation persistence: further evidence', Claremont McKenna College and Wilfrid Laurier University, unpublished paper.

Burdekin, R.C.K., Westbrook, J.R. and Willet, T.D. (forthcoming), 'the political economy of discretionary monetary policy: a public choice analysis of proposals for reform', in R.H. Timberlake and K. Dowd (eds), *Money and The National State*, Independent Institute.

Burdett, K. and Wright, R. (1989), 'Unemployment insurance and short-time compensation: the effects on layoffs, hours per worker, and wages', *Journal of Political Economy*, 97: 1479–96.

Burns, A.F. (1951), 'Mitchell on what happens during business cycles', in *Conference on Business Cycles*, New York: National Bureau of Economic Research, 3–33.

Burns, A. and Mitchell, W.C. (1946), *Measuring Business Cycles*, New York: NBER.

Cagan, P. (1975), 'Changes in the recession behavior of wholesale prices in the 1920s and post-World War II', *Explorations in Economic Research: Occasional Papers of the National Bureau of Economic Reserarch*, 2 (winter): 54–104.

Calomiris, C.W. (1988), 'Price and exchange rate determination during the greenback suspension', *Oxford Economic Papers*, 40: 719–50.

Calomiris, C.W. (1990), 'Policy regimes, the price process, and the Phillips curve: the United States, 1862–1913', Department of Economics, Northwestern University, unpublished paper.

Calomiris, C.W. (1992), 'Regulation, industrial structure and stability in US banking: an historical perspective', in M. Klausner and L.J. White (eds), *Structural Change in Banking*, Homewood, Ill.: Business One Irwin, 19–116.

Calomiris, C.W. (1994), 'Greenback resumption and silver risk: the economics and politics of monetary regime change in the United States, 1862–1900', in M.D. Bordo and F. Capie (eds), *Monetary Regimes in Transition*, New York: Cambridge University Press.

Calomiris, C.W. and Hanes, C. (1994), 'Consistent output series for the antebellum and postbellum periods: issues and preliminary results', *Journal of Economic History*, 54: 409–22; reprinted as Chapter 1 in this volume.

Calomiris, C.W. and Hubbard, R.G. (1987), *International Adjustment under the Classical Gold Standard: Evidence for the US and Britain, 1879–1914*, NBER Working Paper no. 2206, Cambridge, Mass.: National Bureau of Economic Research, mimeo.

Campbell, J.Y. and Perron, P. (1991), 'Pitfalls and opportunities: what macroeconomists should know about unit roots', in O.J. Blanchard and S. Fischer (eds), *NBER Macroeconomics Annual, 1991*, Cambridge, Mass.: MIT Press.

Campbell, R.H. (1957), 'Fluctuations in stocks: a nineteenth-century case study', *Oxford Economic Papers*, 9: 41–55.

Capie, F.H. and Mills, T.C. (1991), 'Money and business cycles in the US and UK, 1870 to 1913', *Manchester School*, 59: 38–56.

Capie, F. and Weber, A. (1985), *Data, Sources and Methods: A monetary history of the United Kingdom*, London: Allen & Unwin.

Capie, F.H., Mills, T.C. and Wood, G.E. (1994), 'Central bank dependence and inflation performance: an exploratory data analyst', in P.L. Siklos (ed.), *Varieties of Monetary Reforms: Lessons and Experience on the Road to Monetary Union*, Boston, Mass.: Kluwer.

Careless, J.M.S. (1970), 'The development of the Winnipeg business community, 1870–1890', *Transactions of the Royal Society of Canada, Series IV*, 8: 239–54.

Carter, S.B. and Sutch, R. (1990), 'The labour market in the 1890s: evidence from Connecticut Manufacturing', in E. Aerts and B. Eichengreen (eds),

Unemployment and Underemployment in Historical Perspective, Leuven, Belgium: Leuven University Press, 15–24.

Carter, S.B. and Sutch, R. (1991), 'Sticky wages, short weeks, and "fairness": the response of Connecticut manufacturing firms to the depression of 1893–94', Historical Labor Statistics Project Working Paper 2, University of California.

Carter, S.B. and Sutch, R. (1992), 'The Great Depression of the 1890s: new suggestive estimates of the unemployment rate, 1890–1905', *Research in Economic History*, 14: 343–76.

Carter, S.B., Ransom, R.L. and Sutch, R. (1991), 'The Historical Labor Statistics Project at the University of California', *Historical Methods*, 24(2): 52–65.

Carter, S.B., Ransom, R.L. and Sutch, R. (1992), *Historical Labor Statistics Newsletter*, Berkeley, Cal.: Institute of Business and Economic Research.

Carter, S.B., Ransom, R.L., Sutch, R. and Zhao, H. (1993), *Codebook and User's Manual: Investigations of the industrial depression in Connecticut, 1894 and 1895, reported in the Tenth Annual and Eleventh Annual Reports of the Connecticut Bureau of Labor Statistics*, Berkeley, Cal.: Institute of Business and Economic Research.

Carter, S.B., Ransom, R.L., Sutch, R. and Zhao, H. (1994), 'The labor market a hundred years ago: new micro-level evidence on long-term change from the depression of 1893–94', unpublished ms.

Catao, L.A.V. and Solomou, S.A. (1993), *Business Cycles during the Gold Standard, 1870–1913*, Working Paper no. 9304, Cambridge University: Department of Applied Economics.

Chambers, E.J. (1964), 'Late nineteenth century business cycles in Canada', *Canadian Journal of Economics and Political Science*, 30(3): 391–412.

Chandler, A.D. (1977), *The Visible Hand: The managerial revolution in American business*, Cambridge, Mass.: Belknap Press.

Church, R.A. (1975), *The Great Victorian Boom, 1850–1873*, London: Macmillan.

Clapham, J.H. (1932), *An Economic History of Modern Britain: Free Trade and Steel, 1850–1886*, Cambridge: Cambridge University Press.

Clapham, J.H. (1938), *An Economic History of Modern Britain: Machines and National Rivalries (1887–1914) with an Epilogue (1914–1929)*, New York: Macmillan.

Clapham, J.H. (1944), *The Bank of England: a History*, vol. II: *1797–1914*, Cambridge: Cambridge University Press.

Clark, K. and Summers, L. (1979) 'Labor market dynamics and unemployment: a reconsideration', *Brookings Papers on Economic Activity*, 1: 13–60.

Cogley, T. and Nason, J.M. (1995), 'Effects of the Hodrick–Prescott filter on trend and difference stationary times series: implications for business cycle research', *Journal of Economic Dynamics and Control*, 19: 237–51.

Collins, M. (1988), 'English banks and business cycles, 1848–80', in P.L. Cottrell and D.E. Moggridge (eds), *Money and Power: Essays in honour of L.S. Pressnell*, London: Macmillan, 1–39.

Connecticut Bureau of Labor Statistics (1894), *Tenth Annual Report for the Year Ending November 30, 1894*, Meriden, Conn.: State Printer.

Connecticut Bureau of Labor Statistics. (1895), *Eleventh Annual Report for the Year Ending November 30, 1895*, Meriden, Conn.: State Printer.

Cooley, T.F. (1995), *Frontiers of Business Cycle Research*, Princeton, NJ: Princeton University Press.

Cooley, T.F. and Ohanian, L.E. (1991), 'The cyclical behavior of prices', *Journal of Monetary Economics*, 28: 25–60.

Corbett, D. (1991), *Unemployment in interwar Germany, 1924–38*, PhD thesis, Harvard University.

Correia, I.H., Neves, J.L. and Rebelo, S. (1992), 'Business cycles from 1850 to 1950: new facts about old data', *European Economic Review*, 36: 459–67.

Cottrell, P.L. (1988), 'Credit, morals and sunspots: the financial boom of the 1860s and trade cycle theory', in P.L. Cottrell and D.E. Moggridge (eds), *Money and Power: Essays in honour of L.S. Pressnell*, London: Macmillan, 41–71.

Crafts, N.F.R. and Mills, T.C. (1994), 'Trends in real wages in Britain, 1750–1913', *Explorations in Economic History*, 31: 176–94.

Crafts, N.F.R., Leybourne, S.J. and Mills, T.C. (1989), 'Trends and cycles in British industrial production, 1700–1913', *Journal of the Royal Statistical Society, Series A,* 152(1): 43–60.

Creamer, D.B. (1950), *Behavior of Wage Rates during Business Cycles*, National Bureau of Economic Research Occasional Paper 34, New York: National Bureau of Economic Research.

Crouzet, F. (1982), *The Victorian Economy*, trans. Anthon Forster, London: Methuen (originally published as *Economie de la Grande-Bretagne victorienne*).

Danthine, J.P. and Donaldson, J. (1993), 'Methodological and empirical issues in real business cycle theory', *European Economic Review*, 37: 1–35.

David, P.A. and P. Solar (1977), 'A Bicentenary Contribution to the History of the Cost of Living in America', *Reserach in Economic History*, 2: 1–80.

Deane, P. and Cole, W.A. (1969), *British Economic Growth, 1688–1959: Trends and Structure*, 2nd edn, University of Cambridge Department of Applied Economics Monograph 8, Cambridge: Cambridge University Press.

DeCanio, S. and Mokyr, J. (1977), 'Inflation and the wage lag during the American Civil War', *Explorations in Economic History*, 14: 311–36.

Decken, H. v.d. and Wagenführ, R. (1936–37), 'Entwicklung und Wandlung der Sachgueterproduktion', *Vierteljahrshefte zur Konjunkturforschung*, NF 11, Series A: 145–63.

DeLong, J.B. and Summers, L.H. (1986a), 'Is increased price flexibility stabilizing?' *American Economic Review*, 76: 1031–44.

DeLong, J.B. and Summers, L.H. (1986b), 'The changing cylical variability of economic activity in the United States', in R.J. Gordon (ed.), *The American Business Cycle: Continuity and Change*, Chicago: University of Chicago Press, 679–734.

Den Haan, W.J. (1996), 'The comovements beween real activity and prices at different business cycle frequencies', San Diego, Cal.: University of California at San Diego, Department of Economics, unpublished ms.

Dessauer-Meinhardt, M. (1940), 'Monthly unemployment records, 1854–1892', *Economica*, 7: 322–6.

Deutsche Bundesbank (1976), *Deutsches Geld- und Bankwesen in Zahlen, 1976–1975*, Frankfurt: Knapp.

Devine, W. (1983), 'From shafts to wires: historicial perspective on electrifications', *Journal of Economic History*, 43(2): 347–72.

Dick, T.J O. and Floyd, J.E. (1991), 'Balance of payments adjustment under the international gold standard: Canada, 1871–1913', *Explorations in Economic History*, 28(2): 209–38.

Dick, T.J.O. and Floyd, J.E. (1992), *Canada and the gold standard: 1871–1913*, Cambridge: Cambridge University Press.

Dick, T.J.O. and Floyd, J.E. (1994), 'Canada and the gold standard, 1871–1914: a durable monetary regime', in M.D. Bordo and F. Capie (eds), *Monetary Regimes in Transition*, New York: Cambridge University Press, 173–200.

Dickey, D.A. and Pantula, S.G. (1987), 'Determining the order of differencing in autoregressive processes', *Journal of Business and Economic Statistics*, 5: 455–61.

Dunlop, J. (1938), 'The movement of real and money wage rates', *Economic Journal*, 48: 413–34.

Durand, J. (1957), 'Development of the labor force concept, 1930–40', *Social Science Research Council Bulletin*.

Dwyer, G.P.J. (1985), 'Money, income and prices in the United Kingdom: 1870–1913', *Economic Inquiry*, 23: 415–35.

Easterbrook, W.T. and Aitken, H.G.J. (1956), *Canadian Economic History*, Toronto: Macmillan.

Easton, S. (1984), 'Real output and the gold standard years, 1830–1913', in M.D. Bordo and A. Schwartz (eds), *A Retrospective on the Classical Gold Standard, 1821–1931*, Chicago: University of Chicago Press, 513–38.

Eavenson, H.N. (1942), *The First Century and a Quarter of American Coal Industry*, Pittsburgh, Pa.: priv. print. [Baltimore Weekly Press].

Ehrlicher, W. (1956), *Geldkapitalbildung und Realkapitalbildung*, Tübingen: Mohr.

Eichengreen, B.J. (1983), 'The causes of British business cycles, 1833–1913', *Journal of European Economic History*, 12(1): 145–61.

Eichengreen, B. and Sachs, J. (1985), 'Exchange rates and economic recovery in the 1930s', *Journal of Economic History*, 65(4): 925–46.

Emery, K.M. (1994), 'Inflation persistence and Fisher effects: evidence of a regime change', *Journal of Economics and Business*, 46: 141–52.

Engel, C. (1933), 'Real exchange rates and relative prices: an empirical investigation', *Journal of Monetary Economics*, 32: 35–50.

Engle, R.F. and Granger, C.W.J. (1987), 'Co-integration and error correction: representation, estimation and testing', *Econometrica*, 55: 251–76.

Erbe, R. (1958), *Die nationalsozialistische Wirtschaftspolitik 1933–1939 im Lichte der modernen Theorie*, Zurich: Polygraphischer Verlag.

Ericsson, N.P. and Irons, J.S. (1995), 'The Lucas critique in practice: theory without measurement', in K.D. Hoover (ed.), *Macroeconometrics: Development, tensions and prospects*, Boston, Mass.: Kluwer, ch. 8.

Erker, P. (1994), *Industrieeliten in der NS-Zeit*, Passau: Rothe.

Evans, D.M. ([1859] 1969), *The History of the Commercial Crises 1857–1858 and the Stock Exchange Panic of 1859*, New York: Augustus Kelly.

Evans, G. and Reichlin, L. (1994), 'Information, forecasts, and the measurement of the business cycle', *Journal of Monetary Economics*, 33: 233–54.

Fair, R.C. (1969), *The Short-run Demand for Workers and Hours*, Amsterdam, North-Holland.

Falkus, M.E. (1975), 'The German Business Cycle in the 1920s', *Economic History Review*, 23: 451–65.

Fay, J.A. and Medoff, J.L. (1985), 'Labor and output over the business cycle: some direct evidence', *American Economic Review*, 75: 638–55.

Feinstein, C.H. (1972), *National Income, Expenditure and Output of the United Kingdom, 1855–1965*, Cambridge: Cambridge University Press.

Feinstein, C.H. (1989), 'Wages and the paradox of the 1880s: a comment', *Explorations in Economic History*, 26: 237–47.

Feinstein, C.H. (1990), 'What really happened to real wages?: Trends in wages, prices, and productivity in the United Kingdom, 1880–1913', *Economic History Review*, 43: 329–55.

Feldstein, M.S. (1976), 'Temporary layoffs in the theory of unemployment', *Journal of Political Economy*, 84: 937–57.

Fels, R. (1959), *American Business Cycles*, Chapel Hill, NC: University of North Carolina Press

Firestone, O.J. (1958), *Canada's Economic Development 1867–1953*, London: Bowes & Bowes.

Firestone, O.J. (1969), *Industry and Education: A century of Canadian development*, Ottawa: University of Ottawa Press.

FitzRoy, F.R. and Hart, R.A. (1985), 'Hours, layoffs, and unemployment insurance funding: theory and practice in an international perspective', *Economic Journal*, 95: 700–13.

Floyd, J.E. (1985), *World Monetary Equilibrium*, Philadelphia: University of Pennsylvania Press.

Fogel, R.W. (1964), *Railroads and American Economic Growth: Essays in econometric history*, Baltimore, MD: Johns Hopkins University Press.

Ford, A.G. (1963), 'Notes on the role of exports in British economic fluctuations', *Economic History Review*, 16: 329–55.

Ford, A.G. (1983), 'The trade cycle in Britain, 1860–1914', in R. Floud and D.N. McCloskey (eds), *1860 to the 1970s*, vol. 2 of *The Economic History of Britain since 1700*, Cambridge: Cambridge University Press.

Fremdling, R. (1988), 'German national accounts for the 19th and early 20th century: a criticial assessment', *Vierteljahrschrift für Sozial- und Wirtschafts-geschichte*, 75: 339–55.

Fremdling, R. (1995), 'German national accounts for the 19th and early 20th century', *Scandinavian Economic History Review*, 43: 77–100.

Frickey, E. (1942), *Economic Fluctuations in the United States: A systematic analysis of long-run trends and business cycles, 1866–1914*, Cambridge, Mass.: Harvard University Press.

Frickey, E. (1947), *Production in the United States, 1860–1914*, Cambridge, Mass.: Harvard University Press.

Friedman, M. (1962), *The Interpolation of Time Series by Related Time Series*, NBER Technical Paper no. 16, New York: National Bureau of Economic Research.

Friedman, M. (1992), *Money Mischief: Episodes in monetary history*, Orlando, Fla: Harcourt Brace Jovanovich.

Friedman, M. and Schwartz, A.J. (1963), *A Monetary History of the United States, 1867–1960*, National Bureau of Economic Research Studies in Business Cycles no. 12, Princeton, NJ: Princeton University Press.

Friedman, M. and Schwartz, A.J. (1982), *Monetary Trends in the United States and the United Kingdom*, Chicago: University of Chicago Press.

Gallman, R. (1960), 'Commodity output, 1839–1899', in National Bureau of Economic Research, *Trends in the American Economy in the Nineteenth Century*, NBER Studies in Income and Wealth no. 24, Princeton, NJ: Princeton University Press, 13–71.

Gallman, R. (1966), 'Gross national product in the United States, 1834–1909', in D.S. Brady (ed.), *Output, Employment and Productivity in the United States after 1800*, NBER Studies in Income and Wealth no. 30, Princeton, NJ: Princeton University Press, 3–90.

Gayer, A.D., Rostow, W.W. and Schwarz, A.J. (1975), *The Growth and Fluctuation of the British Economy, 1790–1850*, Brighton: Harvester Wheatsheaf.

Geary, P.T. and Kennan, J. (1982), 'The employment–real wage relationship: an international study', *Journal of Political Economy*, 90(4): 854–71.

Gehrig, G. (1961), 'Eine Zeitreihe für den Sachkapitalbestand und die Investitionen', in Gehrig *et al.*, *Bestimmungsfaktoren der deutschen Produktion*, Ifo-Studien 7, 1–49.

Gilbert, P. (1930), *Jahresbericht des Reparationsgenten 1928/29*, Berlin: Reimar Hobbing.

Goldin, C. and Margo, R. (1989), 'Wages, prices, and labor markets before the Civil War', NBER Working Paper 3198, mimeo.

Goodhart, C.A.E. (1972), *The Business of Banking, 1891–1914*, London School of Economics Research Monograph, London: Weidenfeld & Nicolson.

Gordon, R.J. (1980), 'A consistent characterization of a near-century of price behavior', *American Economic Review*, 70(2): 243–9.

Gordon, R.J. (1981), 'Output fluctuations and gradual price adjustment', *Journal of Economic Literature*, 19(2): 493–530.

Gordon, R.J. (1982a), 'Price inertia and policy ineffectiveness in the United States, 1890–1980', *Journal of Political Economy*, 90(6): 1087–117.

Gordon, R.J. (1982b), 'Why US wage and employment behavior differs from that in Britain and Japan', *Economic Journal*, 92: 13–44.

Gordon, R.J. (1983), 'A century of evidence on wage and price stickiness in the United States, the United Kingdom, and Japan', in J. Tobin (ed.), *Macroeconomics, Prices and Quantities*, Washington, DC: Brookings Institution, 85–121.

Gordon, R.J. (ed.) (1986), *The American Business Cycle: Continuity and Change*, Chicago: University of Chicago Press.

Gordon, R.J. (1988), 'The role of wages in the inflation process', *American Economic Review Papers and Proceedings*, 78(2): 276–83.

Gordon, R.J. (1990a), *The Phillips Curve Now and Then*, NBER Working Paper no. 3393, Cambridge, Mass.: NBER.

Gordon, R.J. (1990b), 'What is new-Keynesian economics?', *Journal of Economic Literature*, 28: 1115–71.

Gordon, R.J. (1993), *Macroeconomics*, 6th edn, New York: Harper-Collins.

Gordon, R.J. and King, S.R. (1982), 'The output cost of disinflation in traditional and vector autoregression models', *Brookings Papers on Economic Activity*, 13(1): 205–42.

Greasley, D. (1986), 'British economic growth: the paradox of the 1880s and the timing of the climacteric', *Explorations in Economic History*, 23: 416–44.

Greasley, D. (1989), 'British wages and income, 1856–1913: A revision', *Explorations in Economic History*, 26: 248–59.

Green, A.G. and Urquhart, M.C. (1987), 'New estimates of output growth in Canada: measurement and interpretation', in D. McCalla (ed.), *Perspectives on Canadian Economic History*, Toronto: Copp Clark Pitman, 182–99.

Grey, J.A. and Kandil, M. (1991), 'Is price flexibility stabilizing? A broader perspective', *Journal of Money Credit and Banking*, 23(1): 1–12.

Grupe, D. (1957), 'Die Nahrungsmittelversorgung Deutschlands seit 1925', *Agrarwirtschaft*, special issue 34.

Haberler, G. (1937), *Prosperity and Depression*, Cambridge: Harvard University Press.

Hachtmann, R. (1989), *Industriearbeit im Dritten Reich. Untersuchungen zu den Lohn- und Arbeitsbedingungen in Deutschland 1933–1945*, Göttingen: Vandenhoeck & Ruprecht.

Hahn, F., and Solow, R.M. (1986), 'Is wage flexibility a good thing?', in W. Beckerman (ed.), *Wage Rigidity and Unemployment*, London: Duckworth, 1–19.

Hanes, C. (1992), 'Comparable indices of wholesale prices and manufacturing wage rates in the United States, 1865–1914', in *Research in Economic History*, vol. 14, Greenwich, Conn: JAI Press, 269–92.

Hanes, C. (1993), 'The development of nominal wage rigidity in the nineteenth century', *American Economic Review*, 83(4): 732–56.

Hanes, C. (1994), 'Changes in the cyclical behavior of nominal prices, 1869–1990', University of Pennsylvania (unpublished).

Harley, C.K. and McCloskey, D.N. (1983), 'Foreign trade: competition and the expanding international economy', in R. Floud and D.N. McCloskey (eds), *1860 to the 1970s*, vol. 2 of *The Economic History of Britain since 1700*, Cambridge: Cambridge University Press, 50–69.

Harvey, A.C. (1989), *Forecasting, Structural Times Series Models and the Kalman Filter*, Cambridge: Cambridge University Press.

Harvey, A.C. and Jaeger, A. (1993), 'Detrending, stylized facts and the business cycle', *Journal of Applied Econometrics*, 8: 231–47.

Hashimoto, J. (1984), *Daikyokoki no Nihon shihon shugi* [Japanese capitalism during the Great Depression], Tokyo: University of Tokyo Press.

Hatton, T.J. and Williamson, J.G. (1990a), 'Unemployment, implicit contracts, and compensating wage differentials: Michigan in the 1890s', paper presented at the Thirteenth Annual Cliometrics Conference, University of Illinois.

Hatton, T.J. and Williamson, J.G. (1990b), 'Unemployment in the 1890s: microeconomic evidence from Michigan', in E. Aerts and B. Eichengreen (eds), *Unemployment and Underemployment in Historical Perspective*, Leuven: University of Leuven Press, 23–35.

Hausman, J. (1978), 'Specification tests in econometrics', *Econometrica*, 46: 1251–71.

Hawke, G.R. (1970), *Railways and Economic Growth in England and Wales, 1840–1870*, Oxford: Clarendon Press.

Hawtrey, R.G. (1965), *A Century of Bank Rate*, 2nd edn, London and New York: F. Cass and A.M. Kelly.

Hay, K.A.J. (1966), 'Early twentieth century business cycles in Canada', *Canadian Journal of Economics and Political Science*, 32(3): 354–65.

Hay, K.A.J. (1967), 'Money and cycles in post confederation Canada', *Journal of Political Economy*, 75: 262–73.

Hayes, P. (1987), *Industry and Ideology: The IG Farben in the Nazi Era*, Cambridge: Cambridge University Press.

Hirsch, J. (1929), *Wandlungen im Aufbau der deutschen Industrie*, in B. Harms (ed.), *Strukturwandlungen der deutschen Volkswirtschaft*, vol. 1, Berlin: Duncker & Humblot.

Hodrick, R.J. and Prescott, E.C. (1980), 'Post-war US business cycles: an empirical investigation', Working Paper no. 451, Pittsburgh: Carnegie-Mellon University.

Hoffmann, W.G. (1955), *British Industry, 1700–1950*, trans. W.O. Henderson and W.H. Chaloner, Oxford: Blackwell.

Hoffmann, W.G. (1965), *Das Wachstum der Deutschen Wertschaft Seit der Mitte Des 19 Jahrhunderts*, Heidelberg: Springer.

Hoffmann, W.G. (1984), 'Zu hohe Löhne in der Weimarer Republik? Bemerkungen zur Borchardt-These', *Geschichte und Gesellschaft*, 10: 122–41.

Hoffmann, W.G. and Hatfrenrich, C.-L. (1983), 'The growth of net domestic product in Germany, 1850–1913', in R. Fremdling and P. O'Brien (eds), *Productivity in the Economies of Europe*, Stuttgart: Deutsche Verlagsanstalt, 124–32.

Hoffmann, W.G. and Müller, J.H. (1959), *Das deutsche Volkseinkommen 1851–1957*, Tübingen: Möhr.

Holtfrerich, C.-L. (1996), 'Zur Debatte um die deutsche Wirtschaftspolitik von Weimar zu Hitler', *Vierteljahreshefte für Zeitgeschichte*, 44: 119–32.

Hoover, E.D. (1960), 'Retail prices after 1850', in National Bureau of Economic Research, *Trends in the American Economy in the Nineteenth century*, Studies in Income and Wealth no. 24, Princeton, NJ: Princeton University Press.

Hughes, J.R.T. (1956), 'The commercial crisis of 1857', *Oxford Economic Papers*, 8: 194–222.

Hughes, J.R.T. (1960), *Fluctuations in Trade, Industry and Finance: A study of British economic development, 1850–1860*, Oxford: Clarendon Press.

Hultgren, T. (1948), *American Transportation in Prosperity and Depression*, Studies in Business Cycles no. 3, New York: National Bureau of Economic Research.

Hultgren, T. (1953), *Transport and the State of Trade in Britain*, National Bureau of Economic Research Occasional Paper no. 40, New York: National Bureau of Economic Research.

Hultgren, T. (1960), *Changes in Labor Cost During Cycles in Production and Business*, National Bureau of Economic Research Occasional Paper No. 74, New York: National Bureau of Economic Research.

Hunnicutt, B.K. (1988), *Work without End: Abandoning shorter hours for the right to work*, Philadelphia: Temple University Press.

Hunter, L.C. (1979), *A History of Industrial Power in the United States, 1789–1930*, vol. 1: *Waterpower*, Charlottesville, Va: University of Virginia Press.

Imlah, A.H. (1958), *Economic Elements in the Pax Britannica: Studies In British foreign trade in the nineteenth century*, Cambridge, Mass.: Harvard University Press.

Inwood, K. and Stengos, T. (1991), 'Discontinuities in Canadian economic growth, 1870–1935', *Explorations in Economic History*, 28(3): 274–86.

Itoh, M. (1989), *Nihon no Taigai Kinyu to Kinyuseisaku* [Japan's international finance and monetary policy 1914–1936], Nagoya: University of Nagoya Press.

James, H. (1986), *The German Slump: Politics and Economics, 1924–1936*, Oxford: Clarendon Press.

James, H.G. (1985), *The Reichsbank and Public Finance in Germany, 1929–1933*, Frankfurt/M.: Knapp.

James, J.A. (1985), *Shifts in the Nineteenth-century Phillips Curve Relationship*, NBER Working Paper no. 1587, New York: National Bureau of Economic Research.

James, J.A. (1989), 'The stability of the l9th-century Phillips curve relationship', *Explorations in Economic History*, 26(2): 117–34.

James, J.A. (1993), 'Changes in economic instability in l9th-century America', *American Economic Review*, 83(4): 710–31.

James, J.A. (1995), 'Cyclical wage flexibility in early industrial labor markets: the United States, 1840–1891', University of Virginia Department of Economics, unpublished ms.

Jevons, W.S. ([1884] 1964), *Investigations in Currency and Finance*, New York: Augustus Kelly.

Jones, E.B. (1963), 'New estimates of hours of work per week and hourly earnings, 1900–1957', *Review of Economics and Statistics*, 45: 374–85.

Keane, M., Moffit, R. and Runkle, D. (1988), 'Real wages over the business cycle: estimating the impact of heterogeneity with micro data', *Journal of Political Economy*, 96: 1232–66.

Keating, J.W. and Nye, J.V. (1994), 'Permanent and transitory shocks in real output: estimates from nineteenth century and postwar economies', Department of Economics, Washington University, unpublished ms.

Keiser, G. and Benning, B. (1931), 'Kapitalbildung und Investitionen in der deutschen Volkswirtschaft 1924 bis 1928', *Vierteljahreshefte zue Konjunkturforschung Sonderheft*, 22.

Kendrick, J.W. (1961), *Productivity Trends in the United States*, Princeton, NJ: Princeton University Press.

Kerr, D. (1977), 'Wholesale trade on the Canadian plains in the late nineteenth century: Winnipeg and its competition', in H. Palmer (ed.), *The Settlement of the West*, Calgary: Comprint, 130–52.

Keynes, J.M. (1930), *A Treatise on Money*, vol 2: *The Applied Theory of Money*, London: Macmillan.

Keynes, J.M. (1936), *The General Theory of Employment, Interest and Money*, London: Macmillan.

Keynes, J.M. (1938), *A Treatise on Money*, vol. 2: *The Applied Theory of Money*, London: Macmillan.

Keynes, J. M. (1939), 'Relative movements of real wages and output', *Economic Journal*, 49: 35–51.

Keyssar, A. (1986), *Out of Work: The first century of unemployment in Massachusetts*, Cambridge and New York: Cambridge University Press.

Kindleberger, C.P. (1973), *The World in Depression, 1929–1939*, Berkeley, Cal.: University of California Press.

King, R.G. and Watson, M.W. (1994), 'The post-war US Phillips curve: a revisionist econometric history', *Carnegie-Rochester Conference Series on Public Policy*, 41: 157–219.

King, W.T.C. (1936), *History of the London Discount Market*, London: Routledge.

Kitchin, J. (1923), 'Cycles and trends in economic factors', *Review of Economic Statistics*, 5: 10–16.

Klein, B. (1959), *Germany's Economic Preparations for War*, Cambridge, Mass.: Harvard University Press.

Klovland, J.T. (1993), 'Zooming in on Sauerbeck: monthly wholesale prices in Britain 1845–1890', *Explorations in Economic History*, 30: 195–228.

Klovland, J.T. (1994), 'Pitfalls in the estimation of the yield on British consols, 1850–1914', *Journal of Economic History*, 54: 164–87.

Kniesner, T.J. and Goldsmith, A.H. (1987), 'A survey of alternative models of the aggregate US labor market', *Journal of Economic Literture*, 25: 1241–80.

Kroll, G. (1958), *Von der Weltwirtschaftskrise zur Staatskonjunktur*, Berlin: Duncker and Humblot.

Kruedener, J. von (1985), 'Die Überforderung der Weimarer Republic als Sozialstaat', *Geschichte und Gesellschaft*, 11: 358–76.

Kuznets, S. (1951), 'Comment on Joseph Schumpeter', in *Conference on Business Cycles*, New York: National Bureau of Economic Research, 155–62.

Kuznets, S. (1961), *Capital in the American Economy*, Princeton, NJ: Princeton University Press.

Kydland, F.E. (1987), 'The role of money in a business cycle model, Pittsburg, Penn.: Department of Economics, Carnegie-Mellon University, unpublished ms.

Kydland, F.E. and Prescott, E. (1990), 'Business cycles: real facts and a monetary myth', *Federal Reserve Bank of Minneapolis Quarterly Review*, 14: 3–18.

Länderrat des amerikanischen Besatzungsgebiets (ed.) (1949), *Statistiches Handbuch von Deutschland*, Munich: Ehrenwirth.

Layer, R.G. (1955), *Earnings of Cotton Mill Operatives, 1825–1914*, Cambridge, Mass.: Harvard University Press.

Leacy, F.H., Urquhart, M.C. and Buckley, K.A.H. (eds) (1983), *Historical Statistics of Canada*, 2nd edn, Ottawa: Statistics Canada.

Lebergott, S. (1957), 'Annual estimates of unemployment in the United States, 1900–1954', in National Bureau of Economic Research, *The Measurement and Behavior of Unemployment*, Princeton, NJ: Princeton University Press.

Lebergott, S. (1964), *Manpower in Economic Growth: The American record since 1800*, New York: McGraw-Hill.

Lebergott, S. (1966), 'Labor force and employment, 1800–1960', in D.S. Brady (ed.), *Output, Employment and Productivity in the United States after 1800*, National Bureau of Economic Research Studies in Income and Wealth no. 30, Princeton, NJ: Princeton University Press, 116–210.

Lebergott, S. (1986), 'Discussion', *Journal of Economic History*, 46(2): 367–71.

Lebergott, S. (1992), 'Historical unemployment series: a comment', *Research in Economic History*, Greenwich, Conn.: JAI Press, 377–86.

Lebergott, S. and Hall, R.E. (1986), 'Cyclical fluctuations in the labor market, *Handbook of Labor Economics*, vol. 2, Amsterdam: North-Holland, 1001–35.

Lewis, W.A. (1978), *Growth and Fluctuations, 1870–1913*, London: Allen & Unwin.

Lilien, D.M. and Hall, R.E. (1986), 'Cyclical fluctuations in the labor market', in O. Ashenfelter and R. Layard (eds), *Handbook of Labor Economics*, vol. 2, Amsterdam: North-Holland, 1001–35.

Lithwick, N.H. (1970), *Economic Growth in Canada*, 2nd edn, Toronto: University of Toronto Press.

Long, C.D. (1960), *Wages and Earnings in the United States, 1860–1890*, Princeton, NJ: Princeton University Press.

Lucas, R.E. (1972), 'Expectations and the neutrality of money', *Journal of Economic Theory*, 4: 103–24.

Lucas, R.E., Jr. (1973), 'Some international evidence on output–inflation tradeoffs', *American Economic Review*, 63(3): 326–34.

Lucas, R.E. and Stokey, N.L. (1989), *Recursive Methods in Economic Dynamics*, Cambridge: Harvard University Press.

Maddison, A. (1982), *Phases of Capitalist Development*, Oxford: Oxford University Press.

Maddison, A. (1991), *Dynamic Forces in Capitalist Development: A long-run comparative view*, Oxford and New York: Oxford University Press.

Maddison, A. (1995), *Monitoring the World Economy*, 1820–1990, Paris: OECD.

Maier, C.S. (1976), *Recasting Bourgeois Europe: Stabilization in France, Germany and Italy in the Decade after World War I*, Princeton, NJ: Princeton University Press.

Maine Bureau of Industrial and Labor Statistics (1895), *Eighth Annual Report 1894*, Augusta: Burleigh and Flynt.

Margo, R. (1990a), 'The incidence and duration of unemployment: some long-term comparisons', *Economic Letters*, 32: 217–20.

Margo, R. (1990b), 'Unemployment in 1910: some preliminary findings', in E. Aerts and B. Eichengreen (eds), *Unemployment and Underemployment in Historical Perspective*, Leuven: Leuven University Press, 51–60.

Massachusetts Bureau of Statistics of Labor (1890–1900), *Annual Report on the Statistics of Manufactures*, vols. 6–16, Boston, Mass.: State Printer.

McAllister, H.E. (1961), 'Statistical factors affecting the stability of the wholesale and consumers' price indexes Price Statistics Review Committee of the National Bureau of Economic Research', in *Price Statistics of the Federal Government: Review, appraisal, and recommendations*, New York: National Bureau of Economic Research.

McCann, L.D. (1978), 'Urban growth in a stable economy: the emergence of Vancouver as a regional metropolis, 1886–1914', in L.J. Evenden (ed.), *Vancouver: Western Metropolis*, Victoria, BC: University of Victoria, 17–41.

McCulloch, J. (1882), *A Dictionary of Commerce and Commercial Navigation*, London: Longmans, Green.

McNeil, W.C. (1986), *American Money and the Weimar Republic*, New York: Columbia University Press.

Means, G.C. (1935), *Industrial Prices and their Relative Inflexibility*, US Senate Document 13, 74th Congress and 1st Session, Washington, DC: US Government Printing Office.

Medoff, J. (1979), 'Layoffs and alternatives under trade unions in United States manufacturing', *American Economic Review*, 69: 380–95.

Michell, H. (1931), 'Statistics of prices', in K.W. Taylor and H. Michell (eds), *Statistical Contributions to Canadian Economic History*, vol. 2, Toronto: Macmillan.

Miller, S.M. (1988), 'The Beveridge–Nelson decomposition of economic time series: another economical computation method', *Journal of Monetary Economics,* 21: 141–2.

Mills, F.C. (1946), *Price–Quantity Interactions in Business Cycles*, New York: NBER.

Mills, T.C. (1992), 'An economic historians' introduction to modern time series techniques in econometrics', in S.N. Broadberry and N.F.R. Crafts (eds), *Britain in the International Economy*, Cambridge: Cambridge University Press, 28–46.

Mills, T.C. and Wood, G.E. (1993), 'Does the exchange rate regime affect the economy?', *Review of the Federal Reserve Bank of St Louis*, 75: 3–20.

Miron, J.A. and Romer, C.D. (1990), 'A new monthly index of industrial production, 1884–1940', *Journal of Economic History*, 50(2): 321–32.

Mishkin, F.S. (1982), 'Does anticipated monetary policy matter? An econometric investigation', *Journal of Political Economy*, 90(1): 22–51.

Mishkin, F.S. (1991), 'Asymmetric information and financial crises: a historical perspective', in R.G. Hubbard (ed.), *Financial Markets and Financial Crises*, Chicago: University of Chicago Press, 69–108.

Mitchell, B.R. (1975), *European Historical Statistics*, Cambridge: Cambridge University Press.

Mitchell, B.R. (1983), *International Historical Statistics: The Americas and Australasia*, Detroit: Gale.

Mitchell, B.R. (1988), *British Historical Statistics*, Cambridge: Cambridge University Press.

Mitchell, W.C. (1913), *Business Cycles*, Berkeley, Cal: University of California Press.

Mitchell, W.C. (1951), *What Happens during Business Cycles*, Boston, Mass.: Houghton Mifflin.

Mitchell, W.C. and Burns, A.F. (1935), *The National Bureau's Measures of Cyclical Behavior*, NBER Bulletin no. 57, New York: NBER.

Mollin, G. (1988), *Montankonzerne und 'Drittes Reich'. Der Gegensatz zwischen Monopolindustrie und Befehlswirtschaft in der deutschen Rüstung und Expansion 1936–1944*, Göttingen: Vandenhoeck & Ruprecht.

Moore, G.H. and Zarnowitz, V. (1986), 'The development and role of the National Bureau of Economic Research's business cycle chronologies', in R.J. Gordon (ed.), *The American Business Cycle*, National Bureau of Economic Research, Studies in Business Cycles no. 25, Chicago: University of Chicago Press, 735–79.

Morley, J.W. (ed.) (1971), *Dilemmas of Growth in Prewar Japan*, Studies in the Modernization of Japan no. 6, Princeton, NJ, Princeton University Press.

Murphy, K.M. and Topel, R.H. (1987), 'The evolution of unemployment in the United States, 1968–1985', in *NBER Macreconomics Annual 1987*, Cambridge, Mass.: MIT Press, 11–116.

Nakamura, T. (1971), *Senzenki Nihon Keizai no Seicho Bunseki, Iwanami-Shoten*. English trans. published as *Economic Growth in Prewar Japan*, New Haven, Conn.: Yale University Press, 1983.

Nakamura, T. (1978), *Nihon Keizai, sono Seicho to Kozo* [The Japanese Economy: Growth and structure], Tokyo: University of Toyko Press.

Nakamura, T. (1993), *Nihon keizai: Sono seicho to kozo* [The Japanese Economy: Growth and structure], Tokyo: University of Tokyo Press.

Nakamura, T., Yoji and Nishida, Y. (1987), 'Nogyo to Jinushi-sei' [Agriculture and landlord system], in *Nippon Teikokushugi Shi*, Tokyo: University of Tokyo Press, 255–30.

Nanto, D.K. and Takagi, S. (1985), 'Korekiyo Takahashi and Japan's recovery from the Great Depression', *American Economic Review*, 75(2): 369–74.

Neely, C.J. and Wood, G.E. (1995), 'Deflation and real economic activity under the gold standard', *Federal Reserve Bank of St Louis Review*, 77: 27–37.

Nelson, C.R. and Plosser, C.I. (1982), 'Trends and random walks in macroeconomic time series', *Journal of Monetary Economics*, 10(2): 139–62.

Neufeld, E.P. (1972), *The Financial System in Canada, its Growth and Development*, Toronto: Macmillan.

New Jersey Bureau of Statistics of Labor and Industries (1895), *Seventeenth Annual Report for the Year Ending October 31st, 1894*, Trenton, NJ: MacCrellish and Quigley.

New Jersey Bureau of Statistics of Labor and Industries (1896), *Eighteenth Annual Report for the Year Ending October 31st, 1895*, Trenton, NJ: MacCrellish and Quigley.

New York Bureau of Statistics of Labor (1894), *Eleventh Annual Report for the Year 1893*, vol. 2, Albany, NY: James B. Lyon.

Newbold, P. (1990), 'Precise and efficient computation of the Beveridge–Nelson decomposition of economic time series', *Journal of Monetary Economics*, 26: 453–7.

Nishimura, S. (1971), *The Decline of Inland Bills of Exchange in the London Money Market, 1855–1913*, Cambridge: Cambridge University Press.

O'Brien, A.P. (1985), 'The cylical sensitivity of wages', *American Economic Review*, 75: 1124–32.

O'Brien, A.P. (1988), 'Factory size, economies of scale, and the great merger wave of 1899–1902', *Journal of Economic History*, 48(3): 639–49.

Ohkawa, K. *et al.* (1974), *Estimates of Long-term Economic Statistics of Japan since 1868*, Tokyo: Keizai Shinposha.

Okazaki, T. (1993), 'Senkan-ki no Kinyu Kozohenka to Kinyu-kiki' [Change of the financial market structure and financial crisis in prewar Japan], *Keizai Kenkyu* [Economic Review], 44(4): 300–10.

Overy, R. (1982), *The Nazi Recovery*, London: Macmillan.

Owen, J.D. (1989), *Reduced Working Hours: Cure for unemployment or economic burden?*, Baltimore, Md.: Johns Hopkins University Press.

Patrick, H.T. (1971), 'The economic muddle of the 1920s', in J.W. Morley (ed.), *Dilemmas of Growth in Prewar Japan*, Princeton, NJ: Princeton University Press, 211–66.

Perron, P. (1989), 'The great crash, the oil price shock, and the unit root hypothesis', *Econometrica*, 57: 1361–401.

Perron, P. and Vogelsang, T.J. (1992), 'Nonstationarity and level shifts with an application to purchasing power parity', *Journal of Business and Economic Statistics*, 10: 301–20.

Persons, W.M., Silberling, N.J. and Berridge, W.A. (1922), 'An index of British economic conditions, 1903–14', *Review of Economic Statistics*, 4 (suppl. 2): 157–89.

Petzina, D. (1968), *Autarkiepolitik im Dritten Reich*, Stuttgart: Deutsche Verlagsanstalt.

Phelps Brown, E.H. and Hopkins, S. (1950), 'The course of wage rates in five countries, 1860–1939', *Oxford Economic Papers*, 2(2): 226–96.

Phillips, A.W. (1958), 'The relation between unemployment and the rate of change in money wage rates in the United Kingdom, 1861–1957', *Economica*, 25: 283–99.

Pippenger, J. (1986), 'Bank of England operations, 1893–1913', in M.D. Bordo and A.J. Schwartz (eds), *A Retrospective on the Classical Gold Standard, 1821–1931*, Chicago: University of Chicago Press, 203–27.

Plumpe, G. (1990), *Die I.G. Farbenindustrie AG*, Berlin: Duncker and Humblot.

President's Committee to Appraise Employment and Unemployment Statistics (1962), *Measuring Employment and Unemployment*, Washington, DC: US Government Printing Office.

Rees, A.W. (1960), *New Measures of Wage-earner Compensation in Manufacturing, 1914-57*, National Bureau of Economic Research Occasional Paper no. 75, New York: National Bureau of Economic Research.

Rees, A.W. (1961), *Real Wages in Manufacturing, 1890–1914*, National Bureau of Economic Research General Series no. 70, Princeton, NJ: Princeton University Press.

Rich, G. (1988), *The Cross of Gold, Money and the Canadian Business Cycle, 1867–1913*. Ottawa: Carleton University Press.

Rich, G. (1989), 'Canadian banks, gold and the crisis of 1907', *Explorations in Economic History*, 26(2): 135–60.

Riemer, J. (1995), Review of H. Berger and A. Ritschl (1995), *Die Rekonstruktion der Arbeitsteilung in Europa*, in: H-German @MSU.EDU, 30 November 1995.

Ritschl, A. (1990), 'Zu hohe Löhne in der Weimarer Republik? Eine Auseinandersetzung mit Holtfrerichs Berechnungen zur Lohnposition der Arbeiterschaft 1925–1932', *Geschichte und Gesellschaft*, 16: 375–402.

Ritschl, A. (1991), 'Die deutsche Zahlungsbilanz 1936–41 und das Problem des Devisenmangels vor dem Kriegsbeginn', *Vierteljahreshefte für Zeitgeschichte*, 39: 103–23.

Ritschl, A. (1992), 'Über die Höhe und Struktur der gesamtwirtschaftlichen Investitionen in Deutschland 1935–38', *Vierteljahrschrift zur Sozial- und Wirtschaftsgeschichte*, 79: 156–76.

Ritschl, A. (1995), 'Spurious growth in German manufacturing output 1925–1938', Universtät Pompeu Fabra, mimeo.

Ritschl, A. (1996), 'Deutschlands Krise und Konjunktur, 1924–1934. Binnenkonjunktur, Auslandsverschuldung und Reparationsproblem zwischen Dawes-Plan und Transfersperre', Universtät Pompeu Fabra, unpublished book manuscript.

Roediger, D.R. (1987), *Our Own Time: A history of American labor and the working day'*, New York: Greenwood Press.

Roediger, D.R. and Foner, P.A. (1989), *Our Own Time: A history of American labour and the working day*, Greenwich, Conn.: Greenwood Press.

Rolnick, A.J. and Weber, W.E. (1994), *Inflation and Money Growth under Alternative Money Standards*, Working Paper no. 528, Federal Reserve Bank of Minneapolis.

Romer, C.D. (1986a), 'Is the stabilization of the postwar economy a figment of the data?', *American Economic Review*, 76(2): 341–52.

Romer, C.D. (1986b), 'Spurious volatility in historical unemployment data', *Journal of Political Economy*, 94(1): 1–37.

Romer, C.D. (1988), 'World War I and the postwar depression: a reinterpretation based on alternative estimates of GNP', *Journal of Monetary Economics*, 22: 91–115.

Romer, C.D. (1989), 'The prewar business cycle reconsidered: new estimates of gross national product, 1869–1908', *Journal of Political Economy*, 97(1): 1–37.

Romer, C.D. (1991), 'The cyclical behavior of individual production series, 1889–1984', *Quarterly Journal of Economics*, 106(1): 1–31.

Romer, C.D. (1994), 'Remeasuring business cycles', *Journal of Economic History*, 54: 573–609.

Rosenzweig, R. (1983), *Eight Hours for What We Will: Workers and leisure in an industrial city, 1870–1920*, Cambridge and New York: Cambridge University Press.

Rostow, W.W. (1948), *British Economy of the Nineteenth Century*, Oxford: Clarendon Press.

Rostow, W.W. (1978), *The World Economy, History and Prospect*, Austin, Tx.: University of Texas Press.

Rotemberg, J.J. and M. Woodford (1991), 'Markups and the Business Cycle', in O.J. Blanchard and S. Fischer (eds), *NBER Macroeconomics Annual 1991*, vol. 6, Cambridge: MIT Press, 63–128.

Sachs, J. (1980), 'The changing cyclical behavior of wages and prices, 1890–1976', *American Economic Review*, 70(1): 78–89.

Sandberg, L.G. (1968), 'Movements in the quality of British cotton textile exports, 1815–1913', *Journal of Economic History*, 28: 1–27.

Sargent, T.J. (1973), 'Interest rates and prices in the long run', *Journal of Money Credit and Banking*, 5: 385–449.

Sargent, T.J. (1976a), 'The observational equivalence of natural and unnatural rate theories of macroeconomics', *Journal of Political Economy*, 84(3): 631–40.

Sargent, T.J. (1976b), 'A classical macroeconomic model of the United States', *Journal of Political Economy*, 84: 207–37.

Sato, K. (1976), 'Dai Fukyo-ki no Nihon Keizai' [The Japanese economy in the Great Depression], *Keizai Kenkyu* [Economic Review], 27(1): 1–8.

Sato, K. (1981), 'Senkan-ki Nihon no Makuro Keizai to Mikuro Keizai' [Macro- and micro-economy in interwar Japan], in T. Nakamura (ed.), *Senkan-ki no Nihon Keizai Bunseki* [An Analysis of the Interwar Japanese Economy], Yamakawa-Shuppan, 3–20.

Sauerbeck, A. (1886), 'Prices of commodities and the precious metals', *Journal of the Royal Statistical Society*, 49: 581–649.

Schuker, S. (1988), *American Reparations to Germany, 1924–1933*, Princeton, NJ: Princeton University Press.

Schultz, C.L. (1981), 'Some macro foundations for micro theory', *Brookings Papers on Economic Activity*, 2: 521–75.

Schwartz, A.J. (1987), *Money in Historical Perspective*, Chicago: University of Chicago Press.

Scott, A.D. (1958), 'The development of extractive industries', *Canadian Journal of Economics and Political Science*, 28(1): 70–87.

Shearer, R.A., Chant, J.F. and Bond, D. (1984), *The Economics of the Canadian Financial System*, 2nd edn, Scarborough, Ont.: Prentice-Hall Canada.

Sheffrin, S.M. (1983), *Rational Expectations*, Cambridge and New York: Cambridge University Press.

Sherrington, C.E.R. (1934), *A Hundred Years of Inland Transport, 1830–1933*, London: Frank Cass.

Shiells, M. (1987), 'Hours of work and shiftwork in early industrial labor markets of Great Britain, the United States and Japan', *Journal of Economic History*, 47: 497–501.

Shimizu, Y. and Nishida, Y. (1987), 'Nogyo to Jinushi-sei' [Agriculture and landlord system], in K. Oishi (ed.), *Nippon Teikokushugi Shi, Sekai Daikyokoki* [History of Japanese Imperialism: The era of the World Depression], Tokyo: University of Tokyo Press, 255–330.

Shinohara, M. (1961), *Nihon keizai no seicho to junkan* [The Growth and Cyclical Movements of the Japanese Economy], Tokyo: Shobunsha.

Siklos, P.L. (1988), 'Output–inflation trade-offs: some new evidence from postwar US quarterly data', *Journal of Macroeconomics*, 10: 249–60.

Siklos, P.L. (1993), 'Income velocity and institutional change: some new time series evidence, 1870–1986', *Journal of Money Credit and Banking*, 25: 377–92.

Silberling, N.J. (1923), 'British prices and business cycles, 1779–1850', *Review of Economics and Statistics*, 5 (suppl. 2): 223–61.

Silverman, A.G. (1930), 'Monthly index numbers of British export and import prices, 1880–1913', *Review of Economics and Statistics*, 12: 139–48.

Smith, L.A. (1929), *Summarized Data of Lead Production*, Economic Paper no. 5, Washington, DC: US Government Printing Office.

Snyder, C. (1927), *Business Cycles and Business Measurements; Studies in Quantitative Economics*, New York: Macmillan.

Solomou, S. (1994), 'Economic fluctuations, 1870–1913', in R. Floud and D.N. McCloskey (eds), *The Economic History of Britain since 1700*, vol. 2: *1860–1939*, Cambridge: Cambridge University Press, 247–64.

Solon, G., Whatley, W. and Stevens, A.H. (1993), 'Real wage cyclicality between the World Wars: evidence from the Ford and Byers companies', Department of Economics, University of Michigan, unpublished paper.

Solon, G., Barsky, R. and Parker, J.A. (1994), 'Measuring the cyclicality of real wages: how important is composition bias', *Quarterly Journal of Economics*, 109(1): 1–25.

Solow, R.M. (1990), *The Labor Market as a Social Institution: Royer Lectures*, Cambridge, Mass.: Basil Blackwell.

Southall, H. (1986), 'Regional unemployment patterns among skilled engineers in Britain, 1851–1914', *Journal of Historical Geography*, 15: 268–86.

Southall, H. (1989), 'British artisan unions in the New World', *Journal of Historical Geography*, 15: 163–92.

Southall, H. (1991), 'Poor law statistics and the geography of economic distress', in J. Foreman-Peck (ed.), *New Perspectives on the Late Victorian Economy*, Cambridge: Cambridge University Press, 247–64.

Southall, H. and Gilbert, D. (1991), 'A database of nineteenth-century British labour markets', *Economic History Review*, 44: 369–70.

Spoerer, M. (1994), 'German net investment and the cumulative real wage postion, 1925–1929: on a premature burial of the Borchardt debate', *Historical Social Research*, 19: 26–41.

Spoerer, M. (1996), *Von Scheingewinnen zum Rüstungsboom. Die Eigenkapitalrentabilität der deutschen Industrieaktiengesellschaften 1925–1941*, Stuttgart: Steiner.

Sprague, O.M.W. (1910), *History of Crises under the National Banking System*, Washington, DC: US Government Printing Office.

Spree, Reinhard (1977), *Die Wachstumszyklen der deutschen Wirtschaft von 1840 bis 1880*, Berlin: Duncker and Humblot.

Statistisches Bundesamt (1954), 'Die langfristige Entwicklung des Sozialprodukts im Bundesgebiet', *Wirtschaft und Statistik*, 63–6.

Statistisches Reichsamt (1932), 'Das deutsche Volkseinkommen vor und nach dem Kriege', in *Einzelschfiften zur Statistik des Deutschen Reichs*, vol. 24, Berlin: Hobbing.

Stock, J.H. (1990), 'Confidence intervals for the largest autoregressive root in US macroeconomic times series', University of California at Berkeley, Department of Economics, mimeo.

Stock, J.H. and Watson, M. W. (1991), 'A probability model of the coincident economic indicators', in K. Lahiri and G.H. Moore (eds), *Leading Economic Indicators: New approaches and forecasting records*, Cambridge: Cambridge University Press, 63–89.

Stoker, T.M. (1986), 'Simple tests of distributional effects on macroeconomic equations', *Journal of Political Economy*, 94(4): 763–95.

Stucken, R. (1964), *Deutsche Geldpolitik 1918–1961*, Tübingen: Möhr.

Stuebel, H. (1951), 'Die Finanzierung der Aufruestrung im Dritten Reich', *Europa-Archiv*, 6: 4128–36.

Sundstrom, W.A. (1990), 'Was there a golden age of flexible wages? Evidence from Ohio manufacturing, 1892–1910', *Journal of Economic History*, 50(2): 309–20.

Sundstrom, W.A. (1992), 'Rigid wages or small equilibrium adjustments? Evidence from the contraction of 1893', *Explorations in Economic History*, 29(4): 430–55.

Sutch, R. (1988), 'Review of Keyssar, Out of Work', *Journal of Economic History*, 48: 215–17.

Takagi, S. (1989), 'Senkan-ki Nippon Keizai to Hendo Kawasesoba' [The interwar Japanese economy and the floating exchange rate], *Kinyu-Kenkyu* [Bank of Japan], 8(4): 109–40.

Takamura, N. (1987), 'Shihon-chikusei, 2; Keikogyo' [Capital accumulation 2; Light industry], in K. Oishi (ed.), *Nippon Teikokushugi Shi, Sekai Daikyokoki* [History of Japanese Imperialism: The era of the world depression], Tokyo: University of Tokyo Press, 173–216.

Taussig, F. W. (1931a), *Some Aspects of the Tariff Question: An examination of the development of American industries under protection*, 3rd edn, Cambridge, Mass.: Harvard University Press.

Taussig, F.W. (1931b), *The Tariff History of the United States*, 8th edn, New York and London: G.P. Putnam's Sons.

Taylor, J.B. (1986), 'Improvements in macroeconomic stability: the role of wages and prices', in R.J. Gordon (ed.), *The American Business Cycle, Continuity and Change*, NBER Studies in Business Cycles no. 25, Chicago: University of Chicago Press, 639–77.

Temin, P. (1969), *The Jacksonian Economy*, New York: W.W. Norton.

Temin, P. (1971), 'The beginning of the Great Depression in Germany', *Economic History Review*, 24: 240–48.

Temin, P. (1989), *Lessons from the Great Depression* (The Lionel Robbins Lecture, 1989), Cambridge, Mass.: MIT Press.

Thomas, D. S. (1926), 'An index of British business cycles', *Journal of the American Statistical Association*, 21: 60–3.

Thorp, W.L. (1926), *Business Annals: United States, England, France, Germany, Austria, Russia, Sweden, Netherlands, Italy, Argentina, Brazil, Canada, South Africa, Australia, India, Japan, China*, National Bureau of Economic Research General Series no. 8, New York: National Bureau of Economic Research.

Tobin, J. (1993), 'Price flexibility and output stability: an old Keynesian view', *Journal of Economic Perspectives*, 7: 45–65.

Topel, R.H. (1983), 'Inventories, layoffs and the short-run demand for labor', *American Economic Review*, 72: 769–87.

Towne, M.W. and Rasmussen, W.D. (1960), 'Farm gross national product and gross investment in the nineteenth century', in National Bureau of Economic Research, *Trends in the American Economy in the Nineteenth Century*, Studies in Income and Wealth, no. 24, New York: NBER, 255–315.

United States Bureau of Labor Statistics (1929), *Wholesale Prices, 1913 to 1927*, Bulletin 473, Washington, DC: US Government Printing Office.

United States Bureau of Labor Statistics (1982), *Labor Force Statistics Derived From the Current Population Survey: A databook*, 2 vols, Bulletin 2096, Washington, DC: US Government Printing Office.

United States Bureau of Labor Statistics (1985), *Employment, Hours, and Earnings, United States, 1909–84*, vol. 1, Bulletin 1312-12, Washington, DC: US Government Printing Office.

United States Bureau of Labor Statistics (1988), *BLS Handbook of Methods*, Bulletin 2285, Washington, DC: US Government Printing Office.

United States Bureau of Mines (1929), *Summarized Data of Lead Production*, by L.A. Smith, Economic Paper 5, Washington, DC: US Government Printing Office.

United States Bureau of the Census (1929), *Cotton Production and Distribution, Season of 1928–29*, Bulletin 166, Washington, DC: US Government Printing Office.

United States Bureau of the Census (1966), *Long-Term Economic Growth, 1860–1965*, Washington, DC: US Government Printing Office.

United States Bureau of the Census (1975), *Historical Statistics of the United States: Colonial Times to 1970*, Washington, DC: Government Printing Office.

United States Census Office (1895), *Report on Manufacturing Industries in the United States at the Eleventh Census: 1890*, Part I, *Totals for States and Industries*, Washington, DC: US Government Printing Office.

United States Council of Economic Advisors (various years), *Economic Report of the President*, Washington, DC: US Government Printing Office.

United States Department of Agriculture. Bureau of Agricultural Economics (1935), *The Agricultural Situation*, Washington, DC: US Government Printing Office.

United States Weather Bureau (1894), *Report of the Chief of the Weather Bureau*, Washington, DC: US Government Printing Office.

United States Department of Commerce (various years), *Statistical Abstract of the United States*, Washington, DC: US Government Printing Office.

United States Department of Commerce (1975), *Historical Statistics of the United States*, Washington, DC: US Government Printing Office.

United States Department of the Treasury. Bureau of Statistics (October 1896), *Monthly Summary of Finance and Commerce of the United States*, Washington, DC: US Government Printing Office.

United States. President's Committee to Appraise Employment and Unemployment Statistics (1962), *Measuring Employment and Unemployment*, Washington, DC: US Government Printing Office.

Urquhart, M.C. (1986), 'New estimates of gross national product, Canada, 1870–1926: Some implications for Canadian development', in R.E. Gallman and S.L. Engerman (eds), *Long-term Factors in American Economic Growth*, NBER Studies in Income and Wealth no. 51, Chicago: University of Chicago Press, 9–94.

Urquhart, M.C. (1993), *Gross National Product, Canada 1870–1926; The derivation of the estimates*, Montreal: McGill-Queen's University Press.

Urquhart, M.C. (1994), 'Gross national product, Canada 1870–1926: a note', *Review of Income and Wealth*, 40: 223–6.

Urquhart, M.C. and Buckley, K.H.A. (eds) (1965), *Historical Statistics of Canada*, Cambridge: Cambridge University Press.

Voth, H.J. (1994), 'Much ado about nothing? A note on investment and wage pressure in Weimar Germany, 1925–29', *Historical Social Research*, 19: 124–39.

Wagemann, E. (ed.) (1935), *Konjunkturstatistisches Handbuch 1936*, Berlin and Hamburg: Hanseatische Verlagsanstalt.

Wagenführ, R. (1933), 'Die Industriewirtschaft. Entwicklungstendenzen der deutschen und internationalen Industrieproduktion 1860 bis 1932', *Vierteljahreshefte zur Konjunkturforschung*, Sonderheft 31: 3–70.

Wagenführ, R. (1954), *Die deutsche Industrie im Kriege 1939–1945*, Berlin: Duncker & Humblot.

Warren, G.F. and Pearson, F.A. (1932), *Prices*, New York: John Wiley.

Watson, M.W. (1994), 'Business-cycle durations and postwar stabilization of the US economy', *American Economic Review*, 84: 24–46.

Weather Disk Associates (1990), *World Weather Disk* [CD Rom].

Weinstein, M.M. (1980), *Recovery and Redistribution under the NIRA: Studies in monetary economies*, Amsterdam: North-Holland.

Weir, D.R. (1986), 'The reliability of historical macroeconomic data for comparing cyclical stability', *Journal of Economic History*, 46(2): 353–65.

Weir, D.R. (1992), *A Century of US Unemployment, 1890–1990: Revised estimates and evidence for stabilization*, Greenwich, Conn.: JAI Press, 301–46.

Whaples, R. (1990), *The Shortening of the American Work Week: An economic and historical analysis of its context, causes, and consequences*, dissertation in economics, University of Pennsylvania.

Wogin, G. (1980), 'Unemployment and monetary policy under rational expectations: some Canadian evidence', *Journal of Monetary Economics*, 6: 59–68.

Wood, G.H. (1909), 'Real wages and the standard of comfort since 1850', *Journal of the Royal Statistical Society*, LXXII: 91–103.

Wood, H. (1944), 'Hours of work in manufacturing, 1914–43', *Monthly Labor Review*, 67: 838–55.

Wright, C.D. (1893), 'Cheaper living and the rise of wages', *Forum*, 16: 221–8.

Wright, C.D. (1904), *Regulation and Restriction of Output*, United States Department of Commerce and Labor, Eleventh Special Report of the Commissioner of Labor, Washington, DC: US Government Printing Office.

Wright, G. (1988), 'Labor history and labor economics', in A.J. Field (ed.), *The Future of Economic History*, Boston, Mass.: Kluwer Nijhoff, 313–48.

Wynne, M.A. and Balke, N.S. (1993), 'Recessions and recoveries', *Federal Reserve Bank of Dallas Economic Review*, 1–17.

Yamamura, K. (1972), 'Then came the Great Depression: Japan's interwar years', in H.V.D. Wee (ed.), *The Great Depression Revisited: Essays on the economics of the thirties*, The Hague: Martinus Nijhoff, 182–211.

Yellen, J.L. (1984), 'Efficiency wage models of unemployment', *American Economic Review*, 74: 200–205.

Yoshikawa, H. and Shioji, E. (1990), 'Senzen Nihon Keizai no Makuro Bunseki' [A macroeconomic analysis of the prewar Japanese economy], in H.

Yoshikawa and T. Okazaki (eds), *Keizai Riron eno Rekishiteki Perspective* [Historical Perspectives on Economic Theory], Tokyo: University of Tokyo Press, 153–80.

Zarnovitz, V. (1992), *Business Cycles: Theory, history, indicators, and forecasting*, Chicago: University of Chicago Press.

Zivot, E. and Andrews, D.W.K. (1992), 'Further evidence on the great crash, the oil-price shock, and the unit-root hypothesis', *Journal of Business and Economic Statistics*, 10: 251–70.

Index